THE MYTH OF A GENTILE GALILEE

The Myth of a Gentile Galilee is the most thorough synthesis to date of archaeological and literary evidence relating to the population of Galilee in the first century CE. The book demonstrates that, contrary to the perceptions of many New Testament scholars, the overwhelming majority of first-century Galileans were Jews. Utilizing the gospels, the writings of Josephus, and published archaeological excavation reports, Mark A. Chancey traces the historical development of the region's population and examines in detail specific cities and villages, finding ample indications of Jewish inhabitants and virtually none for gentiles. He argues that any New Testament scholarship that attempts to contextualize the Historical Jesus or the Jesus movement in Galilee must acknowledge and pay due attention to the region's predominantly Jewish milieu.

This accessible book will be of interest to New Testament scholars as well as scholars of Judaica, Syro-Palestinian archaeology, and the Roman Near East.

Mark A. Chancey is Assistant Professor in the Department of Religious Studies at Southern Methodist University. He has written articles and reviews for *New Testament Studies*, *Biblical Archaeology Review*, *Currents in Research: Biblical Studies*, and *Africa Journal of Theology*.

SOCIETY FOR NEW TESTAMENT STUDIES

MONOGRAPH SERIES

General editor: Richard Bauckham

118

THE MYTH OF A GENTILE GALILEE

The Myth of a Gentile Galilee

MARK A. CHANCEY

Southern Methodist University
Dallas, Texas

CAMBRIDGE
UNIVERSITY PRESS

PUBLISHED BY THE PRESS SYNDICATE OF THE UNIVERSITY OF CAMBRIDGE
The Pitt Building, Trumpington Street, Cambridge, United Kingdom

CAMBRIDGE UNIVERSITY PRESS
The Edinburgh Building, Cambridge CB2 2RU, UK
40 West 20th Street, New York, NY 10011-4211, USA
477 Williamstown Road, Port Melbourne, VIC 3207, Australia
Ruiz de Alarcón 13, 28014 Madrid, Spain
Dock House, The Waterfront, Cape Town 8001, South Africa

http://www.cambridge.org

© Mark A. Chancey 2002

First published 2002

Printed in the United Kingdom at the University Press, Cambridge

Typeface Times 10/12 pt.   *System* LaTeX 2$_\varepsilon$ [TB]

A catalogue record for this book is available from the British Library

Library of Congress Cataloguing in Publication data

Chancey, Mark A.
The myth of a Gentile Galilee / Mark A. Chancey.
    p.   cm – (Society for New Testament Studies monograph series ; 118)
Based on the author's thesis (doctoral) – Duke University, 1999.
Includes bibliographical references (p.) and index.
ISBN 0-521-81487-1
1. Galilee (Israel) – History.   2. Jews – History – 586 B.C.–70 A.D.   3. Judaism –
History – Post-exilic period, 586 B.C.–210 A.D.   4. Galilee (Israel) – Antiquities.
I. Title.   II. Monograph series (Society for New Testament Studies) ; 118.
DS110.G2 C53   2002
933 – dc21   2001052871

ISBN 0 521 81487 1 hardback

CONTENTS

PREFACE

Little did I know when I departed the first time to participate in excavations at Sepphoris the impact that experience would have on me. I was instantly captivated by fieldwork – the physical challenges, the tangibility of archaeological evidence, the camaraderie that develops while digging. By season's end, I had developed a new interest in Galilean Judaism and its significance for Historical Jesus research. In my subsequent reading, I quickly became aware of a gap between the archaeological evidence I observed in Galilee and the descriptions of Galilee I encountered in much New Testament scholarship. I also soon realized the need for scholars to support generalized descriptions of archaeological finds with references to specific finds and specific publications.

This study is the result of my ensuing investigation of Galilee's population. The consistency of my findings surprised me. In examining the Gospels, Josephus, and published archaeological data, I discovered impressive amounts of evidence for Judaism and very meager evidence for paganism. I found little support for oft-repeated claims that large numbers of gentiles lived in first-century CE Galilee. The implications of these findings are clear: in our attempts to situate Jesus and the Jesus movement in Galilee, we must always keep in mind the region's predominantly Jewish milieu. Because the persuasiveness of my argument depends upon the thoroughness of my research, I have not been sparing in bibliographical detail.

In addition to advancing an argument about Galilee's population, I seek here to provide New Testament scholars with an up-to-date synthesis of the published archaeological data. To make this summary as readable as possible, I have avoided archaeological jargon and relegated technical details to the footnotes. My hope is that this work will serve as a resource for scholars investigating other aspects of Galilee, in addition to its population.

This book is of obvious relevance for those interested in investigating the extent of Greco-Roman culture in Galilee, and I make preliminary observations on that subject. My primary focus, however, is on the considerably narrower topic of who was living in Galilee. A full investigation of Hellenism in Galilee requires its own treatment, and I will turn to that issue in my next book.

This book is based on my doctoral dissertation, "The Myth of a Gentile Galilee: The Population of Galilee and New Testament Studies," which I defended at Duke University in April 1999. I was fortunate to have E. P. Sanders and Eric M. Meyers as my dissertation directors; both provided me with solid guidance and kind encouragement. E. P. Sanders pushed me on multiple occasions to delve more deeply into the data, each time with the hope of catching one more glimpse of ancient Galilee. Eric M. Meyers, as director of the Sepphoris Regional Project excavations, first encouraged my archaeological interests and allowed me to serve on the staff of the dig. I am also greatly indebted to the other readers on my dissertation committee, Richard B. Hays, D. Moody Smith, and Bart D. Ehrman. My discussion of Sepphoris in the third chapter reflects material considered in two previous publications, "The Cultural Milieu of Ancient Sepphoris," *NTS* (47 (2001): 127–145) and "How Jewish was Sepphoris in Jesus' Time?" co-authored with Eric M. Meyers, *BAR* 26:4 (2000): 18–33, 61.

In discussing specific Galilean sites, I have sometimes utilized the Greek name and sometimes the Hebrew, depending on which is better known. In spelling site names, I have generally used the form prevalent in secondary literature; thus, sometimes a *het* is indicated by an ḥ, and sometimes not, though I have tried to be consistent with individual sites. Biblical translations are usually my own, sometimes those of the NSRV; translations of Josephus are usually from the Loeb edition.

I owe thanks to numerous others. Richard Bauckham, editor of the SNTS series, proposed changes that have improved key aspects of my argument. Joanne Hill, my copy editor, deserves my gratitude for her careful reading of my manuscript. The chair of my department at S.M.U., Richard W. Cogley, and my other colleagues have given me a warm welcome to Dallas. The teaching of George Howard, David S. Williams, and Theodore J. Lewis, all at the University of Georgia, first attracted me to the academic study of the Bible. My interaction with students at Duke University, Duke Divinity School, and Southern Methodist University has made me thankful to have entered this profession. The Dorot Foundation and Endowment for Biblical Research awarded me grants enabling travel to Israel. Tracy Anne Allred, my wife, has encouraged me in graduate school, the job search, and these early days at S.M.U.

My deepest gratitude, however, is to my parents, Gladys Chancey and the late Gene Chancey. They first introduced me to the biblical text, and they strove to cultivate in me a love for it. While I have learned much from my formal education, I have learned far more from them. It is in their honor I write.

ABBREVIATIONS

Reference works

ABD   *Anchor Bible Dictionary*. Ed. David Noel Freedman et al. 6 vols. New York: Doubleday, 1992.

EAEHL   *The Encyclopedia of Archaeological Excavations in the Holy Land*. Ed. Michael Avi-Yonah. 4 vols. Englewood Cliffs, N.J.: Prentice Hall, 1975–1978.

NEAEHL   *The New Encyclopedia of Archaeological Excavations in the Holy Land*. Ed. Ephraim Stern. 4 vols. Jerusalem: The Israel Exploration Society and Carta; New York: Simon and Schuster, 1993.

OEANE   *The Oxford Encyclopedia of Archaeology in the Near East*. Ed. Eric M. Meyers. 5 vols. New York and Oxford: Oxford University Press, 1997.

Periodicals

AASOR   *Annual of the American Schools of Oriental Research*
ADAJ   *Annual of the Department of Antiquities of Jordan*
AJA   *American Journal of Archaeology*
BA   *Biblical Archaeologist*
BAIAS   *Bulletin of the Anglo-Israel Archaeology Society*
BAR   *Biblical Archaeology Review*
BASOR   *Bulletin of the American Schools of Oriental Research*
CBQ   *Catholic Biblical Quarterly*
ESI   *Excavations and Surveys in Israel*
HTR   *Harvard Theological Review*
IEJ   *Israel Exploration Journal*
INJ   *Israel Numismatic Journal*
JAOS   *Journal of the American Oriental Society*
JBL   *Journal of Biblical Literature*

JJS	*Journal of Jewish Studies*
JPOS	*Journal of the Palestine Oriental Society*
JSP	*Journal for the Study of the Pseudepigrapha*
JSQ	*Jewish Studies Quarterly*
LA	*Liber Annuus*
NTS	*New Testament Studies*
PEQ	*Palestine Exploration Quarterly*
QDAP	*Quarterly of the Department of the Antiquities in Palestine*
RB	*Revue biblique*
SEG	*Supplementum Epigraphicum Graecum*
ZDPV	*Zeitschrift des deutschen Palästina-Vereins*

Josephus

Ant.	*Jewish Antiquities*
War	*Jewish War*

Rabbinic works

The abbreviations used for rabbinic references are taken from Patrick H. Alexander et al., eds., *The SBL Handbook of Style for Ancient Near Eastern, Biblical, and Early Christian Studies* (Peabody, Mass.: Hendrickson, 1999).

NOTE ON DATING

Archaeological terminology is used for chronological references:

Late Bronze Age = 1500–1200 BCE

Iron I Age = 1200–926 BCE

Iron II Age = 926–586 BCE

Neo-Babylonian Period = 586–539 BCE

Persian Period = 539–332 BCE

Early Hellenistic Period = 332–198 BCE

Late Hellenistic Period = 198–63 BCE

Early Roman Period = 63 BCE–135 CE

Middle Roman Period = 135–250 CE

Late Roman Period = 250–360 CE

Byzantine Period = 360–640 CE

For discussion, see Walter E. Rast, *Through the Ages in Palestinian Archaeology* (Philadelphia: Trinity Press International, 1992).

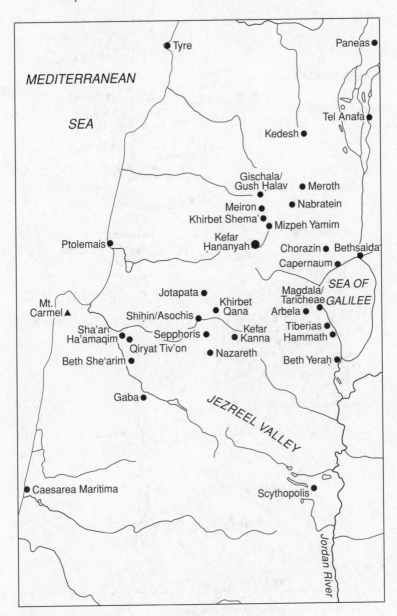

Map 1: Galilee and northern Palestine

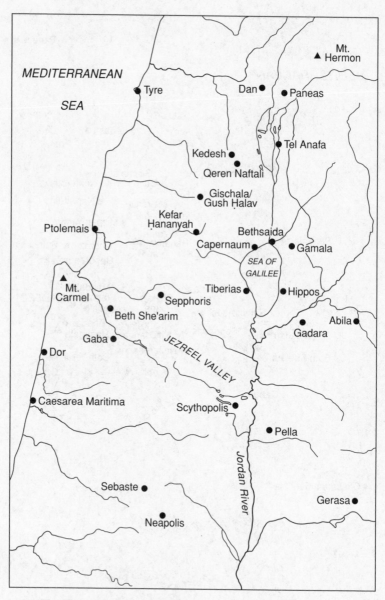

Map 2: Galilee and the surrounding areas

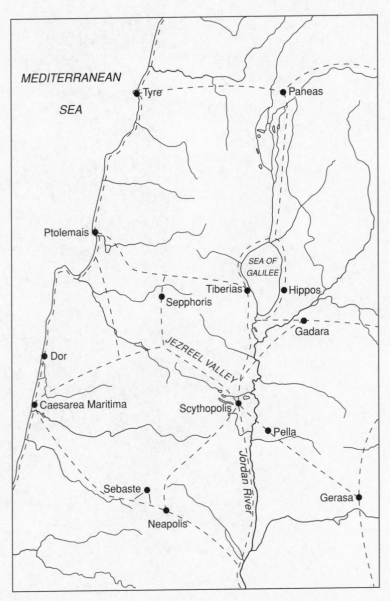

Map 3: Chief roads

INTRODUCTION

The claim that gentiles were numerous in the Galilee of Jesus's day is common in New Testament scholarship. The *Interpreter's Dictionary of the Bible*, one of the most widely distributed and influential of the Bible reference works, goes so far as to suggest that Jews were but a minority there: "Shrines to numerous deities must have existed in the larger cities of Gentile Galilee, especially in a Roman town like Tiberias, and would have been found even in the more Jewish towns. They represented the normal and traditional worship of the Gentile majority in Galilee."[1] This claim is typical of such encyclopedias and dictionaries; a casual perusal reveals that many report a strong gentile presence, sometimes a majority, sometimes a large and highly visible minority. According to this view, Galilee's large pagan population explains why Matthew 4:15 refers to the region as "Galilee of the Gentiles,"[2] derived from the Hebrew גליל הגוים (literally, "circle" or "district of the nations" (Isaiah 8:23 [9:1])). Some reference works emphasize that gentiles from other regions, near and far, often

[1] K. W. Clark, "Galilee," in George Arthur Buttrick et al., eds., *Interpreter's Dictionary of the Bible*, 5 vols. (New York and Nashville: Abingdon, 1962), vol. II, 344–347.

[2] See also F. C. Grant, "Jesus Christ," in Buttrick et al., eds., *Interpreter's Dictionary of the Bible*, vol. II, 869–896; W. R. F. Browning, "Galilee," in W. R. F. Browning, ed., *A Dictionary of the Bible* (Oxford and New York: Oxford University Press, 1996), 145; Arthur M. Ross, "Galilee," in J. D. Douglas, Merrill C. Tenney et al., eds., *The New International Dictionary: Pictorial Edition* (Grand Rapids, Mich.: Zondervan Publishing House; Basingstoke: Marshall Pickering, 1987), 368–369; Henry W. Holloman, "Galilee, Galileans," in Walter A. Elwell et al., eds., *Baker Encyclopedia of the Bible*, 2 vols. (Grand Rapids, Mich.: Baker Book House, 1986), vol. I, 834–836; no author, "Galilee," in John L. Mckenzie, ed., *Dictionary of the Bible* (Milwaukee: Bruce Publishing Company, 1965), 293–294; R. W. Stewart MacAlister and Emil G. Kraeling, "Galilee," in James Hastings, Frederick C. Grant, and H. H. Rowley, eds., *Dictionary of the Bible* (New York: Charles Scribner's Sons, 1963), 313–314; "Galilee," in John E. Steinmueller and Kathryn Sullivan, eds., *Catholic Biblical Encyclopedia: New Testament* (New York: Joseph F. Wagner, Inc.: 1950), 248–249; "Galilee," in Herbert Lockyer et al., eds., *Nelson's Illustrated Bible Dictionary* (Nashville: Thomas Nelson Publishers, 1986), 401–402. The three most recent reference articles avoid this view, however; see Sean Freyne, "Galilee," in *OEANE*, vol. II, 369–376; Sean Freyne, "Galilee (Hellenistic/Roman)," in *ABD*, vol. II, 895–899; Mordechai Aviam, "Galilee: The Hellenistic to Byzantine Periods," *NEAEHL*, vol. II, 453–458.

traversed Galilee; many report both a high gentile population and a high number of gentile visitors. The impression left by these sources is that an unusually high degree of Jewish–gentile interaction was an important part of the particularity of first-century CE Galilee. A certain vagueness permeates many of these scholarly discussions; explanations of why Jewish–gentile interaction was so common, if offered, are typically brief and undetailed.

Though many New Testament scholars have freely referred to the supposedly mixed Galilean population, that image of Galilee has functioned quite differently in various reconstructions of Jesus and early Christianity. Some have made a passing reference to Galilee's diverse inhabitants but have drawn few implications from it, prioritizing Jesus's Jewish context.[3] Others, also stressing the Jewish context, have used Jesus's gentile neighbors as a foil.[4] Still others have argued that Jesus's dealings with Galilee's numerous gentiles explained his open-minded attitude toward humanity.[5]

More recently, the claim of a strong gentile presence in Galilee has been an important component of the argument that Galilee was thoroughly infused with Greco-Roman culture, an argument based largely on purported archaeological finds. Robert W. Funk, for example, writes of "semipagan Galilee, whose inhabitants, because they were often of mixed blood and open to foreign influence, were despised by the ethnically pure Judeans to the south." He also notes, "Greek was widely used in semipagan Galilee, in Hellenistic cities like Sepphoris . . . "[6] Howard Clark Kee suggests that archaeological finds demonstrate the influence of Greco-Roman culture and reveal that Jewish–gentile interaction was quite common.[7] A statement by Marcus J. Borg again reflects the different weight scholars place on the idea of a multicultural Galilee; while noting that archaeological discoveries attest to "a considerable number of Gentiles"

---

[3] E.g., the references to the "mixed race" of Galilee in Günther Bornkamm, *Jesus of Nazareth*, trans. Irene and Fraser McLuskey with James M. Robinson (San Francisco: Harper & Row, 1960), 42; Martin Dibelius, *Jesus*, trans. Charles B. Hedric and Frederick C. Grant (Philadelphia: Westminster Press, 1949), 39–40.

[4] E.g., Adolf von Harnack, *What is Christianity?* trans. Thomas Bailey Saunders (Philadelphia: Fortress Press, 1957), 33–34; Joseph Klausner, *Jesus of Nazareth: His Life, Times, and Teachings* (New York: Macmillan, 1929), 233, 363.

[5] E.g., Shirley Jackson Case, *Jesus: A New Biography* (Chicago: University of Chicago Press, 1927), 199–212.

[6] Robert W. Funk, *Honest to Jesus: Jesus for a New Millennium* (San Francisco: HarperSanFrancisco, 1996), 33, 79.

[7] Howard Clark Kee, "Early Christianity in the Galilee: Reassessing the Evidence from the Gospels," in Lee I. Levine, ed., *The Galilee in Late Antiquity* (New York and Jerusalem: The Jewish Theological Seminary of America, 1992), 19.

there, his own understanding of the historical Jesus stresses his Jewish context.[8]

Burton L. Mack presents a more extreme view: his Galilee has only the thinnest of Jewish veneers. Mack reflects a common practice in Q community reconstruction, the assumption of a Galilean provenance. Arguing that "the traditional picture of Galilean culture . . . " – meaning the picture of a Jewish Galilee – "needs to change," Mack attempts to present a "truer picture" of Galilee, one which recognizes the Hellenistic ethos of this "land of mixed peoples."[9] Though the Hasmonean conquest of Galilee *c.* 103 BCE resulted in its political domination by Jews, "it would be wrong to picture Galilee as suddenly converted to a Jewish loyalty and culture."[10] A hundred years after the conquest, Galilee was a blend of Jewish, local, Greek, and Roman cultures. Thus, many of the first Christians were not Jewish, according to Mack. The members of the Q community, at least, were a "multiethnic, multicultural mix";[11] the Q story of the centurion (whom Mack understands as a Roman, rather than Herodian, officer) is one indication of this mixed constituency.[12] The earliest stratum of Q reflects not apocalyptic eschatology, but Cynic philosophy; it reflects not Jewish worship of Yahweh, but a rather vague monotheism. "The God in question," Mack writes, "is not identified in terms of any ethnic or cultural tradition." Since Mack considers Galilee primarily non-Jewish, this conception of God "fits nicely with Galilean provenance . . . "[13] In de-Judaizing Galilee, Mack has de-Judaized the origins of Christianity.

The fact that Mack depicts himself as correcting the "traditional" picture of a Jewish Galilee is enough to show again that a variety of images of Galilee have long existed in scholarship. So many scholars have repeated the claim of a large gentile population that many regard defense of that claim as unnecessary, but others have articulated different visions of the region. In the scholarly literature, pictures of a rural Galilee have stood side by side with those of an urban Galilee; pictures of a conservative Semitic society, with those of a Hellenized society; and pictures of a solidly Jewish population, with those of a largely gentile population. Many significant studies have downplayed Galilean particularity

[8] Marcus J. Borg, *Meeting Jesus Again for the First Time* (San Francisco: HarperSanFrancisco, 1994), 26; cf. his "The Palestinian Background for a Life of Jesus," in *Searching for Jesus* (Washington, D.C.: Biblical Archaeology Society, 1994), 37–58, esp. 46–47. For another example of the inter-relation in New Testament scholarship of Hellenism and paganism, see Joseph A. Fitzmeyer, "Did Jesus Speak Greek?" *BAR* 18:5 (1992): 61.

[9] Burton L. Mack, *The Lost Gospel: The Book of Q and Christian Origins* (San Francisco: Harper Collins, 1993), 53; cf. *A Myth of Innocence: Mark and Christian Origins* (Philadelphia: Fortress Press, 1988).

[10] Mack, *Lost Gospel*, 59.   [11] Ibid., 214.   [12] Ibid., 154.   [13] Ibid., 127.

altogether, not addressing at any length how its worship, practice, and daily life would have differed from the culture of Jerusalem and the south.[14]

Such disparate images are possible because, to date, no full investigation of the composition of Galilee's population or of the extent of Jewish–gentile contact there has appeared. Previous studies have addressed these topics, but they have not focused on them. When discussing Galilee's population, these studies have often exhibited one of several limitations. Some have been one-sided, utilizing only the literary evidence. For example, Sean Freyne's excellent *Galilee from Alexander the Great to Hadrian* pre-dates the more recent archaeological work and is drawn primarily from textual sources. Martin Goodman's authoritative *State and Society in Roman Galilee* focuses solely on rabbinic materials.[15] Others have presented a synchronic picture, citing archaeological evidence from a wide span of centuries to understand the first-century region.[16] None of these previous studies has attempted to provide a detailed synthesis of both the data found in dig reports of a variety of Galilean sites and the information found in ancient literary sources.

My primary goal in this study is to bridge the gap between textual studies and archaeology, combining both to provide a more detailed and accurate picture of first-century CE Galilee. By making use of Josephus and biblical sources as well as excavation reports, utilizing archaeological data from multiple sites, and differentiating early finds from later finds, this work demonstrates that most Galileans in the first century CE were Jews.[17] Galilee's earlier history explains how it became predominantly Jewish, and, in the first century CE, Josephus and the authors of the

[14] E.g., E. P. Sanders, *Jesus and Judaism* (Philadelphia: Fortress Press, 1985); John P. Meier, *A Marginal Jew*, 2 vols. (New York: Doubleday, 1991, 1994); Elisabeth Schüssler Fiorenza, *Jesus: Miriam's Child, Sophia's Prophet: Critical Issues in Feminist Christology* (New York: Continuum, 1994).

[15] Sean Freyne, *Galilee from Alexander the Great to Hadrian: 323 BCE to 135 CE: A Study of Second Temple Judaism* (Wilmington, Del.: Michael Glazier; Notre Dame, Ind.: University of Notre Dame Press, 1980); Martin Goodman, *State and Society in Roman Galilee, AD 132–212* (Totowa, N.J.: Rowman and Allanheld, 1983). Freyne's more recent works, including *Galilee, Jesus, and the Gospels* (Philadelphia: Fortress Press, 1988) and "Galilee: Galilee in the Hellenistic through Byzantine Periods," *OEANE*, vol. II, 370–376, make more use of archaeological work.

[16] Richard Batey provides an example, claiming the presence in first-century CE Sepphoris of a temple dedicated to Augustus and to Rome based on later numismatic evidence (*Jesus and the Forgotten City: New Light on Sepphoris and the Urban World of Jesus* [Grand Rapids, Mich.: Baker Book House, 1991], 56; on this point, cf. E. P. Sanders, "Jesus in Historical Context," *Theology Today* 50 [1993]: 431).

[17] Rabbinic sources are of limited use for this project, due to its chronological parameters. Pre-Bar Kochbah traditions attesting to Jewish–gentile contacts or providing information about the population of specific communities are rare. Using later sayings to understand

Gospels regarded it as a region where circumcision, Sabbath observance, loyalty to the Jerusalem temple, and purity were major concerns. Archaeological discoveries clearly attest to Jewish burial and purity practices at several sites.[18]

In contrast, evidence for pagans in first-century CE Galilee is surprisingly slim in both the literary and the archaeological records. There appears to be little reason to talk either about Galilee's "predominantly gentile population" or, alternatively, its "sizable and highly visible" gentile minority, and, thus, little reason to place special emphasis on the gentile component of Galilee's population when discussing its cultural milieu. The nature of our data does not allow us to determine what percentage of the population were Jews and what percentage pagans; any attempt to quantify the proportions is mere speculation. What is clear, however, is that gentiles were not an especially large and influential group. Galilee's population included some non-Jews, of course, but their numbers appear to have been relatively small. They have left such a minimal impact in the literary and archaeological records that talking with specificity about the presence of particular groups (e.g., Romans, Greeks, Syrians, Nabateans, Phoenicians) at particular sites is usually impossible. Likewise, while some contact between Galileans and their neighbors, gentile and Jewish, is indisputable – the area is simply not big enough to allow for isolation, particularly in the border regions – there is far less evidence than often supposed for pagans frequently traveling through Galilee.

In examining the composition of Galilee's population and the amount of Jewish–gentile interaction there, I am investigating a sub-topic within the larger discussion of the area's cultural milieu. Providing a comprehensive overview of the extent of Greco-Roman influence – a separate, though obviously related, issue – is not my goal. I am not trying here to resolve such questions as how widely Greek was used or whether or not Cynic philosophers roamed Galilee. Instead, I am arguing that, in light of the ample evidence in Galilee for Judaism and the minimal evidence of

the late Second Temple period population is extremely problematic (Goodman, *State and Society*, 41–53). I will place weight on rabbinic traditions only when an adequate study exists evaluating their relevance for the earlier periods. (For rabbinic references to specific communities, see articles in *ABD, NEAEHL*, and *OEANE*, and Yoram Tsafrir, Leah Di Segni and Judith Green, *Tabula Imperii Romani: Iudaea, Palaestina: Eretz Israel in the Hellenistic, Roman and Byzantine Periods* (Jerusalem: Israel Academy of Sciences and Humanities, 1994).

[18] I understand Galilean Judaism within the larger context of "common Judaism," as discussed by E. P. Sanders in *Judaism: Practice and Belief: 63 BCE–66 CE* (London: SCM Press; Philadelphia: Trinity Press International, 1992) and *The Historical Figure of Jesus* (London: Allen Lane, The Penguin Press, 1993), 33–48. The notion of "common Judaism" does not imply that there were no regional variations.

paganism, discussions of the region in New Testament scholarship should always reflect the Jewish identities of the overwhelming majority of its inhabitants.

A secondary aim is to provide an overview for the broader readership of New Testament scholars of the state of knowledge for Galilee, based on an up-to-date synthesis of published evidence. Though I have made extensive use of archaeological findings, I have written for the non-archaeologist. I have attempted to provide the readers with both descriptive information about Galilee's material culture and a reliable guide to the methodological and interpretive debates about those findings, so that they themselves can determine the significance of individual artifacts or architectural features. Rather than just assembling a catalogue of artifacts pertinent to the question of the nature of Galilee's population, I have sought to contextualize those artifacts within the larger body of data from the region as a whole as well as from individual communities.

My approach is thoroughly historical. This is largely the result of the nature of the evidence, which allows us to draw general historical conclusions but which renders application of certain other theoretical approaches difficult. Social science methodologies have been applied to some questions in Galilean studies, most notably economics and urban–rural relations,[19] but their detailed use for this topic in this time period is challenging. We have no literature from the first century CE of proven Galilean provenance, a lack which hinders the detailed application of ethnicity theory (for example) to population questions. For understanding Galilee's population in later centuries, rabbinic texts are of great use, but demographic shifts in the second century CE render those sources less helpful for first-century CE Galilee. The most significant reason why it is difficult to utilize sociological and anthropological approaches to understand Jewish–gentile relations in Galilee, however, is the sheer lack of evidence of gentiles with which to work. Similarly, the scarcity of literary reports of specific Jewish–gentile encounters in Galilee renders use

---

[19] E.g., several studies by Sean Freyne: "Urban–Rural Relations in First Century Galilee: Some Suggestions from the Literary Sources," in Levine, ed., *Galilee in Late Antiquity*, 75–94; "Herodian Economics in Galilee," in Philip F. Esler, ed., *Modelling Early Christianity* (London and New York: Routledge, 1995), 23–46; "Jesus and the Urban Culture of Galilee," in Tord Fornberg and David Hellholm, eds., *Texts and Contexts: Biblical Texts in their Textual and Situational Contexts* (Oslo: Scandinavian University Press, 1995), 597–622; *Galilee, Jesus, and the Gospels*, 143–155; and "The Geography, Politics and Economics of Galilee and the Quest of the Historical Jesus," in Bruce Chilton and Craig A. Evans, eds., *Studying the Historical Jesus: Evaluations of the State of Current Research* (Leiden: E. J. Brill, 1994), 75–122; cf. John Dominic Crossan, *The Birth of Christianity* (San Francisco: HarperSanFrancisco, 1998), 209–235.

of certain forms of cultural theory, such as contact theory and other post-colonialist approaches, problematic.[20] I hope that future developments in both biblical studies and Syro-Palestinian archaeology will make application of such methods more practical.

Hellenism, Greco-Roman culture, and paganism

While the larger question of how deeply affected Galilee was by Greco-Roman culture is not my primary focus, I recognize the relevance of my project for this issue and will make some preliminary observations about it. Indeed, as will be seen over and over again in my discussion, differentiation between Hellenistic and Greco-Roman culture, on the one hand, and pagan practice, on the other, is crucial for understanding the evidence from Galilee. These phenomena are related, but distinct. "Hellenism" denotes the presence of Greek culture and "Greco-Roman culture," the added influence of Roman culture.[21] "Paganism," however, has a different denotation: the worship of any deity other than the Jewish (and Christian) god. One reason that the amount of evidence for gentiles in Galilee has been exaggerated in some recent studies is that evidence for Hellenistic or Greco-Roman culture has been misinterpreted as evidence for paganism.

The presence of Hellenism at a site does not necessarily indicate the presence of pagans, and the presence of pagans does not necessarily imply the presence of Hellenism. Two hypothetical examples illustrate this point. An ancient community could exhibit a strongly Hellenized atmosphere, characterized by the widespread use of the Greek language, the presence of Greek architectural forms and artistic motifs, and awareness (at least among the educated elite) of Greek thought, without having a large number of gentiles. Such a community could be entirely Jewish, in light of Martin Hengel's work on Hellenism and Judaism.[22] Conversely, a pagan community might not exhibit any characteristics of Hellenistic

---

[20] See Marianne Sawicki's attempt in *Crossing Galilee: Architectures of Contact in the Occupied Land of Jesus* (Harrisburg, Penn.: Trinity Press International, 2000).

[21] For an overview of scholarship on Hellenism and Judaism, see Lee I. Levine, *Judaism and Hellenism in Antiquity: Conflict or Confluence?* (Peabody, Mass.: Hendrickson Publishers, 1998), 3–32.

[22] Martin Hengel, *The "Hellenization" of Judaea in the First Century after Christ*, (London: SCM Press; Philadelphia: Trinity Press International, 1989); *Judaism and Hellenism: Studies in their Encounter in Palestine during the Early Hellenistic Period*, 2 vols., trans. John Bowden (London: SCM Press; Philadelphia: Trinity Press International, 1974).

culture at all; the archaeological record of that site would reflect local indigenous pagan culture.

The relationship between these phenomena is complicated further by the difficulty in determining whether some artifacts – most notably, figurines and artistic depictions of deities – reflect paganism or just Greco-Roman cultural influence. For example, the representations of well-known figures from classical mythology found in the third-fourth-century CE Jewish necropolis at Beth She'arim demonstrate that members of the Jewish community there were quite comfortable with Greco-Roman artistic motifs; they do not demonstrate pagan practices. Unless such depictions are found in a cultic context (e.g., a temple) or are accompanied by cultic objects (e.g., an incense altar) or dedicatory inscriptions, one cannot assume that they reflect paganism.

The challenges of using archaeological data

All studies based on archaeological data are somewhat provisional, and this one is no exception. In discussing Galilee's material culture, I have relied almost exclusively on the published archaeological evidence, rather than attempting to use field notebooks and other unpublished records from various excavations, past and present. The broad scope of the project precludes the use of the latter types of materials on any large scale. When those materials are published, they will clarify further our image of Galilee's population.

Archaeological finds, like texts, are subject to multiple interpretations. I have generally accepted the dates excavators have assigned to specific objects, unless other information in their reports raised questions about those dates. In interpreting and identifying specific artifacts and structures, I have sometimes followed the excavator's suggestions and sometimes disagreed, again on the basis of the published data. When the significance of a find is unclear, I have reported different possibilities and provided bibliographical information so that the reader can investigate the topic and make his or her own judgment about the matter.

Outline of argument

In the first chapter, I review scholarly images of Galilee's population, identifying the reasons why some have contended that large numbers of gentiles dwelt there. The arguments can be quickly summarized: the region's repeated subjugation by foreign powers resulted in a "mixed race";

its position along the major trade routes of the Roman period resulted in highways bustling with foreign traders and travelers; archaeological finds attest to the diversity of peoples.

Understanding Galilee's first-century CE population requires a review of its political and demographic history, the subject of the second chapter. Changes in Galilee's population are traced from the Assyrian conquest to the end of the Early Roman period,[23] when Roman troops were permanently stationed there. Scholars have long noted the successive invasions Galilee suffered between these two events, but the consequences of these repeated invasions have often been misunderstood.

The third chapter provides a site-by-site overview of specific Galilean communities in the Late Hellenistic and Early Roman periods, discussing all of the settlements for which we have significant amounts of data. It draws information from Josephus, the Gospels, and excavation reports to shed light on several questions: Where in Galilee did Jews and gentiles live? Who lived in Upper Galilee, the region between the villages of Kefar Hananyah and the Galilean Beersheba in the south and the foothills of Mount Lebanon in the north? Was the population more mixed in Lower Galilee, between Kefar Hananyah and the Jezreel Valley, where Jesus appears to have been most active?[24] Were gentiles more prevalent in the cities?

Galilee was "surrounded by powerful foreign nations," as Josephus puts it,[25] and the boundaries between Galilee and these regions were often blurred.[26] How much interaction would Galileans have had with their

---

[23] The reference to "Early Roman period," in itself, implies nothing about a Roman presence; it is chronological terminology. See the "Note on dating" in the prefatory material of this work.

[24] On the two Galilees, see *War* 3.35–44. *M. Sheb.* 9:2 adds a third region, the valley of Tiberias. See Eric M. Meyers, "Galilean Regionalism as a Factor in Historical Reconstruction," *BASOR* 221 (1976): 95.

[25] *War* 3.41.

[26] *War* 3.35–44 notes Mount Carmel and the territory of Ptolemais as the western border; Samaria and the territory of Scythopolis as the southern border; Gaulanitis and the territory of Hippos and Gadara as the eastern border; and the territory of Tyre as the northern border. These territories were close together, and the boundaries separating them shifted from time to time. Political Galilee was not always the same as geographical Galilee. For example, Josephus notes in this passage that Carmel had once belonged to Galilee, but in his own time belonged to Tyre (*War* 3.35). Likewise, *Ant.* 8.36 suggests that Galilee had once stretched all the way to Sidon. Josephus describes Ptolemais as a city of Galilee (*War* 2.188), though it was clearly separate from the region. He situates Bethsaida-Julia in both lower Gaulanitis (*War* 2.168) and Perea (*War* 2.252, *Ant.* 20.159), while John (1:43–44, 12:21) and Ptolemy (*Geography* 5.16.4) place it in Galilee. See discussion of Galilee's borders in Freyne, *Galilee from Alexander*, 3–4; Günter Stemberger, "Galilee – Land of Salvation?" in W. D. Davies, ed., *The Gospel and the Land: Early Christianity and Jewish Territorial Doctrine* (Sheffield: JSOT Press, 1994), 409–438, esp. 415–421; Willibald Bösen, *Galiläa*

neighbors? The fourth chapter provides a "cultural map" of the territories that encircled Galilee, describing their cities and villages. It investigates the extent and nature of contact between Galileans and gentiles from these areas. In addition, it considers whether Galilee's role in regional and inter-regional trade would have resulted in large numbers of merchants and traders crossing its territory.

The conclusion summarizes the implications of my findings for New Testament studies. It considers why Matthew 4:15 would refer to the region as "Galilee of the Gentiles," and it discusses the historical plausibility of the very few stories the Gospels preserve of encounters between Jesus and gentiles. Lastly, I consider the relevance of my findings for the ongoing scholarly debate about the extent of Greco-Roman influence in Galilee.

When the published archaeological data have been sifted and the primary ancient texts pored over, the image of Galilee which emerges is that of a predominantly Jewish region. The belief that Galilee had large numbers of gentile inhabitants or visitors does not hold up to testing. Far from being a dominant element of the population in first-century CE Galilee, pagans were a minority, greatly outnumbered by Jews.

als Lebensraum und Wirkungsfeld Jesu (Basel and Vienna: Herder Freiburg, 1985), 18–31; W. Oehler, "Die Ortschaften und Grenzen Galiläas nach Josephus," *ZPDV* 28 (1905): 1–26, 49–74.

1

IMAGES OF GALILEE'S POPULATION
IN BIBLICAL SCHOLARSHIP

No single thread unites the frequent claims that numerous pagans lived in Galilee and that the region was rightly known as "Galilee of the Gentiles." Eminent scholars simply present the description as accepted wisdom. Günther Bornkamm's widely read *Jesus of Nazareth* and Martin Dibelius's *Jesus*, for example, both casually refer to the "mixed race" of Galileans.[1] One can identify recurring arguments, usually based on the purported changes produced by one event or another in Galilee's history, but one is hard-pressed to identify any clear lines of development for this view, at least in the scholarship pre-dating recent excavations.

What differentiates many of the more recent scholarly statements about Galilee is not detailed argumentation but the claim that recent archaeological discoveries irrefutably prove the population's diversity. Indeed, the extensive archaeological activity that began in the early 1970s and has continued to this day is the only true milestone in the scholarly discussion. One can trace archaeology's impact on the debate, from early calls for greater attention to the "Hellenistic" or "cosmopolitan" aspects of Lower Galilee to recent claims of paganism's representation in Galilee's material culture. A review of the spectrum of scholarly positions on Galilee's population will identify the key moments in the region's demographic development as well as the most significant issues raised by archaeological finds.

Before the digs

Galilee has often been depicted as rural, bucolic hinterland, characterized by natural beauty and simplicity of life. Of these portraits, the romanticism of Ernest Renan is unparalleled.[2] For Renan, the region's natural

---

[1] Bornkamm, *Jesus of Nazareth*, 42; Dibelius, *Jesus*, 39–40; cf. Hugh Anderson, ed., *Jesus* (Englewood Cliffs, N.J.: Prentice-Hall, 1967), 24.
[2] Ernest Renan, *The Life of Jesus*, 13th edn. (London: Mathieson and Co., n. d.), 37.

life, that is, its geography, flora, and fauna, granted it an almost para-
disiacal nature, so that "all the dreams of Galilee" had "a charming and
idyllic character." Renan's glowing prose makes the region sound almost
mythical. Galilee, in contrast to gloomy Jerusalem, was "shady" and
"smiling," especially in springtime, when the country was a "carpet of
flowers." The region's animals were "small and extremely gentle," and
its mountains inspired "loftier thought" than any other mountains in the
world.[3] Renan described an essentially rural Galilee, with no large cities
but Tiberias. The population was large and diverse: "This province reck-
oned amongst its inhabitants, in the time of Jesus, many who were not
Jews (Phoenicians, Syrians, Arabs, and even Greeks). The conversions
to Judaism were not rare in mixed countries like this."[4] He provided no
rationale for this description, however.

Guignebert's portrayal is similar. "Peasants for the most part, they
led simple, healthy lives, scarcely touched by the intellectual problems
that perplexed the inhabitants of Judaea." They were "hard-working and
energetic," devoting themselves to farming the region's fertile soil, fishing
in its lake, and prospering from its position on the trade routes. As for their
ethnic and religious composition, it was "very mixed." Jewish customs
predominated, but only because the gentiles living there adopted them
"with more or less sincerity and good will" in order to live peaceably
among the Jews.[5]

In contrast to Renan and Guignebert, Adolf von Harnack stressed the
sophistication of at least some of Galilee's inhabitants. Galilee was populated by many gentiles and influenced by Greco-Roman trends, he argued,
but Jesus's message and ministry were untouched by any significant encounters with larger Hellenistic society.[6] Harnack uses the Hellenistic
atmosphere of Galilee, complete with Greek inhabitants, as a contrasting background for the Jewish Jesus. He was joined in this position by
Joseph Klausner, who argued that "Jesus was in no way influenced" by
these many gentiles.[7]

Other scholars suggested that the area's cultural diversity contributed to
Jesus's open-minded acceptance of individuals of various backgrounds.
Rather than minimizing the impact a mixture of peoples would have
had on Jesus, they emphasized how that diversity affected him. Shirley

---

[3] Ibid., 39.   [4] Ibid., 13–14.

[5] Ch. Guignebert, *The Jewish World in the Time of Jesus*, trans. S. H. Hooke (New York:
E. P. Dutton and Co., 1939), 7–11.

[6] Harnack, *What is Christianity?*, 33–34.

[7] Klausner, *Jesus of Nazareth*, 363; cf. 233.

Jackson Case provides a classic example of this reasoning. Case emphasized the importance of Sepphoris, one of Galilee's two principal cities. Less than four miles from Nazareth, Sepphoris was clearly visible from the hills overlooking Jesus's village. This proximity to Nazareth of a city with a population of both "Jews and foreigners" helped to explain the "unconventionality of Jesus in mingling freely with the common people, his generosity toward the stranger and the outcast, and his conviction of the equality of all classes before God . . . " On Jesus's numerous trips to the city, he would have frequently met pagans.[8] Case thus foreshadowed recent developments in Historical Jesus research.

The idea that Galilee's population was mixed influenced other streams within New Testament scholarship besides Historical Jesus research. Some scholars, most notably Ernst Lohmeyer, Robert Henry Lightfoot, Willi Marxsen, and L. E. Elliot-Binns, argued that Galilee was regarded by some early Christians as the "land of salvation" which served as the setting both for Jesus's earthly ministry and for future revelation. This status was most obvious in the Gospel of Mark, especially in Jesus's instructions for the disciples to go to Galilee following the resurrection (14:28; cf. 16:7). Its focus on Galilee was understood to reflect the presence there of early Christian communities, which were comprised of both Jews and gentiles.[9]

Many geographical studies of Palestine also encouraged a view of Galilee as "Galilee of the Gentiles." Often taking the form of a travelogue, such studies interwove images of ancient and modern Palestine, blending reminiscences of travels in the "holy land"; pertinent passages from the Bible, apocrypha, Josephus, rabbinic materials, church histories, and pilgrimage literature; and local traditions about sites. Gustaf Dalman's Galilee, for example, was far from isolated, given the vast amounts of trade – and the vast numbers of gentile traders – that passed

[8] Shirley Jackson Case in "Jesus and Sepphoris," *JBL* 45 (1926): 14–22, quote from 19, and *Jesus*, 199–212.

[9] Ernst Lohmeyer, *Galiläa und Jerusalem* (Göttingen: Vandenhoeck and Ruprecht, 1936); L. E. Elliot-Binns, *Galilean Christianity* (London: SCM Press, 1956); Robert Henry Lightfoot, *Locality and Doctrine in the Gospels* (New York and London: Harper and Brothers Publishers, n. d.); and Willi Marxsen, *Mark the Evangelist*, trans. James Boyce et al. (Nashville: Abingdon, 1969). On the diversity of Galilee's population, see especially Elliot-Binns (18–19) and Marxsen (note 64 on page 71). G. H. Boobyer ("Galilee and Galileans in St. Mark's Gospel," *Bulletin of the John Rylands Library* 35 [1953]: 334–348) and Werner H. Kelber (*The Kingdom in Mark: A New Place and a New Time* [Philadelphia: Fortress Press, 1974], 130–131) provide other variants of the "land of salvation" theory. Cf. the critiques of such views in Davies, *The Gospel and the Land*, 221–243 and Günter Stemberger, "Galilee – Land of Salvation?" 409–438 in the same volume.

through it.[10] A well-traveled network of roads criss-crossed the region, connecting it to its northern and southern neighbors as well as to the Mediterranean. Nazareth, though only a small village, was a "radiating point of important roads and a thoroughfare for an extensive traffic."[11] Jesus, Dalman believed, would have been greatly influenced by these economic cross currents.[12] The gentile presence in Galilee was due not only to merchants, however; pagans lived there, especially at places like Magdala, with its Greek hippodrome, and the border village Bethsaida.[13] Dalman stressed, however, that despite the sizable numbers of gentiles, most Galileans were Jews. Even Sepphoris was primarily Jewish; in fact, "Jewish Zippori [Sepphoris] was . . . the religious centre of the district."[14]

Few of these claims about Galilee's eclectic population included substantial supporting arguments. If their proponents offered any reasons at all for their views, they typically consisted of one or more elements of the following historical schema, drawn from literary sources:

1   The reference in Isaiah 8:23 (9:1) to "Galilee of the Gentiles" attests to a non-Jewish population in the late eighth century BCE.

2   Following their eighth-century BCE conquest of Israel, the Assyrians depopulated Galilee, carrying away most Israelites in captivity. The settlers the Assyrians introduced to Galilee were non-Jews, as were the neighboring peoples who moved into the region. As subsequent empires – Persian, Ptolemaic, Seleucid, Roman – ruled Galilee, they, too, allowed non-Jewish settlers to come there.[15]

3   In Maccabean times, Galilee's Jewish population was still small enough to be seriously endangered by the gentile majority, necessitating Judas's total evacuation of it to Judea (cf. 1 Maccabees 5:9–23).[16]

4   The region remained outside the Jewish sphere until Aristobulus I conquered it *c*. 103 BCE (*Ant.* 13.318ff.), forcibly converting its inhabitants to Judaism and colonizing the region with Jews

[10] Gustaf Dalman, *Sacred Sites and Ways: Studies in the Topography of the Gospels*, trans. Paul P. Levertoff (New York: Macmillan, 1935). See also Clemens Kopp, *The Holy Places of the Gospels* (New York: Herder and Herder, 1963) and Albrecht Alt, *Where Jesus Worked: Towns and Villages of Galilee Studied with the Help of Local History*, trans. Kenneth Grayson (London: Epworth Press, n. d.).
[11] Dalman, *Sacred Sites*, 63.   [12] Ibid., 11.   [13] Ibid., 126, 165.   [14] Ibid., 76.
[15] E.g., Clark, "Galilee," 344; Bo Reicke, *The New Testament Era*, trans. David E. Green (Philadelphia: Fortress Press, 1968), 68, 117; Guignebert, *Jewish World*, 7–8.
[16] E.g., Clark, "Galilee," 344.

from the south. Roman-era pagans are the descendents of gentiles who managed to escape Hasmonean Judaization. Many scholars argued that this relatively recent conversion meant that those Jews whose roots lay in the pre-Hasmonean population were Jewish only by religion, not by ethnicity. The result was a "mixed race."[17] A few followed this suggestion to its logical conclusion, suggesting that because Jesus was a Galilean, he was not truly a Jew.[18]

5   In the first century CE, gentiles were found throughout Galilee, especially in the cities.[19]

6   Large numbers of Gentile merchants and travellers passed through Galilee, and Roman troops were stationed there.[20]

7   The region continued to be known as "Galilee of the Gentiles," as shown by LXX Isaiah 8:23, LXX Joel 4:4, 1 Maccabees 5:15, and Matthew 4:15.[21] Matthew's reference, in particular, indicates that Galilee contained large numbers of gentiles in the time of Jesus.[22]

[17] E.g., D. S. Russell, *The Jews from Alexander to Herod* (Oxford: Oxford University Press, 1967), 69; Guignebert, *Jewish World*, 11; Humphrey Carpenter, *Jesus* (Oxford: Oxford University Press, 1980), 22; Maurice Goguel, *Jesus and the Origins of Christianity*, 3 vols. (New York: Harper Brothers, 1960), vol. II, 254–255. On both points 3 and 4, see especially Emil Schürer, *The History of the Jewish People in the Age of Jesus Christ*, rev. and ed. Geza Vermes and Fergus Millar, 3 vols. (Edinburgh: T&T Clark, 1973–1987), vol. I, 142 and 216–218 and vol. II, 7–10.

[18] E.g., Walter Grundmann, *Jesus der Galiläer und das Judentum* (Leipzig: Verlag Georg Wigand, 1941), 175; cf. Renan, *Life*, 14; Klausner, *Jesus of Nazareth*, 233; Goguel, *Jesus*, vol. II, 254–255; and the earlier claim by Houston Stewart Chamberlain, *Foundations of the Nineteenth Century,* trans. John Lees, 2 vols. (London: John Lane The Bodley Head, 1910), vol. I, 200–213.

On the Nazi-era context of Grundmann's work, see Susannah Heschel, "Post-Holocaust Jewish Reflections on German Theology," in Carol Rittner and John K. Roth, eds., *From the Unthinkable to the Unavoidable* (Westport, Conn. and London: Greenwood Press, 1997), 57–69; "Transforming Jesus from Jew to Aryan: Theological Politics in Nazi Germany," *Dialog* 35 (1996): 181–187; "Nazifying Christian Theology: Walter Grundmann and the Institute for the Study and Eradication of Jewish Influence on German Church Life," *Church History* 63 (1994): 587–605.

[19] E.g., Clark, "Galilee," 347; Boobyer, "Galilee and Galileans," 334–348; Case, "Jesus and Sepphoris" and *Jesus*, 199–212; cf. Walter Bauer's characterization of "*halbheidnischen Sepphoris*" in "Jesus der Galiläer," *Aufsätze und kleine Schriften* (Tübingen: JCB Mohr [Paul Siebeck], 1967), 102; see also 92–93.

[20] E.g., Dalman, *Sacred Sites*, 11.

[21] Rafael Frankel's discussion of the name "Galilee of the Gentiles" ("Galilee [Pre-Hellenistic]," *ABD*, vol. II, 879), also includes LXX Joshua 12:23[B], but why is unclear. Neither *Septuaginta* (Stuttgart: Deutsche Bibelgesellschaft Stuttgart, 1979) nor the critical edition of Vaticanus (Alan England Brooke and Norman McLean, eds., *The Old Testament in Greek*, vol. I, part 4, *Joshua, Judges, and Ruth* [Cambridge: Cambridge University Press, 1917], 724) notes variant readings which add "of the gentiles" after "Galilee."

[22] E.g., Boobyer, "Galilee and Galileans," 334–348; Reicke, *New Testament Era*, 117.

An extended quote from F. C. Grant's article "Jesus Christ" in *The Interpreter's Dictionary of the Bible* demonstrates the widespread influence of this schema:

> Jesus was a Galilean ... This fact was of far-reaching significance for his whole career. For Galilee was the "Circle of the Gentiles" ... either because it was surrounded by foreign nations or because (in later times) the Jews there were surrounded by foreigners ... [Galilee] had not always been Jewish territory. In the days of Jesus there were many non-Jews, especially Syrians, Phoenicians, Arameans, Greeks, and Romans, living here. Some of these were descended from the peoples who had settled in Palestine during the Exile ... or earlier still, after the destruction of Samaria, then capital of the Northern Kingdom, in 722 BC. Many had, no doubt, crowded into that land during the terrible days of the Maccabean War ... when the Maccabees had evacuated the whole Jewish population to Judea for safety. Later (104 BC) these foreigners were forced to accept Judaism ... The outlook of a Jewish boy, growing to manhood in this region, surrounded by Gentiles, and in contact with foreigners from all parts of the world, was necessarily different from that of a citizen of Jerusalem or of any town in Judea. Across the broad, fertile, Plain of Esdraelon ... came the ancient caravan road from Egypt ... [which] moved on into the distant NE, toward Damascus, Palmyra, Babylon, India, China! How could a boy fail to be impressed with the vastness of the world, with the improbability of God's exclusive concern for one people only, when daily before his eyes came "many from east and west" (Matt. 8:11), Gentiles who might be seeking not only the riches of this world but also the kingdom of God![23]

Few scholars have included in their discussions of Galilee as many points of this historical outline as Grant did. Usually they have referred to only one or two of the arguments described above, if they offered any reason for viewing Galilee's population as mixed.

The influence of archaeology

Many recent works base their understandings of Galilee on the outline described above,[24] but most also cite supposed archaeological evidence.

---

[23] Grant, "Jesus Christ," 877.

[24] Mack, for example, stresses the inefficacy of the Hasmonean conversion (*Lost Gospel*, 59). Bösen repeats the first three points of the schema, though he believes that the Hasmonean

This new dimension in the discussion of Galilee's cultural ethos and population can be traced to the excavations that have followed Israel's victory
in the 1967 war. Although a few Roman-era sites in Galilee had undergone excavation before this time,[25] the 1970s mark the true beginning
of archaeology's influence on conceptions of Galilee in New Testament
scholarship. Continuing holy site archaeology, such as the high-profile
Franciscan project at Capernaum, drew some attention, but it was the
American excavations in Upper Galilee at the sites of Meiron, Gush Ḥalav,
Khirbet Shema', and Nabratein that were to mark the beginning of a new
era in the investigation of ancient Galilee.[26]

Regionalism and Galilee

On the basis of the data unearthed in the Upper Galilee excavations, Eric
M. Meyers proposed that the material culture of Roman and Byzantine
Upper Galilee differed significantly from that of Lower Galilee, demonstrating regional differences.[27] The artwork of Upper Galilee was mostly
aniconic, with simple representative designs such as menorot, eagles,
and geometric designs. Large amounts of Tyrian coinage indicated
Upper Galilee's participation in a trade network connected with the

conquest resulted in a predominantly Jewish population (*Galiläa*, 146–148). The idea that
"Galilee of the Gentiles" accurately highlights Galilee's diverse population is a recurring
view (e.g., Donald A. Hagner, *Matthew 1–13* [Dallas: Word Books, 1993], 73; Daniel
J. Harrington, *The Gospel of Matthew* [Collegeville, Minn.: A Michael Glazier Book pub-
lished by The Liturgical Press, 1991], 71; Francis Wright Beare, *The Gospel According to
Matthew* [San Francisco: Harper and Row, 1981], 121; John P. Meier, *Matthew* [Collegeville,
Minn.: A Michael Glazier Book published by The Liturgical Press, 1990], 33).

[25] The Franciscans had excavated around the holy sites in Nazareth, for example, and
Sepphoris had undergone one season of excavation in 1931.

[26] For an overview of recent excavations, see J. Andrew Overman, "Recent Advances
in the Archaeology of the Galilee in the Roman Period," *Currents in Research: Biblical
Studies* 1 (1993): 35–57.

[27] Meyers, "Galilean Regionalism as a Factor"; Eric M. Meyers, "Galilean Regionalism:
A Reappraisal," in W. S. Green, ed., *Approaches to Ancient Judaism*, 6 vols. (Missoula,
Mont.: Scholars Press for Brown University, 1978–1989), vol. v, 115–131; Eric M. Meyers,
"The Cultural Setting of Galilee: The Case of Regionalism and Early Judaism," in Hildegard
Temporini and Wolfgang Haase, eds., *Aufstieg und Niedergang der römischen Welt*, 2.19.1
(Berlin and New York: Walter de Gruyter, 1979), 686–702; Eric M. Meyers and James
F. Strange, "The Cultural Setting of Galilee: The Case of Regionalism and Early Palestinian
Judaism," in *Archaeology, the Rabbis, and Early Christianity* (Nashville: Abingdon, 1981),
31–47 (a revised version of the article in *Aufstieg und Niedergang der römischen Welt*).

Cf. the critique of Ruth Vale in "Literary Sources in Archaeological Description: The
Case of Galilee, Galilees, and Galileans," *Journal for the Study of Judaism* 18 (1987): 209–
226, and that of Richard A. Horsley in "Archaeology and the Villages of Upper Galilee: A
Dialogue with Archaeologists," *BASOR* 297 (1995): 5–16 and *Archaeology, History, and
Society in Galilee* (Valley Forge, Penn.: Trinity Press International: 1996), 90–95. Meyers
responds to Vale and Horsley in "An Archaeological Response to a New Testament Scholar,"
BASOR 297 (1995): 17–26.

predominantly pagan cities on the coast. Meyers argued, in his original formulations of the regionalism argument, that Upper Galilee's ceramic repertoire had more in common with that of the Golan than with that of Lower Galilee. Thus, numismatic and ceramic evidence both suggested that Upper Galilee was economically oriented more to the north than to the south. The most significant discovery of all in Upper Galilee, perhaps, was what was not found: substantial evidence for the use of Greek, either in inscriptions or in mosaics. Despite economic contacts with the Golan and with the coast, Upper Galilee seemed isolated and culturally conservative, resisting Hellenistic influence.

Lower Galilee, in contrast, exhibited a strikingly different openness to Hellenistic culture. Greek inscriptions were much more common, occurring especially in the lake area and at the burial complex at Beth She'arim. Figurative representative artwork was not uncommon, as seen in the rich imagery of the zodiac mosaic at Ḥammath. Roads passed through Lower Galilee connecting Damascus and the east with the cities on the coast, leading to bustling economic activity and trade in the region. Numismatic and ceramic finds demonstrated participation in far-reaching trade networks extending in all directions. Thus, the cities and villages of Lower Galilee were very much in contact with "the pagan, and hence Greek-speaking west, with its more cosmopolitan atmosphere and multilingual population," Meyers argued.[28] Though Greco-Roman influences were nowhere more visible than in Lower Galilee's principal cities, Sepphoris and Tiberias, they were not limited to the larger communities. The interaction between city and village assured that the cities' cosmopolitan influence was felt throughout the smaller communities of Lower Galilee.

Meyers revised aspects of his thesis in light of subsequent discoveries. Further excavations revealed much more continuity between the pottery of Upper Galilee and Lower Galilee than initially supposed. Imported wares from as far away as Cyprus and Africa and coins from a variety of cities demonstrated that Upper Galilee was also less isolated than originally believed, though still less integrated into trade networks than Lower Galilee.[29] Meyers's basic thesis, however, remained unchanged: far from being a cultural backwater, Lower Galilee exhibited a "cosmopolitan" atmosphere and an exciting synthesis of Jewish and Greco-Roman cultures. This new understanding of Galilee was to have a dramatic

---

[28] Meyers, "Cultural Setting," 697–698.

[29] See "Galilean Regionalism: A Reappraisal," "Archaeological Response," and "Jesus and His Galilean Context," in Douglas R. Edwards and C. Thomas McCollough, eds., *Archaeology and the Galilee: Texts and Contexts in the Graeco-Roman and Byzantine Periods* (Atlanta: Scholars Press, 1997), 57–66.

impact on studies of the Historical Jesus, early Christianity, and rabbinic literature.

In the mid-1980s, excavations began at Sepphoris, and the finds there dramatically attested to the extent of Greco-Roman influence in Galilee in the early centuries of the common era.[30] A triclinium mosaic, dated to the early third century CE, or the approximate time of the redaction of the Mishnah, depicted a procession of the deity Dionysos riding a donkey and a symposium (drinking contest) between Dionysos and Heracles. A market weight bearing an inscription naming the city's *agoranomos* attested to the use of Greek titles for city officials. Numerous other finds also reflected Greco-Roman influence – the Nile mosaic, Roman roads, and lamps decorated with Hellenistic motifs. The theater, partially excavated earlier in the century, received new attention. If built by Antipas, it stood during the time of Jesus, providing popular entertainment for the surrounding villages. Stone vessels and mikvaot (ritual baths), combined with a substantial number of rabbinic traditions, indicated the presence of Jews at Sepphoris, but new evidence indicated that pagans dwelled there, as well. Bronze figurines, possibly of Pan and Prometheus, as well as that of a bull, were discovered; considering them in conjunction with the images of deities, emperors, and temples on the city coins of Sepphoris, some New Testament scholars spoke of the thriving pagan cults within the city. James F. Strange, another of the principal excavators of Sepphoris, described it as a "Roman city" with a "mixed population."[31] "By the second century," Meyers wrote, "Sepphoris had become the home of pagans, Jews, and Jewish-Christians."[32] In short, the excavations at Sepphoris revealed the urban aspects of Lower Galilee and provided proof of its cosmopolitan atmosphere and diverse inhabitants.

As excavated sites multiplied in Galilee, David Adan-Bayewitz and Isadore Perlman took advantage of the newly available data to study ancient pottery production and trade networks. They demonstrated that the pottery of the village Kefar Hananyah, at the border of Upper Galilee and Lower Galilee, dominated the ceramics industry in both Galilees. Trade of the Kefar Hananyah ware extended beyond the borders of Galilee, however, into the gentile communities in the surrounding areas – Acco-Ptolemais on the coast, Tel Anafa to the north, villages of the Golan, and the cities of the Decapolis. The wide distribution of Kefar

---

[30] See the treatment of Sepphoris in chapter 3.

[31] James F. Strange, "Sepphoris," *ABD*, vol. v, 1090–1093.

[32] Eric M. Meyers, "Roman Sepphoris in Light of New Archaeological Evidence and Recent Research," in Levine, ed., *Galilee in Late Antiquity*, 321–338; quote from 329. See also Eric M. Meyers, Ehud Netzer, and Carol L. Meyers, "Sepphoris: Ornament of All Galilee," *BA* 49 (1989): 4–19.

Hananyah's pottery seemed to prove that a well-developed trade network linked Galilee with its neighbors.[33]

"Hellenized" and "urbanized" Galilee

Whereas in previous scholarship, one could find a variety of images of Galilee, in the wake of recent excavations, a dominant view has developed, that of a "Hellenized" and "urbanized" Galilee. Debate continues about the extent and rate of this Hellenization and urbanization, but few scholars reject this terminology entirely. J. Andrew Overman provides a classic expression for "urbanized" Galilee. He argues that Lower Galilee's economic contacts with the coastal cities and the Decapolis "would have resulted in a certain cosmopolitan flavor to the rather small region, and the presence of a variety of influences from the wider Greco-Roman world, and additional toll and tax for the region from this constant flow of goods."[34] His consideration of communities in and around Galilee concludes that the area's cities were "regional centers of Roman power and culture."[35] Overman emphasizes that Jesus's references to scribes, courts, and the *agora* reflect his familiarity with urban life,[36] though his complete lack of any activity in the cities reflects the rural–urban tension which existed in Galilean (and ancient) society as a whole.[37] Overman summarizes, "Life in Lower Galilee in the first century was as urbanized and urbane as anywhere else in the empire."[38]

[33] David Adan-Bayewitz and Isadore Perlman, "Local Pottery Provenience Studies: A Role for Clay Analysis," *Archaeometry* 27 (1985): 203–217; David Adan-Bayewitz and Isadore Perlman, "The Local Trade of Sepphoris in the Roman Period," *IEJ* 40 (1990): 153–172.

[34] J. Andrew Overman, "Who Were the First Urban Christians? Urbanization in Galilee in the First Century," in J. David Lull, ed., *Society of Biblical Literature 1988 Seminar Papers* (Atlanta: Scholars Press, 1988), 161.   [35] Ibid., 165.

[36] Matt. 5:21–26/Luke 12:57–59; Matt. 11:16–17/Luke 7:32.

[37] On urbanization, see several studies by Freyne ("Urban-Rural Relations," "Herodian Economics," "Jesus and the Urban Culture," *Galilee, Jesus, and the Gospels*, 143–155; and "Geography, Politics and Economics") as well as Richard A. Horsley, *Archaeology*, 43–87 and "The Historical Jesus and Archaeology of the Galilee: Questions from Historical Jesus Research to Archaeologists ," in Eugene H. Lovering, Jr., ed., *Society of Biblical Literature 1994 Seminar Papers* (Atlanta: Scholars Press, 1994), 91–135; John S. Kloppenborg Verbin, *Excavating Q: The History and Setting of the Sayings Gospel* (Minneapolis: Fortress Press, 2000), 214–261; and Jonathan L. Reed, "Population Numbers, Urbanization, and Economics: Galilean Archaeology and the Historical Jesus," in *Society of Biblical Literature 1994 Seminar Papers*, 203–221; Meyers, "Jesus and His Galilean Context," 59–63; Douglas R. Edwards, "The Socio-Economic and Cultural Ethos of the Lower Galilee in the First Century: Implications for the Nascent Jesus Movement," in Levine, ed., *Galilee in Late Antiquity*, 53–73; and Douglas R. Edwards, "First-Century Urban/Rural Relations in Lower Galilee: Exploring the Archaeological and Literary Evidence," in D. J. Lull, ed., *Society of Biblical Literature 1988 Seminar Papers* (Atlanta: Scholars Press, 1988), 169–182.

[38] Overman, "Who Were the First Urban Christians?" 168.

For many New Testament scholars, the "urbanization" and "Helleniza-tion" of Galilee indicate that large numbers of pagans – indigenous gentiles as well as Romans and Greeks – lived there. For Strange, the pres-ence of Galilean cities explains not only Jesus's references to institutions like the courts and the *agora*, but also his references to gentiles in such pas-sages as Matthew 5:48 and 6:7. Strange argues that Jews would have met gentiles at "Sepphoris, Tiberias, and above all, Acco-Ptolemais (but also in Hammath, Magdala, and possibly Gennosaur)" as well as on market roads.[39] In addition to the gentiles living in cities and larger communities, Strange suggests that Roman troops were stationed in Galilee. The story of the centurion's servant (Matthew 8:5–13/Luke 7:1–10), he argues, im-plies that a contingent of Roman soldiers was stationed at Capernaum, perhaps as a border patrol or to assist with customs collections.[40]

Like Strange, Howard Clark Kee also argues that the reference to the centurion in Matthew 8:5/Luke 7:2 reflects the "despised Roman occu-pying forces," but, also like Strange, Kee suggests that these were not the only gentiles in Galilee. He argues that "careful analysis of the ar-chaeological sites and remains in the Galilee" suggests that Jesus was likely to have encountered gentiles in his ministry. In his view, Sepphoris was an "important Roman cultural and administrative center" with "all the features of a Hellenistic city . . . including a theater, hippodrome, and temples." Tiberias was a city of "gentile name and origin," though its population had "a predominance of Jews."[41]

Richard Batey also emphasizes the Hellenistic flavor of Sepphoris's culture.[42] Updating Case's earlier argument in light of archaeological discoveries, Batey notes the possibility that Jesus, as a *tekton*, worked at Sepphoris during Antipas's building programs. In his view, Jesus would

---

[39] James F. Strange, "Some Implications of Archaeology for New Testament Studies," in James. H. Charlesworth and Walter P. Weaver, eds., *What has Archaeology to do with Faith?* (Philadelphia: Trinity Press International, 1992), 43–44; cf. Anne Hennessy, *The Galilee of Jesus* (Roma: Editrice Pontificia Università Gregoriana, 1994), 9–10. Bernard J. Lee (*The Galilean Jewishness of Jesus* [New York and Mahwah: Paulist Press, 1988], 53–95) and Bösen (*Galiläa*, 146–148) depict Galilee as primarily Jewish but with gentile minorities in the cities.

[40] Cf. James F. Strange, "First-Century Galilee from Archaeology and from the Texts," in Eugene H. Lovering, Jr., ed., *Society of Biblical Literature 1994 Seminar Papers*, 89–90. See also the frequent references to "Roman occupation" in Sawicki, *Crossing Galilee*, 82–85, 88, 92–96, 178–179.

[41] Kee, "Early Christianity," quotes from 18, 14, 15, and 17.

[42] Richard A. Batey, "Jesus and the Theatre," *NTS* 30 (1984): 563–574; Richard A. Batey, "Is not this the Carpenter?" *NTS* 30 (1984): 249–258; Richard A. Batey, "Sepphoris: An Urban Portrait of Jesus," *BAR* 18:3 (1992): 50–63; Batey, *Jesus and the Forgotten City*; cf. Thomas R. W. Longstaff, "Nazareth and Sepphoris: Insights into Christian Origins," *Anglican Theological Review Supplementary Series* 11 (1990): 8–15. See Stuart Miller's rejoinder to Batey's work in "Sepphoris, the Well-Remembered City," *BA* 55 (1992): 74–83.

have frequently visited the theater at Sepphoris and probably learned the word "hypocrite" – "actor" there.[43] He suggests in one publication that its population was primarily Jewish[44] but elsewhere states that it included Jews, Arabs, Greeks, and Romans.[45] Antipas's Sepphoris had Roman baths as well as a temple to Augustus,[46] and one would have encountered on Galilee's highways pigs "raised for Roman appetites and sacrificial rites."[47]

The impact of the "new Galilee" has been felt elsewhere in Gospels research, such as in provenience studies. Anthony J. Saldarini, for example, argues that given Galilee's "complex and cosmopolitan society," it is as likely a candidate as any for the home of Matthew's audience. "Good-sized cities, such as Sepphoris, Tiberias, Capernaum, and Bethsaida, would have had Jewish and gentile Greek speakers as well as the community resources to educate and support a leader and writer such as the author of Matthew."[48] Likewise, Q has increasingly been placed in Galilee, largely on the basis of references to Galilean communities – Capernaum, Chorazin, and Bethsaida – and to the nearby cities of Tyre and Sidon.[49] Given this Galilean setting, some argue, the Q community must have been made up of both Jews and gentiles.[50]

Jewish Galilee

Despite the frequency with which one encounters the view that large numbers of pagans lived in Galilee, major studies, both pre-dating and post-dating recent excavations, have depicted a primarily Jewish population. In *Jesus the Jew*, Geza Vermes described a Jewish Galilee, though

[43] Batey, "Jesus and the Theatre," 563–565. Cf. Borg's suggestion that Greek and Roman plays were performed at Sepphoris (*Meeting Jesus*, 25–26).

[44] Batey, "Is not this the Carpenter?" 255.

[45] Batey, *Jesus and the Forgotten City*, 14.   [46] Ibid., 81.   [47] Ibid., 140.

[48] Anthony J. Saldarini, "The Gospel of Matthew and Jewish–Christian Conflict in the Galilee," in *Galilee in Late Antiquity*, ed., 26–27.

[49] Matt. 8:5/Luke 7:1; Matt. 11:20–24/Luke 10:13–15; see Kloppenborg Verbin, *Excavating Q*, as well as John S. Kloppenborg, "The Sayings Gospel Q: Recent Opinion on the People Behind the Document," *Currents in Research: Biblical Studies* 1 (1993): 9–34; Christopher M. Tuckett, *Q and the History of Early Christianity* (Edinburgh: T&T Clark, 1996), 102–103; Jonathan L. Reed, "The Social Map of Q," in John S. Kloppenborg, ed., *Conflict and Invention* (Valley Forge, Penn.: Trinity Press International, 1995), 17–36; Jonathan L. Reed, *Archaeology and the Galilean Jesus: A Re-examination of the Evidence* (Harrisburg, Penn.: Trinity Press International, 2000), 170–196; and Jonathan L. Reed, "Places in Early Christianity: Galilee, Archaeology, Urbanization, and Q" (Ph.D. Diss., Claremont Graduate School, 1994).

[50] Mack (*Lost Gospel*) is one proponent of this view. For one recent discussion of this issue, see Tuckett, *Q and the History*, 393–424.

"its overwhelming Jewishness was a relatively recent phenomenon." His understanding of the region's history was similar to the schema outlined above: the region originally had contained many Gentiles, as evidenced by the reference in Isaiah 8:23 to "Galilee of the Gentiles"; the Assyrian conquest resulted in the deportation of most Israelites, though some remained behind to co-exist with the foreign colonists the Assyrians imported. For Vermes, though, the Hasmonean conquest marked the shift of the region back into the Jewish sphere; Aristobulus's "Judaization" had been successful.[51] Galilee's annexation into Hasmonean territory and its position surrounded by gentile neighbors had resulted in a unique Judaism, one marked by Jewish pride despite its geographical separation from Jerusalem. Far from arguing that Galilee's mixed population explained Jesus's openness toward gentiles, Vermes suggested that "it may have been Galilean chauvinism that was responsible for Jesus's apparent antipathy towards Gentiles."[52]

Martin Goodman's analysis of rabbinic texts found a primarily Jewish community in the post-revolts, second-century CE Galilee.[53] His search of early rabbinic traditions for reports of specific encounters between Jews and gentiles in Galilee discovered few examples. Goodman suggests that while generalized rabbinic discussions about appropriate behavior in such meetings may reflect regular contact with non-Jews, more likely they reflect a theoretical concern. He does believe that some interaction between Jews and gentiles occurred, arguing that "social contact with gentiles is . . . probable, at least in some parts of Galilee; commercial contacts are certain,"[54] but he concludes that these contacts were more frequent in the border regions, where Galileans would have encountered pagans from the surrounding cities and villages. The strongest possible evidence for gentiles, according to Goodman, is the presence of pagan symbols on the coins of Sepphoris and Tiberias, but he argues that such images may have been adopted in the wake of the two revolts by Jewish leaders eager to placate the sensibilities of the Roman authorities. If that is the case, then they reflect the political acumen of Galilee's Jewish leadership, not a pagan population.[55]

Sean Freyne's *Galilee from Alexander the Great to Hadrian: 323 B.C.E. to 135 C.E.* also rejected the theory of a gentile Galilee, as evidenced in its subtitle: "A Study of Second Temple Judaism." In contrast to Vermes, Freyne argued for the continuity of the first-century CE population with

---

[51] Geza Vermes, *Jesus the Jew* (Philadelphia: Fortress Press, 1973), 44.

[52] Ibid., 49; cf. Geza Vermes, *Jesus and the World of Judaism* (London: SCM Press, 1983), 1–14.

[53] Goodman, *State and Society*, esp. 41–53.   [54] Ibid., 45.   [55] Ibid., 129.

the pre-Assyrian conquest Israelites. Though the Assyrians had depopulated and resettled Samaria, he suggested, they had not removed the inhabitants of Galilee.[56] Thus, the Jewish character of the region was largely undisturbed throughout the centuries. Jewish–gentile conflicts during the Maccabean campaigns occurred primarily near the gentile coastal cities.[57] Aristobulus "Judaized" the Itureans who had moved into the region as the Seleucid empire crumbled, but no forcible conversion was necessary for most Galileans, who already considered themselves Jews. The first-century CE population, therefore, was predominantly Jewish, just as the populations in the preceding centuries had been.

Freyne wrote *Galilee from Alexander the Great to Hadrian* before much of the archaeological work in Galilee had been executed and published, so his arguments there are based primarily on literary sources. In *Galilee, Jesus, and the Gospels*, he incorporates recent archaeological data in his effort to situate Jesus within a specifically Galilean context. As in his earlier study, Freyne notes the lack of evidence for participation of Galileans at the pagan shrines at Dan or Gerizim and concludes that Galileans were loyal to the Jerusalem temple, though their participation was limited because of distance and some suspicions toward the Jerusalem authorities. Jesus would have encountered gentiles on his travels to surrounding regions, Freyne argues, and he exhibited a universal perspective which emphasized God's care for Jews and gentiles alike.

Freyne has also updated his reconstruction of Galilee's historical development. In recent articles, he acknowledges that the lack of archaeological evidence for settlement between the eighth century BCE and the Hellenistic period suggests that less continuity existed between first-century CE Galilee's Jewish population and the pre-Assyrian deportation Israelites than he originally supposed. Noting a multiplication of Galilean sites in the Late Hellenistic period, he argues that the population grew through colonization after the Hasmonean conquest.[58] In his most recent publications, Freyne allows for a gentile presence in Galilee but places it mostly at the region's margins.

---

[56] A similar position was held by Albrecht Alt, "Galiläsche Probleme," in *Kleine Schriften zur Geschichte des Volkes Israel* (Munich: C.H. Beck'sche Verlagsbuchhandlung, 1953), vol. II, 363–435.

[57] Cf. 1 Macc. 5:9–23.

[58] Freyne, *Galilee, Jesus, and the Gospels*, 169–170; see also Sean Freyne, "Behind the Names: Galileans, Samaritans, *Ioudaioi*," in Eric M. Meyers, ed., *Galilee through the Centuries: Confluence of Cultures* (Winona Lake, Ind.: Eisenbrauns, 1999), 39–56; "Galilee," *OEANE*, vol. II, 370–376; "Galilee," *ABD*, vol. II, 895–899; "Geography, Politics, and Economics"; and "Archaeology and the Historical Jesus," in John R. Bartlett, ed., *Archaeology and Biblical Interpretation* (London and New York: Routledge, 1997), 122–138.

Richard A. Horsley also rejects the idea of a mostly gentile Galilee, though the image he offers in its stead is especially controversial.[59] Horsley dismisses the possibility that Galilee was largely uninhabited after the Assyrian invasion, noting that this view is based primarily on surface surveys, which are often inaccurate. The literary sources, he posits, depict neither a widespread depopulation of the region of Galilee by the Assyrians, nor any massive recolonization by the Assyrian, Persian, Ptolemaic, or Seleucid rulers. Thus, the first-century CE Galileans were descendants of the ancient Israelites. Galilee's distinct history, marked by long-term political separation from Judea and Jerusalem, resulted in a unique culture. Galileans shared a "common Israelite cultural heritage" with the Judeans, but their traditions and customs differed substantially from those of their southern neighbors. Thus, Horsley argues, Galileans were not, properly speaking, "Jews." He proposes that the underlying Greek term ιουδαιος, when used in Palestinian contexts, should be taken quite literally as "Judean," thus excluding Galileans. The Hasmonean "conversion" of the inhabitants of Galilee resulted in their introduction into Jerusalem's sphere of influence and control, not their mass conversion to Judean religion. "Subjection of the Galileans and others to 'the laws of the Judeans' meant, in effect, subordination to the Hasmonean temple-state in a political-economic way inseparable from its religious dimension." Because of the shared Israelite heritage of Galileans and Judeans, the transition to Hasmonean rule of Galilee was not as problematic as it could have been, but the inhabitants were not integrated into the Judean *ethnos*; they remained a distinct people, having "undergone more than eight centuries of separate development."[60] To understand Galilee as a primarily gentile region would be to misunderstand it, but to regard it as "Jewish" would likewise be to remain blind to its own distinctive history and culture.

Meyers's observations of the differences in the material cultures of Upper and Lower Galilee and his work at Sepphoris prompted much of the subsequent discussion of Hellenistic Galilee by New Testament scholars. Even in his earlier articles, however, despite his vigorous call for the recognition of the strong influence of Hellenism in Lower Galilee, Meyers never claimed that the first-century CE population contained many Gentiles. His argument had been that first-century Galilee was in contact with its gentile neighbors, but that its population – including Sepphoris and Tiberias – was predominantly Jewish. He now stresses that

---

[59] Richard A. Horsley, *Galilee: History, Politics, People* (Valley Forge, Penn.: Trinity Press International, 1995) and *Archaeology*.

[60] Horsley, *Galilee*, 50–51. Sawicki (*Crossing Galilee*) follows Horsley in this regard.

changes in the population occurred within the second century CE, when thousands of Roman troops were stationed a few miles to the south at Legio. Meyers's more recent statements leave no doubt that, in his view, the first-century CE population was almost entirely Jewish. He writes, "On the basis of Galilean regionalism, archaeology, the gospels, and Josephus, it is the inescapable and unavoidable conclusion that Jesus's Galilean context was first and foremost a Jewish one both in content and in its political, administrative form."[61]

E. P. Sanders grants the presence of Hellenism in Galilee, though he is skeptical of its extent since evidence for the major institutions of Hellenism, especially the gymnasium, the agent of education and socialization in the Greek world, is noticeably absent. Sanders questions whether mere proximity to cities would have created a common culture shared by both city and village, and he is not convinced that trade between Galilee and surrounding areas indicates that the inhabitants had regular contact with each other. As for the idea that Galilee had large numbers of gentiles, Sanders rejects it entirely, contrasting the extensive evidence for Judaism (particularly in Josephus) with the lack of evidence for paganism. In particular, he dismisses the notion that Roman troops were stationed in first-century CE Galilee, pointing out the irregularity that Roman troops in a client king's territory would have posed and emphasizing the abundance of evidence demonstrating that Roman troops were stationed there only in the second century. He summarizes: "On the whole, in Antipas's Galilee, which was Jesus's Galilee, the law was Jewish, the courts were Jewish, the education was Jewish."[62]

---

[61] Meyers, "Jesus and His Galilean Context," 64.

[62] Sanders, "Jesus in Historical Context," 429–448, quote from 440; see also Sanders, *Historical Figure*, 20–22 and "Jesus' Galilee," in Ismo Dunderberg, Kari Syreeni, and Christopher Tuckett, eds., *Pluralism and Conflicts: Festschrift Heikki Räisänen* (Leiden: Brill, forthcoming). For examples of other scholars who have argued that Galilee was primarily Jewish, see Martin Goodman, "Galilean Judaism and Judaean Judaism," in William Horbury, W. D. Davies, and John Sturdy, eds., *The Cambridge History of Judaism*, vol. III (Cambridge: Cambridge University Press, 1999), 596–617; Frances Xavier Malinowski, "Galilean Judaism in the Writings of Flavius Josephus" (Ph.D. Diss., Duke University, 1973), esp. 66–71; Louis H. Feldman, "How Much Hellenism in Jewish Palestine?" *Hebrew Union College Annual* 57 (1986): 83–111; Louis H. Feldman, *Jew and Gentile in the Ancient World: Attitudes and Interactions from Alexander to Justinian* (Princeton: Princeton University Press, 1993), 24–25; Fergus Millar, *The Roman Near East: 31 B.C.–A.D. 337* (Cambridge, Mass. and London: Harvard University Press, 1993), 347; Ben Witherington, III, *The Jesus Quest: The Third Search for the Jew of Nazareth* (Downers Grove, Ill.: InterVarsity Press, 1995), 38; Anthony J. Saldarini, *Matthew's Christian-Jewish Community* (Chicago and London: University of Chicago Press, 1994), 75–76; Augustine Stock, *The Method and Message of Matthew* (Collegeville, Minn.: A Michael Glazier Book published by The Liturgical Press, 1989), 57; Bösen, *Galiläa*, 146–148.

Conclusion

Scholarly opinions on how to characterize Galilee's populations depend largely on their interpretation of Galilee's complex political history and material culture. Indeed, one wonders if some scholars have started with the view that Galilee's population was mixed and then searched for reasons to explain why this was so. To clarify the nature of Jewish–gentile interaction there in the first century CE, it is necessary to examine more closely key moments in its prior historical development as well as the available evidence from the first century itself.

2

THE POLITICAL AND DEMOGRAPHIC
HISTORY OF GALILEE

For much of antiquity, possession of Galilee shifted hands from power to power. It was conquered successively by the Israelites, the Assyrians, the Babylonians, the Persians, Alexander the Great, the Ptolemies, the Seleucids, and the Hasmoneans. With the demise of the Hasmonean dynasty came the Herodians, and after them direct Roman rule. Some scholars have concluded that each of these waves of conquest left a dramatic imprint on the composition of Galilee's population, so that in the time of Jesus, elements of all of these external, non-indigenous groups dwelled closely together in the small region. Others have focused on key moments in Galilean history, especially the Assyrian conquest and the Hasmoneans' "Judaization" of the region. The question of the extent of the Roman presence in first-century Galilee has also loomed large in recent discussion.

In fact, the accuracy of the image of successive waves of immigrants into Galilee is doubtful. In this chapter, I will provide an overview of Galilee's history. Detailed treatments of Palestine's political history are readily available elsewhere,[1] so I will focus specifically on the development of Galilee's population, starting with the Assyrian conquest and tracing events until the early second century. Because I am here concerned with Galilee's broader historical development, detailed discussions of individual communities will be reserved for chapter 3.

The Assyrian conquest of Galilee

Before the invasion

The nature of the earliest Israelite settlement in Galilee, as in the rest of Palestine, is unclear. In recent years, archaeologists have increasingly

---

[1] For treatments that highlight Galilee, see Freyne, *Galilee from Alexander* and Horsley, *Galilee* and *Archaeology*.

questioned traditional theories of an actual "conquest" by an outside group of refugees from Egypt. Some scholars stress the continuity between the material culture of the primarily village society that emerges in Palestine in the Early Iron Age and that of the older urban culture of the Late Bronze Age, suggesting that the ancient Israelites emerged from the indigenous population. Others argue that drastic changes occurred in the transition of the ages, suggesting the entrance of new groups.[2]

Galilee figures occasionally in the biblical passages describing the purported Israelite settlement.[3] Joshua 19:10–39 records the boundaries of the territorial allotments of the tribes, placing Zebulun and Naphtali in Galilee, Issachar on its southern border, and Asher on the coast.[4] Judges 1:30–33, which summarizes the effectiveness of Israelite attempts to expunge Canaanites from the land, notes that the Galilean tribes Zebulun and Naphtali were only partly successful, with some Canaanites remaining among them as forced labor. The Song of Deborah in Judges 5, one of the oldest passages in the Hebrew Bible,[5] celebrates the victory of Deborah and Barak over Jabin, the Canaanite king of Hazor in Upper Galilee, and includes the Galilean tribes Zebulun, Naphtali, and Issachar in its list of participants in the battle (14–15, 18).[6] Given the paucity of traditions about Galilee and the ambiguity of the archaeological data, our knowledge of its demographic make-up during this period is very scanty.[7]

[2] Classic discussions include Albrecht Alt, *Die Landnahme der Israeliten in Palästina* (Leipzig: Druckerei der Werkgemeinschaft, 1925); George E. Mendenhall, "The Hebrew Conquest of Palestine," *BA* 25 (1962): 66–87; William Foxwell Albright, *Archaeology and the Religion of Israel*, 5th edn. (Baltimore: Johns Hopkins Press, 1968). Reviews of the secondary literature are found in William G. Dever, "Israel, History of (Archaeology and the 'Conquest')," *ABD*, vol. III, 545–558 and Baruch Halpern, "Settlement of Canaan," *ABD*, vol. V, 1120–1143. See also Zvi Gal, *Lower Galilee during the Iron Age* (Winona Lake, Ind.: Eisenbrauns, 1992), 84–93 and Zvi Gal, "The Late Bronze Age in Galilee: A Reassessment," *BASOR* 272 (1988): 79–84; and the essays in *From Nomadism to Monarchy: Archaeological and Historical Aspects of Early Israel*, ed. Israel Finkelstein and Nadav Na'aman (Jerusalem: Yad Izhak Ben Zvi and Israel Exploration Society; Washington: Biblical Archaeology Society, 1994), especially Rafael Frankel, "Upper Galilee in the Late Bronze–Iron I Transition," 18–34, and Zvi Gal, "Iron I in Lower Galilee and the Margins of the Jezreel Valley," 35–46.

[3] See Frankel, "Galilee," and Freyne, *Galilee from Alexander*, 16–21.

[4] See Carol Meyers, "Of Seasons and Soldiers: A Topological Appraisal of the Premonarchic Tribes of Galilee," *BASOR* 252 (1983): 47–59.

[5] On the passage's dating, see J. Alberto Soggin, *Judges* (Philadelphia: Westminster Press, 1981), 80–81; Robert G. Boling, *Judges* (Garden City, N.Y.: Doubleday, 1977), 104–107, 116–120; Dennis T. Olson, "The Book of Judges," in Leander Keck et al., eds., *The Interpreter's Bible* (Nashville: Abingdon Press, 1998), vol. II, 787.

[6] Cf. Joshua 11:1–14.

[7] William G. Dever addresses the difficulties of reconstructing this period in "'Will the Real Israel Please Stand Up?' Archaeology and Israelite Historiography: Part I," *BASOR*

Phoenicians were well settled on the coastal plain,[8] and the population in the interior probably consisted of members from a hodge-podge of different groups.[9]

Fortunately, it is unnecessary to enter in too much depth into this thorny debate. What is clear is that by the tenth century BCE, Galilee was part of the northern kingdom of Israel. During the monarchy, the region was densely settled, and at least fifteen new cities were built. Indeed, Galilee, particularly Lower Galilee, seems to have flourished during the early monarchy,[10] though Syrian incursions resulted in the occasional loss of Israelite territory.[11] Most likely, other peoples continued to dwell among the Israelites (as suggested by Judges 1:30–33), either scattered amongst the villages or grouped in pockets, though on this point, too, our knowledge is vague.[12]

Galilee and the fall of Israel

By the late eighth century BCE, Israel was subject to the watchful eye of the Assyrian Empire, to whom it had paid tribute.[13] Sometime around 733 BCE, King Pekah of Israel undertook a course of action which was to have disastrous consequences. Entering into an alliance with Rezin of Aram, Pekah attacked Jerusalem. His efforts to seize the city were unsuccessful, but Ahaz, king of Judah, felt threatened enough to seek help from Assyria.[14] Tiglath-pileser III, king of Assyria, retaliated against his troublesome vassals *c.* 732 BCE, sweeping through northern Israel and Transjordan and devastating Galilee. A few years later, in 722 BCE, Tiglath-pileser's successor, Shalmaneser V, conquered Samaria, exiling many of its inhabitants and bringing the northern kingdom of Israel to an end.[15]

---

297 (1995): 61–80 and " 'Will the Real Israel Please Stand Up?' Part II: Archaeology and the Religions of Ancient Israel," *BASOR* 298 (1995): 37–58.

[8] William A. Ward, "Phoenicia," *OEANE,* vol. IV, 313–317; Glenn Markoe, "Phoenicians," *OEANE* vol. IV, 325–331.

[9] Frankel, "Galilee," 884.

[10] Gal, *Lower Galilee,* 94–109. This extensive building activity also occurred at smaller sites such as 'Ein Zippori (J. P. Dessel, " 'Ein Zippori, Tel," *OEANE*, vol. II, 227–228 and Carol L. Meyers, "Sepphoris and Lower Galilee: Earliest Times through the Persian Period," in Rebecca Martin Nagy, Carol L. Meyers, Eric M. Meyers, and Zeev Weiss, eds., *Sepphoris in Galilee: Crosscurrents of Culture* [Winona Lake, Ind.: Eisenbrauns, 1996], 15–20).

[11] 1 Kings 15:16–21; 2 Kings 10:32–33; 13:3, 22, 25; 14:25–28. See Horsley, *Galilee,* 27 and *Archaeology,* 21.

[12] See the probable examples discussed in Avraham Faust, "Ethnic Complexity in Northern Israel during Iron Age II," *PEQ* 132 (2000): 2–27.

[13] 2 Kings 15:19–20.   [14] 2 Kings 16:5–7; cf. Isa. 7:1–8:10.

[15] 2 Kings 17:5–6, 23. The account in 2 Kings of the events in this period is considered generally reliable. See Herbert Donner, "The Separate States of Israel and Judah," in

Isaiah 8:23 (9:1) refers to the desolation the Assyrian invasion brought to Galilee, though it also promises future deliverance: "In the former time, he [Yahweh] brought into contempt the land of Zebulun and the land of Naphtali, but in the latter time he will make glorious the way of the sea, the land beyond the Jordan, Galilee of the Nations [גליל הגוים]."[16] This reference, the earliest attestation of the phrase "Galilee of the Nations," has been influential in shaping impressions that eighth-century BCE Galilee's population was eclectic.[17] Whether this view of the name's significance is correct is unclear, however. As suggested above, some diversity in Galilee's population is probable, and it is possible that the name reflects this. Alternatively, the name may have originated in the fact that Canaanite cities surrounded Galilee, making a "circle of nations" – the most literal rendering of גליל הגוים – around the region.[18] Regardless of which view is adopted, it is noteworthy that this passage is the only one in the Hebrew Bible to designate the region "Galilee of the Nations"; other references call it only "Galilee," suggesting that the region normally went by the one-word name.[19]

The depopulation of Galilee

What was the result of the Assyrian conquest of Galilee? If the majority of the inhabitants of Galilee were allowed to remain on their land,

John H. Hayes and J. Maxwell Miller eds., *Israelite and Judaean History* (Philadelphia: Westminster Press, 1977), 381–434; Siegfried Hermann, *A History of Israel in Old Testament Times* (Philadelphia: Fortress Press, 1981), 243–254; and John Bright, *A History of Israel*, 3rd edn. (Philadelphia: Westminster Press, 1981), 269–276.

[16] The references to the "way of the Sea," the "land beyond the Jordan," and "Galilee of the Gentiles" have often been interpreted as references to the three Assyrian provinces of Dor, Megiddo and Gilead. This view was developed by E. Forrer (*Die Provinzeinteilung des assyrischen Reiches* [Leipzig, 1920]) and Albrecht Alt ("Das System der assyrischen Provinzen auf dem Boden des Reiches Israel," *ZDPV* 52 [1929]: 220–242, reprinted in *Kleine Schriften zur Geschichte des Volkes Israel* [Munich: C. H. Beck'sche Verlagsbuchhandlung, 1953], vol. II, 188–205). For contrasting views, see Anson F. Rainey, "Toponymic Problems," *Tel Aviv* 8 (1981): 146–151 and Israel Eph'al, "Assyrian Dominance in Palestine," in Abraham Malamat, ed., *The Age of the Monarchies* (The World History of the Jewish People 1.4.2; Israel: Jewish History Publications; New Brunswick: Rutgers University Press, 1979), 276–289, 364–368.

[17] E.g., John N. Oswalt, *The Book of Isaiah: Chapters 1–39* (Grand Rapids, Mich.: William B. Eerdmans Publishing Co., 1986), 239; J. A. Motyer, *The Prophecy of Isaiah* (Leicester: Inter-Varsity Press, 1993), 100.

[18] See additional discussion of the name in my "Conclusion"; cf. Frankel, "Galilee," 895–896; Freyne, *Galilee from Alexander*, 3; Freyne, "Galilee," *ABD*, vol. II, 895–896; Bösen, *Galiläa*, 13; Alt, "Galiläsche Probleme."

[19] Other references to Galilee are found in Josh. 20:7, 21:32; 1 Kings 9:11; 2 Kings 15:29; 1 Chron. 6:76. Horsley discusses the various passages in *Galilee*, 288–289, n. 1.

they presumably became the ancestors of later inhabitants in the Persian, Hellenistic, and Roman eras. If most Galileans were deported, then continuity was broken between the population of the northern kingdom and the Second Temple population. If some inhabitants were deported and large numbers of foreign colonists were imported, as happened in Samaria,[20] then one might surmise that the subsequent population became a mixture of Israelites, gentiles, and the offspring of the two groups.

Some scholars, most recently Horsley, have suggested that the Assyrian conquest introduced few changes in the Galilean population. Horsley argues that the number of Israelites deported must have been small and would have consisted primarily of skilled workers, soldiers, and the social elite. Furthermore, according to Horsley, since Syrians had controlled much of Galilee, whether those who were deported were Israelites or Syrians is unclear. Horsley rejects as incomplete the archaeological evidence of sparse settlement in the following centuries, citing the notorious inaccuracy of surface surveys.[21]

The evidence suggesting that the Assyrians deported large numbers of Galileans is substantial, however.[22] Second Kings 15:29 includes the Galilean cities Ijon, Abel-beth-maacah, Janoah, Kedesh, and Hazor and "Gilead, and Galilee, all the land of Naphtali" among the northern territories which Tiglath-pileser captured. It concludes, "And he carried the people captive to Assyria."[23] Assyrian inscriptions and Tiglath-pileser's annals also record the exile of Galileans. Two annals, 18 and 24, refer to the expulsion of Galileans and include the numbers, which add up to thousands, exiled from specific communities.[24]

---

[20] On the repopulation of Samaria, see 2 Kings 17:24, 29–31; Ezra 4:2, 10; Isa. 7:8; Bright, *History*, 276; Donner, "Separate States," 434; Hermann, *History*, 251–252.

[21] Horsley, *Archaeology*, 22–23 and *Galilee*, 25–29, relying on Bustenay Oded, *Mass Deportations in the Neo-Assyrian Empire* (Wiesbaden: Reichert, 1979), 54–57, 91–109 and cf. Stuart A. Irvine, "The Southern Border of Syria Reconstructed," *CBQ* 56 (1994): 21–41; cf. Alt, "Galiläsche Probleme," 363–435 and Freyne, *Galilee from Alexander*, 24–25 (Freyne has since accepted Gal's viewpoint that Galilee was only sparsely inhabited ["Galilee," *OEANE*, vol. II, 371–372]).

[22] K. Lawson Younger, Jr., "The Deportations of the Israelites," *JBL* 117 (1998): 201–227, esp. 206–214.

[23] On the possibility that "Gilead and Galilee" are additions to the text, see Irvine, "Southern Border," 25–26.

[24] Younger, Jr., "Deportations," 210–213 and Annals 18 and 24 in H. Tadmor, *The Inscriptions of Tiglath-Pileser III King of Assyria* (Jerusalem: Israel Academy of Sciences and Humanities, 1994), 81–83. As Younger points out, the numbers in Assyrian records (13,420 in Annal 24) correspond roughly to Gal's population estimate (17,600 total for the region) (*Lower Galilee*, 109). Magen Broshi and Israel Finkelstein ("The Population of Palestine in Iron Age II," *BASOR* 287 [1992]: 47–60) estimate that Galilee's population was approximately 47,500, considerably higher than Gal's figure. Even if this higher number is accepted, the proportion of deported Galileans was still considerable.

The archaeological evidence strongly corroborates biblical and Assyrian reports of depopulation. Zvi Gal has persuasively argued that Galilee was mostly uninhabited from the late eighth century BCE until the Persian era.[25] Surface surveys of eighty-three Lower Galilean sites found very little ceramic evidence from the seventh and sixth centuries BCE, in contrast to considerable amounts of pottery for the periods preceding the Assyrian invasion. Familiar ceramic forms (certain mortaria bowls, high-neck decanters, and hole-mouth jars) were largely absent from Galilean sites, and, in contrast to finds at Samaritan sites, Assyrian pottery and local imitations were also uncommon.

Excavations have corroborated the surface surveys. Tel Mador yields evidence of occupation from the tenth and ninth centuries BCE and from the Persian period but only one sherd from the eighth century BCE. Excavations at Tel Qarnei Ḥittin have demonstrated that a sizable city was destroyed in the late eighth century BCE, with no subsequent occupation. The settlement at Hurbat Rosh Zayit, probably a Phoenician community, was likewise destroyed in the mid-eighth century BCE, with no reset-tlement afterwards.[26] Excavations at Hurrat H. Malta, Tel Gath-Hepher, Hazor, Kinneret and Tel Ḥarashim have revealed dramatic decreases in population after the eighth century BCE.[27] The implication is that not only did the indigenous population leave Galilee, but the Assyrians did not repopulate it.[28]

The region was not wholly deserted, however. Although occupation decreased at Hazor, it did not cease altogether. A fortress and a large building (perhaps residential, perhaps palatial) have been discovered there, probably reflecting Assyrian occupation.[29] At Kefar Kanna, an Assyrian presence is suggested by a bronze cup with Assyrian-style decorations.[30] Biblical records of the activities of the southern kingdom occasionally mention Galileans.[31] Soon after Israel's fall, Hezekiah sent messengers

[25] Zvi Gal in several studies: *Lower Galilee*; "Israel in Exile," *BAR* 24:3 (1998): 48–53; "Galilee: Chalcolithic to Persian Periods," *NEAEHL*, vol. II, 449–453; "Galilee: Galilee in the Bronze and Iron Ages," *OEANE*, vol. II, 369–370; "The Lower Galilee in the Iron Age II: Analysis of Survey Material and its Historical Interpretation," *Tel Aviv* 15–16 (1988–1989): 56–64.

[26] Gal, *Lower Galilee*, 36–53.

[27] Gal, "Israel in Exile," 52 and "Galilee," *OEANE*, vol. II, 451.

[28] Gal, *Lower Galilee*, 12–35, 79–83.

[29] R. Reich, "The Persian Building at Ayyelet ha-Shaḥar: The Assyrian Palace of Hazor?" *IEJ* 25 (1975): 233–237 and Amnon Ben-Tor, "Hazor: Fifth Season of Excavations (1968–1969)," *NEAEHL*, vol. II, 604–605.

[30] Frankel, "Galilee," 893. Both the markings for hair on the cup and the frieze of characters on the rim are typically Assyrian (H. Frankfort, *The Art and Architecture of the Ancient Orient* [Baltimore: Penguin, 1954], 103, plate 118A).

[31] Frankel, "Galilee," 893.

north "as far as Zebulun" in his call for a Passover celebration, and a few Galileans responded.[32] Hezekiah's son Manasseh married a Galilean woman, as did Jehoiakim.[33] Josiah's campaign against idolatry in the late seventh century extended "as far as Naphtali."[34] Thus, a few Israelites remained in Galilee, and a few Assyrians (perhaps administrators or soldiers) lived there, but for the most part, the region was unpopulated. In light of both the archaeological and the literary evidence, claims of continuity between the pre-Assyrian conquest population and the Second Temple population, such as the recent ones by Horsley and the earlier ones by Geza Vermes, are difficult to maintain.[35] As Gal concludes, "Lower Galilee was practically deserted by the end of the eighth century."[36]

Galilee in the Persian period

Gal's finds strongly suggest that Galilee remained mostly desolate until the period of Persian rule (*c.* 539–332 BCE). Along with the rest of Palestine, it was part of the large Persian satrapy known as *Ever ha-Nahar*, "Beyond the River."[37] Because biblical sources from this period deal almost exclusively with Jerusalem and the south, and the Zenon papyri are primarily concerned with other areas of Palestine and the Near East, our knowledge of Galilee is extremely limited. Likewise, archaeological remains from the period are relatively uncommon and have not been synthesized recently.[38] A recent survey of Upper Galilee found remains of dozens of small villages, some dating back to the end of the Persian period, demonstrating that old sites were reoccupied and new sites appeared.[39] Many excavated sites have a thin Persian stratum, usually consisting only of pottery sherds. Extensive fragments of Persian architecture are uncommon; remains of a temple discovered at Mizpeh Yamim, located on a southern spur of the Meiron Massif, are a notable exception.[40] Likewise, recovery of well-preserved artifacts, such as the rhyton, cuneiform tablet, and incense burner found at Sepphoris,[41] is infrequent. Galilee's material culture in this period bears more similarities

---

[32] 2 Chron. 30:10–11.   [33] 2 Kings 21:19, 23:36.   [34] 2 Chron. 34:6.

[35] Horsley, *Galilee and Archaeology*; Vermes, *Jesus the Jew*. Vermes's book was published prior to recent archaeological work.

[36] Gal, "Israel in Exile," 52.   [37] Ezra 4; 8:36; Neh. 2:7, 9.

[38] Eric M. Meyers, "Second Temple Studies in the Light of Recent Archaeology: Part I: The Persian and Hellenistic Periods," *Currents in Research: Biblical Studies* 2 (1994): 25–42.

[39] Aviam, "Galilee," *NEAEHL*, vol. II, 453.

[40] Rafael Frankel, "Har Miṣpe Yamim – 1988/1989," *ESI* 9 (1989–1990): 100–102.

[41] See comments by Michael Dayagi-Mendels and Matthew W. Stolper in *Sepphoris*, ed. Nagy et al, 163–167.

to finds from the Phoenician sites on the coast than to finds from Judea or Samaria.[42] This affinity may be due to Phoenician cultural influence, but it probably also reflects the drift of Phoenicians into the otherwise uninhabited territory.[43]

Macedonian and Greek rule

The campaigns of Alexander the Great brought Persian rule of the eastern Mediterranean region to a close. Commercial contacts with Greece are visible in Palestine's archaeological record from the Persian period, and Alexander's conquest and the subsequent Greek kingdoms resulted in increased interaction between Greek and local cultures. Alexander's successors, as is well known, split his empire among them. Galilee was one of the arenas of conflict between the Ptolemies and the Seleucids, with the latter taking it from the former at the end of the third century BCE.[44] Ptolemaic and Seleucid coinage almost invariably appears in the Hellenistic strata of Galilean sites, attesting to their political domination. In general, though, as with the Persian period, our knowledge of Galilee under the Ptolemaic and Seleucid reigns is very limited.[45]

Both kingdoms founded and renamed cities in the border regions of Galilee and in the surrounding territories. The Ptolemies founded cities on previously settled sites, establishing Ptolemais, on the coast at Acco; Scythopolis, at Beth She'an in the plain southeast of Galilee; and Philoteria, to the southwest of the Sea of Galilee (perhaps at Beth Yeraḥ).[46] These foundations may have been accompanied by the arrival of colonists, though our knowledge of the Ptolemaic foundation process in Palestine is scanty. Colonists, if they were introduced, would have included Greeks

[42] Mizpeh Yamim, however, despite the probable Phoenician cultural orientation of its temple, differs from many Galilean sites in that its ceramics have more in common with certain types from Upper Galilee than with the Phoenician types from the coast (Frankel, "Har Miṣpe Yamim").

[43] Ephraim Stern discusses Galilean sites with Persian era remains in *Material Culture of the Land of the Bible in the Persian Period 538–332 B.C.* (Warminster: Aris and Phillips, 1982), 1–9, 240. On the Phoenician character of Galilee's material culture, see ibid., 240 and Gal, "Israel in Exile," 53.

[44] A. H. M. Jones provides a helpful summary of Greek settlement in the area in *The Cities of the Eastern Roman Provinces*, 2nd edn. (Oxford: Clarendon Press, 1971), 226–256; see also A. H. M. Jones, *The Greek City from Alexander to Justinian* (Oxford: Clarendon Press, 1940), 1–50 and Michael Avi-Yonah, *The Holy Land* (Grand Rapids, Mich.: Baker Book House, 1966), 32–51.

[45] For overviews of Galilee in this period, see Freyne, *Galilee from Alexander*, 27–35; Freyne, "Galilee," *OEANE*, vol. II, 371–376; Freyne, "Galilee," *ABD*, vol. II, 895–899; Aviam, "Galilee," *NEAEHL*, vol. II, 453–458.

[46] Freyne, *Galilee from Alexander*, 104–114.

and resettled locals, with perhaps an Egyptian element as well. No cities were founded and no colonists settled in the interior of Galilee, however. While at least some Ptolemaic administrators would have been assigned to Galilee, their numbers are entirely unknown.[47] Thus, we have little evidence of extensive Ptolemaic settlement in the region.

After their takeover of the region, the Seleucids, too, would have assigned administrative officials to Galilee, though, in general, they relied on locals to meet many of their personnel needs.[48] In typical Hellenistic fashion, the Seleucids renamed some Palestinian cities, adding Nysa to the name of Scythopolis, for example. As for new cities, they established Antiochia, to the north near Paneas, and Seleucia, in the Golan.[49] Seleucid colonists typically consisted of Greeks, Macedonians, people from Asia Minor, and locals,[50] but we have no indication that any such colonists were ever brought to Galilee. The Seleucid foundations and colonies seem to have been limited to the surrounding territories.[51]

In short, there is little reason to believe that Greek rule of Galilee led to a massive influx of Greek settlers. In terms of a Greek presence, Galilee does not compare even to the coastal cities of Palestine, much less to the coastal cities of western Asia Minor. A few officials arrived, and troops were stationed in and moved through the region, particularly during times of tension between the Ptolemies and Seleucids. Foreign colonists settled, perhaps, in the cities of the fringes (Scythopolis, Philoteria, Ptolemais) and in the surrounding region (Antiochia, Seleucia), but not in Galilee itself. Even at these places, colonists probably arrived only in limited numbers; the population of Greeks in the world was not boundless, and both the Ptolemies and Seleucids seem to have focused their primary energies elsewhere.[52] The interior of Galilee, in short, was still relatively sparsely populated on the eve of the Maccabean campaigns.[53]

---

[47] Galilee was one of four Ptolemaic hyparchies in Palestine, the others being Judea, Samaria, and Idumea; see Freyne, *Galilee from Alexander*, 28–29 and Roger S. Bagnall, "Palestine, Administration of (Ptolemaic)," *ABD*, vol. V, 90–92.

[48] Galilee and Judea were part of the Seleucid eparchy of Samaria; other Palestinian eparchies were Idumea, Paralia, and Galaaditis; see Freyne, *Galilee from Alexander*, 32–35 and Thomas Fischer, "Palestine, Administration of (Seleucid)," trans. Frederick H. Cryer, *ABD*, vol. V, 92–96.

[49] See Freyne, *Galilee from Alexander*, 113–114.

[50] Getzel Cohen, *The Seleucid Colonies* (Wiesbaden: Franz Steiner Verlag GMBH, 1978), 29–44.

[51] On Seleucid foundations, see ibid., 16–17.

[52] Cf. Jones's discussion of the limited nature of Greek immigration to the east in *Greek City*, 23–26.

[53] One pagan artifact possibly dating to this period is a votive altar or stele (its exact function is uncertain), with four sides, two decorated with snakes and one with a rounded

Galilee and the Maccabees

Simon's expedition to Galilee

Galilee next appears in the historical record in accounts of the Maccabean revolt, and 1 Maccabees 5:9–23 has been an especially influential passage in shaping views of its population. This account of Simon's military activity in Galilee, placed within a larger report (chapter five) of the rescue of Jews in both Galilee and Gilead, has often been cited to show that by the Maccabean revolt, Jews were a small minority in the region known as "Galilee of the Gentiles."[54] The account begins with a report of gentile hostility toward the Jews. Galilean messengers to Judas and his brothers claim that "the people of Ptolemais and Tyre and Sidon, and all Galilee of the Gentiles (πᾶσαν Γαλιλαίαν ἀλλοφύλων) had gathered together against them 'to annihilate us.'" Simon "went to Galilee and fought many battles against the gentiles, and the gentiles were crushed before him." Apparently unable or unwilling to hold the area, Simon withdrew the Jews of Galilee and Arbatta (exact location unknown) to Jerusalem. Schürer concluded, "It is thus clearly evident that the Jews in Galilee and Gilead still formed a Diaspora among the Gentiles; and the early Maccabees by no means set out to Judaise those regions, but on the contrary, withdrew their Jewish population."[55] Simon's evacuation of the Jews, Schürer thought, left the region almost wholly gentile until the subsequent Hasmonean conquest some sixty years later.

"Galilee of the Gentiles"

First Maccabees 5:15 at first glance appears to provide evidence that the region was commonly called "Galilee of the Gentiles," during both the time of the Maccabean revolt itself and the time of the composition of 1 Maccabees, but a more careful look reveals otherwise. The geographical referent is clearly not the larger region of Galilee, but the portion near the coast, which was dominated by gentiles.[56] This is where the conflict

knob, found near Bar'am (Nahman Avigad, "A Votive Altar from Upper Galilee," *BASOR* 167 [1962]: 18–22).

[54] E.g., J. C. Dancey, *A Commentary on 1 Maccabees* (Oxford: Basil Blackwell, 1954), 104; B. Bar-Kochva, "Manpower, Economics, and Internal Strife in the Hasmonean State," in H. van Effenterre, ed., *Armées et Fiscalité dans le Monde Antique* (Paris: Editions du Centre National de la Recherche Scientifique, 1977), 192; and the widely influential Schürer, *History*, vol. I, 142 and vol. II, 7–10.

[55] Schürer, *History*, vol. I, 142; cf. vol. II, 8.

[56] Dancey (*Commentary*, 104) suggests the term refers to "the hinterland of the coastal cities"; see also Robert Doran, "The First Book of Maccabees," in Leander Keck et al., eds.,

occurs: gentile assaults originate in Ptolemais, Tyre, and Sidon, and Simon routs his opponents as far as "the gates of Ptolemais" (5:22).

The phrase Γαλιλαία ἀλλοφύλων also appears in LXX Joel 4:4: "What are you to me, Tyre and Sidon πᾶσα Γαλιλαία ἀλλοφύλων?" This passage brings with it its own problems, however, because πᾶσα Γαλιλαία ἀλλοφύλων is either a mistranslation of the Hebrew פלשת גלילות, "districts of the Philistines," or it reflects an alternative textual tradition. The Septuagint frequently uses ἀλλοφύλος to translate פלשת, but the use of Γαλιλαία here may reflect a misreading of גלילות, the plural form of גלילה, "district." Perhaps the translators chose Γαλιλαία ἀλλοφύλων as an archaizing allusion to Isaiah 8:23, though the Septuagint renders גליל הגוים there as Γαλιλαία τῶν ἐθνῶν, not Γαλιλαία ἀλλοφύλων. At most, LXX Joel 4:4 suggests that at the time of translation, the part of Galilee near the coast was known as Γαλιλαία ἀλλοφύλων.

Complicating even further the relevance of 1 Maccabees 5:15 for determining Galilee's name is the fact that ἀλλοφύλος is probably intended to echo biblical language. On a literal level, the word means "foreigner." Though, in later usage, it often signifies "gentile,"[57] in the Septuagint, it is not used where the Masoretic reading is גוי. Instead, ἀλλοφύλος occurs hundreds of times (as in Joel 4:4) where the Masoretic text has פלשת, "Philistine," and it is especially prevalent in Judges, 1 and 2 Samuel, and 1 and 2 Kings. In using ἀλλοφύλος to refer to the Jews' enemies,[58]

The New Interpreter's Bible (Nashville: Abingdon Press, 1996), vol. IV, 77 and Schürer, *History*, vol. II, 8. W. Fairweather and J. Sutherland Black provide the alternate possibility (though with no supporting evidence) that the term refers to Upper Galilee, given "the mixed character of its population" (*The First Book of Maccabees* [Cambridge: Cambridge University Press, 1936], 120); cf. H. A. Fischel, *The First Book of Maccabees* (New York: Schocken Books, 1948), 48. In contrast to those who would limit the geographical referent of the phrase, Jonathan A. Goldstein translates it "heathen Galilee" (*1 Maccabees* [Garden City, N.Y.: Doubleday and Co., Inc. 1976], 299).

[57] E.g., *Ant.* 1.338, 4.183; *War* 5.194, Acts 10:28.

[58] 3:41; 4:12, 22, 26, 30; 5:15, 66, 68; 11:68, 74. Both the RSV and the NRSV alternately translate it as "gentile," "foreigner," or "Philistine," choosing "Philistine" primarily for geographical references ("land of the Philistines" [γῆ ἀλλοφύλων] in 3:41; 4:22; 5:66, 68). Though the geographical accuracy of this translation choice is questionable – the Philistines were associated with the coastal areas further south (see Seymour Gitin, "Philistines: Late Philistines," *OEANE*, vol. IV, 311–313) – the translation accurately reflects 1 Maccabees' echo of biblical language; γῆ ἀλλοφύλων is often used in the LXX to translate ארץ פלשתים (e.g., 1 Sam. 27:1, 29:11, 30:16, 31:9; 1 Kings 4:21; 2 Kings 8:2, 1 Chron. 10:9; 2 Chron. 9:26; cf. 1 Sam. 13:20). The NRSV and RSV also choose "Philistine" in 4:30 for the "camp of the Philistines" in the reference to Jonathan's victory over Philistines in 1 Sam. 14. Despite the possibility of translating ἀλλοφύλως as "Philistine," no one has suggested translating Γαλιλαία ἀλλοφύλων in 1 Macc. 5:15 as "Galilee of the Philistines." The English translation "Galilee of the Gentiles" in 1 Macc. 5:15 appears dependent on Isa. 8:23 and Matt. 4:15.

the author of 1 Maccabees connects the Maccabean struggle with those against the Philistines described in the Deuteronomistic history.[59]

The occurrence of Γαλιλαία ἀλλοφύλων in 5:15 may also reflect a pun on the part of the author. First Maccabees does not exclusively use ἀλλόφυλος to refer to gentiles. Far more references to τὰ ἔθνη occur, and this latter term appears frequently in 5:9–23.[60] In 1 Maccabees 5:1, the writer refers to the threat to Israel from "the nations roundabout" (τὰ ἔθνη κυκλόθεν).[61] Perhaps πᾶσαν Γαλιλαίαν ἀλλοφύλων in 5:15, in addition to being a reference to the coastal area, is a play on words of sorts, combining an archaizing allusion to Isaiah 8:23 (Γαλιλαία τῶν ἐθνῶν) with an attempt to bring together the writer's Deuteronomistic use of ἀλλόφυλος and his references to "the nations roundabout" (τὰ ἔθνη ἐν κύκλῳ αὐτῶν). The word play is more visible if one considers the Hebrew root of Γαλιλαία, גלל, or "circle." For the reader familiar with Hebrew Γαλιλαίαν ἀλλοφύλων echoes of "circle of the foreigners," which ties in nicely with the writer's emphasis on "the nations roundabout [most literally, "in a circle about"] them."

The phrase Γαλιλαία ἀλλοφύλων occurs only in these two passages, both times in reference to coastal areas. It may reflect archaizing language, and in 1 Maccabees its occurrence seems related to the author's emphasis on "the nations roundabout" Israel. In neither passage is it clear that the phrase denotes the larger region of Galilee or that it was the common name for the entire region.

The rescue campaign

Most scholars have accepted the basic historicity of Simon's campaign, though some have expressed reservations.[62] Second Maccabees omits the expedition altogether.[63] The description in 1 Maccabees is undetailed:

[59] This association of the Maccabees' opponents and the Philistines reflects the author's unrelenting hostility to gentiles and his glorification of the Maccabees; see Seth Schwartz, "Israel and the Nations Roundabout: 1 Maccabees and the Hasmonean Expansion," *JJS* 41 (1991): 16–38; Bezalel Bar-Kochva, *Judas Maccabeus: The Jewish Struggle against the Seleucids* (Cambridge: Cambridge University Press, 1989), 217–218; Goldstein, *1 Maccabees*, 260.

[60] 5:9, 10, 19, 21, 22; cf. 5:1. Given this fact, the use of ἀλλόφυλος in 5:15 is even more curious.

[61] 5:1; cf. 1:11. See Schwartz, "Israel and the Nations."

[62] Horsley, *Galilee*, 40. Schwartz raises questions about the accuracy of 1 Maccabees 5 as a whole, though he concentrates primarily on the campaign in Gilead ("Israel and the Nations"). Bar-Kochva accepts the historicity of the evacuation (*Judas Maccabeus*, 554).

[63] Second Maccabees 6:8 does report persecution of Jews in Ptolemais and "the neighboring Greek cities."

Simon went to Galilee, where he "fought many battles against the Gentiles and the Gentiles were crushed before him. He pursued them to the gate of Ptolemais; as many as three thousand of the Gentiles fell, and he despoiled them" (5:21–22). Such brevity may reflect only a lack of sources, or the lack of detail may indicate that the entire incident is exaggerated. The author of 1 Maccabees uses the campaigns in chapter five to depict the Maccabees as the fulfillers of a biblical prophecy. In rescuing the Jews of Galilee and Gilead, they are beginning the ingathering of Jews to Jerusalem.[64] Thus, 5:9–23 may reflect the author's glorification of the Maccabees more than historical events.

Other Maccabean campaigns in Galilee

First Maccabees 9:1–2 possibly alludes to conflict in Galilee, though its vague language makes interpretation difficult. After Judas's defeat of Nicanor's army (7:39–50), Demetrius I, a claimant to the Seleucid throne after the death of Antiochus, sent Bacchides and Alcimus to Judah to battle the Maccabees (9:1). According to 9:2, "they went by the road that leads to Mesaloth in Arbela, and they took it and killed many people." A traditional reading of this passage suggests that Bacchides encamped at Arbel near the Sea of Galilee and fought against Galileans loyal to the Maccabees. Unfortunately, the reported route of Bacchides and Alcimus is notoriously difficult to identify. The Greek is unclear: ἐπορεύθησαν ὁδὸν τὴν εἰς Γαλγαλα καὶ παρενέβαλον ἐπὶ Μαισαλωθ τὴν ἐν Αρβηλοις. Galgala may refer to Galilee or to Gilgal, and the reference to Mesaloth is also vague. Josephus clarifies the location of this incident in *Ant.* 12.421, omitting the reference to Mesaloth altogether and reporting that Bacchides came to "Judea and encamped at Arbela, a city in Galilee." Bar-Kochva and Horsley suggest instead that the Hebrew original behind the Greek refers to the heights (מסלות) of Beth-el (בית-אל), a location near Jerusalem, where Bacchides subsequently encamped.[65]

Other accounts of conflict in Galilee are less problematic. According to 1 Maccabees 11:63–74 and *Ant.* 13.158–162 (which relies on

---

[64] Ezek. 39:27, Jer. 31:6–12, 2 Chron. 15:19, Obad. 20–21, Zech. 10:6–8. John J. Collins (*Daniel, First Maccabees, Second Maccabees with an Excursus on the Apocalyptic Genre* [Wilmington, Del.: Michael Glazier, Inc., 1981], 188) and Goldstein (*1 Maccabees*, 300) point out the theme of the ingathering, though they accept the historicity of Simon's expedition. On the Maccabees as fulfillers of biblical prophecies, see Diego Arenhoevel, *Die Theokratie nach dem 1 und 2 Makkabäerbuch* (Mainz: Matthias-Grünewald-Verlag, 1967), 58–69, especially 62.

[65] Bar-Kochva, *Judas Maccabeus*, 552–559; Horsley, *Galilee*, 40; cf. *Ant.* 12.421. Freyne accepts the Galilean locale (*Galilee from Alexander*, 39).

1 Maccabees), Demetrius II encamped at Kedesh in the western part of Upper Galilee *c.* 144 BCE. Jonathan marched against these forces, defeating them in the plain of Hazor in Upper Galilee and pursuing them back to Kedesh. (The motivation Josephus provides for Demetrius demonstrates that Josephus himself viewed Galilee as a Jewish region. Demetrius seeks to draw Jonathan to Galilee "as an ally of that latter country" figuring that "he would not allow the Galileans, who were his own people, to be attacked" [*Ant.* 13.154].) Jonathan later marched north again, this time to Hammath in Lebanon, to prevent an attack by Demetrius on "his own country" (1 Maccabees 11:24ff.). After Jonathan's death in Ptolemais, Trypho attempted but failed to destroy his forces in Galilee and the plain of Esdraelon (1 Maccabees 13:46–52).

Galilee in the Maccabean period

What conclusions can be drawn from these passages? Only the most basic: Galilee was outside the sphere of control of the early Maccabean leadership, though they were willing to venture north occasionally. Aside from the campaign recorded in 1 Maccabees 5:9–23, all action in Galilee occurs between Maccabean forces and Syrians, not with local gentiles. If the report of the expedition to Galilee in 1 Maccabees 5:9–23 is accurate, it indicates only that conflict between Jews and gentiles occurred near the coastal region. Its account of a complete evacuation of Jews is especially suspect, given its usefulness for portraying the Maccabees as the fulfillers of biblical promises of the ingathering of the Jews to Jerusalem. In any case, whether chapter five is historically reliable or not, it allows us to make few generalizations about Galilee's population. We cannot tell what proportion of the population was Jewish before the Maccabees, and we cannot assume that all Jews left Galilee during the wars of Jonathan and Simon.

The Hasmoneans and Galilee

Galilee remained outside the control of the Jerusalem-based Hasmoneans for some time, despite occasional Hasmonean campaigns to the north. John Hyrcanus (ruled 135–104 BCE) ventured as far north as Samaria. His sons Aristobulus I and Antigonus I added Scythopolis as well as territory south of Mount Carmel to the long list of territories assaulted during their father's reign.[66] Galilee itself did not come into Hasmonean hands until after the death of Hyrcanus.

---

[66] *War* 1.66, *Ant.* 13.280.

Aristobulus and the "Judaization" of Galilee

Upon his father's death, Aristobulus secured the Hasmonean throne for himself. His reign was brief, lasting only one year (104–103 BCE), but during that year he conquered Galilee. Perhaps no event is as significant for understanding Galilee's subsequent population as Aristobulus's conquest. Our only preserved account of it, which Josephus provides in his summary of Aristobulus's accomplishments, is brief. Josephus reports that

> in his reign of one year, with the title of Philhellene, he conferred many benefits on his country, for he made war on the Ituraeans and acquired a good part of their territory for Judaea and compelled the inhabitants, if they wished to remain in their country, to be circumcised and to live in accordance with the laws of the Jews.

Josephus continues with a quote of Timagenes by way of Strabo:

> This man was a kindly person and very servicable to the Jews, for he acquired additional territory for them, and brought over to them a portion of the Ituraean nation, whom he joined to them by the bond of circumcision.[67]

Schürer posited that the territory of Iturea that Aristobulus seized included Galilee, and most scholars have followed him on this point.[68] Galilee's subsequent history (discussed below) demonstrates that in the first century BCE, it was part of the Hasmonean sphere.

A proper understanding of Aristobulus's conquest of Galilee, his "conversion" of Galileans to Judaism, and the subsequent Hasmonean settlement there is absolutely essential for understanding its population a hundred years later at the dawn of the New Testament era. Were the inhabitants of first-century CE Galilee descendants of the prior pagan population who had converted whole-heartedly to Judaism?[69] Or, was their "Jewishness" purely superficial, the result of an imposition on their ancestors by the Hasmoneans, an imposition that had failed to impact their

---

[67] *Ant.* 13.318–319. Seth Schwartz suggests that Josephus foreshadows in this passage Aristobulus's annexation in *Ant.* 13.35–58 ("The 'Judaism' of Samaria and Galilee in Josephus's Version of the Letter of Demetrius I to Jonathan [*Antiquities* 13.48–57]," *HTR* 82 [1989]: 377–391).

[68] Schürer, *History*, vol. I, 216–218; vol. II, 7–10. The demarcation of the territory taken by Aristobulus is difficult to determine.

[69] E.g., Vermes, *Jesus the Jew* and *Jesus and the World of Judaism*, 1–14.

underlying pagan beliefs?[70] Were those "Judaized" descendants of the northern Israelite tribes, and thus reasonably open to the similar traditions of the south?[71] Or had the conquest of Aristobulus led to a new Jewish settlement of Galilee, so that the first-century CE population had little continuity with that of the late second century BCE?

The question of who was living in Galilee on the eve of Aristobulus's conquest is difficult to answer. As discussed above, the lack of evidence for habitation in Galilee after the Assyrian invasion suggests that only a very few Galileans would have been descendants of the northern Israelites or descendants of any gentiles who had lived alongside them. Signs of Assyrian occupation of Galilee are minimal and that of colonization is nonexistent, so it is unlikely that the Assyrians had left behind gentile settlers.

Phoenicians probably dwelled in Galilee at the close of the second century BCE, some descendants of those who had penetrated through the western mountain range during the Persian era, and others, more recent arrivals. Coins from the coastal cities are common in the Hellenistic strata of numerous sites, attesting to economic relations with the Phoenician cities. Phoenician construction techniques were used in a Hellenistic wall at Jotapata and as far east as Tel Anafa; at the latter site, large quantities of Late Hellenistic Phoenician pottery and coins are found.[72]

As for other groups, it is unlikely that many were Greeks, since so few had arrived in the Ptolemaic and Seleucid eras. First Maccabees 5 reports the presence of Jews near the coastal region, and if we regard its report of their total evacuation to the south as, at the least, an exaggeration, we might suppose that a few Jews, exact numbers and origin unknown, dwelled in Galilee in the middle of the second century BCE.[73] And, of course, there were the Itureans.

---

[70] E.g., Mack, *Lost Gospel*, 59.

[71] E.g., Freyne, *Galilee from Alexander*, 23–26; Horsley, *Archaeology*, 21–23, and *Galilee*, 25–29.

[72] David Adan-Bayewitz and Mordechai Aviam, "Iotapata, Josephus, and the Siege of 67: Preliminary Report on the 1992–1994 Seasons," *Journal of Roman Archaeology* 10 (1997): 137, 161 and additional sources cited in my chapter 3; Sharon C. Herbert, "Anafa, Tel," *OEANE*, vol. I, 117–118 and additional sources cited in my chapter 4. Construction techniques used on a Hellenistic tower at Sha'ar Ha'amaqim also have possible Phoenician parallels (Arthur Segal and Yehuda Naor, "Sha'ar Ha'amaqim," *NEAEHL*, vol. IV, 1339–1340 and "Sha'ar Ha'amaqim, 1991," *ESI* 12 [1993]: 22–23). Cf. the use of Phoenician construction techniques at the coastal city of Dor (Ephraim Stern, "Dor," *NEAEHL*, vol. I, 357–368, esp. 362–263).

[73] Samuel Klein, however, argued for a sizable Jewish population in Galilee at this time, given the presence of Jewish communities there even prior to the Maccabean wars ("Die ältesten jüdischen Siedlungen in Galiläa," in *Galiläa von der Makkabäerzeit bis 67* [Vienna: Verlag "Menorah," 1928], 1–21).

The Itureans were an Arab tribe based primarily to the north and northeast of Galilee, on and around Mount Lebanon and Anti-Lebanon.[74] Apparently taking advantage of the weakness of the Seleucids, at some point they began migrating into Galilee, though how far they reached is unknown. Archaeologists have discovered Iturean sites on Mount Hermon and in the Golan,[75] but remains in Galilee have been more difficult to identify.[76] Though parts of Galilee were clearly under Iturean control, no finds indicate that any massive influx of Itureans ever occurred. Proportionally, the Itureans were just one more element in the Galilean population mix.[77]

Whom, then, did Aristobulus compel to be circumcised and to accept the laws of the Jews? Some scholars have recently suggested that Josephus's forceful language masks the benign nature of alliances the Hasmoneans made, not only with the Itureans, but also with the Idumeans, an Arab people conquered by Hyrcanus. If both the Idumeans and Itureans already practiced circumcision, a common custom among Semitic peoples, that requirement would not have been problematic. All benefited, according to the alliance theory, from the additional defensive strength provided by numbers.[78] This argument is difficult to prove, however, particularly in regard to the Itureans. Josephus reports straightforwardly that

---

[74] On the Itureans, see Ernest Axel Knauf, "Ituraea," *ABD*, vol. III, 583–584; Willy Schottroff, "Die Ituräer," *ZPDV* 98 (1982): 125–152; Peter Richardson, *Herod: King of the Jews and Friend of the Romans* (Columbia: University of South Carolina Press, 1996), 68–72; Schürer, *History*, vol. I, 561–573.

[75] Mosheh Hartel, "Khirbet Zemel, 1985/1986," *IEJ* 37 (1987): 270–272; Shimon Dar, "The Greek Inscriptions from Senaim on Mount Hermon," *PEQ* 120 (1988): 26–44. Zvi Uri Ma'oz notes sixty-seven Ituraean sites in the Golan ("Golan: Hellenistic Period to the Middle Ages," *NEAEHL*, vol. II, 535–536).

[76] Archaeologists have certainly not identified any "Iturean phase" of settlement in Galilee. Iturean ware itself has been identified *per se* only recently (Hartel, "Khirbet Zemel"; Shimon Dar, *Settlements and Cult Sites on Mount Hermon, Israel: Ituraean Culture in the Hellenistic and Roman Periods* [Oxford: BAR, 1993], 16–190); cf. Freyne, "Galilee," *OEANE*, vol. II, 372 and Aviam, "Galilee," *NEAEHL*, vol. II, 453.

[77] Cf. Freyne, "Galilee," *OEANE*, vol. II, 372.

[78] *Ant.* 13.257–258. Morton Smith, "The Gentiles in Judaism 125 B.C.E. – 66 C.E.," in Shaye J. D. Cohen ed., *Studies in the Cult of Yahweh* (Leiden: E. J. Brill, 1996), vol. I, 263–319; Shaye D. Cohen, "Religion, Ethnicity and Hellenism in the Emergence of Jewish Identity," in Per Bilde et al., eds., *Religion and Religious Practice in the Seleucid Kingdom* (Aarhus: Aarhus University Press, 1990), 204–223; and Aryeh Kasher, *Jews, Idumaeans and Ancient Arabs* (Tübingen: J. C. B. Mohr [Paul Siebeck], 1988), 116–137. On the possible practice of circumcision by Idumeans and Itureans, see Cohen, "Religion," 214–215; Smith, "Gentiles," 272; Steven Weitzman, "Forced Circumcision and the Shifting Role of Gentiles in Hasmonean Ideology," *HTR* 92 (1999): 37–59; cf. *Ant.* 1.214 and the comment by Herodotus (2.104.3) that the "Syrians" in Palestine practice circumcision.

the Idumeans became Jews,[79] and they certainly figure prominently in his subsequent narratives. The brevity of his description leaves our questions about their conversion's process and nature unanswered, but, in any case, it is notable that he provides no such statement regarding the Itureans.[80]

Presumably, then, whatever Itureans chose to remain in Galilee after the Hasmonean conquest subjected themselves to Hasmonean rule. Already circumcised, these Itureans who stayed probably yielded to the Jewish law of the land. Phoenicians and any pagans of other non-Semitic backgrounds were probably compelled to undergo circumcision; archaeological data (see below) suggests that many left Galilee. Perhaps some gentiles here and there, particularly in the hinterland, escaped the circumcision requirement, but probably not in large numbers. Galilean Jews, whether descendants of the northern Israelite tribes or more recent immigrants, presumably welcomed Hasmonean rule.[81]

Alexander Jannaeus and Galilee

Josephus provides only brief references to Galilee in his accounts of the exploits of Aristobulus's brother and successor, Alexander Jannaeus (103–76 BCE). We learn that Jannaeus had spent time in Galilee in his youth,[82] and that nearby Strato's Tower and Ptolemais were among the coastal cities he attacked early in his reign. His assault on Ptolemais led to the intervention of Cleopatra's son, Ptolemy Lathyrus, who arrived from Cyprus to confront Jannaeus. Ptolemy attacked at least two Galilean sites before his eventual retreat from the region. Asochis, near Sepphoris, fell to his forces. By noting that Ptolemy's attack on Asochis fell on the Sabbath, Josephus implies that the timing favored Ptolemy, thus suggesting that the inhabitants were primarily Jews. Ptolemy's attack on Sepphoris was less than successful, and after substantial casualties he abandoned the assault.[83]

---

[79] *Ant.* 13.257–258.

[80] Nor does other evidence corroborate such peaceful relations between the Itureans and the Hasmoneans: the Byzantine historian Syncellus (I, 559) records an assault on Jewish forces during the time of Alexander Jannaeus (cited by Israel Shatzman, *The Armies of the Hasmoneans and Herod* [Tübingen: J. C. B. Mohr (Paul Siebeck): 1991], 83).

[81] A. K. M. Adam has suggested that the Hasmoneans imposed their Judean form of Judaism, attempting to supplant Galilean Jewish customs with their own ("According to Whose Law? Aristobulus, Galilee and the ΝΟΜΟΙ ΤΩΝ ΙΟΥΔΑΙΩΝ" *JSP* 14 [1996]: 15–21). Adam's argument, however, assumes a larger number of Jews in Galilee than probably existed.

[82] *Ant.* 13.322.   [83] *Ant.* 13.337–338; cf. *War* 1.86.

The archaeological evidence for population shifts

Numismatic finds shed some light on what occurred in Galilee after the Hasmonean conquest. Hasmonean coins are ubiquitous in the Hellenistic and Roman strata of sites in both Lower and Upper Galilee. Hasmonean coins are often cited as proof of Jewish habitation, but, in and of themselves, they are insufficient evidence. Though they reflect economic connections with the south and the Hasmoneans' political domination of the region, such domination extended over both Jewish and non-Jewish areas. Proper interpretation of the coins is further complicated by their lengthy circulation, which extends well into the first century CE and occasionally beyond.[84]

More illuminating than the mere presence of Hasmonean coins are changes in a given site's numismatic profile. The finds at two Galilean sites suggest the introduction of new coinage after the Hasmonean takeover. At Jotapata, Seleucid coins from the late second century BCE were absent and Phoenician coins from this period and after were rare, despite the frequency of earlier issues. At precisely the time when these issues disappear, however, Hasmonean coinage appears, with six coins of John Hyrcanus and sixty of Alexander Jannaeus.[85] A similar situation occurs with the coins of Meiron.[86] At the very least, Galilee's numismatic evidence indicates its political and economic integration into the Hasmonean kingdom.

Fortifications that are most likely associated with the Hasmoneans also appear at several sites. At Jotapata, older fortifications were renovated and expanded in the Hasmonean period.[87] Hasmonean coins at Khirbet el-Tufaniyeh in western Upper Galilee suggest that the defenses there may have been built in this period.[88] Hasmonean forces seem to have taken over an earlier fortification at Sepphoris.

Many older sites, particularly smaller settlements, were abandoned in the second century BCE, and new sites sprang up in the time of Alexander Jannaeus.[89] At Sha'ar Ha'amaqim, in southwestern Galilee, fortifications

[84] Does the discovery at a given site of coins of Alexander Jannaeus indicate that during that king's reign the site was associated with the Hasmoneans, or did later occupants introduce earlier coinage? Since numismatic finds at sites are often published apart from their stratigraphic contexts, such questions are difficult to answer.

[85] Adan-Bayewitz and Aviam, "Iotapata."

[86] Joyce Raynor and Yaakov Meshorer, with Richard S. Hanson, *The Coins of Ancient Meiron* (Winona Lake, Ind.: ASOR, Eisenbrauns, 1988), 83–85.

[87] Adan-Bayewitz and Aviam, "Iotapata."

[88] Shatzman, *Armies*, 86–87. On Hasmonean defenses in Galilee, see ibid., 83–87.

[89] This is shown by a survey reported in Aviam, "Galilee," *NEAEHL*, vol. II, 453; cf. Freyne, "Galilee," *OEANE*, vol. II, 372.

dating back to the third or second century BCE seem to have gone out of use in the early first century BCE; the site was reoccupied later in the same century. At Mizpeh Yamim, a pagan temple (probably dedicated to a Phoenician deity) seems to have gone out of use in the second century BCE, perhaps in the latter half. Tel Anafa, located just beyond the boundaries of Galilee in the Huleh basin, also provides evidence of the changes which occurred in the area following the Hasmonean annexation. Founded in the Seleucid period, it was a wealthy and prosperous settlement, probably inhabited by Phoenicians and perhaps Greeks. Several Late Hellenistic buildings have been identified, and at the end of the second century CE, a stuccoed building and a large three-room bathhouse were erected. Near the end of the reign of Alexander Jannaeus, however, Tel Anafa was abandoned, though it was later reoccupied by a different group during the reign of Herod Philip.[90]

In discussions of Aristobulus's imposition of Judaism in Galilee, scholars have often focused on the fate of those gentiles who chose to remain on their land (i.e., did they "convert" to Judaism, and what did that mean?). The archaeological evidence, while admittedly not yet extensive, suggests that many chose to escape Jewish rule altogether, abandoning their communities and fleeing into the surrounding areas. The appearance of new sites in the Late Hellenistic era suggests that new settlers moved into Galilee, the most likely candidates being Judean colonists. Perhaps they came to reclaim ancestral territory, or perhaps they were attracted by Galilee's climate and arable land. In any case, the expanded settlement which began in the Late Hellenistic period continued into the Roman period.[91]

Herodian and Roman rule

Upon the death of Jannaeus's wife and successor, Salome (67 BCE), chaos ensued as her sons Hyrcanus II and Aristobulus II battled for power. Pompey's arrival in Palestine in the midst of this turmoil in 63 BCE permanently altered the political landscape. Ultimately Jerusalem was besieged, the temple entered by Pompey himself, Aristobulus taken captive to Rome (twice), and Hyrcanus appointed high priest and, eventually, ethnarch.[92] Pompey also seized for Rome the territory that had been conquered by the Hasmoneans. The list of liberated cities is long:

---

[90] See discussion in the third and fourth chapters.
[91] Aviam, "Galilee," *NEAEHL*, vol. II, 454.
[92] *Ant.* 14.54–73, 79, 96–97, 191; *War* 1.138–158, 173, 194.

Hippos, Scythopolis, Pella, Samaria, Jamnia, Marisa, Azotus, Arethus, Gaza, Joppa, Dora, Strato's Tower. "All these towns," Josephus notes, "he restored to their legitimate inhabitants and annexed to the province Syria."[93] Located in the interior of Galilee, Sepphoris remained within Jewish territory.

The Roman reorganization of Palestine began even before Aristobulus's final defeat, with the appointment of Gabinius as *strategos* of Syria. Gabinius divided the country into five regional councils based at Jerusalem, Gadara, Amathus, Jericho, and Sepphoris.[94] The selection of Sepphoris as administrative capital for Galilee suggests its prominence. Josephus does not suggest that Romans administered these councils; they were probably run by local elites. The duration of this administrative organization was probably brief; Josephus's comment that Gabinius reordered the government according to the wishes of Antipater suggests that Jerusalem soon emerged as the dominant political center at the expense of the regional councils.[95]

Even after Pompey's arrival, occasional conflict still erupted in Palestine as various factions sought to dominate the region. Parthian incursions from the east added to the tension, and warring between Roman generals in the aftermath of Julius Caesar's death only complicated matters. Galilee was again a battleground, once at Mount Tabor, where Gabinius defeated the forces of Alexander, son of Aristobulus II,[96] and once again at Taricheae, where Cassius enslaved a reported thirty thousand Jews.[97]

The Herodian dynasty

Throughout these disturbances, the Idumean Antipater had been gaining prominence and power. He had wisely backed Hyrcanus, who had become the Romans' choice to assume leadership; he had taken advantage of connections with the Nabateans, persuading them to give Hyrcanus refuge; he had ingratiated himself to Gabinius and Cassius; and, most importantly, he had supported Julius Caesar in Egypt. His ultimate reward was granted in 48 BCE, when Caesar appointed him *epitropos* of Judea, reaffirming at the same time Hyrcanus as high priest.[98]

---

93 *Ant.* 13.74–76, *War* 1.155–157 (quote from 1.157).   94 *Ant.* 14.91, *War* 1.170.
95 *War* 1.178; cf. Horsley, *Galilee*, 53.   96 *Ant.* 14.102, *War* 1.177.
97 *Ant.* 14.120, *War* 1.180.   98 *Ant.* 14.143, *War* 1.197–200.

Herod the great

Antipater's son, Herod, is better known in history than Antipater himself, and it is notable that he began his political career in Galilee during his father's reign.[99] His father appointed him administrator of the region *c.* 47 BCE, while he was still quite young.[100] His first major accomplishment was the subjection of forces led by a certain Hezekiah, who had been plaguing settlements along the Syrian border.[101] While Herod's action drew praise from the Syrians, some Jews attacked it as unjust and illegal; he was ultimately pardoned for any indiscretion by Hyrcanus.[102] Herod was adept in his service to the Romans. He collected the necessary tribute from Galilee and was rewarded with an appointment over Syria, though the extent of the territory placed under him is unknown.[103] Herod also defeated and expelled Tyrians who had seized Galilean territory in support of the Hasmonean Antigonus, who was still active in his efforts to seize the throne.[104]

In the civil war that erupted among Roman generals after Caesar's death, Herod at first backed Cassius against Antony. Despite Herod's support for his rival, Antony, after his victory *c.* 42 BCE, appointed him and his brother Phasael as tetrarchs over the Jews.[105] When the Parthians marched into Palestine and Antigonus seized Jerusalem, conflict erupted in Galilee, with some Galileans backing Herod, others, Antigonus.[106] Herod was forced to flee, but his exile was short-lived. Because of his opposition to the Parthians, Antony and the Roman Senate declared him king.[107] After the defeat of Antigonus and the Parthians, the remainder of Herod's reign appears to have been peaceful.

[99] On Herod's career, see Richardson, *Herod*, esp. 52–80 and 153–173.

[100] In *Ant.* 14.158, Josephus describes him as a "mere lad" of fifteen years when he received this assignment, though, as Ralph Marcus points out in the notes on this passage in the Loeb edition, Josephus elsewhere says that Herod died at about age seventy (*Ant.* 17.148). If he was around seventy in 4 BCE, he would have been approximately twenty-five in 47 BCE.

[101] *War* 1.203–205, *Ant.* 14.158–160. Freyne's suggestion that Hezekiah was a Hasmonean noble who favored Antigonus over Hyrcanus is plausible but unconfirmable (*Galilee from Alexander*, 63), as is Richardson's suggestion that the forces were Itureans (*Herod*, 71).

[102] *Ant.* 14.163ff., *War* 1.208ff.

[103] *Ant.* 14.280, *War* 1.221. See Freyne, *Galilee from Alexander*, 64; Richardson, *Herod*, 70.

[104] *Ant.* 14.297–299, *War* 1.238–239.   [105] *Ant.* 14.326, *War* 1.244.

[106] *Ant.* 14.395–450, *War* 1.290–316. Freyne (*Galilee from Alexander*, 66–67) and Horsley (*Galilee*, 54–56) provide summaries of these events.

[107] *Ant.* 14.385, *War* 1.285.

Galilee receives little attention in Josephus's account of Herod's later rule, and Galileans receive even less.[108] Nevertheless, by considering Herod's numerous building projects elsewhere, we are able to make inferences about Galilee's cultural climate. Herod was a benefactor for projects in Asia Minor, the isles of the eastern Mediterranean, Greece (including Athens), and the coastal cities of Palestine. His own territory was also the site of numerous significant projects, the most famous being the rebuilding of the Jerusalem temple. In Samaria, he founded Caesarea Sebaste and provided it with a temple to Roma and Augustus. He built the new city Caesarea Maritima on the site of the former Strato's Tower, constructing an artificial harbor, a theater, an amphitheater, a hippodrome, an agora, and, as at Sebaste, a temple to Roma and Augustus. At Paneas he built another temple to Roma and Augustus beside the traditional shrine to Pan. Thus, he ringed Galilee with temples to the imperial cult and other construction projects.[109]

Galilee does not seem to have been the beneficiary of such massive building projects, and, since Herod had his political start in Galilee, this lack of activity is especially noteworthy.[110] The royal palace and the arsenal at Sepphoris, attacked shortly after Herod's death, were presumably his constructions,[111] but aside from these we know of no high-profile projects in the region. In his predominantly Jewish territories, Herod built no pagan temples or gymnasia; his decision to build neither institution in Galilee suggests that the region's inhabitants were probably for the most part Jews.[112] Likewise, his failure to sponsor the construction of

---

[108] The land originally assigned to Herod included not only Galilee, but also Perea, Iturea, Judea and Idumea. Iturea, along with other territories, was later granted to Cleopatra, and Batea, Trachonitis, and Auranitis were added to Herod's territory. See Richardson's summary in *Herod*, 70–71.

[109] *Ant.* 15.266–276, 328–341 and 16.136–149, *War* 1.401–428. Josephus's summaries of the building programs of Herod the Great are telling. In addition to the construction projects described above, Herod sponsored the construction of gymnasia for Tripolis, Damascus, and Ptolemais; halls, porticoes, temples, and agoras for Berytus and Tyre; theaters for Damascus and Sidon; and baths, fountains, and colonnades for Ascalon. Thus, Herod sponsored these Hellenistic institutions in the cities surrounding Jewish Palestine, not in Judea or in Galilee. Josephus's characterization of Herod in regard to his building projects varies in *War* and *Antiquities*. In *War*, Herod's projects reflect his generosity and magnanimity. In *Antiquities*, his sponsorship of Hellenistic institutions reflects his impiety. Perhaps Josephus relied on a pro-Herod, pro-Hellenistic culture source for *War* (Nicolaus?) and an anti-Herod source for *Antiquities*. In any case, it is notable that none of the accounts of his building activities, including the pro-Hellenistic report in *War*, refers to temples or gymnasia in Jewish territories. See E. P. Sanders, "Jesus in Historical Context," 432–438; cf. Richardson, *Herod*, 174–202.

[110] Richardson, *Herod*, 175.   [111] *Ant.* 17.271, *War* 2.56.

[112] Cf. Josephus's explicit comment in *Ant.* 15.328–330 that Herod erected no temples in Jewish territories.

other Hellenistic buildings in Galilee may reflect sensitivity to Jewish sentiments.

Galilee under Antipas

At the death of Herod in 4 BCE, popular revolts broke out throughout his kingdom.[113] In Galilee, the son of Hezekiah, who had troubled northern villages when Herod was first assigned to Galilee, assaulted the royal palace at Sepphoris.[114] Widespread demonstrations prompted Varus, legate of Syria, to intervene. Arriving from Syria, his troops, according to Josephus, burned down Sepphoris and enslaved its inhabitants before proceeding to the south, where they quelled the remainder of the disturbances.[115] Peace restored to the region, Augustus split Herod's kingdom among his sons, granting Galilee, along with Perea, to Antipas; Judea, Idumea, and Samaria to Archelaus; Batanea, Trachonitis, Auranitis, and other territories that had formerly been subject to the Iturean king Zenodorus to Philip.[116]

We learn about developments within Galilee as Josephus discusses Antipas's accomplishments.[117] Antipas imitated his father in launching massive construction projects, but unlike his father, he did not neglect Galilee.[118] He rebuilt Sepphoris, naming it "Autocratoris" and establishing it as, in Josephus's words, "the ornament of Galilee."[119] Around 20 CE, he began construction of a new city, Tiberias,[120] in a controversial location. The general area, along the shores of the Sea of Galilee near the springs of Ḥammath, was appealing, but the exact location Antipas chose for his city was an old graveyard. Settlers were difficult to come by, and he had to bring in by force people from all directions.[121] A Herodian palace and a stadium mentioned by Josephus probably date to this time.[122]

---

[113] *Ant.* 17.206–298, *War* 2.1–79.   [114] *Ant.* 17.271–272, *War* 2.56.

[115] *Ant.* 17.286–303 (on Galilee, see 17.288–289), *War* 2.56. Excavations at Sepphoris have not yet confirmed Josephus's report of this mass destruction.

[116] *Ant.* 17.318–320, *War* 2.93–100.

[117] Josephus also reports an incident in the south involving a Galilean during Antipas's reign. While Coponius was procurator of Judea (6–9 CE), a rebellion broke out, attributed to Judas the Galilean, but it was speedily suppressed (*War* 2.117–118, *Ant.* 18.4–11, 23–25; cf. Acts 5:37). In *War* and Acts, Judas is identified as a Galilean; in *Antiquities* he is said to come from Gamla in Gaulanitis. Josephus's varying usage reflects the flexibility of boundaries between the two regions.

[118] His projects were not limited to Galilee. In Perea, he built a city named Julia, about which we have little information (*Ant.* 18.36–38, *War* 2.168).

[119] *Ant.* 18.27.   [120] *Ant.* 18.36–38, *War* 2.168.

[121] *Ant.* 18.36–38, *War* 2.168.   [122] *Ant.* 18.149, *Life* 331, *War* 2.618.

In neither of these cities did Antipas erect temples, either to the emperor or to pagan deities. His coins are free of the images of either Caesar or the gods, bearing instead reeds, palm branches, wreaths, palm trees, and dates.[123] The absence of personal images on his coins and the absence of temples in his new cities are striking when compared to the typical coins and constructions of the period.[124] Combined, these absences imply that the majority of Antipas's subjects would have resented the images and institutions of paganism. Whether Antipas's actions imply his own Jewish piety or simply prudence is debatable, but it is notable that both Luke and Josephus report his attendance at festivals in Jerusalem.[125] Regardless of his personal motivation for such actions, an anti-pagan attitude on the part of his subjects is visible decades later at the start of the Revolt, when they burned the palace decorated with images at Tiberias.[126]

Roman administration of Galilee in the first century CE

Galilee vacillated between Herodian and Roman administration for years. Antipas ruled until 39 CE, when Caligula deposed him and gave his territory to Agrippa I, who was already ruler of Philip's former territory.[127] In 41 CE, Agrippa I received Judea as well, briefly reuniting all of Herod the Great's territory. In 44 CE, however, all Palestine, including Galilee, became part of the province Judea, under direct Roman administration. Galilee remained part of the province for the rest of the century, with the exception of the territories of Taricheae and Julias, which were given, along with Abila, *c.* 54/55 CE to Agrippa II, ruler of Philip's former territory to the northeast of Galilee.[128]

We have little information about the nature of Roman administration of Galilee. As Fergus Millar generalizes, "the realities of the process by which the Roman state lived off its subjects, in this [Palestine] as in other areas, escape us."[129] No literary or archaeological evidence suggests that the introduction of direct Roman rule resulted in the introduction of new

---

[123] Yaakov Meshorer, *Jewish Coins of the Second Temple Period*, trans. I. H. Levine (Tel Aviv: Am Hassefer Publishers Ltd. and Massada, 1967), 72–75, 133–135; Yaakov Meshorer, *Ancient Jewish Coinage* (Dix Hills, N.Y.: Amphora Books, 1982), vol. II, 35–41, 242–243.

[124] In contrast to Antipas, Philip, whose territory contained both Jews and gentiles, apparently had no qualms about issuing coins with pagan motifs (Meshorer, *Jewish Coins*, 76–77 and *Ancient Jewish Coinage*, vol. II, 42–50).

[125] Luke 23:7, *Ant.* 18.122–123.   [126] *Ant.* 18.149.

[127] *Ant.* 18.252, *War* 2.183.   [128] *Ant.* 20.159, *War* 2.252.

[129] Millar, *Roman Near East*, 110.

settlers. While Galilee had a favorable climate, and Lower Galilee in particular had much arable land, nothing suggests that people in the Empire at large were particularly aware of these characteristics and would have flocked there to exploit its natural riches. As for other economic opportunities, Galilee was integrated into far-reaching trade networks, but these did not require any Roman presence to sustain them. While Roman traders probably settled in larger cities and ports, such as Ptolemais and Caesarea Maritima (cities known to have had Romans among their occupants), reasons why many would have been attracted to the interior of Galilee are difficult to imagine. Perhaps Rome assigned some bureaucrats to Galilee, but we have no reason to believe their numbers, if they came at all, were large; local leadership networks probably sufficed for the Romans' purposes.

No Roman troops are reported to have accompanied the introduction of direct Roman rule, and it is extremely unlikely any were left over from the period of Herodian rule. Stationing units in the territory of a friendly client king such as Antipas would have been very unusual, and we have no solid evidence to suggest Roman policy in Galilee differed from the norm.[130] Thus, the popular image of Roman soldiers patrolling the highways and villages of first-century CE Galilee is erroneous. A substantial military presence was not established in the region until *c.* 120 CE.[131]

Nor did Roman colonists ever attempt to imitate Roman society in Galilee, though *coloniae* were established in surrounding areas. To the north, Augustus had founded his only Near Eastern colony at Berytus, granting land to Latin-speaking veterans. Claudius had elevated Ptolemais to the level of *colonia* and settled veterans from his Syrian legions there. Vespasian rewarded Caesarea Maritima for its support with the status of *colonia* and introduced veterans into its population, and he founded the new city of Neapolis in Samaria near biblical Shechem, though the identity of its inhabitants is unclear. In the early second century CE, Hadrian established Aelia Capitolina in Jerusalem itself. At no point,

---

[130] See Sanders, "Jesus's Galilee." In general, the client kingdoms served as a source of troops, not a depository for them. In particularly unstable realms, the Romans might provide a garrison to support their clients; see David Braund, *Rome and the Friendly King: The Character of the Client Kingship* (London and Canberra: Croom Helm; New York: St. Martin's Press, 1984), 94. The only possible evidence for a Roman military presence in Antipas's Galilee is the story of the centurion at Capernaum in Matt. 8:5–13/ Luke 7:1–10, and this report is subject to other interpretation. See discussion under "Capernaum" in chapter 3.

[131] The nearby Decapolis likewise didn't receive a legion until Trajan's reign in the second century.

however, either in the first century CE or later, did the Romans ever attempt to colonize Galilee.[132]

Galileans and the temple

Two events in these years demonstrate Galilean fidelity to the Jerusalem temple.[133] The first occurred when Gaius Caligula ordered a statue of himself to be erected in the temple. Petronius, legate to Syria, knew the uproar this would produce and successfully delayed action until Caligula's assassination in 41 CE. During the crisis, however, thousands of Jews left their fields unattended for weeks to petition Petronius at Ptolemais and Tiberias, asking him to refrain from defiling the temple.[134] While Josephus does not specify that the Jewish protesters were Galileans, given the northern locations of their demonstrations, Galilean participation is likely.[135]

The second event occurred while Cumanus administered the province Judea (48–52 CE). Galilean pilgrims, on their way to Jerusalem for Passover, were attacked by Samaritans. In *Antiquities*, Josephus reports that "a great number" of Galileans were slain; in *War*, a single Galilean. Tacitus also refers to the hostilities between Galileans and Samaritans but does not mention the initial pilgrim incident. In any case, tensions quickly escalated. The Galileans appealed for justice to Cumanus, who ignored them, reportedly having been bribed by the Samaritans. This neglect encouraged Jewish outrage, and Jews promptly began attacking Samaritan villages. The end result, after intervention by Roman troops stationed in Syria, was the quieting of disturbances and Claudius's removal of Cumanus from office.[136]

Both incidents depict Galilean loyalty toward the temple, and the Gospels corroborate this picture. Luke places Jesus in the temple for his circumcision and at age twelve at Passover, though these stories likely reflect Luke's narrative interest in Jerusalem more than events in Jesus's

---

[132] Fergus Millar, "The Roman *Coloniae* of the Near East: A Study of Cultural Relations," in Heikki Solin and Mika Kajava, eds., *Roman Eastern Policy and Other Studies in Roman History* (Helsinki: Societas Scientiarum Fennica, 1990), 7–58; Millar, *Roman Near East*: on Berytus, 36, 279; on Ptolemais, 65; on Caesarea, 73; on Neapolis, 368–369; on Aelia Capitolina, 348–349.

[133] On Galileans and the temple, see Freyne, *Galilee, Jesus, and the Gospels*, 178–189 and *Galilee from Alexander*, 259–304. Kloppenborg Verbin's review of the evidence (*Excavating Q*, 223–229) is overly negative; a regional variation in the payment of the temple tax does not preclude a basic orientation toward the temple.

[134] *Ant.* 19.261–309, *War* 2.192–203.   [135] Freyne, *Galilee from Alexander*, 166.

[136] *Ant.* 20.118–136, *War* 2.232–235; Tacitus, *Annals* 12.54.

life.[137] Luke elsewhere attests to Galilean pilgrimages to the temple, cryptically referring to "Galileans whose blood Pilate had mingled with their sacrifices."[138] All four Gospels depict contact between Galilee and the south, most notably in Jesus's final Passover pilgrimage. In John, Jesus frequently moves between Judea and Galilee, attending three different Passovers.[139] Regardless of which of these details in the Gospels one deems historical and which one rejects as the authors' embellishments, what is most significant is that all four Gospels assume that the temple was a natural place of worship and pilgrimage for Jesus as a Galilean. The very fact that he chose it as the site for his demonstration at Passover indicates its centrality in his – and most likely in other Galileans' – symbolic world.

Galilee during the Jewish War

Josephus's discussions of Galilee's role in the Revolt are rich in detail. Because Galilee was the scene of his own activity, his observations are first-hand. He freely shares his perceptions of the area, and though his accounts of the war are shaped by his apologetic needs, they are still the best source of information we have.[140]

The process by which the Jerusalem authorities assigned military commanders to Galilee suggests a history of contacts between the north and the south. They clearly felt Galilee was within their authority and would respond, to some degree, at least, to their leadership. The men they initially appointed, Josephus and two others, were priests. To a great extent, this reflects the composition of the Jerusalem *protoi* themselves, but Josephus also suggests that priestly lineage was an asset in gaining credibility with the Galileans.[141] He claims to have refused priestly

---

[137] Luke 2:21–52. See Hans Conzelmann, *The Theology of St. Luke*, trans. Geoffrey Buswell (London: Faber & Faber, 1960), 27–94; Joseph A. Fitzmeyer, *The Gospel According to Luke (I–IX)* (Garden City, N.Y.: Doubleday and Co., Inc., 1981), 164–171; and J. Bradley Chance, *Jerusalem, The Temple, and the New Age in Luke-Acts* (Macon, Ga.: Mercer University Press, 1988).

[138] Luke 13:1. Whether Luke is reporting an otherwise unattested incident or is indicating Galilean participation in one of the conflicts recorded by Josephus during Pilate's governorship (*War* 2.169–177, *Ant.* 18.55–64) is unclear. See Schürer, *History*, vol. I, 385 and E. Mary Smallwood, *The Jews under Roman Rule* (Leiden: E. J. Brill, 1976), 163; Freyne, *Galilee from Alexander*, 219, 227, 290.

[139] John 2:13, 6:4, 11:55.

[140] On the Revolt in Galilee, see Freyne, *Galilee from Alexander*, 78–91; Horsley, *Galilee*, 72–88; and Uriel Rappaport, "How Anti-Roman was the Galilee?" in Levine, ed., *Galilee in Late Antiquity*, 95–102.

[141] *Life* 28; cf. *War* 2.568–569. On the discrepancy in Josephus's accounts – in *Life* he claims to have been sent to Galilee to minimize its involvement in the Revolt, in *War* to

tithes offered to him by the Galileans,[142] and while his brief reference
to the incident is self-serving (the Galileans were subservient to him,
but he treated them with generosity) and thus perhaps exaggerated (or
fictitious), it is consistent with his depiction of the people's Jewish
ethos. When the Jerusalem authorities attempted to relieve Josephus
of his command, they sent forces led by a delegation of men of both
priestly and Pharisaic backgrounds. While Josephus surely overstates
the intensity of Galilean loyalty to him, his description of the delegation's plans to gain their sympathies again sheds light on his own view
of the Galileans. According to him, the delegation planned to demonstrate that they were his equal both in Jerusalem origin, in knowledge
of the Jewish laws, and in priestly lineage. The loyalty of the Galileans,
Josephus indicates, would be given to the most observant of very observant Jews.[143]

As in Judea, conflicts in Galilee were due to a variety of tensions: pro-
and anti-Roman and pro- and anti-Agrippan sentiment, class conflict,
urban–rural distrust, communities' needs for self-protection, opportunities for self-advancement, and varying degrees of openness to Greco-
Roman culture. Ethnic tensions were also a dimension of the Revolt
and resulted in Jewish–gentile conflicts in the areas surrounding Galilee
and in conflicts between Galilean marauders and neighboring communities. Early hostilities occurred at Caesarea Maritima, to the southwest
of Galilee on the coast, where thousands of Jews were massacred. Jews
retaliated against "Syrian villages" and nearby cities. Josephus enumer-
ates Jewish attacks on areas surrounding Galilee, including cities in the
Decapolis, such as Gerasa, Pella, Scythopolis (located at the southeastern border of Galilee), Gadara, and Hippos; unspecified communities in
the Golan; Kedesh (identified as a "Tyrian village"); Ptolemais on the
coast; Gaba, to the southwest; and Caesarea itself. All of these communities were predominantly gentile, some with Jewish minorities.[144]
The violence escalated, with "the whole of Syria" becoming "a scene
of frightful disorder," Josephus writes, as Jewish minorities in numerous
villages were attacked. The Jews of Scythopolis were slaughtered, even

lead it against the Romans – see Shaye D. Cohen, *Josephus in Galilee and Rome: His Vita
and Development as a Historian* (Leiden: E. J. Brill, 1979).

[142] *Life* 80; cf. Freyne, *Galilee from Alexander*, 281.

[143] *Life* 195–198; cf. *War* 2.626–631 and *Life* 309.

[144] *War* 2.458–460, *Life* 42, 341–342. Gaba, which had been settled with cavalry men by
Herod the Great (*War* 3.36, *Life* 115), was probably predominantly gentile; see discussion in
chapter 4. Jews also attacked more southern sites, such as Heshbon, Philadelphia, Sebaste,
Ascalon, Anthedon, and Gaza.

those whose loyalty to the city had extended to active defense against Jewish raiders.[145] In Agrippa's kingdom, Jews from Batanea who sought the king's assistance were murdered by his assistant Noarus.[146]

Despite this lengthy list of conflicts between Jews and gentiles in neighboring territories as well as between Galilean villages and neighboring communities, Josephus does not give the impression that Jewish–gentile conflict was a major cause of confrontations within Galilee itself. He does report a curious assemblage of forces that gathered to assault Gischala, an assemblage drawn from the Decapolis city of Gadara, the coastal city of Tyre, and the Galilean villages of Gabara and Sogane,[147] but whether or not these forces were predominantly gentile is unclear. Gabara (elsewhere identified as one of the three greatest cities of Galilee)[148] later aligned itself with John of Gischala[149] and was ultimately destroyed by Vespasian.[150] Sogane was among the sites Josephus reports to have fortified, suggesting its Jewishness.[151]

Not all Galileans fought against the Romans. Sepphoris invited in Roman garrisons and issued coins proclaiming itself "Eirenopolis," "city of peace." Tiberias vacillated between resistance and submission to the Romans and Agrippa, ultimately choosing the latter option,[152] though not before its Greek minority had been massacred.[153] Other communities doubtless kept as low a profile as possible, attempting not to offend any of the involved parties.

Many communities actively participated in the Revolt, however, such as Japha and the community at Mount Tabor.[154] Taricheae was also a battleground, though Josephus claims that the Jewish combatants there were outsiders, not inhabitants of the city.[155] The principal Roman sieges in the area occurred, however, at Gischala, Jotapata, and nearby Gamla. Gischala ultimately surrendered peacefully once John of Gischala escaped the Romans under cover of night,[156] but the sieges of Jotapata and Gamla ended with their complete destruction.[157] Resistance in Galilee

---

[145] *War* 2.462–476 (quote from 462); cf. *Life* 24–27. *War* 2.477–480 describes other cities where Jewish–gentile tensions led to violence, as well as cities where Jewish minorities were not attacked.

[146] *War* 2.481–483, *Life* 54–58.

[147] *Life* 43–45; Freyne, *Galilee from Alexander*, 79.

[148] *Life* 123.   [149] *Life* 123–124.   [150] *War* 3.132–134.

[151] *Life* 186–188, *War* 2.573–575.   [152] See discussion in the next chapter.

[153] *Life* 65–67.   [154] *War* 3.289–306, 4.54–61.

[155] *War* 3.492–502.   [156] *War* 4.84–120.

[157] On Jotapata, see *War* 3.141–288, 316–408. Josephus pointedly notes the presence at Jotapata of Galileans from other villages, including a Jew from Saba, and of two men from

itself ceased after the siege of nearby Gamla, though some Galileans fled to Jerusalem to continue the struggle.[158]

To summarize, we find no evidence of extensive confrontation between the Jews and gentiles of Galilee. The massacre of Greeks at Tiberias is the exception, rather than the rule. We also have no evidence that the choices of participation and pacifism fell along Jewish–gentile lines. Josephus's writings provide no support for the idea that the cities adopted pro-Roman policies because of largely pagan citizenries. He nowhere characterizes Sepphoris as a non-Jewish city; in contrast, he describes its abstinence from the Revolt as a betrayal of the temple "common to us all."[159] As for Tiberias, the factions within the city that competed for power as the Romans drew closer seem to have been primarily Jewish. Indeed, indigenous Galilean gentiles are conspicuously absent from Josephus's accounts of the war.

The aftermath of the Revolt

Roman occupation

The Revolt had been costly enough for Rome that it took new measures to discourage future uprisings. For the first time, it stationed large numbers of Roman troops within the province Judea.[160] In the past, the Roman garrison in Palestine had consisted of a small auxiliary contingent at the Antonia Fortress in Jerusalem, overlooking the temple, and another auxiliary contingent at Caesarea Maritima.[161] For the most part, these troops seem to have been recruited in Sebaste and Caesarea.[162] The bulk of Rome's military forces in the region, however, had been stationed to the north in Syria, where they were available to respond to any crisis that might erupt in Judea. As noted above, though, we have no indication of any influx of soldiers into Galilee when it was subsumed into the larger province of Judea mid-century.

the village of Ruma. On Gamla, see *War* 4.1–83. Excavations at both sites have confirmed Josephus's reports of destruction.

[158] *Life* 354.   [159] *Life* 348.

[160] Menahem Mor provides a thorough analysis of Roman troop deployments in "The Roman Army in Eretz-Israel in the Years AD 70–132," in Philip Freeman and David Kennedy, eds., *The Defence of the Roman and Byzantine East* (Oxford: BAR, 1986), vol. II, 757–601. Lawrence Keppie discusses the larger near eastern context of troop movements in "Legions in the East from Augustus to Trajan," in the same volume 411–429; cf. Millar, *Roman Near East*, 56–111.

[161] Mor, "Roman Army," 577–580; Zeev Safrai, "The Roman Army in Galilee," in Levine, ed., *Galilee in Late Antiquity*, 104.

[162] *Ant.* 19.356–366, 20.121, 20.176; *War* 2.236, 3.66.

After 70 CE, however, an entire legion, the X Fretensis, which had participated in the war, remained in Judea. Initially, at least, its auxiliary units remained with it.[163] In 120 CE or shortly thereafter, the Legio VI Ferrata was reassigned from Syria to Galilee.[164] At some point, a garrison was assigned to Sepphoris, though when is unknown.[165] The deployment of the Legio VI Ferrata marked the first time that Galileans felt the effects of a long-term presence of Roman troops. Soldiers remained there until the fourth century, when both legions were reassigned. From 120 CE until the fourth century CE, as Safrai points out, Judea was home to the largest number of Roman troops of any comparably sized Roman province, and half of these troops were stationed in the relatively small Galilee.[166]

Units of the Legio VI Ferrata were stationed just south of the Nazareth ridge at Kefar 'Otnay, giving the settlement its new name, Legio.[167] The Legio camp has yet to be fully excavated, but two enclosures and a theater have been found there. Safrai estimates that the camp probably housed a cohort, or approximately a thousand soldiers. Civilian settlements of support personnel as well as military families usually sprang up around such bases; perhaps the theater was associated with these settlers.[168] Other units of the Legio VI Ferrata were stationed at Tiberias; Mount Hazon; Tel Shalem, south of Beth Shean; and probably at outposts elsewhere throughout the country.[169]

---

[163] *War* 7.5; Safrai, "Roman Army," 104.

[164] On the arrival of the Legio VI Ferrata, see Benjamin Isaac and Israel Roll, "Judea in the Early Years of Hadrian's Reign," *Latomus* 38 (1979): 54–66; B. Lifshitz, "Sur la date du transfert de la legio VI Ferrata en Palestine," *Latomus* 19 (1960): 109–111; and David Kennedy, "Legio VI Ferrata: The Annexation and Early Garrison of Arabia," *Harvard Studies in Classical Philology* 84 (1980): 283–309. Some evidence suggests that the Legio II Traiana was briefly stationed in Galilee prior to the VI Ferrata; see Mor, "Roman Army," 579; Isaac and Roll, "Judea," 54–66; Benjamin Isaac and Israel Roll, "Legio II Traiana in Judaea," *Zeitschrift für Papyrologie und Epigraphik* 33 (1979): 149–156; Benjamin Isaac and Israel Roll, "Legio II Traiana – A Reply," *Zeitschrift für Papyrologie und Epigraphik* 47 (1982): 131–132.

[165] See Stuart S. Miller's discussion of *t. Shabb.* 13:9 and related traditions in *Studies in the History and Traditions of Sepphoris* (Leiden: E. J. Brill, 1984), 24, 31–45, 56–59.

[166] Safrai, "Roman Army," 103–114 (esp.103–105); Ze'ev Safrai, *The Economy of Roman Palestine* (London and New York: Routledge, 1994), 339–349, esp. 339–340; see also Benjamin Isaac, *The Limits of Empire: The Roman Army in the East*, rev. edn. (Oxford: Clarendon Press, 1992), 104–118 and Mor, "Roman Army," 575–602.

[167] *M. Git.* 1.5, 7.7 indicates that Kefar 'Otnay's inhabitants were a mixture of Jews and Samaritans; cf. Isaac, *Limits*, 432–433.

[168] Safrai, *Economy*, 345–346.

[169] Safrai ("Roman Army," 105–106) and Isaac (*Limits*, 432–435) present the archaeological evidence. In addition to the sites listed above, note also the presence at Kefar Hananyah of roof tiles with impressions of the Legio VI Ferrata (David Adan-Bayewitz,

Rabbinic materials contain hundreds of reports of encounters between Galileans and Roman troops.[170] As might be expected, the character of relations varied, from the positive (Roman troops assisting in putting out a fire at Shiḥin)[171] to the negative (sexual assault).[172] The Romans especially made their presence felt on holidays. One rabbi reported that no festival occurred without a patrol at Sepphoris, another that no festival occurred at Tiberias without Roman officials.[173]

The change in Sepphoris's coinage probably reflects the growing Roman presence in the region. Already in the time of Trajan (98–117 CE), two of its coins bore images of the emperor. Coins issued in the reign of Antoninus Pius (138–161 CE) depict both deities and temples and show that the city was known as "Diocaesarea."[174] Municipal coins of Tiberias appearing in the time of Trajan also bear images of deities, and later issues depict both deities and temples.[175]

Judean migration to Galilee

Another change occurred in Galilee's population, beginning after the first revolt and continuing after the Bar Kochbah revolt. With the destruction of Jerusalem in 70 CE and the expulsion of its Jewish inhabitants and establishment of Aelia Capitolina after the Bar Kochbah revolt, at least some Judeans began migrating to Galilee. Our understanding of this population shift is admittedly sketchy, but we can catch several glimpses of it. In the aftermath of the first revolt, Judean rabbis moved north. After initially settling at Javneh (Jamnia), rabbis established schools first at Usha, in southwestern Galilee, then at Shefar'am and Beth She'arim, and ultimately at Sepphoris and Tiberias.[176] Priestly courses also settled in Galilee following the Bar Kochbah revolt, though the exact date of their arrival is uncertain.[177]

"Kefar Hanania," *IEJ* 37 [1986]: 178–179) and Horvat Hazon (D. Bahat, "A Roof Tile of the Legio VI Ferrata and Pottery Vessels from Horvat Hazon," *IEJ* 24 [1974]: 160–169). On Roman roads in Galilee, see Benjamin Isaac and Israel Roll, *Roman Roads in Judaea I: The Legio–Scythopolis Road*, BAR International Series 141 (Oxford: BAR, 1982).

[170] Aharon Oppenheimer, "Roman Rule and the Cities of the Galilee in Talmudic Literature," in Levine, ed., *Galilee in Late Antiquity*, 115–125, esp. 121–125; Safrai, *Economy*, 345–349; Isaac, *Limits*, 115–118.

[171] *T. Shabb.* 13:9.   [172] *Y. Ned.* 12, 13, 42d.   [173] *B. Shabb.* 145b.

[174] Yaakov Meshorer, *City-Coins of Eretz-Israel and the Decapolis in the Roman Period* (Jerusalem: The Israel Museum, 1985), 36–37. The name "Diocaesarea" for Sepphoris is also attested on a nearby milestone. See discussion in chapter 3 below.

[175] Ibid., 34–35.

[176] Goodman, *State and Society*, 93, 111; Smallwood, *Jews*, 473ff.

[177] Miller, *Studies*, 116–132; Meyers, "Archaeological Response," 20.

This shift northward included more than the religious elite, however. The sheer amount of expansion and construction in Galilee in the Middle Roman period strongly suggests that large numbers of Judean Jews migrated there.[178] This process may be visible at Meiron, where neutron activation analysis of sherds indicates that pots were imported from outside Galilee. These vessels may have been present as a result of trade, but it is also possible they were brought by Judeans moving north.[179] A late second- or early third-century CE Greek inscription from Tiberias provides an additional example for this migration; it records the interment of a Jew whose grandfather was from Horesa, in Judah.[180] The growth of Galilee's Jewish population is also visible in the multiplication of settlements throughout the Middle and Late Roman periods,[181] and in the growing numbers of synagogues which begin appearing in dozens of villages from the third century CE onward. With the temple gone and the gradual emergence of the rabbis as authorities, Galilee became the spiritual center of Judaism.[182]

Galilee's population in the first century CE

Galilee's historical development does not demonstrate that Early Roman Galilee had a mixed population; in fact, it suggests the opposite case. In the first century CE, its inhabitants seem to have been primarily Jewish, with only a few pagans. Not until the second century CE do we have strong evidence of large numbers of gentiles in Galilee, and these are Roman soldiers and their accompanying entourage.

Very few first-century Galileans would have been descendants of the pre-Assyrian conquest Israelites and gentiles, given the Assyrians'

---

[178] This construction occurs at a number of Galilean sites, in both Upper and Lower Galilee (see chapter 3).

[179] Eric M. Meyers, James F. Strange, and Carol L. Meyers, *Excavations at Ancient Meiron, Upper Galilee, Israel 1971–1972, 1974–1975, 1977* (Cambridge, Mass.: The American Schools of Oriental Research, 1981), 146, 156–157. Recent analysis of a fragment of a Herodian lamp found at Meiron corroborates the analysis of the sherds, demonstrating that the lamp was made at the same location as lamps found in Judea (Eric Christian Lapp, "The Archaeology of Light: The Cultural Significance of the Oil Lamp from Roman Palestine" [Ph.D. Diss., Duke University, 1997], 22–23).

[180] Yosef Stepansky, "Two Mausolea on the Northern Fringes of the Roman-Period Cemetery of Tiberias," *Atiqot* 38 (1999): 226–227; Emanuel Damati, "A Greek Inscription from a Mausoleum in Tiberias," *Atiqot* 38 (1999): 227–228.

[181] Freyne, "Galilee," *OEANE*, vol. II, 371–372.

[182] Despite Richard A. Horsley's reservations ("Archaeology and the Villages," esp. 8–10; *Archaeology*, 40–41; *Galilee*, 97–98), the question is not whether such a northern shift occurred, but to what extent and at what pace. See Meyers, "Archaeological Response," 20–21; Goodman, *State and Society*, 32–33, 93.

depopulation of the region. The Ptolemies' and Seleucids' impact on the population's composition had been minimal. Some Galileans were probably of Phoenician or Iturean lineage, given these neighboring groups' pre-Hasmonean expansion into the available land. (Indeed, cultural affinities with the Phoenicians lasted into the first century CE, at least in western Galilee. When Cestius and the Romans marched on Chabulon, a Galilean community near the border of Ptolemais, early in the Jewish Revolt, they burned down houses built in the style of Tyre, Sidon, and Berytus.[183]) Some Galilean Jews may have been descendants of those living in Galilee at the time of the Maccabean conflicts, though their numbers are impossible to establish.

The Hasmonean annexation of the territory had marked the beginning of a new chapter in Galilee's history, however. Archaeological evidence suggests that many Galileans had chosen to escape Hasmonean rule, abandoning their communities entirely. The Hasmoneans, on the other hand, had introduced new settlers, and from this time on, Jews seem to have dominated its population.[184]

Thus, the idea that Galilee's population included numerous pagans is unsupported by the region's history. In the first century CE, some gentiles dwelt there, but their numbers do not seem to have been large. An occasional Roman or Greek may have chosen to live in Galilee, but he or she would have been a rarity, not the norm. The only place where Josephus explicitly states there was a Greek population is in Tiberias, and this group was wiped out early in the Revolt. Even in this case, whether Josephus is referring to ethnic Greeks or using the term more inclusively for gentiles in general is unclear. For the most part, gentiles are low profile–even invisible–in the historical record of first-century Galilee.

[183] *War* 2.504.

[184] My findings thus support the historical schema proposed in Freyne, "Galilee," *OEANE*, vol. II, 371–373. Reed has independently corroborated the basic elements of this picture in *Archaeology*, 23–43.

3

GALILEAN COMMUNITIES IN THE LATE
HELLENISTIC AND EARLY ROMAN PERIODS

A more detailed investigation of individual cities and villages confirms the image of a predominantly Jewish Galilee. In this chapter, I will investigate the populations of specific Galilean communities from the Late Hellenistic period through the beginning of the second century CE to determine what evidence exists in each for Jews and non-Jews. My survey will include communities that are generally acknowledged to be significant in the Early Roman period, such as Sepphoris and Tiberias; settlements mentioned in the New Testament and in the writings of Josephus; and other sites that are well known or that have yielded significant archaeological data from the Hasmonean and Early Roman periods (see Map 1).[1] For the most part, this chapter will consider sites in Galilee's interior. Some sites that are arguably within geographical Galilee (such as Scythopolis on the southeastern border and the remote Upper Galilean sites of Kedesh and Tel Anafa) were clearly outside of political Galilee in the New Testament period; they will be considered in the next chapter. The exceptions to this are Bethsaida and Beth Yeraḥ, included here because of their proximity to other lake-side sites.

The nature of our evidence

The literary sources

Josephus is by far the most helpful literary source for this issue. While one must read his writings with a skeptical awareness of his penchant for exaggeration, such caution is most warranted when he is discussing his own actions and motivations or those of his opponents and rivals. His

---

[1] A number of sites are not discussed because they are unexcavated, have yielded few remains from the Late Hellenistic and Early Roman periods, or are insufficiently published, e.g., Bar'am, Gebul, Kafra, Baca, Mamliaḥ, Sirin, Lavi, Beth Gan, Beth Maon, Rama, Selame, Accaboron, Dabburiyya, and Ḥorvat Ammudim.

description of the Galilean backdrop for his wartime activities often provides rich details about specific villages and towns, as does his narration of events during the Hasmonean and Herodian periods.

The Gospels are also of obvious significance. Despite their complicated processes of development, they preserve, to varying degrees, memories of Jesus's Galilean setting. Pericopes set in specific communities are especially useful for our purposes.[2]

Strabo, writing near the turn of the millennium, refers only briefly to Galilee, but his passing comment merits discussion. He writes that Galilee, along with Philadelphia, Samaria, and Hiericus (presumably, Jericho), is inhabited by "mixed stocks of people from Egyptian and Arabian and Phoenician tribes."[3] Strabo's description is problematic for three reasons. First, his ethnographic comments are often muddled. In the same passage, he inaccurately claims that Idumaeans are Nabateans who have been banished from their homeland (the two are actually separate Arab peoples). Similarly, he identifies Jews as descendants of the Egyptians whom Moses led to Judea. Second, the parameters of the territory Strabo means by "Galilee" are unclear; they might include pagan territory, such as villages associated with the coastal cities. Third, and most importantly, Palestine does not seem to have been one of the areas Strabo visited.[4] In describing it, he relied on older sources, and the information they contained seems to have been dated. For example, he writes that

> some writers divide Syrians as a whole into Coele-Syrians and Syrians and Phoenicians, and say that four other tribes are mixed up with these, namely, Judaeans, Idumaeans, Gazaeans, and Azotians, and that they are partly farmers, as the Syrians and Coele-Syrians, and partly merchants as the Phoenicians.[5]

Idumea, Gaza, and Azotus had all been subsumed into Jewish territory by the Hasmoneans, so Strabo's description of their inhabitants as separate ἔθνη is, at the least, an oversimplification. Menahem Stern suggests that Strabo drew this description of Palestine from second-century BCE sources.[6] In light of Galilee's historical development, Strabo's characterization of its population as mixed also suggests a reliance on

---

[2] Because of their later date, rabbinic materials are less useful for understanding Galilee in this period; see discussion in Introduction.

[3] Strabo, *Geography* 16.2.34.

[4] Menahem Stern, *Greek and Latin Authors on Jews and Judaism* (Jerusalem: The Israel Academy of Sciences and Humanities, 1974), vol. I, 261.

[5] *Geography* 16.2.2.   [6] Stern, *Greek and Latin Authors*, 262–264.

pre-Hasmonean sources. His passing generalization is not a source on which we should place much weight.

The archaeological materials

Our archaeological data from first-century CE Galilee is limited; we have more than in the Early Hellenistic period, reflecting Galilee's growth, but considerably less than in the Middle and Late Roman periods. Using what we do have requires the site-by-site sifting of information, and the differentiation of materials from earlier and from later periods.

Characterizing ethnographic make-up of a population from archaeological evidence is a tricky enterprise at best. Unfortunately, the only "ethnic" distinction visible in Galilee's archaeological record is that between Jew and non-Jew (and that distinction is only occasionally visible). The artifacts found in Galilee that possibly indicate pagan cultic practices do not lend themselves to identifying the specific "ethnicity" of their users or creators. In the survey below, I prioritize evidence reflecting religious practices neither because "religion" is necessarily the "core value" of cultural identity nor because "religion" was a separate sphere of life, but for the simple reason that religious practices often leave remains that are archaeologically distinct.[7]

The most common discoveries, pottery sherds, provide us with little help in addressing this question. Two villages, Shiḥin and Kefar Ḥananyah, appear to have dominated the pottery industry of Galilee, and their wares are found in the surrounding regions, as well. While imports are found at various Galilean sites, these seem to indicate the integration of Galilee into trade networks rather than the presence of various ethnic minorities.[8] Ceramic remains may on occasion shed light on the inhabitants of Galilean sites,[9] but these occasions are exceptions, not examples of the rule.[10]

---

[7] Cf. Eric M. Meyers, "Identifying Religious and Ethnic Groups through Archaeology," in Avraham Biran and Joseph Aviram, eds., *Biblical Archaeology Today, 1990: Proceedings of the Second International Congress in Biblical Archaeology* (Jerusalem: Israel Exploration Society and Israel Academy of Sciences and Humanities, 1993), 738–745 and "Archaeological Response," 21.

[8] For example, remains of Rhodian wine jars, a common find, are no indication of the presence of Rhodians.

[9] Tel Anafa, discussed in the next chapter, is the rare example of a site where the ceramic repertoire is so distinctly different from that of the rest of Galilee that its excavators suggest that it is a non-Jewish site.

[10] Two articles, with contrasting arguments, illustrate the difficulty of identifying the users of ceramics. James C. Waldbaum ("Greeks *in* the East or Greeks *and* the East? Problems in the Definition and Recognition of Presence," *BASOR* 305 [1997]: 6) argues

Ceramics aside, then, generally accepted evidence for pagan religious practices includes cultic sites as well as dedicatory inscriptions and grave inscriptions that mention deities; figurines or other portraits of deities, pagan symbols, and images of temples or deities on city coins are also possible indicators. Evidence for Judaism includes remains of synagogues; mikvaot or stone vessels, both indicators of Jewish purity concerns; secondary burial of bones; and epigraphic evidence. Each individual artifact is open to interpretation.

Pagan temples and Jewish synagogues would be our strongest evidence – but both are largely absent from the archaeological record from this period. Pagan cultic sites are found only in the areas surrounding Galilee; the temple at Kedesh on the fringe of Upper Galilee dates to the early second century CE. While synagogues dot the Galilean landscape in the third and fourth centuries CE,[11] no undisputed synagogue remains from the first century CE have been found in Galilee (though, as we shall see, a strong claim has been issued that a structure in Capernaum was a first-century synagogue, and a less persuasive claim for a structure in Magdala).[12] Both pagan and Jewish symbols and iconography are rare.

that imported pottery is not a sure indicator of the presence of a given group while Andrea M. Berlin, ("From Monarchy to Markets: The Phoenicians in Hellenistic Palestine," *BASOR* 306 [1997]: 75–78) suggests that the presence of Phoenician ware suggests the presence of Phoenicians.

[11] On the development of the synagogue, see Eric M. Meyers, "Synagogue," in *ABD*, vol. VI, 251–260; Steven Fine and Eric M. Meyers, "Synagogues," in *OEANE*, vol. V, 118–123; and the collection of essays in Steven Fine, ed., *Sacred Realm: The Emergence of the Synagogue in the Ancient World* (New York and Oxford: Oxford University Press and Yeshiva University Museum, 1996), esp. Eric M. Meyers, "Ancient Synagogues: An Archaeological Introduction," 3–20. For surveys of synagogues in Galilee, see Zvi Ilan, "Galilee, Survey of Synagogues," *ESI* 5 (1986): 35–37; Gideon Foerster, "The Ancient Synagogues of the Galilee," in Levine, ed., *Galilee in Late Antiquity*, 289–320; Eric M. Meyers, "The Current State of Galilean Synagogue Studies," in Lee I. Levine, ed., *The Synagogue in Late Antiquity* (Philadelphia: American Schools of Oriental Research, 1987), 127–138; Eric M. Meyers, "Ancient Synagogues in Galilee: Their Religious and Cultural Setting," *BA* 43 (1980): 97–108; Eric M. Meyers, "Synagogues of Galilee," *Archaeology* 35 (1982): 51–58.

[12] First-century CE synagogues are rare throughout Palestine. Only three structures, at Masada, Herodium, and Gamla, are generally accepted as such; Ehud Netzer claims to have found another at Jericho, built in the mid-first century BCE ("A Synagogue from the Hasmonean Period Recently Exposed in the Western Palace of Jericho," *IEJ* [1999]: 49: 203–221). Though Howard Clark Kee has rejected the identification of the (first three) structures as synagogues and questioned the existence of architecturally distinct synagogues at all prior to the third century CE ("The Transformation of the Synagogue after 70 C.E.: Its Import for Early Christianity," *NTS* 36 [1990]: 1–24; "The Changing Meaning of Synagogue: A Response to Richard Oster," *NTS* 40 [1994]: 281–283; "Defining the First-Century C.E. Synagogue: Problems and Progress," *NTS* 41 [1995]: 481–500; "Early Christianity," 2–22), Kenneth Atkinson's recent review of the evidence persuasively refutes his arguments

As for epigraphic evidence, we have few dedicatory inscriptions and few grave inscriptions from Hellenistic and Early Roman Galilee. Inscriptions that provide information about named individuals are rare and their interpretation debatable. We cannot assume that a Greek or Latin name, whether preserved in an inscription or in literary sources, necessarily indicates that an individual was not Jewish. In both Diaspora and Palestinian contexts, in both the Hellenistic and Roman eras, Jewish use of non-Semitic names was not uncommon. Examples of Greek names can be seen among the Hasmoneans – Hyrcanus, Aristobulus, Alexander – as well as among the Herodians – Antipater, Antipas, Agrippa, Philip. Usage was not limited to the rulers, though; Jewish use of Greek names can be found among the mercenaries of third-century BCE Egypt, and Greek and Latin names are found in the burial inscriptions from the second century CE and later at Beth She'arim.[13]

Burial customs are of mixed usefulness for identifying Jews and gentiles. Tomb architecture in and of itself often tells us little. Tombs were typically cut out of rock or built within caves, and Jews and non-Jews alike typically employed *kokhim* – individual burial slots – within tomb complexes.[14] More helpful is evidence of ossilegium (secondary burial of bones), which seems to be a typically Jewish custom during this time period. Remains of ossuaries – small chests into which bones were transferred after the flesh had decayed – provide clear evidence of a Jewish grave.[15]

Limestone vessels are among the clearest indicators of Jewish inhabitants. Jews believed that ceramic vessels could become impure and thus

---

("On Further Defining the First-Century C.E. Synagogue: Fact or Fiction?" *NTS* 43 [1997]: 491–502).

[13] See Hengel, *Judaism and Hellenism*, vol. I, 61–65; cf. Victor Tcherikover, *Hellenistic Civilization and the Jews*, trans. Shimon Applebaum, 3 vols. (Philadelphia: Jewish Publication Society of America; Jerusalem: Magnes, Hebrew University Press, 1959), vol. II, 346–347; Moshe Schwabe and Baruch Lifshitz, *Beth She'arim* (New Brunswick, N.J.: Rutgers University Press, 1974), vol. II: *The Greek Inscriptions*, 209–213. The adoption of foreign names occurred with other peoples as well, such as the Celts in Galatia, where Greek names became common among the upper classes (Jones, *Cities*, 119–121).

[14] Oren Tal, "Roman-Byzantine Cemeteries and Tombs around Apollonia," *Tel Aviv* 22 (1995): 107–120.

[15] Byron McCane, "Burial Techniques," *OEANE*, vol I, 386–387; Byron McCane, "Ossuary," *OEANE*, vol. IV, 187–188; Byron McCane, "Jews, Christians, and Burial in Roman Palestine" (Ph.D. Diss., Duke University, 1992); Eric M. Meyers, "Secondary Burials in Palestine," *BA* 33:1 (1970): 2–29; Eric M. Meyers, *Jewish Ossuaries: Reburial and Rebirth* (Rome: Biblical Institute Press, 1971); Rachel Hachlili, "Burials: Ancient Jewish," *ABD*, vol. I, 789–794.

render their liquids impure. Stone vessels, in contrast, were impervious to impurity. Their special status was due to the fact that, unlike ceramic vessels, they had not been fired (cf. *M. Kelim* 4.4). Stone vessels are only rarely discovered outside of Jewish areas. Within Palestine, they are found more frequently in Judea than in Galilee, presumably because proximity to the temple heightened the importance of ritual purity. The presence of stone vessels may indicate the presence of priestly families, Pharisees, or just of more purity-minded Jews; categorizing their users is not necessary for our purposes. Following the Jewish Revolt and the Bar Kochbah revolt, they went out of use, but they are common finds in late Second Temple strata.[16] Reina, a village north of Nazareth, served as a production center for limestone measuring cups and other vessels.[17]

Jewish ritual baths, or mikvaot, are similarly helpful. Also used for purification, they took the form of stepped immersion pools with bottoms cut directly into bedrock.[18] They are found all over Palestine and seemingly have few parallels in the Diaspora.[19]

[16] Roland Deines provides the most extensive treatment of stone vessels in *Jüdische Steingefäße und pharisäische Frömmigkeit* (Tübingen: J. C. B. Mohr [Paul Siebeck], 1993). (While his thesis that stone vessels indicate Pharisaic influence is problematic, his compilation of the sites where they have been discovered is impressive.) See also Yitzhak Magen, "Ancient Israel's Stone Age: Purity in Second Temple Times," *BAR* 24:5 (1998): 46–52; Yitzhak Magen, "The Stone Vessel Industry during the Second Temple Period," in *"Purity Broke Out in Israel"* (Catalogue no. 9, The Reuben and Edith Hecht Museum, University of Haifa, 1994), 7–28; Yitzhak Magen, "Jerusalem as a Center of the Stone Vessel Industry during the Second Temple Period," in Hillel Geva, ed., *Ancient Jerusalem Revealed* (Jerusalem: Israel Exploration Society; Washington, D.C.: Biblical Archaeology Society, 1994), 244–256; and Jane M. Cahill, "Chalk Vessel Assemblages of the Persian/Hellenistic and Early Roman Periods," *Qedem* 33 (1992): 190–274.

[17] Zvi Gal, "A Stone-Vessel Manufacturing Site in the Lower Galilee," *Atiqot* 20 (1991): 179–180; Magen, *"Purity Broke Out,"* 8.

[18] On mikvaot, see E. P. Sanders, *Jewish Law from Jesus to the Mishnah* (London: SCM Press; Philadelphia: Trinity Press International, 1990), 214–227 and references cited in index under "Purity laws: immersion, immersion pools"; Sanders, *Judaism*, 222–230; Ronny Reich, "Ritual Baths," *OEANE*, vol. IV, 430–431; Ronny Reich, "The Hot Bath-House (*balneum*), the *Miqweh*, and the Jewish Community in the Second Temple Period," *JJS* 39 (1988): 102–107. It is important to note that scholars may differ on whether a particular pool is a mikveh; see, for example, the criticisms of Hanan Eshel in "A Note on 'Miqvaot' at Sepphoris," in Edwards and McCollough, eds., *Archaeology and the Galilee*, 131–134 and "They're Not Ritual Baths," *BAR* 26:4 (2000): 42–45; and Eric M. Meyers's response in "Yes, They Are,"*BAR* 26:4 (2000): 46–48. For the purposes of this study, I have generally accepted a given site's excavator's interpretation of such pools.

[19] Justin Martyr's reference (*Dialogue with Trypho* 14.1) to Jewish usage of cisterns for purification shows that the practice was known outside of Palestine, and a synagogue on Delos may have contained an immersion pool. See Sanders, *Judaism*, 223; cf. Sanders, *Jewish Law*, 360 n. 11.

Lower Galilee

Galilee's population increase is reflected in the remains of both cities and villages. Josephus mentions three "great cities" of Galilee, Sepphoris, Tiberias and Gabara.[20] Gabara, however, plays almost no role in his narrative, and extensive archaeological remains have not been recovered there. Josephus devotes considerable attention, however, to events at Sepphoris and Tiberias. Of these two, only Sepphoris has undergone extensive excavation. Our discussion of Lower Galilee will begin there, at Sepphoris and nearby villages. Afterwards we will consider the evidence from Tiberias and other sites in the lake region, and then we will examine sites in southwestern Galilee.

Sepphoris and the surrounding areas

Sepphoris

No site in Galilee has attracted more attention recently than Sepphoris, known in Hebrew as *Zippori*.[21] Centered around a hill top, midway between the Mediterranean and the Sea of Galilee (eighteen miles from each), Sepphoris was a thriving city in the Roman and Byzantine eras. Given Sepphoris's prominence in Galilee and its proximity (about four miles) to Nazareth, the absence of references to it in the Gospels is curious. Though various explanations for its omission from the Gospels have been offered[22] – Jesus never visited there; Jesus purposely avoided the city because of the strong Herodian presence; as a rural Galilean, Jesus held the city in low regard; the city's residents rejected Jesus's teaching – all are speculative.

[20] *Life* 188.
[21] My discussion of Sepphoris incorporates material included in my "The Cultural Milieu of Ancient Sepphoris," *NTS* 47 (2001): 127–145 and "How Jewish was Sepphoris in Jesus' Time?" with Eric M. Meyers, *BAR* 26:4 (2000): 18–33, 61. For overviews of the history, significance, and lay-out of Sepphoris, see Carol L. Meyers and Eric M. Meyers, "Sepphoris," *OEANE*, vol. IV, 527–536; Eric M. Meyers, Ehud Netzer, and Carol L. Meyers, *Sepphoris* (Winona Lake, Ind.: Eisenbrauns, 1992) and "Sepphoris: Ornament of All Galilee"; Eric M. Meyers, "Roman Sepphoris"; James F. Strange, "Sepphoris," *ABD*, vol. V, 1090–1093; Zeev Weiss, "Sepphoris," in *NEAEHL*, vol. IV, 1324–1328; Zeev Weiss and Ehud Netzer, "Architectural Development of Sepphoris during the Roman and Byzantine Periods," in Edwards and McCollough, eds., *Archaeology and the Galilee*, 117–130; Michael Avi-Yonah, "Sepphoris," *EAEHL*, vol. IV, 1051–1055; and E. P. Sanders, "Jesus' Relation to Sepphoris," in Rebecca Martin Nagy, Carol L. Meyers, Eric M. Meyers, and Zeev Weiss, eds., *Sepphoris in Galilee: Crosscurrents of Culture* (Winona Lake, Ind.: Eisenbrauns, 1996), 75–79.
[22] Bösen, *Galiläa*, 69–75; Reed, *Archaeology*, 100–108.

When Herod Antipas rebuilt the city at the end of the first century BCE, he turned it into the "ornament of all Galilee," according to Josephus.[23] Josephus is not alone in his glowing description; scholars emphasizing the Greco-Roman ethos of Galilee point to this city, with its splendid mosaics, aqueduct, paved and colonnaded streets, agora, and Roman theater, as their prime example, as do those who postulate a Galilee with a strong pagan presence.[24] Because of the attention Sepphoris has received in recent scholarship, a full discussion of its first-century atmosphere and population is warranted. Sepphoris is the rare Galilean site for which we have both extensive literary sources and archaeological remains. It is well excavated and relatively well published. Josephus frequently refers to it in his discussion of the Jewish Revolt, and rabbinic traditions seem to preserve memories from the Second Temple period. We might suspect that here, if anywhere in Galilee, explicit evidence for non-Jews can be found.

History and development of Sepphoris. Josephus provides us with enough information to sketch an outline of the history of Sepphoris from the beginning of the first century BCE until the Jewish Revolt; archaeological findings testify to its importance in the Roman and Byzantine periods; and frequent rabbinic references provide the occasional glimpse of life in Sepphoris.

The earliest history of the city is unclear. *M. Arakhin* 9.6 mentions the "the old castra" of Sepphoris in a list of walled cities going back to the time of Joshua, son of Nun, but the veracity of this tradition is dubious, given the small amount of supporting archaeological data.[25] Iron Age remains consist of a few pottery sherds; Persian era finds consist of sherds, a vase fragment with cuneiform inscriptions, a limestone incense burner, and a terracotta rhyton (decorated horn-shaped drinking vessel).[26]

Excavations are only beginning to shed light on Sepphoris in the Hasmonean era. The western side of the acropolis was used as a quarry until the first century BCE, when construction began there.[27] Architectural remains of that period are scant. One recently discovered structure

---

[23] *Ant.* 18.27.

[24] Batey, *Jesus and the Forgotten City*, 14; cf. Strange, "Sepphoris," *ABD*, vol. V, 1091 and my Introduction and chapter 1.

[25] See Miller, *Studies*, 15–30 for discussion. The passage also mentions other Galilean sites: the "fortress of Gush Ḥalav" and "old Yodefat" (perhaps Jotapata).

[26] See the comments by Michael Dayagi-Mendels and Matthew W. Stolper in *Sepphoris*, ed. Nagy et al., 163–167. Perhaps at the end of the Iron Age or the beginning of the Persian era, settlement had shifted from Ein Zippori, a tel to the southeast (C. Meyers, "Sepphoris and Lower Galilee," 16), though the paucity of post-eighth century BCE remains at Ein Zippori and of pre-Persian remains at Sepphoris makes this difficult to demonstrate.

[27] Weiss and Netzer, "Architectural Development," 117.

near the acropolis measured more than twenty meters long and had walls nearly two meters thick at points. The sheer size of this building and the thickness of its walls suggest that it was a military fortress, and the presence of two mikvaot attests to its use by Jews. Dozens of coins from the period of Alexander Jannaeus (103–76 BCE) and pottery from the Late Hellenistic period reflect its use by the new Hasmonean conquerors of Galilee.[28]

Sepphoris first appears in the literary record in Josephus's account of Alexander Jannaeus's reign as one of the cities attacked by Ptolemy Lathyrus.[29] Josephus's commentary on Sepphoris is brief, noting only that the assault was unsuccessful and that Ptolemy lost many men.[30] Given Ptolemy's success at nearby Asochis (a capture of "ten thousand men and a great deal of booty besides," according to Josephus's surely inflated account), and his subsequent rout of Jannaeus's forces at the Jordan, Sepphoris's successful defense suggests a strongly fortified city.

Josephus next mentions Sepphoris in the context of the administrative organization of Gabinius, *strategos* of Syria, *c.* 57 BCE, following his victories over Alexander the son of Aristobulus. The references are brief and passing: Gabinius divided the people (ἔθνος) into five portions and established five councils[31] or unions,[32] which governed from Jerusalem, Gadara, Amathus, Jericho, and Sepphoris. Gabinius's selection of Sepphoris suggests that it had already achieved a prominent standing. The councils do not seem to have been lasting institutions; Josephus makes no mention of them after the rise of Antipater to the position of *epitropos* of Judea in 48 BCE and the appointment of his son Herod a year later to administer Galilee.[33]

We can piece together a sketchy history of Sepphoris in the Herodian period. Herod the Great captured it in the winter of 39/38 BCE after its

---

[28] E. Meyers, "Sepphoris on the Eve of the Great Revolt"; Kenneth G. Hoglund and Eric M. Meyers, "The Residential Quarter on the Western Summit," in 39; Eric M. Meyers, Carol L. Meyers, and Kenneth G. Hoglund, "Zippori (Sepphoris) – 1994," *ESI* 16 (1997): 46–47; cf. Jürgen Zangenberg, "Jüngste Ausgrabungen im neutestamentlichen Sepphoris," *Weld und Umwelt der Bibel* 10:4 (1998): 76–77. For references to other Hellenistic remains, see Eric M. Meyers, Ehud Netzer and Carol L. Meyers, "Sepphoris (Ṣippori), 1987 and 1988," *IEJ* 40 (1990): 219; Eric M. Meyers, Carol L. Meyers, and Kenneth G. Hoglund, "Sepphoris (Ṣippori), 1993," *IEJ* 44 (1994): 250; and Joan Keller, "The Glass from Sepphoris (1983–1991): A Preliminary Report," http://www.colby.edu/rel/Glass.html, which notes the presence of Hellenistic glass.

[29] *Ant.* 13.324–355. It is sometimes claimed that Ptolemy attacked Sepphoris on a Sabbath (see, for example, Strange, "Sepphoris," *ABD*, vol. V, 1091). Josephus, however, describes a Sabbath attack on nearby Asochis (probably Shiḥin); whether the subsequent attack on Sepphoris happened on the same day is unclear.

[30] *Ant.* 13.337–338; cf. *War* 1.86.   [31] *Ant.* 14.91.   [32] *War* 1.170.

[33] *Ant.* 14.143, 158; *War* 1.197–200.

abandonment by the Hasmonean Antigonus.[34] Following Herod's death
in 4 BCE, one of the groups struggling for power assaulted his royal palace
there and seized the arms therein.[35] Acting to stabilize the increasingly
chaotic conditions, Varus, legate of Syria, marched south. His forces,
"after capturing Sepphoris . . . reduced its inhabitants to slavery and burnt
the city,"[36] though excavations have so far produced only scattered evidence of any conflagration.[37] After Varus crushed the rebellion, Herod's
son, Antipas, received Galilee. Antipas fortified Sepphoris, rebuilding
it as "the ornament of all Galilee," and named it "Autocratoris," probably to honor the emperor.[38] The administrative center of Galilee seems
to have shifted to Antipas's new city, Tiberias, when it was constructed
c. 20 CE.[39] It remained there until *c.* 61 CE, when Nero turned Tiberias
over to Agrippa II[40] and made Sepphoris home to the royal bank and the
archives.[41]

Sepphoris, though "the strongest city in Galilee" according to
Josephus,[42] refused to rebel against the Romans during the Jewish
Revolt.[43] Early in the conflict, it readily admitted a garrison of Roman
soldiers from Caesennius Gallus's troops[44] and later it accepted a contingent from Vespasian.[45] Meyers has suggested on the basis of ceramic and
numismatic evidence that the old Hellenistic era fortress was dismantled
at this time, as a symbolic display of its submission to the Romans.[46]
Josephus reports his own failed attempts to drive the Romans out of the
city.[47] The city occasionally suffered other attacks during the Revolt due
to intra-Jewish rivalries and urban–rural tensions.[48]

[34] *Ant.* 14.414, *War* 1.304.   [35] *Ant.* 17.271–272, *War* 2.56.
[36] *Ant.* 17.289; cf. *War* 2.68.
[37] C. Meyers and E. Meyers, "Sepphoris," *OEANE*, vol. IV, 530. A deteriorated Roman
cuirass from the first century BCE or the first century CE could date to this event, or
alternately, to the Great Revolt; see James F. Strange, Dennis E. Groh, Thomas R. W.
Longstaff, and C. Thomas McCollough, "Sepphoris, 1998," *IEJ* 49 (1999): 126–128.
[38] *Autocrator* is the Greek translation of the Latin imperial title *Imperator*; see note in
Josephus, *Jewish Antiquities Books XVIII–XIX*, trans. Louis H. Feldman (Cambridge, Mass.
and London: Harvard University Press, 1965), 24.
[39] *Ant.* 18.36–38, *War* 2.168.   [40] *War* 2.252, *Ant.* 20.159.   [41] *Life* 38.
[42] *War* 2.511.
[43] While Josephus describes Sepphoris as initially "eager for hostilities" (*War* 2.574),
in *Life*, he frequently refers to its pro-Roman sentiments (see 30, 37, 39, 104, 124, 232,
346–347, 373, 394).
[44] *War* 2.511, *Life* 394 (where the commander is named Cestius Gallus).
[45] *War* 3.31, *Life* 411.
[46] E. Meyers, "Sepphoris on the Eve of the Great Revolt." The fortress was dismantled
between 53 CE and 70 CE. A cache of weaving tools from a first-century CE stratum suggests that it may have been used for industrial, rather than military, purposes by that time.
[47] *War* 3.62, *Life* 394–397.
[48] *War* 2.574, 630, 645–646; *Life* 82, 111, 373–380, 384.

Two different coins struck at Sepphoris *c*. 68 CE support Josephus's account of the city's actions during the Revolt. The reverses of both bear the inscription "Under Vespasian, Eirenopolis-Neronias-Sepphoris" (ΕΠΙ ΟΥΕCΠΑΙΑΝΟΥ ΕΙΡΗΝΟΠΟΛΙC ΝΕΡѠΝΙΑ CΕΠΦѠ). These inscriptions testify to the city's respect for Vespasian as well as to a new name for Sepphoris, honoring both its role as a "peaceful city" and Nero. One coin bears an additional inscription that functioned as pro-Roman propaganda, the Latin letters "SC," a common legend on Roman coins.[49]

After this point, with the cessation of Josephus's narratives, the political history of Sepphoris becomes less clear, though coins provide us with hints of developments. The names "Neronias" and "Eirenopolis" dropped from usage. When the city issued four series of coins during Trajan's reign (98–117 CE), all bore the inscription ΣΕΠΦѠΡΗΝѠΝ ("of the people of Sepphoris").[50] At some point in the second century CE, the city was renamed "Diocaesarea," a name honoring Zeus and the emperor.[51] City coins minted under Antoninus Pius (138–161 CE) bore this new name, which reflects the changing cultural climate of Sepphoris.[52]

The growth of Sepphoris in the first two centuries CE. Major construction occurred in the Early Roman period, initiated by Herod Antipas's rebuilding of the city. The summit of the hill was well settled, and as the first century CE progressed, the city seems to have expanded eastwards onto an adjoining plateau. The very nature of archaeological excavations, however, prevents us from drawing a full picture of what the city looked like in this time. Centuries of rebuilding on top of old occupation layers destroyed much evidence from earlier times. This fact,

[49] See the comments by Yaakov Meshorer in *Sepphoris*, ed. Nagy et al, 195–196 and Yaakov Meshorer, "Sepphoris and Rome," in O. Morkholm and N. M. Waggoner, eds., *Greek Numismatics and Archaeology: Essays in Honor of Margaret Thompson* (Belgium: Cultura Press, 1979), 159–171; H. Hamburger, "The Coin Issues of the Roman Administration from the Mint of Caesarea Maritima," *IEJ* 20 (1970): 81–91; Henri Seyrig, "Irenopolis-Neronias-Sepphoris: An Additional Note," *Numismatic Chronicle* 15 (1955):157–159; Henri Seyrig, "Irenopolis-Neronias-Sepphoris," *Numismatic Chronicle* 10 (1950): 284–289.

[50] Nagy et al., eds., *Sepphoris*, 196–197.

[51] A nearby Roman milestone, probably erected *c*. 120 CE, provides additional evidence for the new name. At an uncertain date, a second, cruder Greek inscription providing the distance to "Diocaesarea" was added to the original Latin inscription. Benjamin Isaac and Israel Roll note that coins of Tiberias from *c*. 120 CE depict Zeus (with whom Hadrian was identified) seated in a temple, as do coins from Neapolis. They suggest that the change of Sepphoris's name to "Diocaesarea" may have coincided with developments in these other cities. If the name change does date to 120 CE, it shortly follows the stationing of Roman troops at nearby Legio (Isaac and Roll, "Judaea," 63–66; cf. Baruch Lifschitz, "Sur la date du transfert de la Legio VI Ferrata en Palestine," *Latomus* 19 [1960]: 109–111).

[52] Nagy et al., eds., *Sepphoris*, 197; Meshorer, "Sepphoris and Rome," 165.

coupled with archaeologists' understandable decisions to go no further down in particular areas once substantial architectural remains are uncovered, results in the common characteristic of most excavated sites of the region: the juxtaposition of remains from a broad span of time, with exposed Hellenistic strata (few though they are) side by side with remains from all centuries of Roman and Byzantine rule.

Thus, many of the impressive remains that one sees today when visiting Sepphoris post-date the Early Roman era; they tell us little about first-century CE Sepphoris. While one aqueduct dates to the first century CE, the more massive aqueduct system (including a swimming pool and a reservoir), partly visible to the east, dates to the second century CE.[53] Two bathhouses apparently post-date the expansion of the city onto the eastern plateau, though one of them may date to the early phase of that expansion.[54] One of the most famous of the Sepphoris finds, the Roman villa with its triclinium mosaic celebrating the life of Dionysos, dates to the early third century CE.[55] The mosaics of the Nile festival building, with such vivid depictions of the Nile and its accompanying Nilometer, Alexandria, hunting scenes, and Amazons, date to the Byzantine era.[56] A recently discovered synagogue, with a mosaic depicting astrological symbols as well as the binding of Isaac and traditional temple furnishings, probably was constructed in the fifth century.[57]

No discovery at Sepphoris has generated more controversy than that of the theater, which seated 4,500–5,000 spectators.[58] Batey has argued

[53] Tsvika Tsuk, "Bringing Water to Sepphoris," *BAR* 26:4 (2000): 34–41; "The Aqueducts of Sepphoris," in Eric M. Meyers, ed., *Galilee through the Centuries: Confluence of Cultures* (Winona Lake, Ind.: Eisenbrauns, 1999), 161–176; "The Aqueducts of Sepphoris," in Nagy et al., eds., *Sepphoris*, 45–49; "Şippori: The Aqueducts," *ESI* 1 (1982): 105–107; "Şippori: The Aqueducts," *ESI* 9 (1989–1990): 20.

[54] Weiss and Netzer, "Architectural Development," 121.

[55] Eric M. Meyers, Ehud Netzer and Carol L. Meyers, "Artistry in Stone: The Mosaics of Ancient Sepphoris," *BA* 50 (1987): 223–231 and *Sepphoris* 34–59; Carol L. Meyers, Eric M. Meyers, Ehud Netzer, and Zeev Weiss, "The Dionysos Mosaic," in Nagy et al., eds., *Sepphoris*, 111–115; Carol L. Meyers, Eric M. Meyers, Ehud Netzer, and Zeev Weiss, "Sepphoris (Şippori), 1986 (I) – Joint Sepphoris Project," *IEJ* 37 (1987): 277.

[56] E. Meyers, Netzer, and C. Meyers, "Artistry in Stone," 223–231; Zeev Weiss and Ehud Netzer, "The Mosaics of the Nile Festival Building," in Nagy et al., eds., *Sepphoris*, 127–131.

[57] Ehud Netzer and Zeev Weiss, *Zippori* (Jerusalem: n.p., distributed by Israel Exploration Society, 1994); Zeev Weiss and Ehud Netzer, "The Synagogue Mosaic," in Nagy et al., eds., *Sepphoris*, 133–139; Zeev Weiss and Ehud Netzer, *Promise and Redemption: A Synagogue Mosaic from Sepphoris* (Jerusalem: Israel Museum, 1996); Zeev Weiss, "The Sepphoris Synagogue Mosaic," *BAR* 26:5 (2000): 48–61, 70.

[58] On the theater, see especially Leroy Waterman, *Preliminary Report of the University of Michigan Excavations at Sepphoris, Palestine, in 1931* (Ann Arbor: University of Michigan Press, 1937), 6–12; E. Meyers, Netzer, and C. Meyers, *Sepphoris*, 30–33; on the decoration,

that "the presence of a theatre at Sepphoris was symbolic of the larger crosscultural currents in which Jesus matured."[59] Yet the first-century CE dating of the theater is contested. S. Yeivin, associated with the original excavation, dated it to Herod Antipas's rebuilding of the city, arguing, "There is no other period in the history of the town when the erection of a similar building was likely, whereas Herod Antipas tried, no doubt, to ape, on his own small scale, the large program of public buildings initiated by his father." Yeivin pointed to the presence of Hasmonean coins in the debris above the orchestra floor as support for this dating.[60] W. F. Albright, however, expressed reservations based on stylistic grounds, suggesting a late second- or even third-century CE origin instead.[61] The more recent archaeological excavations of the 1980s and 1990s have led to no unanimity on this issue. Strange claims that the latest pottery fragments found on the bedrock under the theater date to the Early Roman period,[62] while Meyers writes that "extensive soundings under its foundations indicate a later date, perhaps as late as the early to mid-second century, when the city underwent extensive rebuilding after the First Jewish Revolt."[63] I am inclined to accept this later date, but the issue will remain disputed until the publication of the ceramic evidence.

What, then, can we determine about Early Roman Sepphoris from archaeology?[64] A recent study by Jonathan Reed suggests that the population of first-century CE Sepphoris, based on the physical size of the city,

see Zeev Weiss and Ehud Netzer, "Zippori – 1992–1993," *ESI* 14 (1994): 41. On theaters in the larger Greco-Roman world, see Mary T. Boatwright, "Theaters in the Roman Empire," *BA* 53 (1990): 184–192.

[59] Batey, "Jesus and the Theatre," 563–570; quote from 570. Batey suggests that Jesus's familiarity with that institution explains his use of the term ὑποκριτής.

[60] S. Yeivin, "Historical and Archaeological Notes," in Waterman, *Preliminary Report*, 29.

[61] W. F. Albright, review of Leroy Waterman, *Preliminary Report of the University of Michigan Excavations at Sepphoris, Palestine, in 1931*, *Classical Weekly* 31 (1938): 148.

[62] See James F. Strange, "Six Campaigns at Sepphoris: The University of South Florida Excavations, 1983–1989," in Levine, ed., *Galilee in Late Antiquity*, 342–343.

[63] C. Meyers and E. Meyers, "Sepphoris," *OEANE*, vol. IV, 533. Zeev Weiss and Ehud Netzer support this later dating ("Hellenistic and Roman Sepphoris: The Archaeological Evidence," in Nagy et al., eds., *Sepphoris*, 32 and "Architectural Development," 122).

[64] On Early Roman finds, see Strange, "Some Implications," 40 and "Six Campaigns," 346–349; Zeev Weiss and Ehud Netzer, "Hellenistic and Roman Sepphoris," 29–37; and Hoglund and Meyers, "Residential Quarter," esp. 39–41; C. Thomas McCollough and Douglas R. Edwards, "Transformations of Space: The Roman Road at Sepphoris," in *Archaeology and the Galilee*, 139–140; Eric M. Meyers, Carol L. Meyers, and Ehud Netzer, "Sepphoris, (Șippori) 1985, (I)" *IEJ* 35 (1985): 295–297; Eric M. Meyers, Carol L. Meyers, and Kenneth G. Hoglund, "Sepphoris, (Șippori) 1994," *IEJ* 45 (1995): 68–71 and "Zippori (Sepphoris) – 1994," 46–47; James F. Strange, Ehud Netzer and Zeev Weiss, "Sepphoris, (Șippori) 1991–1992," *IEJ* 43 (1993): 190–196; James F. Strange, Dennis E. Groh, and Thomas R. W. Longstaff, "Sepphoris, 1996," *IEJ* 49 (1999): 122–123; James F. Strange,

was between 8,000–12,000 inhabitants[65] – smaller than Batey's estimate of 30,000,[66] but still sizable. With confidence, we can say that both the western summit and the eastern plateau were settled, and that Sepphoris had urban architectural features – paved and colonnaded streets, water installations (including possibly a bathhouse on the eastern plateau and some sort of public water work nearer the acropolis), multi-storey buildings, and public architecture, including a large basilical style building on the eastern plateau.[67] At least some of the roads were oriented on a grid. Additional second-century CE expansion to the east of the acropolis required new or renovated streets, including a colonnaded *decumanus* and the *cardo*, as well as a new aqueduct. Sepphoris clearly was a city of major import for Galilee and its presence undermines stereotypical depictions of the region as a backwater or totally rural province. Recent studies of Galilee that emphasize this fact have done a service for those who seek to understand the Palestinian context of early Christianity and Judaism.

The "Greco-Roman Ethos" of Sepphoris. Scholars who point to Sepphoris as the prime example of the how thoroughly Greco-Roman culture had affected first-century CE Galilee have, however, sometimes overstated their case. Strange's helpful model of an "urban overlay" that Rome imposed on local cultures provides an opportunity to discuss this point. Discussing the mixture of cultures in Roman Palestine, Strange proposes that "Roman culture advanced over the local Jewish

Dennis E. Groh, and C. Thomas McCollough, "Sepphoris, 1997," *IEJ* 49 (1999): 124–126; Strange, Groh, Longstaff, and McCollough, "Sepphoris, 1998," 126–128.

[65] Reed, *Archaeology*, 80; cf. his earlier estimate of a maximum of 24,000 ("Population Numbers," 214).

[66] Batey, *Jesus and the Forgotten City*, 14.

[67] On the basilical building, the foundation of which dates to the Early Roman period, see James F. Strange, Dennis E. Groh, Thomas R. W. Longstaff and C. Thomas McCollough, "The University of South Florida Excavations at Sepphoris, Israel: Report of the Excavations: May 11–July 14, 1998," http://www.colby.edu/rel/Sep98.html; James F. Strange, Dennis E. Groh, and C. Thomas McCollough, "The University of South Florida Excavations at Sepphoris, Israel: Report of the Excavations: May 8–23, 1997," http://www.colby.edu/rel/Sep97.html; James F. Strange, Thomas R. W. Longstaff, and Dennis E. Groh, "The University of South Florida Excavations at Sepphoris, Israel: Report of the Excavations: 10 June–12 July, 1996," http://www.colby.edu/rel/Sep96.html; and James F. Strange, "The University of South Florida Excavations at Sepphoris, Israel: Report of the Excavations: 12 June–14 July 1995," http://www.colby.edu/rel/Sep95.html; "The University of South Florida Excavations at Sepphoris, Israel: Report of the Excavations: 14 June–15 July, 1994," http://www.colby.edu/rel/Sep94.html; and "The University of South Florida Excavations at Sepphoris, Israel: Report of the Excavations: 3 May–18 July, 1993," http://www.colby.edu/rel/Sep93.html; James F. Strange, Thomas R. W. Longstaff, and Dennis E. Groh, "Zippori – 1991," *ESI* 13 (1993): 29–30.

culture rather like a warm weather front advances over the terrain."[68] He explains:

> In other words, this "urban overlay," especially as it came to expression in artifacts and architecture, bore the major institutions, ideas, and symbols of Roman culture in Judea [and, Strange's subsequent discussion makes clear, Galilee]. The local Jewish culture, on the other hand, bore its own institutions, ideas, and symbols . . . To clarify further, the symbols of specifically Roman culture, sometimes on a co-opted Hellenistic base, include baths, hippodromes, theaters, amphitheaters or circuses, odeons, nymphaea, figured wall paintings, statues, triumphal monuments, temples (Augustaea, Tiberia), etc . . . Symbols of the Jewish foundation include the Second Temple, synagogues or places of assembly, art forms with Jewish symbols (menorah, ethrog, lulab), and tombs.[69]

Strange's model is useful for understanding the interplay of Roman urban culture and indigenous culture in Palestine, but it is far more applicable to later periods than to the first century CE, and to cities surrounding Galilee (e.g., Sebaste, Scythopolis, and Caesarea Maritima), than to Sepphoris (or Tiberias, for that matter). In the Early Roman period, Sepphoris had a basilical building, possibly a theater, if the disputed earlier dating is accepted, and perhaps a bathhouse. Some buildings' interiors were decorated with frescoes. As of yet, however, none of the other features Strange highlights as part of the Roman "urban overlay" have been discovered in Sepphoris, from the first century CE or later.

As for the languages in use at Sepphoris in the Late Hellenistic and Early Roman periods, we have surprisingly little information. One early find dates to the second century BCE – a jar fragment with an inscription written in square Hebrew characters. The first five of the seven visible letters (אפמלסלש) seem related to the Greek word ἐπιμελετης ("manager, overseer"); if so, then as a loan-word it reflects the growing importance in the region of Greek.[70] Aside from civic coins, with their Greek inscriptions, we have little evidence for the linguistic environment of Sepphoris until the mid-second century CE, to which a lead market weight dates. Inscribed in Greek on both sides, it reads: "under the market inspection

---

[68] Strange, "Some Implications," 31.   [69] Ibid., 32–33.

[70] See E. Meyers, "Sepphoris on the Eve of the Great Revolt," 130–131; comments by Joseph Naveh in Nagy et al., eds., *Sepphoris*, 170.

of [αγορανομουτων] Simon son of Aianos and Justus son of... "[71] The name "Simon" is Semitic in origin (שמעון); "Justus" is Latin. The Semitic name probably indicates that one of the market inspectors was Jewish, though we can't be certain; whether the name "Justus" indicates a gentile or simply a Jew with a Latin name is likewise unclear. Such limited data tell us very little about what languages were in use in first-century Sepphoris. The chief significance of these inscriptions is that they allow us to document the initial stages of Galilee's later linguistic trends.

Not until the beginning of the third century CE do we begin to have substantial evidence for understanding Sepphoris's linguistic environment. The Mishnah, codified under Judah ha-Nasi at Sepphoris, demonstrates a strong Jewish presence and the use among the rabbis of Hebrew. The Dionysos mosaic, dating to roughly the same period, has Greek labels for the various scenes of the symposium (drinking contest) of Heracles and Dionysos. A nearby room in the same villa is paved with a mosaic decorated with the word ΥΓΕΙ, and fragments of an amphora also found nearby bore the name "Tryphon." A Greek mosaic inscription accompanying a depiction of Orpheus, found in another recently uncovered building, dates to the late third or even fourth century.[72] By the Late Roman and Byzantine periods, we have substantially more evidence for both Aramaic and Greek at Sepphoris.

Josephus and the Rabbis. Though one might infer the presence of pagans in Sepphoris from its unwillingness to send troops to defend the temple during the revolt, Josephus does not say this. Instead, he stresses Sepphoris's pragmatic reasons for siding with Rome. Realistically aware of the power of Rome, Sepphoris put its own security first.[73] Though the city forbade its citizens to take service with the revolutionaries,[74] its support for Rome was not due to any ethnic tension between Jews and gentiles. Rather, Josephus describes the support of the Sepphoreans for the Romans as an action against the "allies of their tribe" (κατὰ τῶν ὁμοφύλων συμμάχους).[75] The temple in Jerusalem they failed to defend was the temple "common to us all."[76] The only gentiles in Sepphoris

---

[71] See comments by Yaakov Meshorer in Nagy et al., eds., *Sepphoris*, 201; cf. his earlier report, "The Lead Weight: Preliminary Report," *BA* 49 (1986): 16–17. For the dating of the weight, see Eric M. Meyers, Carol L. Meyers, and Ehud Netzer, "Sepphoris, (Ṣippori) 1985, (I)," *IEJ* 35 (1985): 295–297.

[72] (No author), "The Mosaic Pavements of Roman and Byzantine Zippori," www.hum. huji.ac.il/archaeology/zippori/mosaic.htm.

[73] *War* 3.31.   [74] *Life* 347.   [75] *War* 3.32.   [76] *Life* 348.

that Josephus mentions are the Roman soldiers who were stationed there during the Revolt[77] and a pair of refugees from Trachonitis. Josephus had to restrain the Sepphoreans from forcibly circumcising the latter two.[78]

Rabbinic traditions preserve memories of Sepphorean priests. One of these is Joseph ben Elim, who once served as a substitute for the high priest on the Day of Atonement, according to *Tosefta Yoma* 1:4.[79] *Tosefta Sotah* 13:7 tells the story of another, who became known as ben Ḥamsan. Taking more than his share of the Two Loaves and the Shewbread, he still received only a bean-sized piece of bread, thus earning his unfavorable nickname ("Ḥamsan" refers to one who is greedy and snatches).[80] Another priest, Arsela, "the Israelite" who led the scapegoat into the wilderness one Yom Kippur, is identified in some manuscripts as a Sepphorean (*M. Yoma* 6.3).[81] Stuart Miller concludes that all we can tell from these stories is that second-century rabbis remembered the participation in the temple cult of individuals from Sepphoris.[82]

Archaeological evidence for Jews and pagans. The physical evidence for Jewish inhabitants in Early Roman Sepphoris is unambiguous: mikvaot[83] and over a hundred fragments of stone vessels[84] unmistakably demonstrate that many Sepphoreans were concerned with Jewish ritual purity customs. Ceramic incense shovels, similar in appearance to

[77] Rabbinic traditions also mention the presence of a contingent of non-Jewish soldiers at Sepphoris, but these traditions probably post-date the revolts; see discussions of *t. Shabb.* 13:9 and similar traditions in Miller, *Studies*, 24, 31–45, 56–59.

[78] *Life* 112–113.

[79] *B. Yoma* 12b–13a preserves an abbreviated version of this story, and *y. Yoma* 1, 38c–d provides additional information; cf. the corresponding account in Josephus, *Ant.* 17.165ff. (Miller, *Studies*, 63–88).

[80] See also *y. Yoma* 6, 43c and *b. Yoma* 39a–b (Miller, *Studies*, 88–102).

[81] Miller, *Studies*, 129.

[82] Ibid., 102. Though the presence of the priestly course (*mishmar*) of Jedaiah is attested in *y. Taanit* 4, 68d, Miller dates this particular tradition to the fourth century, suggesting that the *mishmar* can be traced in Sepphoris to the third century at the earliest (*Studies*, 131–132 and note 1. on 62; Stuart S. Miller, "Jewish Sepphoris: A Great City of Scholars and Scribes," in Nagy et al., eds., *Sepphoris*, 61).

[83] Strange, "Six Campaigns," 345; James F. Strange, Dennis E. Groh and Thomas R. W. Longstaff, "Sepphoris," *RB* 96 (1989): 241 and "Sepphoris (Ṣippori) 1987," *IEJ* 38 (1988): 189; James F. Strange and Thomas R. W. Longstaff, "Sepphoris (Ṣippori)-1986 (II)," *IEJ* 37 (1987): 279; Eric M. Meyers, Carol L. Meyers, and Ehud Netzer, "Sepphoris (Ṣippori) 1987, (I)," *IEJ* 37 (1987): 276; Weiss and Netzer, "Zippori – 1992–1993," 41. At least two mikvaot, those found in the fortress, date back to the Late Hellenistic period (E. Meyers, "Sepphoris on the Eve of the Great Revolt," 137–138). Despite the reservations of Hanan Eshel ("Note," 131–132; "They're Not Ritual Baths," 42–45), the identification of at least most of these installations as miqvaot is secure (Eric M. Meyers, "Yes, They Are," 46–48).

[84] The Early Roman date of these stone vessels is well established; the upcoming report of the Sepphoris Regional Project will provide more data on their archaeological contexts.

those depicted in later Jewish art and with characteristics corresponding to biblical and rabbinic descriptions, are probably additional indicators of Judaism.[85] Analysis of the bones recovered in the western residential area near the acropolis found that pig bones are extremely infrequent until the Byzantine period, suggesting that the Roman-era inhabitants, at least in this part of the city, kept kosher.[86]

In light of such finds, as well as the references of Josephus and the rabbis, the presence of Jews at first-century CE Sepphoris is indisputable. What evidence exists for the presence of pagans? Examples of Greco-Roman culture in the city's material record are easier to identify than examples of paganism, particularly in the first two centuries CE. A bronze plaque (approximately 4.9 cm by 4.9 cm) dating to either the first century BCE or the first century CE illustrates the problem. It depicts a winged figure atop a horned animal, perhaps a goat. In front of the rider is a table (an altar?) with a cone-shaped object, which may be bread. Who is the winged figure? Is the bread some type of offering? All that can be said with certainty about such imagery is that it reflects Greco-Roman influence, not that it reflects pagan cultic practices.[87] Later finds, such as the previously mentioned Dionysos and Orpheus mosaics, are similarly difficult to interpret.

Lamps dating from the late second century CE to the third century CE also display distinctive Hellenistic motifs. Erotic scenes are present on the medallions of some, and one shows the head of a Medusa.[88] We cannot say whether the users of these lamps were Jewish or pagan. Their decorations reflect the influence of Hellenistic culture, but not the cultic practices or ethnic identities of their owners.[89]

Two tiny (6 and 7.5 cm) bronze figures, one of either Pan or a satyr, the other of Prometheus, possibly attest to pagan practices, though their exact function is unsure. While they might have been used as household idols or for other cultic purposes, they may just as easily have been decorative; such figurines were often furniture attachments. The figurines were found in a cistern near the acropolis, in an area that appears to have been predominantly Jewish, given the discovery there of mikvaot and stone vessels. Their presence, like that of the plaque and the lamps, unmistakably shows

[85] Leonard V. Rutgers, "Incense Shovels at Sepphoris?" in E. Meyers, ed., *Galilee*, 177–198.

[86] Billy J. Grantham, "Sepphoris: Ethnic Complexity at an Ancient Galilean City" [Ph.D. Diss., Northwestern University, 1996).

[87] See comments by Ellen Reeder in Nagy et al., eds., *Sepphoris*, 174.

[88] See lamps 112–114 in ibid., 220–221.

[89] Some lamps from the fourth century CE bear more traditional motifs; two depict a menorah and one an aedicula from a Torah shrine (ibid., 221–222).

the influence of Hellenistic culture and art, but not necessarily of pagan cultic practices or religious beliefs. In any case, they, too, post-date the first century, probably belonging to the second or the third.[90]

Strange's expedition has uncovered three objects that are less ambiguous: a bronze bowl, a small (2.5 cm high) bronze incense altar, and a (7 cm) bronze bull, which he associates with Serapis. These items (especially the altar), found together in a cistern beneath a wall in a Roman villa, provide the strongest evidence for paganism in Sepphoris. They most likely date to the fourth century CE, however, and so are of little use for understanding the earlier period.[91]

The coins of Sepphoris. The coins of Sepphoris give us some information about who was living there – or, at least, who was in charge. As noted above, the two issued in 68 CE reflect the city's pro-Roman stance during the Revolt. Neither bears the image of the emperor, present on all later issues, or of a pagan deity or temple. The reverse of one bears an inscription within a circle and a wreath; that of the other depicts a double cornucopia with a caduceus between the two. The cornucopia itself is very common on Jewish coins,[92] though it is not an exclusively Jewish symbol,[93] but the caduceus, often associated with the staves of Hermes and Asclepius, is much rarer on Jewish coins. This combination of the double cornucopia and the caduceus is even more infrequent, though it does appear on coins of Herod the Great, Archelaus, and Agrippa II, as well as on other Palestinian (non-Jewish) coins.[94] The parallel between the image on Sepphoris's coin and that of Agrippa II is notable, since the latter was struck at Paneas slightly prior to that of Sepphoris around 67 CE and also bears an inscription reflecting that city's renaming in honor of Nero. By adopting this symbol on their coin, Sepphoris may have been subtly affirming its traditional link to the Herodian dynasty.

---

[90] C. Meyers and E. Meyers, "Sepphoris," *OEANE*, vol. IV, 532 and comments of Sarah H. Cormack in Nagy et al., eds., *Sepphoris*, 171–172.

[91] Strange, "Six Campaigns," 345 and "Some Implications," 40. See the comments of Dennis E. Groh in Nagy et al., eds., *Sepphoris*, 173.

[92] Meshorer, *Ancient Jewish Coinage*, vol. I, 67 and vol. II, 27–28; Paul Romanoff, *Jewish Symbols on Ancient Jewish Coins* (New York: American Israel Numismatic Association, Inc., 1971), 26–27.

[93] Augustus Spijkerman, *The Coins of the Decapolis and Provincia Arabia* (Jerusalem: Franciscan Printing Press, 1978), 239. For examples, see two coins of Gadara, one from 28/29 CE and the other from 50/51 CE (coins 12 and 20 on 130–133).

[94] Meshorer, *Ancient Jewish Coinage*, vol. II, 27; cf. Meshorer, *Jewish Coins*, 66. For Herodian coins depicting the double cornucopia and caduceus, see coins 53–53C, 56–56a, and 99 in *Jewish Coins* and coins 17–17m, 1–1f, and 5 in *Ancient Jewish Coinage*, vol. II, 237, 239, and 250; cf. comments in Seyrig, "Irenopolis-Neronias-Sepphoris," 286, note 3.

The four coins issued under Trajan (98–117 CE) differ from the two Revolt coins in that their obverses bear the emperor's image. Around each bust is the inscription ΤΡΑΙΑΝΟΣ ΑΥΤΟΚΡΑΤѠΡ ΕΔѠΚΕΝ, and each reverse bears the ethnic ΣΕΠΦѠΡΗΝѠΝ. A different symbol is found on each of the four reverses: a laurel wreath, a caduceus, two ears of grain or corn, and a palm tree.[95] These symbols all appear on Jewish coinage, but all occur on non-Jewish coinage as well.[96] Thus, they may reflect an effort to depict representations acceptable to both Jews and pagans. If so, they may reveal a city whose population and cultural ethos are in flux.

The next set of coins minted at Sepphoris, during the time of Antoninus Pius, provide stronger evidence for a non-Jewish presence – at the least a non-Jewish administration. Again, portraits of the emperor adorn the obverses, and the inscriptions on the reverses record the city's new name, ΔΙΟΚΑΙCΑΡΙΑ ΙΕΡΑ ΑCΥΛΟC ΚΑΙ ΑΥΤΟΝΟΜΟC ("of Diocaesarea, Holy City of Shelter, Autonomous"), a name that honors both the emperor and Zeus. On the reverses appear images of the Capitoline Triad within a temple, as well as the goddess Tyche within a temple. A later coin, dating to the time of Julia Domna (died *c.* 217 CE), has a different depiction of a temple with Tyche within.[97]

These numismatic images of temples, our only evidence for pagan temples at Sepphoris, date to the middle of the second century CE. Even then, the existence of the depicted temples is not assured. Because archaeologists have not yet uncovered any remains of temples, other interpretive possibilities should be kept in mind, such as a propagandistic depiction of Roman culture.[98]

The population of Sepphoris in the Early Roman period. In sum, references in Josephus and rabbinic materials indicate that Sepphoris in the Early Roman period was a primarily Jewish city; we find no evidence in either body of literature for the presence of pagans (other than soldiers and the two refugees during the Revolt). Our most unambiguous archaeological evidence is in agreement with this image of a predominantly Jewish city: ritual baths and stone vessels. These findings provide

[95] Meshorer, "Sepphoris and Rome," 163–164; comments in Nagy et al., eds., *Sepphoris*, 195–196.

[96] Even the palm tree, often associated with Jewish coinage because of its appearance on coins of the Hasmoneans, Herodians, and the two revolts, shows up on non-Jewish first-century CE coins (Meshorer, *Ancient Jewish Coinage*, vol. II, 83–84).

[97] Meshorer, *City-Coins*, 36–37; Meshorer, "Sepphoris and Rome," 165; comments by Meshorer in Nagy et al., eds., *Sepphoris*, 197; E. Meyers, Netzer, and C. Meyers, *Sepphoris*, 13.

[98] Strange, "Some Implications," 38; cf. Goodman, *State and Society*, 41, 46.

unmistakable proof of a concern on the part of some inhabitants with Jewish purity customs. Ceramic incense shovels probably provide additional signs of Jewish inhabitants.

The published materials attesting to the presence and influence of pagans in Sepphoris post-date the Hellenistic and Early Roman periods. No evidence at all is found for temples until the time of Antoninus Pius, and even then the significance of that evidence – images on coins – may be debated. No cultic objects are found until the second century CE at the very earliest. Many of the architectural features, such as the gymnasium, associated with gentile cities were absent from Sepphoris. In short, whatever pagans were found in the Sepphoris of the Hasmoneans and the Herodians are thus far invisible in the archaeological record – and in the literary record, as well. With the Jewish Revolt, foreign troops are stationed in Sepphoris, though we are unsure of the length of their stay, and in the second century, we slowly begin to find evidence of a growing non-Jewish presence.[99] But in first-century CE Sepphoris, a mixed population consisting of not only Jews but also Arabs, Greeks, and Romans is nowhere to be found.

Nazareth

Sepphoris's neighbor, Nazareth, was just a small village in the first century CE, having been founded some time in the third century BCE. By one estimate, it occupied approximately sixty acres and probably had around 480 inhabitants.[100] It is not mentioned at all prior to the Gospels, and they provide only minimal information about it. All four regard the village as the hometown of Jesus, and John suggests that it was not a notable town.[101] According to the synoptics, Nazareth had a synagogue, which served as the setting for Jesus's preaching and rejection by the villagers.[102] Josephus makes no reference to it at all.

Tombs from the Early and Middle Roman periods (and later) have been found around Nazareth, demarcating its ancient boundaries,[103] as

[99] E. Meyers, "Roman Sepphoris," 328–329 and "Jesus and His Galilean Context," 57–66.

[100] Strange, "Nazareth," *ABD*, vol. IV, 1050–1051; see also overviews in James F. Strange, "Nazareth," *OEANE*, vol. IV, 113–114; Vassilios Tzaferis and Bellarmino Bagatti, "Nazareth," *NEAEHL*, vol. III, 1103–1106; and Bellarmino Bagatti, "Nazareth," *EAEHL*, vol. III, 919–922.

[101] Matt. 4:13, 13:54, 21:11; Mark 1:9, 6:1; Luke 4:16; John 1:45.

[102] Luke 4:16; cf. Mark 6:1, Matt. 13:54.

[103] See Clemens Kopp, "Beiträge zur Geschichte Nazareths," *JPOS* 18 (1938): 187–233; Bellarmino Bagatti, *Excavations in Nazareth*, trans. E. Hoade (Jerusalem: Franciscan

well as in the vicinity of the nearby modern city, Nazareth 'Illit. Of these, one, dating to the first or second century CE, contained an ossuary, indicating the practice of secondary burial.[104] The tombs of Nazareth are less known among students of Early Roman Palestine than the famous Greek inscription found there, probably dating to the mid-first century CE, of an imperial decree prohibiting grave-robbing.[105]

More famous still are Nazareth's Christian holy sites, which have been extensively excavated. In fact, they are practically the only parts of the ancient settlement that have been excavated, due to the density of construction and population in the modern city. Significant remains from the Roman and Byzantine eras have been discovered near and under the Church of the Annunciation, the Church of St Joseph, and the site presently occupied by the Sisters of Nazareth. Various chambers, tunnels, cavities, pits, cisterns, oil presses and granaries have been found, attesting to the village's agricultural activity.[106]

The remains underneath the Church of the Annunciation have received the most attention by far.[107] Particularly important are architectural fragments – capitals and column bases and moldings – which Bagatti, the primary excavator, interprets as remains of a synagogue dating from the second through the fourth century CE.[108] Joan E. Taylor has argued, however, that "the form of the building . . . bears no resemblance whatsoever to a

---

Printing Press, 1969), 237–249; E. T. R. [no further identification of author provided], "A Rock-Cut Tomb at Nazareth," *QDAP* 1 (1932): 53; Bellarmino Bagatti, "Una singolare tomba a Nazaret," *Rivista di Archeologia Cristiana* 43 (1967): 7–14. Joan E. Taylor dates an Aramaic funerary inscription to the first century, though her reason is uncertain (*Christians and the Holy Places: The Myth of Jewish-Christian Origins* [Oxford: Clarendon Press, 1993], 133); cf. Jean-Baptiste Frey, ed., *Corpus Inscriptionum Iudaicarum*, 2 vols. (Rome: Pontificio Instituto di Archeologia Cristiana, 1952), vol. II, 173, no. 988.

[104] Nurit Feig, "Nazareth 'Illit,' " *IEJ* 33 (1986): 116–117; for the tomb with the ossuary, see no author, "Nazareth 'Illit," *ESI* 1 (1982): 78–79. An additional tomb was found in the general area of Nazareth, near H. Tirya (Arfan Najjar and Nissim Najjar, "Nazareth," *ESI* 16 [1997]: 49).

[105] *SEG* 8, #13; 13, #59; 16, #828; cf. Eric M. Meyers and James F. Strange, *Archaeology, the Rabbis, and Early Christianity* (Nashville: Abingdon, 1981), 83–84.

[106] The primary publication for Nazareth is Bagatti, *Excavations*; cf. Italian original, Bellarmino Bagatti, *Gli Scavi di Nazaret*, vol. I (Jerusalem: Tipografia Dei PP Francescani, 1967). Of earlier reports, among the more substantial is Bellarmino Bagatti, "Ritrovamenti Nella Nazaret Evangelica," *LA* 5 (1955): 5–44.

[107] See Bagatti, *Excavations*, 77–218.

[108] Bagatti argues that the fragments are remains of a Jewish-Christian synagogue that reflects a continuous Jewish-Christian presence since the time of Jesus (ibid., 138–146, 171–172; cf. Bellarmino Bagatti, *The Church from the Circumcision* [Jerusalem: Franciscan Printing Press, 1971]; Emmanuele Testa, *Il Simbolismo dei Giudo-Cristiani* [Jerusalem: Tipografia dei PP Francescan, 1962]; Emmanuele Testa, *Nazareth Giudo-Cristiana* [Jerusalem: Tipografia dei PP Francescan, 1969]). Taylor launches a devastating attack on the Bellarmino-Testa thesis in *Christians and Holy Places*.

synagogue," pointing out that the structure was oriented toward the north, facing away from Jerusalem – an atypical orientation for a synagogue.[109] Furthermore, fragments such as these could come from either a synagogue or a church. In short, the remains are not necessarily from a synagogue at all; even if they are, they date to a later period than the first century CE.

Other especially relevant finds in Nazareth include a stepped basin, the bottom of which is decorated with a mosaic, found underneath St Joseph's church. Bagatti interpreted this basin as a mikveh, but as Taylor has pointed out, the decoration of a mikveh with a mosaic is extremely unusual. In any case, the basin dates to the Late Roman or Byzantine period. Bagatti also refers to fragments of large (26 cm diameter), vase-like stone vessels, of uncertain date, and two stone feet, one marble and one of stone, also of uncertain date, found in a cistern beneath the Church of the Annunciation. Bagatti suggests that Crusaders may have deposited the votive feet in the church at some point. Given uncertainty regarding their place and date of origin, we cannot consider them evidence of paganism in first-century CE Nazareth.[110]

Asochis/Shiḥin

Josephus reports that Asochis was near Sepphoris,[111] and one story he narrates suggests that it was a Jewish community. In his description of Ptolemy Lathyrus's attack on the village during the reign of Jannaeus, Josephus mentions that the attack occurred on the Sabbath; his reference to the day of the assault suggests that timing was one factor in Ptolemy Lathyrus's victory.[112] Asochis is usually identified with the "Shiḥin" mentioned in rabbinic sources, a village within sight of Sepphoris which was known for its high quality storage jars.[113] Though its exact location is not certain, a hill to the north of Sepphoris is a likely candidate. Surveys there discovered large quantities of Roman pottery, including wasters, which indicate that the village at that site served as a center for pottery production. Neutron activation analysis of these wasters as well as of ceramics discovered at other Galilean sites revealed that a majority of the storage jars used in Galilee, as well as 45 percent of the pottery at Sepphoris,

[109] Taylor, *Christians and Holy Places*, 230–267 (quote from 257).

[110] On the mikveh, see Bagatti, *Excavations*, 228–231; on the stone feet, see ibid., 318; cf. Taylor, *Christians and Holy Places*, 230–267.

[111] *Ant.* 13.338; cf. *Life* 233, 384. Rabbinic traditions record that a fire at Shiḥin was visible at Sepphoris; soldiers stationed there aided in extinguishing it; see sources in n. 114.

[112] *Ant.* 13.338; cf. *War* 1.86. Josephus reports that he himself quartered there (*Life* 384), suggesting that the village was sympathetic to the Revolt.

[113] *T. Ter.* 7.14, *b. Shabb.* 120b, *b. Shabb.* 121a and *y. Shabb.* 16, 15d.

came from this site. The most notable of the survey's finds, for our purposes, are fragments of limestone vessels, though, as surface finds, they were discovered out of context. The site awaits full excavation, and the ceramic finds, as well as features visible on the surface – a waste pit, cisterns, an olive press, a kiln – suggest that it will yield significant data regarding production and trade of pottery in Galilee.[114]

Cana

Cana, the setting for two of Jesus's miracles in John,[115] is another example of a settlement for which the exact location is unknown. Josephus once set up his headquarters there;[116] he later refers to a base in the Plain of Asochis,[117] or the present-day Bet Netofa valley. If he is referring to the same place in both passages, then Cana lay in the valley to the north of Sepphoris and Nazareth. Most scholars point to either Kafr Kanna (located approximately five km north of Nazareth) or Khirbet Qana (fourteen km north of Nazareth) as the likely candidate for biblical Cana's location.[118]

Neither of these sites has been fully excavated. The ruins of Khirbet Qana include tombs, cisterns, caves, the foundations of several buildings and the remains of at least one sizable structure. Sherds attest to occupation from the first through the sixth centuries CE.[119] A possible Roman-era columbarium has been found; given Jews' aversion to cremation, its presence would suggest non-Jewish inhabitants. The columbarium's exact date of use is unclear, however, making it of questionable relevance for understanding first-century CE Cana.[120]

[114] James F. Strange, Dennis E. Groh, and Thomas R. W. Longstaff, "Excavations at Sepphoris: Location and Identification of Shikhin," *IEJ* 44 (1994): 216–227; James F. Strange, Dennis E. Groh, Thomas R. W. Longstaff, with David Adan-Bayewitz, Frank Asaro, Isadore Perlman, and Helen V. Michel, "Excavations at Sepphoris: Location and Identification of Shikhin," *IEJ* 45 (1994): 171–187; see the revision of these two articles in James F. Strange, Dennis E. Groh, and Thomas R. W. Longstaff, "The Location and Identification of Ancient Shikhin (Asochis)," www.colby.edu/rel/shikhin.html. On the pottery trade, see Adan-Bayewitz and Perlman, "Local Trade," and David Adan-Bayewitz, *Common Pottery in Roman Galilee: A Study of Local Trade* (Ramat-Gan: Bar-Ilan University Press, 1993).
[115] John 2:1–11 and 4:46.   [116] *Life* 86.   [117] *Life* 206.
[118] James F. Strange, "Cana of Galilee," *ABD*, vol. I, 827; Richard M. Mackowski, "Scholars' Qanah: A Re-examination of the Evidence in Favor of Khirbet Qanah," *Biblische Zeitschrift* 23 (1979): 278–284; Bellarmino Bagatti, "Le Antichità di Kh. Qana e di Kefr Kenna in Galilea," *LA* 15 (1964–1965): 251–292; E. W. G. Masterman, "Cana of Galilee – at Khirbet Kana," *Palestine Exploration Fund Quarterly Statement* (1914): 179–183; and Hermann Guthe, "Beiträge zur Ortskunde Palästinas: Kana in Galilee," *Mitteilungen und Nachrichten des deutschen Palästina-Vereins* 18 (1912): 81–86.
[119] James F. Strange, "Survey of Lower Galilee, 1982," *IEJ* 32 (1982): 254–255.
[120] Bagatti, "Antichità," 260; Mackowski, "Scholars' Qanah," 281.

Until recently, finds at the alternate site, Kefar Kanna, consisted primarily of tombs, ranging in date from the Late Hellenistic to the Middle Roman period. At least one of these tombs, dating to the late first century or early second century CE, contained fragments of ossuaries, attesting to the Jewish practice of secondary burial.[121] The series of excavations that began in 1998 will clarify the nature of the site further; the findings are so recent that they are currently unpublished.

Jotapata

Jotapata lay to the north of Sepphoris, separated from the city by a ridge and a valley. Founded in the late fourth or early third century BCE on a hill surrounded on three sides by steep ravines, its occupation lasted until its destruction in the Revolt. After the Revolt, settlement shifted to a different site at the foot of the hill. Excavations have revealed an extensively fortified town on the hill itself. In the Late Hellenistic period, a fortress-like structure, two towers, and town walls were built. Though some of these defenses were dismantled in the Early Roman period, others remained in use. Additional walls, including one of casemate construction, and earthworks were erected in the Early Roman period.[122] Arrowheads from iron bows, catapults, ballista stones, a rolling stone, an iron knife, the shaft from an iron spear, and portions of a siege ramp remain from the Roman campaign.[123] After the Revolt, occupation on the hill ceased, though the plateau was resettled later in the century or in the early second century CE.

Josephus provides us with extensive information about the war-time conflict at Jotapata, as well as his leadership during the siege and his clever survival.[124] He reports having fortified the site,[125] and perhaps some of the first-century constructions were built at his direction,

---

[121] Nissim Najjar, "Kafr Kanna (A)," *ESI* 16 (1997): 47–48 and Stanislao Loffreda, "Un lotto di ceramica da Karm er-Ras presso Kafr Kanna," *LA* 25 (1975): 193–198. On the ossuaries, see Hana Abu Uqsa and Nissim Najjar, "Kafr Kanna (B)," *ESI* 16 (1997): 48–49 and A. Berman, "Kafr Kanna," *ESI* 7–8 (1988–1989): 107–108.

[122] Adan-Bayewitz and Aviam, "Iotapata"; see also Douglas R. Edwards, "Jotapata," *OEANE*, vol. III, 251–252; Mordechai Aviam, "Tel Yodefat, Oil Press," *ESI* 9 (1989/1990): 106; Douglas R. Edwards, Mordechai Aviam, and David Adan-Bayewitz, "Yodefat, 1992," *IEJ* 45 (1995): 191–197; David Adan-Bayewitz, Mordechai Aviam, and Douglas R. Edwards, "Yodefat – 1992," *ESI* 16 (1997): 42–44.

[123] Adan-Bayewitz and Aviam, "Iotaptata," 139, 143, 148, 162; Edwards, "Jotapata," *OEANE*, vol. III, 252; Edwards, Aviam, and Adan-Bayewitz, "Yodefat, 1992," 196.

[124] *War* 3.110–114, 141–288, 316–339, 340–408.

[125] *War* 2.573, *Life* 188. Josephus reports that it was the "most formidable" of the sites he had fortified (*War* 3.111).

though this cannot be demonstrated with certainty. Throughout these accounts, he describes the inhabitants and defenders of Jotapata as Ἰουδαῖοι. Archaeological finds corroborate Josephus's description. Artifacts that suggest the inhabitants' Jewishness include a first-century ostracon from a store jar with Semitic letters, stepped pools, some of which are possibly mikvaot, and approximately eighty fragments of lime-stone vessels.[126]

The sea of Galilee region

Tiberias

Though Antipas devoted considerable resources to the rebuilding of Sepphoris, it was not the only object of his attention. He began the con-struction of a new capital city for Galilee c. 20 CE,[127] naming it Tiberias in honor of the emperor.[128] Establishing the city was no easy task; in addition to funding and planning requirements, Antipas faced difficulty in finding inhabitants for his new capital. Though the location he chose for the city was a lakeside site near the well-known springs of Hammath, in "the best region of Galilee" according to Josephus, it was also on top of old tombs. Occupation of such territory, according to Jewish law, resulted in ritual impurity. To populate his new city, Antipas forcibly set-tled Galileans from surrounding areas, including both local officials and poor people imported from "any and all places of origin" (πανταχόθεν), as well as slaves, many of whom he himself freed. For the latter, Antipas himself funded the construction of homes, with the condition that these beneficiaries would not later abandon his city.[129]

Possession of Tiberias shifted between Herodian rulers and Roman overseers throughout the first century. After exiling Antipas to Gaul

[126] Edwards, "Jotapata," *OEANE*, vol. III, 252; Edwards, Aviam and Adan-Bayewitz, "Yodefat, 1992," 195–196; Adan-Bayewitz, Aviam, and Edwards, "Yodefat – 1992," 44; Adan-Bayewitz and Aviam, "Iotapata," 151–153, 164.

[127] Coins minted at Tiberias first appear in the twenty-fourth year of Antipas's reign, which would be 20 CE (Yizhar Hirschfeld, "Tiberias," *OEANE*, vol. V, 203 and James F. Strange, "Tiberias," *ABD*, vol. VI, 547). Michael Avi-Yonah, however, suggested 18 CE as the foundation date ("The Foundation of Tiberias," *IEJ* 1 [1950–1951]: 160–169).

[128] Hirschfeld, "Tiberias," *OEANE*, vol. V, 203–206; Yizhar Hirschfeld, "Tiberias," *NEAEHL*, vol. IV, 1464–1470; Gideon Foerster, "Tiberias," *EAEHL*, vol. IV, 1173–1176; Gideon Foerster, "Tiberias: Excavations in the South of the City," *NEAEHL*, vol. IV, 1470–1473; Strange, "Tiberias," *ABD*, vol. VI, 547–549; and Tessa Rajak, "Justus of Tiberias," *Classical Quarterly* 23 (1973): 345–368.

[129] *Ant.* 18.36–38; cf. *War* 2.168. The cemetery would continue to present a problem to Jews concerned with ritual impurity until it was declared pure by Rabbi Simeon Bar Yohai (*Gen. Rab.* 79h; *y. Shabb.* 9, 1–38d).

c. 39 CE, Caligula turned the city over to Agrippa I, a former *agoranomos* of the city.[130] When Agrippa I died in 44 CE, rule seems to have shifted over to Roman procurators. In 61 CE, Nero added Tiberias, along with Taricheae, Julias, and other cities, to the territory of Agrippa II. Tiberias thus became part of a kingdom with a mixed population of Jews and gentiles, while the capital of Galilee shifted back to Sepphoris.[131] By the second century CE, Tiberias had again come under Roman rule, and coins from the time of Trajan demonstrate that it was renamed Tiberias Claudia.[132] Epiphanius records the beginning, but not completion, of the construction of a temple dedicated to Hadrian during his reign, and city coins from this period depict a temple of Zeus. Given the identification of Hadrian with Zeus, these images may reflect the Hadrianeum reported by Epiphanius.[133] The city continued to prosper under Roman rule, and, despite any such pagan institutions, became a center of Palestinian Jewry.

Given Jesus's extensive activity in the Sea of Galilee region, one wonders if he ever entered Tiberias. As with Sepphoris, the Gospels are silent on this point, and so Galilee's chief cities play virtually no role in Jesus's recorded activities. John, however, does make passing mention of the city, referring twice to the "Sea of Tiberias" (6:1, 21:1), and once to people traveling by boat from Tiberias (6:23).

Archaeological remains of Tiberias. Ancient Tiberias is less excavated than Sepphoris. Portions of it lie underneath the modern city, and much of what has been excavated has not been well published. Though the majority of archaeological finds are from the Byzantine and later periods, substantial remains from the Roman era attest to the city's extensive development. These include a Roman-style bathhouse (fourth century CE); a theater, perhaps seating as many as five thousand, at the foot of nearby Mount Berenice (second or third century CE); a cardo by the sea (from the second century CE); and evidence of a drainage system. First-century CE remains include a gate complex, made of basalt stones and flanked by two round towers, originally constructed without walls. This complex apparently stood to the south of the city, and a paved street ran northward into the city's interior.[134]

---

[130] *Ant.* 18.252; see 18.149 for Agrippa's appointment as *agoranomos*.

[131] *Ant.* 20.159, *War* 2.252, *Life* 37–38.

[132] Meshorer, *City-Coins*, 34. Claudius is similarly honored on a coin appearing *c.* 53 CE (see discussion below).

[133] Epiphanius, *Adv. Haereses* 30.12.1; Meshorer, *City-Coins*, 34, coin 81; and Foerster, "Tiberias," *NEAEHL*, vol. IV, 1464.

[134] See citations above; Yizhar Hirschfeld, "Excavations at Tiberias Reveal Remains of Church and Possibly Theater," *BA* 54 (1991): 170–171; and [no author] "Notes and News,"

These discoveries, while providing glimpses of ancient Tiberias, tell us little of the composition of its first-century population, which was probably between 6,000 and 12,000.[135] More relevant to this issue, perhaps, are two smaller finds, both discovered underneath the floor of a large second- or third-century CE building: a fragment of a stone jar and a bone figurine of a female. The stone vessel indicates a Jewish presence. The figurine, given the Jewish abhorrence of images, likely belonged a pagan owner, but could conceivably reflect the degree of Hellenization among at least some of Tiberias's Jewish population. Accompanying ceramic finds date from the first or second century CE.[136]

A large Roman tomb found on the nearby mountain side also provides relevant data. Constructed in the late first or the second century CE, it consisted of two chambers. Its underground chamber contained thirty-five skeletons, and most of its twenty-eight loculi of the upper chamber also contained skeletons. Two of the skeletons found in this upper chamber were found in an ossuary, indicating Jewish burial customs.[137]

Epigraphic evidence. Like Sepphoris, Tiberias has so far yielded a paucity of first-century CE epigraphic evidence.[138] Aside from the inscriptions on coins, the only published inscriptions securely dated to the first century are found on two lead weights. The first of these weights was found at Tiberias itself; the second, though found at Magdala, seems to be dated according to the era of Tiberias and thus probably originated in that city.[139] The weights' inscriptions name the city's *agoranomoi*. The first reads, "In the thirty-fourth year of Herod the tetrarch, *agoranomos* of Gaius Julias."[140] The date provided by the inscription suggests that

IEJ 3 (1953): 265. Hirschfeld reports the finding of remains from the first two centuries CE underneath a "basilica" on the south road leading into Tiberias ("Tiberias," *ESI* 16 [1997]: 38).

[135] Reed, *Archaeology*, 82.

[136] Yizhar Hirschfeld, "Tiberias," *ESI* 9 (1989/1990): 107–109. He suggests the figurine "reflects the appearance of a Tiberian noblewoman in the second century C.E." ("Tiberias: Preview of Coming Attractions," *BAR* 17:2 [1991]: 51). He also reports the discovery of a possible mikveh in the second- or third-century stratum of this same building ("Tiberias," *NEAEHL*, vol. IV, 1468).

[137] Fanny Vitto, "Tiberias: The Roman Tomb," *NEAEHL*, vol. IV, 1473.

[138] A sarcophagus, possibly from the first century CE, more likely from the third, contains a lengthy Greek inscription, which is, for the most part, a typical burial formula, applauding the virtues of the deceased (M. Schwabe, "Ein griechisches Grabepigramm aus Tiberias," *JPOS* 16 [1936]: 158–165).

[139] Shraga Qedar, "Two Lead Weights of Herod Antipas and Agrippa II and the Early History of Tiberias," *INJ* 9 (1986–1987): 29–35. Strange also reports the discovery of weights of Tiberias with Greek inscriptions at Yodefat in "Tiberias,"*ABD*, vol. IV, 549.

[140] ΕΠΙ ΗΡѠΔΟΥ / ΤΕΤΡΑΡΞΟΥ / ΛΔΛ ΑΓΟΡΑ / ΓΑΙ / ΟΥ ΙΟΥΛΙΟΥ / ΕΤΑΛΕΝΤΟ. As Qedar notes ("Two Lead Weights," 29), the reading of the sixth line is unclear.

the weight was used *c.* 31 CE. At that time, the *agoranomos* held a Latin name, "Gaius Julias." We are left with little other information about who this Gaius Julias was. Does his name indicate that he was a Roman, as Shraga Qedar contends, or that, at minimum, he was not a Jew?[141] Or does it demonstrate one Jew's openness toward Roman culture? The second weight bears an inscription on both the obverse and the reverse. The obverse reads, "Year 43 of the great king Agrippa lord"; the reverse, "[In the term of office of the] *agoranomoi* Iaesaias [son of] Mathias and Animos [son of] Monimos."[142] Given the circumstance that Agrippa I reigned only eight years, the weight probably dates to the time of Agrippa II. The names of these *agoranomoi* are Semitic, though the second name, Animos son of Monimos, is of uncertain origin. Qedar goes too far when he suggests that they reflect a Jewish *agoranomos* and a "Syrian Semite" *agoranomos*.[143] The difficulty of drawing such conclusions is obvious: we know little more about these individuals than their names.

The coins of Tiberias. The city of Tiberias apparently issued no municipal coins until the time of Trajan, but the coins of Herod Antipas often bear Greek inscriptions naming it. Antipas's coins, like those of war-time Sepphoris, bear symbols acceptable to Jew and gentile alike: reeds, palm branches, palm trees, wreaths, and dates.[144] In contrast to the coins of Antipas, the coins of Agrippa I and Agrippa II frequently bore images of both emperors and pagan deities. Some of the issues of Agrippa I commemorated the family of Caligula, with images of several members of his family as well as Nike figures.[145] Agrippa II minted a variety of series of coins, which frequently bore busts of emperors and images of Tyche and Nike.[146] Though Tiberias is often cited as the mint for these

[141] Ibid., 33.

[142] ΛΜΓ/ΒΑ CΙΑ/ΕШC ΜΕ/ΓΑΛΟΥΑ/ ΓΡΙΠΠΑ Κ/ΥΡΙΟ and ΑΓΟΡΑΝΟ/ΜΟΥΝΤШΝ /ΙΑΕCΑΙΟΥ Μ/ΑΘΙΟΥ, Κ ·ΑΙ Α/ ΝΙΜΟ C ΜΟΝ/ΙΜΟΥ Qedar notes uncertainty on the translation of Κ ·ΑΙ Α / ΝΙΜΟ. If k· is an abbreviation for και, the name is "Aianimos." If, however, Κ ·ΑΙ is simply και, then the name is "Animos."

[143] Qedar, "Two Lead Weights," 33.

[144] Meshorer, *Jewish Coins*, 72–75, 133–135, and *Ancient Jewish Coinage*, vol. II, 35–41, 242–243.

[145] The obverse of one bore a bust of the emperor, and the reverse depicted a rider, perhaps Agrippa himself or perhaps Germanicus (father to Caligula), riding a chariot adorned with a Nike figure. Another bore a bust of Antonia, the grandmother of Caligula, on the obverse; the image of a female figure holding in her hand a small Nike figure, and inscriptions honoring Drusilla, sister to Caligula, on the reverse. The third bore a bust of a young Agrippas II on the obverse, a double cornucopia on the reverse (Meshorer, *Ancient Jewish Coinage*, vol. II, 166–167; *Jewish Coins*, 78–80).

[146] Meshorer, *Ancient Jewish Coinage*, vol. II, 65–95, 250–258; *Jewish Coins*, 81–87.

coins, this is uncertain.[147] These coins reliably tell us about the images the two Agrippas were trying to project for their kingdom, as well as their own loyalties to Rome; they do not tell us who was living in first-century Tiberias.

Several denominations of coins appeared in 53 CE, during the period of direct Roman rule of the city between the rule of the two Agrippas. All bore similar symbols: an obverse with a palm branch and inscription "of Claudius Caesar" and a reverse bearing the inscription "Tiberias" surrounded by a wreath. These coins, with representations inoffensive to Jews, obviously emanate from the city, though the minting authority is disputed.[148]

An additional coin from the first century is also noteworthy. Its reverse contains the name Tiberias and the date "year eighteen," probably referring to the reign of Agrippa II. The coin bears no ruler's image, but its obverse depicts the ubiquitous image of a palm branch and the inscription NIK CEB. This Greek inscription is found on no other known coin from the ancient world; at first glance, it could conceivably be taken as an inscription honoring Nike. Most likely, however, it is a Greek translation and abbreviation of the Latin "Victoria Augustus," an imperial title and a common Latin inscription on western coins.[149]

Once municipal coins (rather than royal issues) begin to appear in the second century, they bear pagan images. The earliest of these are four issues minted under Trajan, each bearing his bust. Their reverses bear the images of the familiar double cornucopia with a palm branch in between; an anchor; Hygeia, goddess of health; and a city goddess. Coins minted under Hadrian depict the (aforementioned) temple with a seated figure of Zeus; a city goddess; and a galley. Later coins from the Roman period bear the images of Poseidon, Hygeia and Asklepios.[150]

The coins of Tiberias do not provide evidence for a large pagan population in the first century. Most Herodian coins cannot be confidently associated with the city; those that are (such as the issues of Antipas) do not bear pagan motifs. Not until the municipal issues

---

[147] Meshorer, for example, provides little evidence to support his contention that Tiberias was the mint for Agrippa I's coins (*Ancient Jewish Coinage*, vol. II, 54, 57, 247). Perhaps Agrippa I minted some coins at Caesarea Philippi as Agrippa I did.

[148] Ibid., vol. II, 166–167, 279. Meshorer proposes that Agrippa II commissioned them; Arie Kindler (*The Coins of Tiberias* [Tiberias: Hamei Tiberia, 1961], 17) suggests a procurator.

[149] Ya'akov Meshorer, "Ancient Jewish Coinage Addendum I," *INJ* 11 (1990–1991): 104–132, revising earlier comments in Meshorer, *Ancient Jewish Coinage*, vol. II, 166–167, coin 4.

[150] Meshorer, *City-Coins*, 34–35.

of the second century do images of the emperor, deities, and temples appear.

Josephus and Tiberias. The writings of Josephus remain our primary source for information about first-century CE Tiberias. His discussion of Antipas's difficulties in settling the city suggest that many of the local population were Jews who did not desire to enter into a constant state of ritual impurity. He also provides a glimpse into the mid-century city in his account of the Caligula crisis. When the emperor announced that his image was to be placed in the Jerusalem temple, Petronius, the Roman legate to Syria, and Palestinian Jews met at Tiberias.[151] This suggests a sizable Jewish presence at the city or, at minimum, a hospitality to Jews.

Josephus provides several other details about Tiberias. By the time of the Revolt, at least, it was a walled city.[152] Ten *protoi*[153] and a *boule* of six hundred[154] governed the city. Public assemblies were held in the stadium[155] as well as in the *proseuche*, which was sizable enough to serve as the meeting place for the *boule*.[156] The Herodian palace was lavishly decorated, with a roof inlaid with gold and artistic representations of animals within.[157] Josephus refers to its market overseer as an *agoranomos*,[158] strengthening the case for Tiberias as the origin for the two lead weights described above.

Josephus describes the war-time political dynamics of Tiberias in fascinating detail, discussing at length the leaders and their agendas (or at least his estimations of their agendas). Three primary factions competed for the city's leadership. The pro-Roman, pro-Agrippa faction was headed by one Julius Capellus, with the assistance of Herod son of Miarus, Herod son of Gamalus, and Compsus son of Compsus. The second party, made up "of nobodies" and led by Jesus, son of Sapphias, desired war with the Romans. The third group was led by Justus son of Pistus. (Justus would later pen a history of the conflict condemning Josephus's leadership; *Life* is Josephus's response to the charges of Justus.) According to Josephus's acrimonious account, Justus feigned pacifism, hoping that a war would bring political changes to the city and result in his own rise to power.[159] To complicate the political landscape further, various rebel

---

[151] *War* 2.193, *Ant.* 18.269–283.   [152] *War* 3.461.
[153] *Life* 69, 296; cf. *War* 2.639.   [154] *War* 2.639, 641; *Life* 64, 169, 279, 284.
[155] *Life* 331, *War* 2.618.   [156] *Life* 277–280.   [157] *Life* 65, 68.
[158] *Ant.* 18.149.
[159] *Life* 32–37 (cf. *Life* 66 on the followers of Jesus, son of Sapphias); note the mixture of Latin and Semitic names.

leaders, including Josephus, also vied for the loyalty of the city's popu-
lace. Though Josephus claims to have fortified the city himself,[160] such
action (if actually undertaken) did little to endear him to the Tiberians.
Their city vacillated between support of him; of other leaders such as John
of Gischala, Jonathan, and Justus; and of Agrippa II and the Romans.[161]

The situation at Tiberias appears to have deteriorated into chaos as
these different groups attempted to outmaneuver each other. Jesus led
his followers in razing Herod's palace, with its images of animals, ac-
complishing the task for which Josephus claims to have been sent to
Galilee. He next turned on the city's Greeks, slaughtering them, an action
suggesting that gentiles comprised only a minority of the population.[162]

In the midst of this turmoil occurred some of Josephus's more remarkable claimed exploits. He escaped an assassination attempt by John –
an attempt in which, he colorfully writes, the "iron [blade] was at his
throat" – by fleeing in a boat to Taricheae.[163] When Tiberias declared for
Agrippa and the Romans, Josephus sailed upon it, he reports, with a fleet
of two hundred and thirty boats, manned only by seven soldiers in addition to the boats' crews. Falling for the deception, the city surrendered to
his forces. Josephus promptly sailed the *boule* of six hundred as well as
two thousand other citizens back to Taricheae.[164] Ultimately, Tiberias fell
to Vespasian, who had marched on it with the intention to "crush Jews
wherever they arose."[165] Out of respect for Agrippa II, Vespasian spared
most of it from destruction.[166]

Perhaps a few of Josephus's vivid accounts of his cleverness and valor –
and they are rich in detail – are even true, but his descriptions of the setting
and workings of Tiberias, rather than these possibly fanciful claims, aid
us more in our present inquiry. Josephus's narration implies that many of
the citizens observed the Sabbath, and much of the community's political discourse and wrangling occurred in the city's *proseuche*, suggesting
again that Jews formed the majority of the city's population. When Josephus and his forces arrived at Tiberias, John of Gischala welcomed them
but requested that they billet elsewhere lest they disturb the city's Sabbath, which fell on the following day. On the Sabbath, the townspeople
assembled at the *proseuche* to chart their course of action. Opinions varied so much that only the mid-day reprieve for dinner ("our custom on
the Sabbath," Josephus notes) saved the group from riot. On both of the
next two days, the crowd reassembled at the *proseuche* for further discussion. At the final meeting, Josephus reports that he and his guards

[160] *War* 2.573; *Life* 188.   [161] *War* 2.599–646; *Life* 84–96.   [162] *Life* 65–67.
[163] *Life* 94–96; *War* 2.614–619 (quote from 619).   [164] *War* 2.635–646.
[165] *War* 3.445.   [166] *War* 3.461.

were engaged in "the ordinary service and . . . prayer" when Jesus pub-
licly confronted him about his leadership. The result of this confrontation,
Josephus says, led to another treacherous attempt on his life from which
he barely escaped.[167]

Josephus's retrospective judgment on Tiberias is not a flattering one,
shaped as it is by his need to respond to Justus's charge that Josephus
himself was to blame for the city's participation in the Revolt.[168] Josephus
counters this charge by arguing that it was Justus who led the Tiberians in
hostilities against the cities and villages of the Decapolis, and Justus who
garrisoned the city until the arrival of Vespasian.[169] Josephus blames the
Tiberians' actions on their "warlike mind-set" and notes as further evidence of their support for the Revolt the presence of Tiberians at the siege
of Jerusalem.[170] As with other reported events at Tiberias, these incidents
reflect the influence of Jews, rather than pagans, in war-time Tiberias.

The population of Tiberias in the Early Roman period. Archaeological remains are of only limited usefulness in determining the
composition of first-century Tiberias's population. A fragment of a stone
jar suggests the presence of Jews, and a bone figurine possibly indicates
the presence of gentiles, but one can draw no generalizations about the
city as a whole on the basis of such limited findings. Though pagan motifs
occur on second-century CE coins, none is found on coins known to have
been produced at Tiberias in the first century. The lead weights naming the
city's *agoranomoi* (if, in fact, the weights emanate from Tiberias), provide evidence of the city's mixed cultural atmosphere (as do the names
mentioned in Josephus's summaries of the city's factions), but whether
one can identify the officials as Jews or pagans on the basis of only names
is debatable.

The image of Tiberias's population in Josephus's histories is dramatically clearer. Antipas's difficulties in settling the original city suggest that
the inhabitants of surrounding areas were Jewish. During the Caligula
crisis, Jews gathered at the city to protest the emperor's demands. Once
the Revolt started, the city's small minority of Greeks was slaughtered.
Town meetings happened in the community's *proseuche*, and many of
the citizens were Sabbath-observant. Some participated in raids on neighboring gentile cities, and other Tiberians participated in the defense of
Jerusalem. In short, the evidence from Josephus shows that the majority
of the first-century city's citizens was Jewish.

[167] *Life* 276–303.   [168] *Life* 336–367, esp. 349–354.   [169] *Life* 341, 351–352.
[170] *Life* 353–354.

Ḥammath

Ḥammath, famous for its hot springs, lies approximately three kilometers south of Tiberias.[171] Pottery, coins, and architecture indicate habitation in the Hellenistic period, though the exact date of foundation is unclear.[172] Though its settlement pre-dates that of Tiberias itself, the two communities eventually merged into one.[173]

Ḥammath's best-known archaeological find is its synagogue – a fifth-century CE basilical synagogue, decorated with a zodiac mosaic and Greek, Aramaic, and Hebrew inscriptions, built atop a third- or fourth-century CE broadhouse-style synagogue.[174] The synagogue's rich decorations have attracted so much attention that another discovery from an earlier stratum is largely unknown: a large public building from the first or early second century CE which Dothan suggests could be a gymnasium or a *palaestra* – as he describes it, "the only probable *palaestra* ever excavated in Israel."[175]

Dothan bases this identification on the structure's architectural design. Rooms and halls existed on at least three sides of the building, surrounding a courtyard, and the building had at least two entrances. Dothan argues that because the building was smaller than most gymnasia, it was most likely a *palaestra*. Dothan also notes the proximity of "what seems to be part of 'Herodian' *thermae* – or at least of hot water reservoirs and conduits"; such *thermae* were often associated with gymnasia and *palaestrae*.[176] To

[171] According to *t. Meg.* 4.3, the springs were approximately one Roman mile from Tiberias. Josephus (referring to Ḥammath as "Ammathus") mentions them (*Ant.* 18.36, *Life* 85, and *War* 2.614) as does Pliny (*Natural History* 5.71). Presumably the name is derived from these springs (the Hebrew for hot springs is חמה; cf. *War* 4.11, where Josephus himself provides the etymology).

[172] Moshe Dothan suggests that Seleucid coins may indicate a date as early as 170 BCE, though a date between Antiochus IV and Alexander Jannaeus seems more probable in light of the numismatic evidence he cites, with the small number of Seleucid coins suggesting a later date within that range (*Hammath Tiberias: Early Synagogues and the Hellenistic and Roman Remains* [Jerusalem: Israel Exploration Society; Haifa: University of Haifa Department of Antiquities and Museums, 1983], 10–14). On other difficulties of Dothan's interpretations, see review by Eric M. Meyers of *Hammath Tiberias: Early Synagogues and the Hellenistic and Roman Remains* in *JAOS* 104 (1984): 577–578.

[173] For overviews of Ḥammath Tiberias, see Gary A. Herion, "Hammath," *ABD*, vol. III, 37–38; Douglas L. Gordon, "Hammath Tiberias," *OEANE*, vol. II, 470–471; Moshe Dothan, "Hammath-Tiberias," *NEAEHL*, vol. II, 573–577; Moshe Dothan, "Tiberias, Hammath," *EAEHL*, vol. IV, 1178–1184.

[174] Dothan, *Hammath Tiberias*, 20–70.

[175] Ibid., 1; cf. 15–19. Because the building is only partially excavated, its exact measurements are unknown, though Dothan suggests that it was 60 m by 40 m (Dothan, "Hammath-Tiberias," *NEAEHL*, vol. II, 574). The structure was destroyed in the middle of the second century CE, perhaps in the earthquake of 130 CE.

[176] Dothan, *Hammath Tiberias*, 16.

provide further support for his thesis, he appeals to the cultural diversity of Tiberias, which he claims had a "prominent Greek and alien population until the Jewish War," as well to the "Hellenistic influence among the Jews" there.[177]

Dothan's identification of this structure is problematic and controversial. His proposed outline of the building – rectangular with multiple rooms and a courtyard – does bear general resemblance to other gymnasia and *palaestrae*,[178] but a comparison of his outline with the actual walls and remains uncovered by the excavation suggests that the details of his outline may be optimistic. The absence of columns and capitals – a defining characteristic of gymnasia and *palaestrae* – in this stratum of the structure also seriously undermines Dothan's thesis, though he suggests that two limestone drums and two column bases found in a later stratum may originally have come from the earlier phase. As possible parallels for the structure, Dothan refers to a gymnasium at Petra and a possible gymnasium at Jericho,[179] but little has been found of the structure at Petra and most archaeologists now regard the proposed gymnasium at Jericho as a palace.[180] Dothan ultimately acknowledges that "we have too little evidence about this public building to be able to draw definite conclusions concerning its use."[181] In publications post-dating the excavation report, he grants the possibility that it was a synagogue, given the construction of the later synagogues atop it.[182]

Even if we were to accept Dothan's interpretation of the building as a *palaestra*, we would be left again with the difficulty of distinguishing

---

[177] Ibid., 19; cf. Lee I. Levine's criticism in his review of *Hammath Tiberias: Early Synagogues and the Hellenistic and Roman Remains* in *IEJ* 34 (1984): 284–288.

[178] See Jean Delorme, *Gymnasion: Etude sur les Monuments consacré a l'éducation en Grèce* (Paris: Editions E. de Boccard, 1960), plates V–XXVIII. On gymnasia and *palaestrae*, see Stephen J. Glass, "The Greek Gymnasium: Some Problems," in Wendy J. Raschke, ed., *The Archaeology of the Olympics* (Madison: University of Wisconsin Press, 1988), 155–173.

[179] Dothan, *Hammath Tiberias*, 17–18.

[180] Avraham Negev, "Petra," *NEAEHL*, vol. IV, 1185; Gideon Foerster, "Jericho: Exploration since 1973," *NEAEHL*, vol. II, 687.

[181] Dothan, *Hammath Tiberias*, 16.

[182] Dothan, "Hammath-Tiberias," *NEAEHL*, vol. II, 575 and "Tiberias, Hammath," *EAEHL*, vol. IV, 1180; cf. Dothan, *Hammath Tiberias*, 77, n. 97; and "The Synagogue at Hammath-Tiberias," in Lee I. Levine, ed., *Ancient Synagogues Revealed* (Jerusalem: Israel Exploration Society; Detroit: Wayne State University Press, 1982), 64. Among the more intriguing finds in this building was a glass goblet with floral decoration and a tin-lead coating (Dothan, *Hammath Tiberias*, 18). Though in some publications Dothan described this vessel as centaur-shaped (Dothan, "Tiberias, Hammath," *EAEHL*, vol. IV, 1180; "The Synagogue at Hammath-Tiberias," 64), in the excavation report he refrains from this comparison, describing it instead as a "glass kanthoras of a slim inverted bell shape" (18) with a possible ritualistic function (77, n. 97).

between Greco-Roman influence and gentile inhabitants. Who would have used such a building? Can we assume that only non-Jews would have gone there, or could its visitors have been Hellenized Jews? In any case, without a more detailed description of the parallels between this structure and other *palaestrae*, Dothan's identification is unconvincing. In short, we do not know what this structure was, beyond a large public building.

Beth Yeraḥ

Located to the southwest of the Sea of Galilee, Beth Yeraḥ has yielded substantial amounts of ancient remains. Most of the more significant discoveries have either pre-dated or post-dated the first century CE, though the site was definitely occupied at that time. Hellenistic finds include a stamped jar handle with a Greek inscription, fortification walls and towers, and houses. Because some of the Hellenistic remains, including a house, date back as far as Ptolemaic rule, Beth Yeraḥ is a proposed site for the Ptolemaic foundation Philoteria, about which little is known.[183] Roman-era finds include a fourth- or fifth-century CE bathhouse, complete with a frigidarium, hypocaust cellar, caldarium, and tepidarium; a second- or third-century CE Roman fortress, and a synagogue. Greek inscriptions have been found, but their dates are uncertain. A marble head of Tyche provides the most explicit evidence for a pagan presence, but, its exact date, too, is unknown.[184]

Magdala/Taricheae

Further north along the coast from Tiberias and Ḥammath is the proposed site for Magdala, generally identified with the Taricheae of Josephus's writings. Both names are associated with the fish industry. "Magdala" is thought to be the same community as Migdal Nunnaya ("Tower of Fish,"

---

[183] Cf. Polybius 5.70.3–4.

[184] Alexander H. Joffe, "Beth Yeraḥ," *OEANE*, vol. I, 312–314; Ruth Hestrin, "Beth Yeraḥ," *NEAEHL*, vol. I, 255–259. On the marble head of Tyche and the Greek inscriptions, see L. Sukenik, "The Ancient City of Philoteria (Beth Yeraḥ)," *JPOS* 2 (1922): 101–107. Donald T. Ariel describes an Early Hellenistic Rhodian jar handle in "Two Rhodian Amphoras," *IEJ* 38 (1988): 31–35. On the Roman bathhouse and fort, see B. Maisler, M. Stekelis, and M. Avi-Yonah, "The Excavations at Beth Yerah (Khirbet el-Kerak) 1944–1946)," *IEJ* 2 (1952): 165–173, 218–229, esp. 218–223. Additional references to Hellenistic and Roman-era materials are found in P. Bar-Adon, "Beth Yerah," *IEJ* 5 (1955): 273; O. Yogev and E. Eisenberg, "Beth Yeraḥ," *ESI* 4 (1985): 14–16; see also Richard Delougaz and Richard C. Haines, *A Byzantine Church at Khirbat al-Karak* (Chicago: University of Chicago Press, 1960).

mentioned in the later text *b. Pesah.* 46b), while "Taricheae" obviously derives from ταριχεία, "factory for salting fish" (cf. the reference to a salted-fish industry at Taricheae in Strabo, *Geography*, 16.2.45).[185]

Taricheae is one of the many Galilean communities which Josephus claims to have fortified.[186] He provides passing details about the physical features of the town – it had gates[187] as well as a hippodrome[188] – but, as with Tiberias, his reports of his own activities there prove to be the richer source of information. In one account of the plundering of Agrippa's convoy, Josephus says he entrusted the seized goods to one Annaeus, whom he describes as Taricheae's leading citizen.[189] In his other version of this incident, however, Josephus claims to have given the goods to two individuals, Dassion and Jannaeus, the son of Levi, whom he describes as friends of Agrippa.[190] Annaeus and Jannaeus are presumably the same person, whose name is clearly Semitic.

Josephus was quite active in Taricheae, attempting to find refuge there and using it as a base for his operations in the region, including his (reported) capture of Tiberias. He reports being conscientious in dismissing his soldiers on the Sabbath, lest the Taricheans be frustrated by a military presence on that day.[191] He was unable to avoid offending the Taricheans' sensibilities when he settled in their midst nobles from the kingdom of Agrippa II. When these refugees failed to observe local customs to the satisfaction of the Taricheans, Josephus was forced to evacuate them across the sea to the territory of Hippos. If these refugees are the same as the two who fled to Sepphoris, they were not circumcised; if this was one of the reasons for offense at Taricheae, then it demonstrates the city's adherence to Jewish tradition.[192]

Josephus's various descriptions of the Taricheans' zeal for the Revolt and loyalty to him are quite different. In his account in *War* of the speech he delivered in the city's hippodrome, he portrays the Taricheaens as his enthusiastic supporters.[193] The account of the speech in *Life* is even more vivid, for there he is challenged by Jesus, son of Sapphias, who rises,

---

[185] The exact location of the city is uncertain because Josephus places Taricheae some thirty stadia from Tiberias (*Life* 157), but Pliny (*Nat. Hist.* 5.15) situates it further south. Josephus is the more reliable of the two sources, and so a site north of Tiberias is accepted as the probable location. See James F. Strange, "Magdala," *ABD*, vol. IV, 463–464 and the comments of William F. Albright, "Contributions to the Historical Geography of Palestine," *AASOR* 2–3 (1921–1922): 24–47.

[186] *War* 2.573, *Life* 188.   [187] *War* 2.634–635.   [188] *War* 2.599; *Life* 132, 138.

[189] *War* 2.596.   [190] *Life* 130.

[191] Josephus's two accounts of this event vary (*Life* 155–168, *War* 2.632–641), but both reflect the area's Sabbath observance.

[192] *Life* 149–154; cf. 112–113.   [193] *War* 2.599–608.

Torah scroll in hand, to confront his leadership.[194] In contrast, when he describes the city's fall to Vespasian and Titus, he specifies in both *War* and *Life* that outsiders, rather than local citizens, were the instigators of resistance to the Romans.[195]

Among the earlier archaeological remains of Taricheae is the foundation of a tower, now under water, which may be the structure reflected in the name "Magdala,"[196] and a private building which contained ceramics from the first two centuries CE and coins from the first century BCE to the second century CE. Damaged in the late first century CE, the building was rebuilt and used until the second century CE.[197]

A small (8.1 m × 7.2 m) rectangular building at Taricheae has been identified by its excavator as a "mini-synagogue." The excavator points to the building's interior columns (some of which are heart-shaped, as in later synagogues), Doric capitals, and possible benches against the north walls as evidence for this identification.[198] Two phases of the building have been excavated and published; one floor dates to the first century BCE and another to the first century CE. The identification of this structure as a synagogue has not won widespread acceptance. The "benches" have been plausibly interpreted as a flight of steps, and water canals around the south, east and west walls of the building suggest that it could be a springhouse.[199]

Arbela

Arbela is well known for nearby cave complexes which have been used for refuge throughout the centuries.[200] The caves themselves seem to have

[194] *Life* 132–136.   [195] *War* 3.492; cf. 3.532; *Life* 97, 142–143.

[196] Ehud Galili, Uzi Dahari and Jacob Sharvit, "Underwater Survey along the Coast of Israel," *ESI* 10 (1991): 160–165.

[197] Hana Abu Uqsa, "Migdal," *ESI* 13 (1993): 28; Mordechai Aviam, "Magdala," *OEANE*, vol. III, 399–400.

[198] Virgilio C. Corbo, "Scavi archeologici a Magdala, 1971–1973," *LA* 24 (1974): 19–37; Virgilio C. Corbo, "La Città Romana di Magdala: Rapporto preliminaire dopo la quarta campagna di scavo, 1975," in *Studi Archeologici*, vol. I of *Studia Hierosolymitana in onore del P. Bellarmino Bagatti*, ed. Emmanuele Testa (Jerusalem: Franciscan Printing Press, 1976), 355–378; Virgilio C. Corbo, "La mini-synagogue de Magdala," *Le Monde De La Bible* 57 (1989): 15. Strange accepts this identification and reports that the excavators "believe that the building was converted to a fish pond after A.D. 70," suggesting that the Jewish population departed after the Revolt ("Magdala," *ABD*, vol. IV, 463–464).

[199] Aviam, "Magdala," *OEANE*, vol. III, 399–400; cf. the suggestion the structure was a bathhouse in Eric M. Meyers and A. Thomas Kraabel, "Archaeology, Iconography, and Non-literary Written Remains," in Robert A. Kraft and W. E. Nickelsburg, eds., *Early Judaism and its Modern Interpreters* (Atlanta: Scholars Press, 1986), 179.

[200] *Ant.* 14.415–430; *War* 1.305–313, 2.573; *Life* 188, 311; see discussion of *Ant.* 12.421 and 1 *Macc.* 9:2 in chapter 2 above. See also Zvi Ilan and Avraham Isdarechet, "Arbel," *NEAEHL*, vol. I, 87–89; Paul L. Redditt, "Arbela," *ABD*, vol. I, 354.

been rendered habitable in the Hellenistic period,[201] and occupation in the nearby village may go back to this time.[202] The limestone synagogue visible today reflects the fourth-century CE village, and the other ruins (mostly of basalt) also post-date the first century.[203]

Capernaum

Though Josephus makes only passing references to Capernaum,[204] the town is prominent in the synoptic Gospels' accounts of Jesus's ministry. In Matthew, it is Jesus's base of operation.[205] For Mark, it is the hometown of Simon, Andrew, James, and John.[206] Matthew and Luke follow Mark in their report of Jesus's call of a tax collector there.[207] The local synagogue is the setting for Jesus's preaching[208] as well as an exorcism.[209] Jesus performs other miracles in the village, as well, including the healing of Simon's mother-in law at Simon's house[210] and the healing of the paralytic man.[211] Though John does not situate as much of Jesus's ministry in Capernaum as the synoptics do, he does preserve the memory of some activity there – the long-distance healing from Cana of a Capernaum official's son and Jesus's teaching in the synagogue.[212] Each Gospel author, of course, places his own narrative "spin" on the Capernaum stories, but the overall impression the Gospels make is unmistakable: Capernaum had a sizable Jewish population.

Only in the pericope of the centurion's servant do we find any literary evidence at all for gentiles.[213] For both Matthew and Luke, the story serves to illustrate the importance of faith and to foreshadow the church's openness to gentiles. In both, Jesus marvels at the centurion's certitude that his servant will be healed, even at a distance, and exclaims, "Not even in Israel have I found such faith." Luke emphasizes the gentile identity of the centurion even more by having him contact Jesus through the Jewish

---

[201] Zvi Ilan, "Arbel, Survey of Caves," *ESI* 9 (1989–1990): 17–18. Ilan mentions water installations and 3 mikvaot in the caves, but provides no date for them.

[202] Zvi Ilan ("Ḥorvat Arbel," *ESI* 6–7 [1988–1989]: 8–9) places the foundation date in the second century BCE, but without explanation.

[203] Zvi Ilan, "Horvat Arbel," *IEJ* 39 (1989): 100–102; Ilan, "Ḥorvat Arbel," *ESI* 6–7 [1988–1989]: 8–9; cf. Ilan and Izdarechet, "Arbel," *NEAEHL*, vol. I, 87–89.

[204] *War* 3.519; *Life* 403 (though the manuscript tradition varies in the spelling of the town's name).

[205] Matt. 4:13, 9:1.   [206] Mark 1:29.

[207] Mark 2:13–17, Matt. 9:9–13, Luke 5:27–32. John 1:44 and 12:21, however, report that Bethsaida was the home of Andrew and Peter.

[208] Mark 1:21.   [209] Mark 1:23–28, Luke 4:33–37.

[210] Matt. 8:16, Mark 1:32–34, Luke 4:40–41.

[211] Matt. 9:1–8, Mark 2:1–12, Luke 5:17–26.   [212] John 4:46–54, 6:59.

[213] The story is found in two versions, one in Matt. 8:5–13, the other in Luke 7:1–10.

elders. These elders attest to this man's "love for our nation" and inform Jesus that the centurion built the local synagogue.[214]

Some scholars have been quick to locate Roman troops in Capernaum on the basis of this story.[215] As discussed in chapter 2, however, we have few, if any, references in literary sources, whether Josephus, Roman histories, rabbinic materials or other, for Roman troops stationed in pre-war first-century Galilee; it is possible that some occasionally passed through en route to another destination. In any case, neither Matthew nor Luke specifies that the officer is Roman, only that he is gentile. Even if we accept the story as historical, for all we know the centurion could be a non-Jewish officer in Antipas' army.[216] This one story, taken from Q and ably used by both Gospels for their own theological agendas, is slender evidence indeed for postulating a Roman military presence.[217]

By the first century CE, Capernaum was a small town or village.[218] Though the excavators have argued that its streets formed a grid pattern, with residences grouped in *insulae*,[219] Reed has rightly criticized such claims, pointing out that the city's arrangement does not reflect such central planning.[220] Archaeologists have recovered substantial Hellenistic and Roman-era remains,[221] including a multi-room mausoleum, in which

---

[214] Luke 7:3–4.

[215] Strange, "First-Century Galilee," 89–90; Clark, "Galilee," 347; Joel B. Green, *The Gospel of Luke* (Grand Rapids, Mich.: William B. Eerdmans, 1997), 284–285; Thomas G. Long, *Matthew* (Louisville: Westminster John Knox Press, 1997), 89; Eduard Schweizer, *The Good News According to Matthew* (Atlanta: John Knox Press, 1975), 211; W. D. Davies and Dale C. Allison, *A Critical and Exegetical Commentary on the Gospel According to Saint Matthew* (Edinburgh: T&T Clark, 1991), vol. II, 18–19; Guido Tisera, *Universalism According to the Gospel of Saint Matthew* (Frankfurt am Main: Peter Lang, 1993), 105.

[216] Shatzman has shown that Herod the Great's army was organized along Roman lines (*Armies*, 205–210); if Antipas's army was organized similarly, then the argument that the term "centurion" implies a Roman presence is weakened further. Cf. Robert H. Gundry, *Matthew: A Commentary on His Handbook for a Mixed Church under Persecution*, 2nd edn. (Grand Rapids, Mich.: William B. Eerdmans, 1994), 141; Meier, *Matthew*, 83; Beare, *Gospel*, 207.

[217] Cf. the similar story in John 4:46–54, where there is no hint that the "official" is a gentile or a soldier.

[218] Stanislao Loffreda ("Capernaum," *NEAEHL*, vol. I, 292) suggests that the village took up some 10–12 acres. Reed, however, proposes a maximum size of 17 hectares (approximately 42 acres), with a population of 600–1500 (*Archaeology*, 151–152; cf. the earlier "The Population of Capernaum," *Occasional Papers of the Institute for Antiquity and Christianity* 24 [1992]: 1–19; Reed, "Population Numbers," 209–212).

[219] Virgilio C. Corbo, "Capernaum," *ABD*, vol. I, 866.

[220] Reed, *Archaeology*, 152–153.

[221] Stanislao Loffreda, "Capernaum," *NEAEHL*, vol. I, 291–295 and "Capernaum," *OEANE*, vol. I, 416–419; Corbo, "Capernaum," *ABD*, vol. I, 866–869. The primary excavation reports for Capernaum are Virgilio C. Corbo, *Gli Edifici della Città*, vol. I of *Cafarnao* (Jerusalem: Franciscan Printing Press, 1975); Stanislao Loffreda, *La Ceramica*,

several sarcophagi were found.[222] A recently discovered Roman bath-house dates to the second or third century CE.[223] Stone vessels found in the excavation of the areas around the synagogue[224] and the so-called "St Peter's house" (see below) attest to a concern for Jewish ritual purity on the part of at least some of the inhabitants.[225]

The white limestone synagogue that now dominates the grey basalt ruins of ancient Capernaum was once thought to be the synagogue in which Jesus preached,[226] but subsequent excavations have proven that it is from a later period. The date of its construction has been a hotly debated topic. Though some archaeologists have insisted, based on typological similarities with other Galilean synagogues, that it was built in the second or third century CE, most now acknowledge that numismatic and ceramic evidence date it to the fourth or fifth century.[227]

Underneath the synagogue, however, are the remnants of earlier structures, including basalt walls, staircases, channels for water, and stone pavements.[228] Some of these features are from residences, but

---

vol. II of *Cafarnao* (Jerusalem: Franciscan Printing Press, 1974); Augustus Spijkerman, *Catalogo della Monete Città*, vol. III of *Cafarnao* (Jerusalem: Franciscan Printing Press, 1975); Emmanuele Testa, *Graffiti della Casa di S. Pietro*, vol. IV of *Cafarnao* (Jerusalem: Franciscan Printing Press, 1972); and Vassilios Tzaferis et al., *Excavations at Capernaum, vol. I: 1978–1982* (Winona Lake, Ind.: Eisenbrauns, 1989); Vassilios Tzaferis, "New Archaeological Evidence on Ancient Capernaum," *BA* 46 (1983): 198–204.

[222] Virgilio C. Corbo, "Il Mausoleo di Cafarnao," *LA* 27 (1977): 145–155.

[223] John C. H. Laughlin, "Capernaum: From Jesus' Time and After," *BAR* 19:5 (1993): 54–61.

[224] Gaudence Orfali, *Capharnaüm et ses Ruines* (Paris, 1922), 64 and fig. 115.

[225] See Deines, *Jüdische*, 147–152.   [226] Orfali, *Capharnaüm*, 83–84.

[227] The literature on the dating is substantial. Virgilio C. Corbo, Stanislao Loffreda, and Augustus Spijkerman, *La Sinagoga di Cafarnao dopo gli Scavi del 1969* (Jerusalem: Tipografia dei PP. Francescani, 1970) provide an early and important report, arguing for the later date. See also Stanislao Loffreda, "The Late Chronology of the Synagogue of Capernaum," in Levine, ed., *Ancient Synagogues Revealed*, 52–56; Stanislao Loffreda, *Recovering Capharnaum*, 2nd ed. (Jerusalem: Franciscan Printing Press, 1993, 32–40) and "Capernaum," *NEAEHL*, vol. I, 292; and Virgilio C. Corbo, "Capernaum," *ABD*, vol. I, 867. Those who defended a second- to third-century CE date include Gideon Foerster, "Notes on Recent Excavations at Capernaum," in *Ancient Synagogues Revealed*, ed. Levine, 57–59 and "Notes on Recent Excavations at Capernaum," *IEJ* 21 (1971): 207–211; Michael Avi-Yonah, "Some Comments on the Capernaum Excavations," in Levine, ed., *Ancient Synagogues Revealed*, 60–62. James F. Strange and Hershel Shanks provide a helpful overview of the debate in "Synagogue Where Jesus Preached Found at Capernaum," *BAR* 9:6 (1983): 25–28.

[228] Virgilio C. Corbo, *Gli Edifici della Città*, 117–169; Virgilio C. Corbo, "Edifici antichi soto la sinagoga di Cafarnao," in Emmanuele Testa, ed., *Studia Hierosolymitana in onore del P. Bellarmino Bagatti*, vol. I, *Studi Archeologici* (Jerusalem: Franciscan Printing Press, 1976), 159–176; Virgilio C. Corbo, "Resti della Sinagoga del Primo Secolo a Cafarnao," in Emmanuele Testa, ed., *Studia Hierosolymitana III in onore del P. Bellarmino Bagatti*, vol. III, *Studi Archeologici* (Jerusalem, 1982), 313–357; Stanislao Loffreda, "Ceramica ellenistica-romana nel sottosuolo della sinagoga di Cafarnao," in *Studia Hierosolymitana III*,

others – thick basalt walls and a basalt cobblestone pavement found underneath the nave of the synagogue – seem to have come from a larger building. Ceramic evidence clearly dates the construction of the pavement to the first century CE at the latest. The basalt walls are likewise early, possibly constructed at the same time as the pavement. The excavators argue that these architectural fragments are the remains of an earlier synagogue dating to the first century CE. They have dubbed this earlier synagogue the "Centurion's Synagogue," believing it to be the site of Jesus's sermon in Capernaum.[229] Given the custom of establishing holy sites on top of earlier holy sites, this identification of some of the underlying remains as a synagogue is not unlikely.[230] If so, then it is among the very few first-century synagogues that are distinct in the archaeological record.

Located approximately thirty meters south of the limestone synagogue is the so-called "St Peter's house." Excavators claim to have discovered in the remains of a typical Late Hellenistic or Early Roman building the actual house of Peter, which they argue served as the meeting place for a Jewish-Christian house church as early as the first century CE. They present several arguments for their identification. The house underwent unusual renovations in the second half of the first century CE, when its ceiling, walls and floor were extensively plastered. Walls erected in fourth century renovations bear dozens of Christian graffiti in Aramaic, Greek, Latin, and Syriac. These graffiti indicate that the house became a Christian pilgrimage site, and the excavators claim in two of these graffiti to have found the name "Peter." The fourth-century CE pilgrim Egeria

273–312; Loffreda, *Recovering Capharnaum,* 41–49; Loffreda, "Capernaum," *NEAEHL,* vol. I, 291–295. Strange and Shanks provide a helpful summary in "Synagogue Where Jesus Preached," 28–31.

[229] The excavators disagree on the sequence of construction of the basalt wall and the pavement. Corbo suggests that the floor and wall were built at the same time; Loffreda suggests that the basalt wall belongs to an intermediate stage between the first-century CE and the Late Roman synagogues. Likewise, the exact relation of these earlier structures to the later limestone synagogue is complicated. When excavators first discovered walls underneath the limestone synagogue's nave, prior to their discovery of the pavement, they noted the possibility that the walls were built as foundations for the later synagogue. They also noted, however, that one wall under the southwest corner of the limestone synagogue was out of alignment; the wall above it had not been built directly upon it. When further excavations discovered the pavement, the foundation wall thesis became untenable.

[230] Kee rejects this identification, interpreting the earlier remains as houses, but he offers no detailed analysis of either the basalt walls or the pavement ("Defining the First-Century C.E. Synagogue," 495–496). (Cf. the suggestion of Strange and Shanks that some of the "earlier remains [underneath the limestone synagogue] may well be of a home converted into a synagogue . . ." ["Has the House where Jesus Stayed in Capernaum been Found?" *BAR* 8:6 (1982): 29–30].)

reported visiting the house of St Peter, and in the fifth century, an octagonal church was constructed atop this house, indicating the site's significance for Christians. The excavators argue that the cumulative weight of all of this evidence indicates that the house is, in fact, that of Peter.

While the significance of "St Peter's house" is clear for the Byzantine era, its earliest remains are less spectacular. At the time of its construction, it was a typical residence. Though excavators claim to have found evidence that the house was already used as the gathering place for Jewish Christians in the late first century CE,[231] this thesis is simply undemonstrable.[232] The fragments of stone vessels found in the vicinity of the house tell us more about the first-century population than later Christians' veneration of the site does.

Chorazin

Chorazin, one of the objects of Jesus's condemnation in Matthew 11:21–24/Luke 10:13–16, lies four kilometers north of the sea of Galilee.[233] Its most famous ruin is a basalt synagogue from the third through the sixth centuries CE which is decorated with Hellenistic imagery, including a medusa or Helios figure. Other finds include a basalt seat bearing an Aramaic inscription, cisterns, streets, and the remains of buildings, as well as a fourth-century mikveh and otsar.[234] Thus far, all finds post-date the time of Jesus; the earliest pottery dates to the late first century or early second century CE.[235]

---

[231] Virgilio C. Corbo, "La Casa di S. Pietro a Cafarnao," *LA* 18 (1968): 5–54; Virgilio C. Corbo, *The House of St. Peter at Capharnaum*, trans. Sylbester Saller (Jerusalem: Franciscan Printing Press, 1969); Loffreda, *Recovering Capharnaum*, 50–66. The graffiti are found in Emmanuele Testa, *Graffiti della Casa di S. Pietro*, vol. IV of *Cafarnao*; for those the excavators interpret as references to Peter, see #152 on pp. 173–178 and #128 on pp. 164, 169. Strange and Shanks provide an accessible summary in "Has the House where Jesus Stayed," 26–37.

[232] See Strange and Shanks, "Has the House where Jesus Stayed," 35–36; James F. Strange, "The Capernaum and Herodium Publications, Part 2," *BASOR* 233 (1979): 63–69; and Joan E. Taylor, "Capernaum and its 'Jewish-Christians:' A Re-examination of the Franciscan Excavations," *BAIAS* 9 (1989–1990): 7–28. See also the critique of the Jewish-Christian community thesis in Taylor ("Capernaum") and in James F. Strange, "The Capernaum and Herodium Publications," *BASOR* 226 (1977): 69.

[233] Steven Fine, "Chorazin," *ABD*, vol. I, 490–491; Zeev Yeivin, "Chorazain," *EAEHL*, vol. I, 299–301; Nahman Avigad, "Chorazin: The Synagogue," *EAEHL*, vol. I, 301–303; Robert W. Smith, "Chorazin," *ABD*, vol. I, 911–912; Zeev Yeivin, "Chorazin," *NAEAHL*, vol. I, 301–304.

[234] Zeev Yeivin, "Ancient Chorazin Comes Back to Life," *BAR* 13:5 (1987): 22–39 and Zeev Yeivin, "Korazim-1983/1984," *ESI* 3 (1984): 66–71.

[235] In addition to the references above, see [no author] "Korazin," *ESI* 1 (1982): 64–67.

Bethsaida

Bethsaida, also rebuked by Jesus, lies slightly northeast of the Sea of Galilee, in the border area where Galilee and the Golan meet.[236] According to John, the disciples Philip, Andrew, and Peter hailed from Bethsaida, rather than from Capernaum.[237] Jesus is reported to have healed a blind man there, and Luke places the miracle of the multiplication of the loaves and fish there.[238]

Bethsaida came into Philip's hands upon the death of his father, Herod the Great. Philip expanded the city *c.* 30 CE, adding both residents and additional fortifications. He renamed it Julia, most likely in honor of either Augustus's wife and Tiberius's mother, Livia-Julia, or perhaps in honor of Augustus's daughter Julia.[239] Philip himself chose the city as the site of his grave and was buried there *c.* 33 CE.[240] At his death, Tiberius added his territories, including Bethsaida-Julia, to Syria. Apparently it remained a part of that province until the accession of Nero in 54 CE, at which time it was handed over to Agrippa II (as were Abila, Taricheae and Tiberias).[241] Skirmishes occurred in the general vicinity of Julia during the Revolt, including one which led to a broken wrist for Josephus. Josephus's description of the efforts of Sulla, one of Agrippa II's

[236] Josephus places it variously in lower Gaulanitis (*War* 2.168), Perea (*War* 2.252, *Ant.* 20.159), on the edge of Lake Gennesaritis (*Ant.* 18.28), and near the Jordan (*Life* 399), but John (1:43–44, 12:21) places it within Galilee, as does Ptolemy (*Geography* 5.16.4). Josephus and Ptolemy refer to Bethsaida by its new name, Julia (see discussion below); cf. Pliny the Elder, *Nat. Hist.* 5.71.

[237] John 1:44, 12:21.

[238] Mark 8:22–26; Luke 9:10–17 and parallels Mark 6:31–44, Matt. 14:13–21; John 6:1–14; see Fred Strickert, *Bethsaida: Home of the Apostles* (Collegeville, Minn.: Michael Glazier, Liturgical Press, 1998), 115–130.

[239] Josephus reports that Philip renamed the city after Augustus's daughter Julia (*Ant.* 18.28). Heinz-Wolfgang Kuhn and Rami Arav ("The Bethsaida Excavations: Historical and Archaeological Approaches," in Birger A. Pearson et al., eds., *The Future of Early Christianity* [Minneapolis: Fortress Press, 1991], 87–89), Strickert (*Bethsaida*, 91–107), John T. Greene ("The Honorific Naming of Bethsaida-Julias," in Rami Arav and Richard A. Freund, eds., *Bethsaida: A City by the North Shore of the Sea of Galille*, vol. II, Bethsaida Excavations Project [Kirksville, Mo.: Truman State University Press, 1999], 307–331) and Mark D. Smith ("A Tale of Two Julias: Julia, Julias, and Josephus," in ibid., vol. II, 333–346) note, however, that this Julia had been banished in 2 BCE and died in 14 CE, well before Philip's refounding of the city. Since Augustus's wife Julia died in 29 CE, Philip's renaming of the town a year later was likely in memory of her. The fact that Philip also honored Augustus's wife Julia on his coins supports this argument (cf. Meshorer, *Ancient Jewish Coinage*, vol. II, 245, nos. 6 and 6a and vol. II, 278; Fred Strickert in "The Coins of Philip," in Arav and Freund, eds., *Bethsaida*, vol. I, 165–189 and "The Founding of Bethsaida-Julias: Evidence from the Coins of Philip," *Shofar* 13/4 [1995]: 40–51).

[240] *Ant.* 18.108.   [241] *War* 2.252, *Ant.* 20.159; cf. *War* 3.57.

officers, to cut off the town's supply lines to Galilee suggests that it was sympathetic to the Revolt.[242]

Three different sites have been suggested for Bethsaida, all in the same general vicinity: et-Tell, el-Araj, and el-Mess'adiyye. Of these, only et-Tell, a large mound, has yielded significant Hellenistic and Roman-era finds, making it the most likely candidate.[243] Several houses have been discovered, along with city walls and a large public building. Not unexpectedly, excavators have recovered implements for both fishing and agriculture.[244] The village flourished until its destruction at the end of the first century or early in the second.[245]

The excavators suggest that some finds stand out as significant indicators of pagans at Bethsaida. They claim to have made a dramatic discovery: the remains of a first-century CE temple of the imperial cult, with walls, column fragments, and a bronze incense shovel, right on the border of Galilee in a village that Jesus visited. They argue that the building has the architectural lay-out of a Roman temple, with a *pronaos*, a *naos*, and an *opisthodomous* (a back room).[246] As additional possible evidence, they

[242] *Life* 398–406; John T. Green, "Bethsaida-Julias in Roman and Jewish Military Strategies, 66–73 C.E.," in Arav and Freund, eds., *Bethsaida*, vol. I, 203–227.

[243] On the issues regarding the identification of Bethsaida, see Rami Arav, "Bethsaida," *OEANE*, vol. I, 302–305; James F. Strange, "Beth-saida," *ABD*, vol. I, 692–693; Chester McCown, "The Problem of the Site of Bethsaida," *JPOS* 10 (1930): 32–58; James F. Strange, "Survey of Lower Galilee, 1982," *IEJ* 32 (1982): 255; John F. Shroder Jr. and Moshe Inbar, "Geologic and Geographic Background to the Bethsaida Excavations," in Arav and Freund, eds., *Bethsaida*, vol. I, 65–66; and Bargil Pixner, "Searching for the New Testament Site of Bethsaida," *BA* 48 (1985): 207–216.

[244] Rami Arav, "Bethsaida Excavations: Preliminary Report, 1994–1996," 3–114 in Arav and Freund, eds., *Bethsaida*, vol. II; Rami Arav, "Bethsaida Excavations: Preliminary Report, 1987–1993," 3–64 in Arav and Freund, eds., *Bethsaida*, vol. I and Arav, "Bethsaida," *OEANE*, vol. I, 302–305; Strickert, *Bethsaida*, 47–66; Sandra Fortner, "The Fishing Implements and Maritime Activities of Bethsaida-Julias (et-Tell)," in Arav and Freund, eds., *Bethsaida*, vol. II, 269–282; Rami Arav, "Bethsaida – 1990/1991," *ESI* 12 (1993): 8–9 and "Bethsaida – 1992," *ESI* 14 (1994): 25–26; Rami Arav, "Et-Tell and El-Araj," *IEJ* 38 (1988): 187–188; Rami Arav and J. Rousseau, "Bethsaïde, ville Perdue et Retrouvée," *RB* 100 (1993): 415–428; Rami Arav, "Bethsaida, 1996–1998," *IEJ* 49 (1999): 128–136; and Heinz-Wolfgang Kuhn, "Zum neuesten Stand der Grabungen auf et-Tell," *Welt und Umwelt der Bibel* 10:4 (1998): 78–80.

[245] The excavators disagree on the date and cause of destruction. Arav ("Bethsaida," *OEANE*, vol. I, 303) credits the Jewish Revolt for the city's demise (though he reports the presence of second-century CE ceramics in "Bethsaida, 1989," *IEJ* 41 [1991]: 184–185). Fred Strickert argues that Bethsaida was destroyed by an earthquake in the second century CE ("2 Esdras 1.11 and the Destruction of Bethsaida," *Journal for the Study of the Pseudepigrapha* 16 [1997]: 111–122; *Bethsaida*, 161–177; "The Destruction of Bethsaida: The Evidence of 2 Esdras 1:11," in Arav and Freund, eds., *Bethsaida*, vol. II, 347–372).

[246] Arav, "Bethsaida Excavations: Preliminary Report, 1994–1996," 18–24; Rami Arav, Richard A. Freund, and John F. Shroder, Jr., "Bethsaida Rediscovered," *BAR* 26:1 (2000):

point to the head of a clay figurine of a female with curled hair (which they suggest represents Livia-Julia) as well as to fragments of three additional figurines (though no date for them is provided).[247]

Full evaluation of these claims will have to await fuller publication, but thus far they are less than convincing. Despite the attempt to show that the building's rooms correspond to those of a typical Roman temple, the structure could be nothing more than a rectangular public building. Incense shovels are found in buildings other than temples, and no cultic objects, altar, or dedicatory inscriptions have yet been discovered. Neither the identification of the figurine as Livia-Julia nor its cultic use has yet been proven nor disproven, and all that can be said with confidence is that the figurine shows that some inhabitants of Bethsaida felt free to disregard the Jewish abhorrence of images. Given the fact that Josephus describes building projects of the Herods in some detail, his omission of a reference to a temple at Bethsaida is strong evidence that none existed. For the most part, then, the archaeological finds from et-Tell do not tell us whether first-century Bethsaida's inhabitants were Jewish or gentile.

Southwestern Galilee

Beth She'arim

Beth She'arim is one of the best-known sites in Galilee.[248] With its extensive tomb complexes, richly decorated sarcophagi, and inscriptions in Greek, Hebrew, Aramaic, and Palmyrene,[249] it provides substantial information about Jewish burial practices as well as the cultural and linguistic environment of Galilee. Extensive use of the tombs at Beth She'arim

44–56; Strickert, *Bethsaida*, 103–106; cf. Rami Arav and Richard Freund, "An Incense Shovel from Bethsaida," *BAR* 23:1 (1997): 32. Freund, however, interprets the incense shovel in its Jewish context in "The Incense Shovel of Bethsaida and Synagogue Iconography in Late Antiquity," in Arav and Freund, eds., *Bethsaida*, vol. II, 413–457.

[247] Rami Arav in several publications: "Bethsaida Excavations: Preliminary Report, 1994–1996," 32–33, including fig. 21; "Bethsaida, 1989," 184–185; "Et-Tell (Bethsaida) – 1989," *ESI* 9 (1989–1990): 98–99; "Bethsaida Excavations: Preliminary Report, 1987–1993," 21; also Strickert, *Bethsaida*, 105–106.

[248] Nahman Avigad and Benjamin Mazar, "Beth She'arim," *NEAEHL*, vol. I, 236–248; Nahman Avigad and Benjamin Mazar, "Beth She'arim," *EAEHL*, vol. I, 229–247; Lee I. Levine, "Beth She'arim," *OEANE*, vol. I, 309–311.

[249] Benjamin Mazar, *Catacombs 1–4*, vol. I of *Beth She'arim* (New Brunswick, N.J.: Rutgers University Press, 1973), 193–209; Moshe Schwabe and Baruch Lifshitz, *The Greek Inscriptions*, vol. II of *Beth She'arim* (New Brunswick, N.J.: Rutgers University Press, 1974).

began at the end of the second century CE, and the vast majority of remains from both the tombs and the village, including the synagogue, are from the third and fourth centuries CE.[250] In the village itself, a few Early Roman remains have been discovered: pottery; lamps; indications of a wall around the city; walls of buildings resting on bedrock; and coins of Herod, Agrippa I, Roman procurators, and second-century CE Tyre, as well as older coins of Alexander Jannaeus.[251] Aside from Josephus's passing remarks,[252] we have no other literary references to it until the rabbinic period.

Despite the frequency with which New Testament scholars cite Beth She'arim's inscriptions to demonstrate the use of Greek in Galilee,[253] only a few of the village's tombs date to the first century CE, and these do not contain inscriptions.[254] Nor are the Jewish symbols (such as the menorah) so prevalent in the tombs of the Middle and Late Roman periods found among the Early Roman tombs.[255] In short, the tombs at Beth She'arim tell us considerably more about Middle Roman and Late Roman Galilean Judaism than about the Early Roman inhabitants.[256]

Qiryat Tiv'on

Roman-era tombs were also discovered at Qiryat Tiv'on, near Beth She'arim. Cooking vessels, glass vessels, a bronze mirror, and oil lamps, all from the first and second centuries CE, were found within them. One rock-cut tomb contained coffins, and, more importantly, multiple ossuaries – seven made of limestone and one of clay. One of these ossuaries bears a Greek inscription naming the interred, "Maria Caoulos," providing rare epigraphic evidence from this period.[257]

---

[250] Mazar, *Catacombs 1–4*, vol. I of *Beth She'arim*, 18. [251] Ibid., 16–17, 212–213.

[252] *Life* 118–119 (assuming Besara is equivalent to Beth She'arim).

[253] Cf., for example, Kee, "Early Christianity," 20–22; and Stanley E. Porter, "Jesus and the Use of Greek in Galilee," in Bruce Chilton and Craig A. Evans, eds., *Studying the Historical Jesus: Evaluations of the State of Current Research* (Leiden: E. J. Brill, 1994), 147.

[254] Nahman Avigad, *Catacombs 12–23*, vol. III of *Beth She'arim* (New Brunswick, N.J.: Rutgers University Press, 1976), 260–261.

[255] Ibid., 268–274.

[256] See also Senzo Nagakubo, "Investigations into Jewish Concepts of Afterlife in the Beth She'arim Greek Inscriptions" (Ph.D. Diss., Duke University, 1974); Zeev Weiss, "Social Aspects of Burial in Beth She'arim: Archeological Finds and Talmudic Sources," in Levine, ed., *Galilee in Late Antiquity*, 357–372.

[257] Fanny Vitto, "Qiryat Tiv'on," *IEJ* 24 (1974): 279 and "Kiriat Tiv'on," *RB* 79 (1972): 574–576.

Sha'ar Ha'amaqim

Sha'ar Ha'amaqim, at the foot of Qiryat Tiv'on, seems to have been abandoned in the late second or the first century BCE, only to be reoccupied later in the first century BCE. Archaeological remains from several buildings have been discovered, as have ashlars from the lower courses of a tower and a surrounding wall. The tower was most likely built during the third to second centuries BCE, perhaps during the conflict between the Ptolemies and the Seleucids. A subterranean water system from the Hellenistic period contained Seleucid coins from the reign of Antiochus III (223–187 BCE) to Antiochus VIII (125–113 BCE) from Acco, Antiochia, Tyre, and Sidon. Pieces of a Corinthian capital and a "pseudo-Doric capital" as well as first-century BCE plowshares have also been discovered. By the late second century BCE or early first century CE, the tower seems to have gone out of use. In the Roman period, stones from the tower were re-used and the tower itself seems to have been converted into a raised platform.[258] Sherds as well as coins attest to some occupation of the site into the second century CE, though who its inhabitants were is not clear.[259]

Upper Galilee

Pagan inhabitants in Upper Galilee left their mark in the archaeological record primarily on the fringes of the region, where the boundaries blur between it and the neighboring territories. Tel Anafa and Kedesh were pagan communities. The unexcavated remains of a temple, apparently in use in the Early Roman period, have been surveyed further to the north at Jebel Balat, and a dedicatory inscription to Diana and Apollo, perhaps from the second century CE, was discovered northwest of Kedesh.[260] All of these communities were outside the bounds of first-century Galilee.[261]

---

[258] Segal and Naor, "Sha'ar Ha'amaqim," *NEAEHL*, vol. 4, 1339–1340 and "Sha'ar Ha'amaqim, 1991," 22–23. The excavators note that the construction of the tower – some courses consist entirely of headers, others of both headers and footers, and some courses have headers with drafted margins – is rare in Israel, with parallels at Samaria, Dor, and Acco.

[259] Shatzman (*Armies*, 86) and Richardson (*Herod*, 178) suggest that Sha'ar Ha'amaqim is a likely candidate for the site of Gaba, but most scholars place Gaba at Tel Shosh (see discussion in next chapter).

[260] Aviam, "Galilee," *NEAEHL*, vol. II, 453–454.

[261] Tel Anafa, unmentioned in literary sources, was probably part of Philip's territory, and Josephus (*War* 2.459) describes Kedesh as a Tyrian village (though 1 Macc. 11:63 clearly regards it as within Galilee).

Within the interior of Upper Galilee, there is very little evidence for pagan inhabitants, from the later Roman period or earlier times.

Upper Galilee, like Lower Galilee, had mostly Jewish inhabitants. Josephus refers frequently to its communities, and his comments reflect its Jewish character. The archaeological evidence for Late Hellenistic and Early Roman habitation is thus far limited. While a 1990 survey found evidence of ninety-three sites from the Late Hellenistic period, most of these are as yet unexcavated.[262] The sites that have been excavated and published have yielded, for the most part, only sherds and coins from the Hasmonean and Herodian periods.[263] The numerous synagogues in Upper Galilee from the Late Roman and Byzantine periods suggest that in those centuries, the region's population was primarily Jewish.

Kefar Ḥananyah

According to rabbinic tradition, Kefar Ḥananyah marked the boundary between Upper and Lower Galilee.[264] Located on a hill to the east of Ḥananyah Valley, the ancient village lay approximately twenty-three kilometers north of Sepphoris.[265] Kefar Ḥananyah dominated Galilee's pottery industry for over six centuries, and trade of its cookwares reached into the neighboring regions as well. *M. Sheb.* 9.2 mentions that the village was a pottery producer. Archaeometric analysis of pottery from a variety of sites both within Galilee and from the surrounding areas shows that Kefar Ḥananyah was the producer of the majority of the cookware for Galilee and of a sizable portion of that of the Golan and other surrounding regions from the mid-first century BCE through the early fifth century CE. Pottery wasters from the Early Roman and Middle Roman periods and a Late Roman kiln provide evidence of the processes of production, as does a pit with ash.[266]

---

[262] Aviam, "Galilee," *NEAEHL*, vol. II, 453.

[263] Eric M. Meyers, "Archaeology and Rabbinic Tradition at Khirbet Shema', 1970 and 1971 Campaigns," *BA* 35 (1972): 5.

[264] *M. Sheb.* 9.2.

[265] This corresponds roughly to the distance from Sepphoris implied in the discussion in *t. Bekh.* 7.3; see David Adan-Bayewitz, *Common Pottery in Roman Galilee: A Study of Local Trade* (Ramat-Gan: Bar-Ilan University Press, 1993), 30–31.

[266] Cf. *Lam. Zuta* 1.4, *y. Pe'ah* 7.4, 20a; *b. Ket.* 112a; *Gen. Rab.* 86.5; see David Adan-Bayewitz, "Kefar Hananyah," *OEANE*, vol. III, 276–277; David Adan-Bayewitz, "Kefar Hananya, 1987," *IEJ* 39 (1989): 98–99; David Adan-Bayewitz, "Kefar Hananya, 1989," *IEJ* 41 (1991): 186–188; Adan-Bayewitz, *Common Pottery*; David Adan-Bayewitz, "Kefar Hananyah," *OEANE*, vol. III, 276–278; Adan-Bayewitz and Perlman, "Local Trade," 153–172; Adan-Bayewitz and Perlman, "Local Pottery."

Other than the significance of the ceramics industry, however, very little is known of the Early Roman village. Two possible synagogues and a mikveh seem to have been used in a later period; their exact date is uncertain.[267] The exact archaeological context of a handle from a limestone cup is unknown, but, given what we know of the use of stone vessels, probably dates to the first century CE or earlier.[268] Numerous roof tiles with the mark of Legio VI Ferrata attest to either the presence of Roman troops or the manufacture of tiles in the post-Bar Kochbah period.[269]

Mizpeh Yamim

Mizpeh Yamim is notable for our purposes not because it was thriving settlement during the Late Hellenistic era, but because at precisely this time the buildings there went out of use. Located on a southern spur of the Meiron Massif, Mizpeh Yamim has the remains of a pagan temple, the only one yet discovered in the interior of Galilee from the Second Temple period. The temple consisted of two rooms (6×13.7 m and 4×4.8 m), the larger of which contained benches along all four walls and an altar in the northwest corner. Persian-era remains demonstrate that the building was erected in that period, and sheep/goat bones and skulls attest to sacrifices. A second phase of construction, in which earlier steps leading to the altar were filled in, occurred in the Hellenistic period, as shown by sherds and a Tyrian coin from the latter half of the second century BCE. Three bronze figurines, of a ram, a lion cub, and an Apis bull, were discovered, as well as a Persian-era *situla* with Egyptian inscriptions, images of Egyptian deities, and a Phoenician inscription to Astarte. All of these bronze finds originally dated to the Persian period but remained in use for the duration of the temple. In addition, a slate figurine of Isis, Osiris, and Horus was recovered near the altar. To the west of the temple stood a complex consisting of a building and a courtyard, where another Persian-era bronze figurine, of Osiris, was recovered. The temple functioned until some time in the second century BCE. Both the slate figurine and the

---

[267] Adan-Bayewitz, "Kefar Hananyah," *OEANE*, vol. III, 276; Zvi Ilan, "H. Kefar Hananya, Survey," *IEJ* 33 (1983): 255; Ilan, "Galilee, Survey of Synagogues," 35–37.

[268] Adan-Bayewitz, "Kefar Hananya, 1987," 98–99. A bronze candelabrum from a later period contains an Aramaic inscription mentioning the "holy place of Kefar Hananyah" and bears depictions of two menorahs with lulavs and shofars (Frey, ed., *Corpus Inscriptionum Iudaicarum*, vol. II, 164–165).

[269] Adan-Bayewitz, "Kefar Hananya," *OEANE*, vol. III, 277; Adan-Bayewitz, "Kefar Hanaya, 1986," 178–179; Adan-Bayewitz, "Kefar Hananya, 1987," 98–99; Adan-Bayewitz, "Kefar Hananya, 1989," 186–188.

Apis bull were broken, perhaps by the Hasmoneans when they took over the area.[270]

Gischala/Gush Ḥalav

Gischala is well known from the narratives of Josephus as the hometown of his chief rival, John, son of Levi, for whom Josephus has no kind words. According to *War*, John was a trouble-maker who initially amassed his forces not from his own community but from Tyrian villages and Syria.[271] Indeed, Josephus portrays the residents of Gischala as peaceful farmers who would have avoided conflict with the Romans if not for the influx of John's outsiders.[272] The account in *Life* is somewhat different; there John initially discouraged the villagers from revolt, but his attitude changed after Gischala was attacked by inhabitants of Gadara, Gabara, Sogane, and Tyre. In preparation for conflict with the Romans, John himself fortified the village.[273] After the fall of Gamla, Gischala was the last Galilean hold-out against the Romans, who promptly set siege. John's negotiations with the Romans provide evidence for the Jewish character of Gischala; he convinced Titus to refrain from any activities, whether war-making or peace-making, on the sabbath. When Titus granted the request, John seized the opportunity to slip out of Gischala and flee to Jerusalem. With John gone, the village surrendered and the siege ended peacefully.[274]

Substantial architectural remains, most notably a basilical synagogue initially built in the third century CE and a mausoleum from the fourth century CE, attest to Gischala's importance in the Middle Roman and later periods.[275] Evidence from the first century and earlier consists mainly of

---

[270] Rafael Frankel and Raphael Ventura, "The Miṣpe Yamim Bronzes," *BASOR* 311 (1998): 39–55; Rafael Frankel, "Har Miṣpe Yamim – 1988/1989," *ESI* 9 (1989/1990): 100–102; Nagy et al., eds., *Sepphoris*, 168–170.

[271] *War* 2.585–589, 623–625.   [272] *War* 4.84.

[273] *Life* 43–45. In *War* 2.575, 590, Josephus insists John's fortification was at his own instruction.

[274] *War* 4.84–120.

[275] Gischala became known in these later periods as a center of olive oil production (*Sifre* 135b, 148a). On the archaeological evidence, see Eric M. Meyers, Carol L. Meyers, with James F. Strange, *Excavations at the Ancient Synagogue of Gush Ḥalav* (Winona Lake, Ind.: Eisenbrauns, 1990); Eric M. Meyers, "Excavations at Gush Halav in Upper Galilee," in Levine, ed., *Ancient Synagogues Revealed*, 75–77; Eric M. Meyers, "Ancient 'Gush Ḥalav' (Gischala), Palestinian Synagogues and the Eastern Diaspora," in Joseph Gutmann, ed., *Ancient Synagogues: The State of Research* (Chico, Cal.: Scholars Press, 1981), 61–78. Michael Avi-Yonah refers to another synagogue located underneath the present village's church in "Synagogues," *EAEHL*, vol. IV, 1135–1136. On the mausoleum, see Fanny Vitto, "Gush Halav: The Mausoleum," *NEAEHL*, vol. II, 549–550 and "Gush Halav," *RB* 82 (1975): 277–278. Other significant finds include a ring, of uncertain date, with the Greek

sherds and coins, with a notable find being an ostracon from between the first century BCE and the first century CE with a partial inscription in Greek: "APICT . . . "[276] The dates of recovered coins extend back into the second century BCE.[277] The limited quantities of Hellenistic coinage as well as ceramic evidence suggest that the village was quite small in the Hellenistic period, though fragments of painted plaster found in the fill under the synagogue may attest to at least one sizable building.[278]

Khirbet Shema'

The archaeological picture at Khirbet Shema', the traditional burial site of the Pharisee Shammai, is similar to that of Gischala.[279] Excavations in industrial and agricultural areas as well as around the village's synagogue and necropolis have turned up Late Hellenistic, Early Roman and Middle Roman ceramic remains, but not in any substantial qualities. Most of the site's numismatic evidence comes from the Middle and Late Roman periods.[280] While there are a number of Hellenistic coins – Ptolemaic, Seleucid, Tyrian, and Hasmonean (especially those of Alexander Jannaeus) – only a few are from the Early Roman period. The settlement seems to have thrived between the second and the fifth centuries CE. Its

inscription DOMETILA (see E. Meyers, C. Meyers, and Strange, *Excavations at the Ancient Synagogue*, 125 and Eric M. Meyers, James F. Strange, Carol L. Meyers, and Richard S. Hanson, "Preliminary Report on the 1977 and 1978 Seasons at Gush Halav [El Jish]," *BASOR* 233 [1979]: 53–56), and a rock-cut tomb with ossuaries, again of uncertain date (Mordechai Aviam, "Gush Halav," *ESI* 5 [1986]: 44–45).

[276] E. Meyers, C. Meyers, and Strange, *Excavations at the Ancient Synagogue*, 126; cf. E. Meyers, Strange, C. Meyers, and Hanson, "Preliminary Report," 56.

[277] Eric M. Meyers, "Gush Halav," *NEAEHL*, vol. II, 546–549; Carol L. Meyers, "Gush Halav," *OEANE*, vol. II, 442–443. These finds were recovered from the lower village. On the nearby tell Mordechai Aviam has discovered Early Roman sherds and substantial amounts of Late Hellenistic sherds ("Gush Halav," *ESI* 3 [1984]: 35). Because the earliest ceramics on the site date to the Iron Age II, the reference in *M. Arak.* 9.2 to a walled city there in the time of Joshua is of doubtful accuracy.

[278] E. Meyers, C. Meyers, and Strange, *Excavations at the Ancient Synagogue*, 62.

[279] Eric M. Meyers, A. Thomas Kraabel, James F. Strange, *Ancient Synagogue Excavations at Khirbet Shema', Upper Galilee, Israel, 1970–1972* (Durham, N.C.: Duke University Press, 1976); Eric M. Meyers, "Shema,' Khirbet," *ABD*, vol. V, 1197–1198; Eric M. Meyers, "Shema', Khirbet," *NEAEHL*, vol. IV, 1359–1361; Eric M. Meyers, "Shema', Khirbet," *OEANE*, vol. V, 26–27; Eric M. Meyers, "Shema', Khirbet," *EAEHL*, vol. IV, 1095–1097. Khirbet Shema' is generally associated with Talmudic Tekoa (E. Meyers, Kraabel, and Strange, *Ancient Synagogue Excavations*, 11–16; cf. the earlier reservations about identifying the two in Eric M. Meyers, "Archaeology and Rabbinic Tradition," 1–31).

[280] Tyrian coins are surprisingly prevalent, with issues from the late third century BCE through the second century CE (E. Meyers, Kraabel, and Strange, *Ancient Synagogue Excavations*, 146–151, 167).

synagogue dates to this period,[281] and primary usage of its mausoleum occurred in the fourth century CE, though some tombs possibly date to the late second and third century CE.[282] The synagogue provides obvious evidence for Jewish inhabitants, as do two mikvaot, but all of these post-date the Early Roman period.[283] As for paganism, the sole possible piece of evidence is a red carnelian gem, bearing a depiction of a female who may be Athena. The image is similar to depictions of Athena in the first centuries BCE and CE, though the gem itself was found in fourth-century CE fill.[284]

Meiron

Meiron is located approximately one kilometer north of Khirbet Shema'.[285] Like Khirbet Shema' and Gischala, it is known for its synagogue, in this case a basilica-style structure oriented toward Jerusalem from the end of the third century C.E.[286] As with other sites in Upper Galilee, most of its finds date to the Middle Roman period and later; its heyday seems to have been the third and fourth centuries CE. There are some earlier finds: Hellenistic sherds, Hasmonean and Hellenistic lamp fragments, and Early Roman ceramic and architectural remains. The corpus of numismatic evidence includes Hasmonean and Tyrian coins, as well as issues of Agrippa II.[287] There are a few remnants of Early Roman architecture,[288] as well as a tomb complex used from the Herodian period to the fourth century CE that demonstrates the practice of ossilegium at Meiron.[289] A Herodian stone cup is evidence of the practice of Jewish purity customs,[290] and the later synagogue as well as a mikveh (probably

[281] Ibid., 33–102.   [282] Ibid., 119–145.

[283] On the mikvaot, see ibid., 40, 113–117.   [284] Ibid., 250–253.

[285] Meiron may be one of the sites Josephus claims to have fortified; in *War* 2.573 he includes in his list the settlement "Mero," but in *Life* 188, he lists "Ameroth," leaving open the possibility that he is referring to Meroth.

[286] See E. Meyers, Strange, and C. Meyers, *Excavations at Ancient Meiron*; Eric M. Meyers, "Meiron," *ABD*, vol. IV, 682–683; Eric M. Meyers, "Meiron," *OEANE*, vol. III, 469–470; Eric M. Meyers, "Meiron," *EAEHL*, vol III, 856–862; Eric M. Meyers, "Meiron," *NEAEHL*, vol III, 1024–1027; Nurit Feig, "Meron," *ESI* 7–8 (1988/1989): 127–128. While in E. Meyers, Strange and C. Meyers, *Excavations at Ancient Meiron*, 3, the excavators associate Meiron with the "Meroth" of *War* 2.573 and 3.39, in "Meiron," *ABD*, vol. IV, 682–683, Meyers accepts that "Meroth" is the site excavated by Zvi Ilan and Emanuel Damati (see discussion below).

[287] Raynor and Meshorer, *Coins of Ancient Meiron* (Winona Lake, Ind.: ASOR, Eisenbrauns, 1988); Richard S. Hanson, *Tyrian Influence in the Upper Galilee* (Cambridge, Mass.: American Schools of Oriental Research, 1980); and E. Meyers, Strange, and C. Meyers, *Excavations at Ancient Meiron*, 155–157.

[288] E. Meyers, Strange, and C. Meyers, *Excavations at Ancient Meiron*, 27.

[289] Ibid., 107–120; see also Emanuel Damati, "Meiron," *ESI 10* (1991): 72–73.

[290] E. Meyers, Strange, and C. Meyers, *Excavations at Ancient Meiron*, 152.

from the Middle Roman period) provide evidence for a Jewish population in later periods.[291] The only possible evidence for a pagan presence
at Meiron is a figurine of a muscular man (Hercules?) grasping a ser-
pent found in the earliest stratum (200–50 BCE);[292] a lamp discus with
a winged figure (Nike?) demonstrates Hellenistic influence in the second
or third century CE.[293]

Nabratein

Nabratein's synagogue is somewhat earlier than the other synagogues of
Upper Galilee, dating to shortly after the Bar Kochbah war. The Middle
and Late Roman periods are well attested there, and substantial amounts of
Early Roman pottery and some Hellenistic pottery have been found.[294] At
least one pre-135 building was excavated, with plastered pits, a plastered
floor, and substantial amounts of pottery, including limestone vessels and
basins.[295]

Meroth

Meroth marked the northern boundary of Galilee, according to
Josephus.[296] The earliest coins on site are from the second century BCE,
but there are few other Late Hellenistic remains.[297] Early Roman finds
include an underground plastered reservoir [298] and perhaps the village's

---

[291] For the mikveh, see ibid., 43. Excavators point to a jar from between 250 CE and 365
CE with the Hebrew inscription "esh" ("fire") as additional evidence for Judaism (66).
(See also their discussion of an ostracon from the same period with a Greek inscrip-
tion Ιουλιαμου, "My Julia," or "of Juliamos"); cf. the critiques of Gideon Foerster in
"Excavations at Ancient Meron [sic] (Review Article)," *IEJ* 37 (1987): 262–269.

[292] E. Meyers, Strange, and C. Meyers, *Excavations at Ancient Meiron*, 152.

[293] Ibid.

[294] Eric M. Meyers, "Nabratein (Kefar Neburaya)," *NEAEHL*, vol. III, 1077–1079; Eric
M. Meyers, "Nabratein," *OEANE*, vol. IV, 85–87, and Nahman Avigad, "Kefar Neburaya,"
EAEHL, vol. III, 710–711; Eric M. Meyers, James F. Strange, and Carol L. Meyers, "The Ark
of Nabratein – A First Glance," *BA* 44 (1981): 237–243 and Eric M. Meyers and Carol L.
Meyers, "Finders of a Real Lost Ark," *BAR* 7:6 (1981): 24–39.

[295] Eric M. Meyers, James F. Strange, and Carol L. Meyers, "Preliminary Report on the
1980 Excavations at en-Nabratein, Israel," *BASOR* 244 (1981): 13; Eric M. Meyers, James
F. Strange, and Carol L. Meyers, "Second Preliminary Report on the 1981 Excavations at
en-Nabratein, Israel," *BASOR* 246 (1982): 46. On the limestone vessels, see Eric M. Meyers,
James F. Strange, and Carol L. Meyers, "Nabratein, 1980," *IEJ* 31 (1981): 108–110.

[296] *War* 3.40. Meroth may have been one of the sites Josephus fortified (*War* 2.573, *Life*
188); see discussion under "Meiron" above.

[297] Zvi Ilan and Emanuel Damati, "Kh. Marus (Merot), 1985–1986," *IEJ* 37 (1987):
54–57.

[298] Zvi Ilan and Emanuel Damati, "Khirbet Marus – 1984," *ESI* 3 (1984): 73.

fortifications.[299] A tomb dates to the first or second century CE[300] and ceramic remains include fragments of Herodian lamps.[301] Nearby caves also contained sherds from the Hellenistic and Early Roman periods.[302] Meroth's synagogue was constructed in the late fourth or early fifth century CE. When it was rebuilt a century or so later, it was decorated with the only zodiac mosaic discovered in Upper Galilee.[303]

Conclusion

Remains from Galilee from the Hasmonean conquest to the Bar Kochbah revolt are so limited that it is difficult to generalize about where Jews and gentiles lived solely on the basis of archaeological evidence. Even at Sepphoris, supposedly a prime example of a community of both Jews and gentiles, few artifacts prior to the mid-second century CE suggest a pagan presence. Lamps and mosaics display Greco-Roman motifs, but these post-date the New Testament period by decades or centuries; in any case, given the blending of Greco-Roman and Jewish culture, such motifs cannot be automatically assumed to indicate a pagan presence. The Pan and Prometheus figurines, as well as the bronze bowl, altar, and bull, likewise date from a later period. No gymnasium, the hallmark institution of the Greek city, has been discovered at Sepphoris. No evidence exists for temples there until the city coins of the second and third centuries CE, and it is important to note that thus far, no remains of temples have been discovered to correspond to those images.

The situation is similar at other Galilean sites. The finds at Mizpeh Yamim are indisputably pagan, but the temple there went out of use in the second century BCE. The marble head of Tyche from Beth Yeraḥ, near the southeastern borders of Galilee, is possible evidence of paganism, but it is of indeterminate age. City coins of Tiberias bear images of deities and temples, but all were minted after the first century CE. Figurines have been discovered at Tiberias and Bethsaida, as well as in an early stratum at Meiron, but they present the interpreter with the difficulty of establishing their use and function – are they cultic objects or merely decorative works that serve as examples of Greco-Roman influence? If

---

[299] Zvi Ilan, "Meroth," *NEAEHL*, vol. III, 1028–1031; [no author] "Khirbet Marus," *ESI* 1 (1982): 70; Ilan and Damati, "Khirbet Marus – 1984," 76.

[300] Zvi Ilan and Emanuel Damati, "Meroth (Kh. Marus) – 1986," *ESI* 5 (1986): 68.

[301] Ilan and Damati, "Kh. Marus (Merot), 1985–1986," 57.

[302] Zvi Ilan, "Har Evyatar, Caves of Refuge," *ESI* 7–8 (1988–1989): 75.

[303] Ilan, "Meroth," *NEAEHL*, vol. III, 1028–1031; Zvi Ilan and Emmanuel Damati, "The Synagogue at Meroth," *BAR* 15:2 (1989): 20–36.

the first-century CE rectangular structure at Bethsaida is shown to be a temple for the imperial cult, it would stand in stark isolation as clear and irrefutable evidence of paganism, but, thus far, the excavators' arguments for identifying it so are unpersuasive.

In short, the archaeological evidence for paganism in the interior of Galilee is limited and ambiguous, not only in the Late Hellenistic and Early Roman periods, but in the later centuries of Roman rule. It is simply not the case that excavations have recovered numerous artifacts testifying to high numbers of non-Jews living in the interior of Galilee. Such evidence exists only in communities on the border and in nearby regions.

The evidence for Judaism is stronger. The ruins of Middle and Late Roman era synagogues can be seen throughout Galilee, and mikvaot are found in the post-Bar Kochbah strata of some Galilean sites, such as Sepphoris, Chorazin, Arbel, Khirbet Shema' and Meiron. The amount of Jewish materials from Early Roman contexts is also substantial.[304] Fragments of stone vessels have been discovered at Reina, Sepphoris, Nazareth, Asochis, Jotapata, Tiberias, Capernaum, Kefar Hananyah, Meiron, and Nabratein; Magen reports additional discoveries at Ibelin and Bethlehem of Galilee (as well as nearby Migdal Ha-Emeq).[305] Mikvaot have been found in early strata at Sepphoris and Jotapata. Evidence for secondary burial in this period exists at Kafr Kanna, Tiberias, Qiryat Tiv'on, Meiron, and near the modern city Nazareth 'Illit; additional discoveries at Dabburiyya and Huqoq may date to this time.[306] Though the identification of a rectangular structure at Taricheae as a synagogue is doubtful, the remains of a basalt structure underlying the limestone synagogue at Capernaum may well come from a first-century CE synagogue.

Though our archaeological evidence for Judaism is greater than that for paganism, we should neither exaggerate its quantity nor minimize the challenge of generalizing about a community's population from such limited evidence. Even such an unambiguous find as fragments of stone vessels allows us only to attest to the presence of Jews at a specific site – not to determine that all of the inhabitants of the site were Jews. The surprising fact is that the archaeological record from a given site often tells us nothing about who its inhabitants were, at least in the earlier

[304] Reed has independently corroborated this general picture in *Archaeology*, 43–53.

[305] Magen, *"Purity Broke Out,"* 25.

[306] See Nissim Najjar's brief report of stone ossuaries from the late first century or second century CE ("Dabburiyya," *ESI* 16 [1997]: 50–51). The ossuaries at Huqoq were found before ceramic and lamp typologies had been determined; the excavator assigned them to the first century CE, but they could be later (B. Ravani, "Rock-Cut Tombs at Huqoq: The Excavations," *Atiqot* 3 [1961]: 121–127; P. P. Kahane, "Rock-Cut Tombs at Huqoq: Notes on the Finds," *Atiqot* 3 [1961]: 128–147).

centuries of Roman rule. This is not because the populations of these sites were neither Jews nor gentiles, of course, but because the distinction between Jews and non-Jews in the material culture of the Late Hellenistic and Early Roman periods is usually invisible.

Fortunately, we also have Josephus and the Gospels to provide us with additional information. Josephus says nothing to indicate that a large number of non-Jews lived in Sepphoris, and he mentions Greeks in Tiberias only in the context of their massacre by Jews during the Revolt, suggesting their minority status. Tiberias's *proseuche* served as the setting for "town hall" meetings, and Josephus noted a Sabbath consciousness on the part of its residents. His references to smaller Galilean communities suggest Jewish populations there as well.

The Gospels report that synagogues existed throughout Galilee, mentioning specific ones at Capernaum and at Nazareth. Their descriptions of Galilean villages, though undetailed, are consistent in their implications: Jesus was a Jew traveling, teaching, and working wonders among other Jews. Other than Matthew's and Luke's references to a gentile centurion at Capernaum, the Gospels provide no evidence for pagans within Galilee itself.

Thus, nothing in Josephus or the Gospels suggests that Galilee was primarily gentile, or even that its population contained a large gentile minority amongst a Jewish majority. The impression they give is unambiguous: in the first century CE, Galilee's population was overwhelmingly Jewish. Archaeological evidence does nothing to disconfirm this view. On the contrary, though its record from this period is often silent on the issue of religious and cultural orientation, when it speaks, it almost always attests to the presence of Jews.

4

GALILEE AND THE CIRCLE OF NATIONS

Josephus described Galilee as a region "encircled by foreign nations."[1] Many scholars have regarded this encirclement as a defining factor in Galilee's cultural milieu.[2] Not only was Galilee itself full of gentiles, it has often been argued, but gentiles from the adjacent regions often made their way into Galilee. In addition, traders and travelers from more distant lands passed through on the major highways of the day. Galileans frequently took advantage of these same highways to venture frequently into the adjacent regions.

Are such claims accurate? In this chapter, I will summarize the evidence for Galilean interaction with "foreigners." Understanding this issue requires, first, knowledge of the surrounding territories – their histories, cultural atmospheres, and inhabitants (see Map 2). (As will be seen, determining the cultural identity of a given site's occupants – e.g., Roman, Greek, Syrian, Nabatean, Phoenician, Iturean, or other – is sometimes less complicated outside of Galilee than within Galilee.) It requires, secondly, a summary of the archaeological and literary evidence for contact between Galileans and non-Galileans, with particular attention to trade and the road networks. While some interaction between Galileans and non-Galileans indisputably occurred, its extent, like so many of the stereotypical characteristics of Galilee, has been overstated in much recent scholarship.

The "foreign nations"

The Golan Heights

To the east and northeast of Galilee are the Golan Heights. Altars, statues, inscriptions, and synagogues allow considerable discussion of

---

[1] *War* 3.41.   [2] See the sources cited in chapter 1.

the presence of gentiles and Jews at specific sites in the Late Roman and Byzantine periods. The earlier remains, however, are much sparser. Sherds prior to the second century BCE are uncommon, and architectural remains even more so, suggesting that the region was only thinly populated until the late Hellenistic period.[3]

Most, though not all, of the population were pagans. Itureans were among the earliest settlers in this period, arriving in the area around Mount Hermon by the mid-second century BCE. Ceramic finds at numerous sites attest to their continuing presence in the Roman period.[4] Nabateans may have settled there, as well, given their occasional efforts to expand northwards, but their presence is less visible in the archaeological record.[5] Other Semitic peoples from neighboring regions also dwelt in the area; Josephus describes the inhabitants as "Jews and Syrians."[6]

The Jewish presence also extended back at least to the mid-second century BCE and probably grew following Alexander Jannaeus's conquest of the region.[7] After Pompey's administrative reorganization in 63 BCE, the Golan was most likely taken out of Jewish hands, though Josephus is not explicit on this issue.[8] Caesar later granted it to Herod the Great, and

[3] The finds of a recent survey reflect the region's population growth, identifying 78 sites in the second century BCE, 108 in the first century CE, and 173 in the sixth century CE (Ma'oz, "Golan," *NEAEHL*, vol. II, 534–546); cf. Zvi Uri Ma'oz, "Golan Heights," *ABD*, vol. II, 1055–1065; Zvi Uri Ma'oz, "Golan," *OEANE*, vol. II, 417–424; Rami Arav, "Golan," *ABD*, vol. II, 1057–1058; Dan Urman, *The Golan: A Profile of a Region during the Roman and Byzantine Periods* (Oxford: BAR, 1985); Dan Urman, "The Golan During the Roman and Byzantine Periods: Topography, Settlements, Economy" (Ph.D. Diss., New York University, 1979). Robert C. Gregg and Dan Urman provide the most thorough discussion of the archaeological remains in *Jews, Pagans, and Christians in the Golan Heights* (Atlanta: Scholars Press, 1996).
[4] Ma'oz, "Golan," *NEAEHL*, vol. II, 535. See also Hartel, "Khirbet Zemel"; Dar, "Greek Inscriptions"; Shimon Dar and Yohanon Mintzker, "Sena'im, Mount," *NEAEHL*, vol. IV, 1322–1324.
[5] At times in the first centuries BCE and CE, their kingdom included parts of southeastern Syria, stretching along the eastern edge of the Decapolis; for a brief period between 85 and 64 BCE and perhaps again in the mid-first century CE, it reached as far north as Damascus (cf. 2 Cor. 11:32). See Wayne T. Pitard, "Damascus," *OEANE*, vol. I, 103–106; P. C. Hammond, *The Nabataeans: Their History, Culture and Archaeology* (Gothenburg, Sweden: Paul Aströms Verlag, 1973), 33–39; John Irving Lawlor, *The Nabataeans in Historical Perspective* (Grand Rapids, Mich.: Baker Book House, 1974), 42, 115–118; and Millar, *Roman Near East*, 56–57.
[6] *War* 3.58.
[7] *Ant.* 13.393–394; *War* 1.103–105; on the Golan during the Maccabean period, see 2 Macc. 10:24–37 and 12:10–31.
[8] Josephus does not refer to the area in his lists of freed and rebuilt communities in *War* 1.155–158 and *Ant.* 14.75–76.

the Jewish population seems to have increased further under him and his successors.[9] After his death, it was passed first to his son Philip,[10] then, in 34 CE, directly to the Romans,[11] and later back to Herodian rule under Agrippa I (37–44 CE) and Agrippa II (53–92/93 CE).[12] By the mid-first century CE, Jews were a sizable minority.

Given the Golan's Jewish presence and proximity to Galilee, it was drawn inevitably into the Jewish Revolt. At the outbreak, Jews raided pagan villages in Gaulanitis,[13] and eventually all Gaulanitis as far as the village of Solyma rebelled against Agrippa II.[14] Whether this Golan up-rising consisted exclusively of Jews or was a more widespread movement against Agrippa II is unclear. Josephus claims to have fortified Sogane and Seleucia, implying that they were primarily Jewish communities,[15] and he lists other specific locales affected by the Revolt. Jews at Caesarea Philippi were killed, Gamla was totally destroyed, and inhabitants of Gaulanitis and Trachonitis fled to Taricheae, where they were captured by Vespasian.[16]

The number of Jewish inhabitants in the Golan in the immediate after-math of the Revolt is unknown. While some suggest that Jewish occupation ceased and did not resume until the fourth century CE, others argue for continuity in habitation for some communities and an influx of new Jewish settlers in the second century CE. Until additional excavations are carried out, this issue will remain unresolved.[17]

Mount Hermon

Mount Hermon and its environs had been the site of pagan cults for cen-turies prior to the Roman period.[18] In earlier times the mountain had been associated with the Canaanite god: Joshua 11:17 refers to "Baal-Gad in the valley of Lebanon below Mount Hermon," and 1 Chronicles 5:23 and Judges 3:3 refer to "Baal-Hermon." Mount Hermon's slopes were liter-ally dotted with cultic sites from the second century BCE to the Roman

---

[9] *Ant.* 15.360. Gregg and Urman suggest that certain Jewish inscriptions may date to the Herodian dynasty (*Jews*, 306), but with little supporting evidence. Herod also purposely introduced loyalist settlers to the east of Gaulanitis, settling Idumeans in Trachonitis and Babylonian Jews in Bataneae (*Ant.* 16.285, 17.23–31).

[10] *Ant.* 17.189, 319; *War* 2.95.   [11] *Ant.* 18.108.

[12] *Ant.* 18.237; *War* 4.2, *Life* 187; cf. rule of Trachonitis in *Ant.* 17.23–31.

[13] *War* 2.458–460.   [14] *Life* 185–186.   [15] *Life* 187; *War* 2.574.   [16] *War* 3.542.

[17] See the contrasting views of Ma'oz, "Golan," *NEAEHL*, vol. II, 536 and Gregg and Urman, *Jews*, 291, 305–310.

[18] Dar, *Settlements and Cult Sites*; Shimon Dar, "Hermon, Mount," *NEAEHL*, vol. II, 616–617; Rami Arav, "Hermon, Mount," *ABD*, vol. III, 158–160.

era. At least twenty pagan temples have been discovered, along with accompanying inscriptions, altars, stelae, statues, and figurines. Despite the plenitude of evidence for pagan cults, the specific deities worshipped are not always obvious. Statues of eagles at one site suggest veneration of Baal-Shamin, while an image on an altar at the same site depicts Helios.[19] Elsewhere, a temple from the first four centuries CE contains an inscription to the "Greatest and Holiest God."[20] While a few Jews probably also lived in the vicinity of Mount Hermon, no clear archaeological evidence of their presence has been found on the mountain itself.[21]

Dan

At the southern foot of Mount Hermon stood Dan, best known as the location of the sanctuary chosen by Jeroboam for his temple to Yahweh, complete with a golden calf.[22] Cultic use of the site continued into the Hellenistic period, when a new temple precinct was built. A third- to second-century BCE Greek inscription reads "To the God who is in Dan, (Z)oilos made a vow," and a statue of Aphrodite from the same period was recovered in a nearby field.[23] In the Roman period, a new temenos was constructed, illustrating the continuing veneration of the god.[24]

Paneas

Paneas, another site at the foot of Mount Hermon, was also long associated with pagan cultic activity.[25] A grotto shrine to Pan was already in use by the third century BCE,[26] and the city's name reflects veneration of that deity. After receiving the city from Augustus, Herod the Great constructed a white marble temple in honor of him and Roma,[27] beginning a long association of the city with the emperor. When Philip inherited the northeastern portion of Herod's territories, he renamed the city Caesarea,

---

[19] Dar, *Settlements and Cult Sites*; Dar, "Greek Inscriptions"; Dar and Mintzker, "Sena'im, Mount."

[20] Arav, "Hermon, Mount," 158–160.   [21] Dar, *Settlements and Cult Sites*, 26–27.

[22] Judges 18:2, 30; 1 Kings 12:29. Archaeologists have recovered the remains of a tenth-century BCE cult center and altar.

[23] Avraham Biran, "To the God who is in Dan," in Avraham Biran, ed., *Temples and High Places in Biblical Times* (Jerusalem: Nelson Glueck School of Biblical Archaeology of Hebrew Union College – Jewish Institute of Religion, 1981), 142–151.

[24] Avraham Biran, "Dan, Tel," *NEAEHL*, vol. I, 323–332; Avraham Biran, "Dan (Place)," *ABD*, vol. II, 12–17; David Ilan, "Dan, Tel," *OEANE*, vol. II, 107–112.

[25] Zvi Uri Ma'oz, "Banias," *NEAEHL*, vol. I, 136–143; Vassilios Tzaferis, "Banias," *OEANE*, vol. I, 270–271; John Kutsko, "Caesarea Philippi," *ABD*, vol. I, 803.

[26] Polybius, *Histories* 16.18.2, 28.1.3.   [27] *War* 1.404; *Ant.* 15.363–364.

established his capital there, and initiated a new phase of construction.[28] Agrippa II also began impressive construction projects there, including a recently discovered 400-foot long palatial complex.[29] He honored the emperor by renaming the city "Neronia," as indicated by both literary evidence and his coins.[30] Both Vespasian and Titus billeted troops there in the Revolt, and Josephus describes in detail Titus's compulsion of Jewish prisoners to engage in combat with each other and with beasts.[31] Agrippa's Roman cultural inclination is seen clearly on coins appearing in 85/86 and 86/87 CE: they bear Latin inscriptions, the first Herodian coins to do so.[32] After Agrippa II's death, Caesarea Philippi was placed under direct Roman rule. Greek and Latin inscriptions from buildings attest to the city's continuing growth in the second century CE.

The city was primarily gentile. Josephus refers to the "Syrians" of Caesarea Philippi,[33] and many of the inhabitants were probably of Iturean descent. Physical evidence of pagan cults abounds. The grotto dedicated to Pan is still visible, as are the aedicula niches for statues adorning it. Large numbers of Middle and Late Roman lamps, probably votive offerings given by individual worshippers, have been found in the shrine's vicinity, suggesting it was heavily visited.[34] Second- through fourth-century CE inscriptions record veneration of the Nymphs, Hermes, Dio-Pan, and Nemesis. Excavations have revealed portions of the temple dedicated to Augustus, and other shrines, including one to Nemesis and another to Zeus and Pan, were constructed in later centuries. An unusually large corpus of statuary, dating from the late first century CE to the late fourth or early fifth century CE, contains at least 245 marble fragments from at least twenty-eight different sculptures, including images of the Syrian Goddess, Heracles, Nemesis, Roma, and other deities.[35]

---

[28] *War* 2.95, 168; *Ant.* 17.319, 18.28.

[29] John F. Wilson and Vassilios Tzaferis, "Banias Dig Reveals King's Palace," *BAR* 24:1 (1998): 54–61, 85; cf. suggestion by Ma'oz that Herod built the palace ("Banias," *NEAEHL*, vol. I, 140–141).

[30] *Ant.* 20.211; Meshorer, *Ancient Jewish Coinage*, vol. II, 73–74; Meshorer, *Jewish Coins*, 85–87.

[31] *War* 3.443–444; 7.23–24, 27–37.

[32] Meshorer, *Ancient Jewish Coinage*, vol. II, 80–87; Meshorer, *Jewish Coins*, 151–152.

[33] *Life* 51, 53, 59.

[34] Andrea M. Berlin, "The Archaeology of Ritual: The Sanctuary of Pan at Banias/Caesarea Philippi," *BASOR* 315 (1999): 27–46.

[35] E. Friedland, "Graeco-Roman Sculpture in the Levant: The Marbles from the Sanctuary of Pan at Caesarea Philippi (Banias)," in J. H. Humphrey, ed., *The Roman and Byzantine Near East* (Portsmouth, R.I.: Journal of Roman Archaeology), vol. II, 7–22; Ma'oz, "Banias," *NEAEHL*, vol. I, 140–141; Berlin, "Archaeology of Ritual," 34; Vassilios Tzaferis, "Cults and Deities Worshipped at Caesarea Philippi-Banias," in Eugene Ulrich et al., eds., *Priests, Prophets, and Scribes* (Sheffield: Sheffield Academic Press, 1992), 190–204.

The city's coins also reflect a pagan ethos. Those of Philip are devoid of the symbols often found on Jewish coins, such as the palm tree or cornucopia. Instead, they bear his bust and that of the emperor, the first Herodian issues to do so, and a tetrastyle temple, probably to Augustus.[36] Agrippa II's coins depict symbols acceptable to Jews as well as images of himself, the emperor, Tyche, Nike and Pan.[37] After its attachment to the province of Syria, the city's coins depict Pan, Tyche, and Zeus.[38]

Jewish inhabitants were a minority; Josephus notes that at least some preferred to use ritually pure oil.[39] During the Revolt, Varus, one of Agrippa II's officials, had many Jews, including twelve of the community's most respected members, put to death "to ingratiate himself with the Syrians of Caesarea,"[40] according to Josephus. Varus was rumored to have plotted further against the Jews of Caesarea (who Josephus claims to have numbered "many thousands") before Agrippa removed him from his post.[41]

Tel Anafa

Tel Anafa, located 9.5 kilometers southeast of Panias and 10–12 kilometers north of Lake Huleh, is a distinctive, even anomalous, site.[42] It has yielded an extraordinary assemblage of luxury items, including gems, fine wares, and, most notably, ornate cast glass vessels. Its ceramic repertoires are strikingly different from those discovered elsewhere in the area, providing an unusual example (for the region) where pottery forms suggest that the inhabitants (in two distinct phases of occupation) were not Jewish. Given its unusual characteristics, Tel Anafa merits a full discussion.

[36] Meshorer, *Ancient Jewish Coinage*, vol. II, 42–49, 244, 246 and *Jewish Coins*, 76–77, 135–137.

[37] Meshorer, *Ancient Jewish Coinage*, vol. II, 77–78 and *Jewish Coins*, 81–87, 141–150.

[38] Zvi Uri Ma'oz, "Coin and Temple – The Case of Caesarea Philippi-Paneas," *INJ* 13 (1994–1999): 90–100; Ya'akov Meshorer, "The Coins of Caesarea Paneas," *INJ* 8 (1984–1985): 37–58; Meshorer, *City-Coins*, 68–69; M. Rosenberger, *City-Coins of Palestine*, 3 vols. (Jerusalem, 1972–1977), vol. III, 38–47.

[39] *Life* 74–76; cf. *War* 2.591–592.   [40] *Life* 53, 54.   [41] *Life* 61, *War* 2.481–483.

[42] Sharon Herbert, ed., *Tel Anafa, I: Final Report on Ten Years of Excavation at a Hellenistic and Roman Settlement in Northern Israel*, 2 vols. (Ann Arbor, Mich.: Kelsey Museum, 1994); Sharon Herbert, ed., *Tel Anafa II, i: The Hellenistic and Roman Pottery* (Ann Arbor, Mich.: Kelsey Museum; Columbia, Mo.: Museum of Art and Archaeology of the University of Missouri, 1997); Sharon C. Herbert, "Anafa, Tel," *OEANE*, vol. I, 117–118; Herbert, "Anafa, Tel," *NEAEHL*, vol. I, 58–61; Saul S. Weinberg, "Anafa, Tel," *EAEHL*, vol. I, 65–69. Herbert notes that while the area is today considered part of Galilee, in antiquity it would have been considered outside its limits (*Tel Anafa, I, i*, 4).

The ancient community's name is unknown.[43] The settlement may have originated in the Persian era, and coins, ceramics, and a few architectural finds suggest its occupation in the Ptolemaic and Seleucid periods. Abundant finds of all types clearly demonstrate that its height came *c*. 125–80 BCE.[44] The principal discovery from this latter period is an unusually large stuccoed and lavishly decorated building, approximately 38 meters square. The walls were painted, with white for some portions and geometric designs for others, and architectural fragments bear Corinthian, Doric, and Ionic motifs. A three-room private bath complex was adjacent to the building, with a black and white mosaic floor and a large basin for heated water. The structure displays distinctive Phoenician construction techniques, and excavators have compared it to Greek peristyle private houses.[45] In the early years of the second century BCE, the building was subdivided into distinct units, and new buildings, also lavish in style and decoration, were constructed. Corroborating the image of a wealthy site are the non-architectural finds: "thousands of molded glass bowls, numerous metal vessels and ornaments, molded lamps, and fine red-slipped pottery."[46] One season's excavation even unearthed a small cache of fourteen gems, including garnets and amethysts.[47]

Coins reveal the community's participation in trade networks including Tyre and Sidon, and ceramic finds reflect an even more far-reaching trade. Eastern Sigillata A was used, and other pottery was imported from the Phoenician cities, the Huleh valley, Ptolemais, southern Italy, Rhodes, Kos, Knidos, Chios, and perhaps Asia Minor and Alexandria. Numerous amphora handles from Rhodes and elsewhere in the Aegean attest to the occupants' considerable consumption of imported wine. Sharon Herbert suggests that the nature and quantity of the imports reflect the inhabitants' luxurious living and sophisticated tastes.[48]

---

[43] Gideon Fuks provides little evidence for his suggestion that it is Arsinoe of Coele Syria ("Tel Anafa: A Proposed Identification," *Scripta Classica Israelica* 5 [1979]: 178–184).

[44] Herbert, ed., *Tel Anafa, I, i*, 12–13 and *Tel Anafa II, i*, 16–29.

[45] Herbert, ed., *Tel Anafa, I, i*, 14; Herbert, "Anafa, Tel," *NEAEHL*, vol. I, 59; Herbert, "Anafa, Tel," *OEANE*, vol. I, 117–118. See also the earlier Saul S. Weinberg, "Tel Anafa: The Hellenistic Town," *IEJ* 21 (1971): 86–109; Saul S. Weinberg, "Tel Anafa (Shamir)," *IEJ* 18 (1968): 195–196.

[46] Herbert, "Anafa, Tel," *NEAEHL*, vol. I, 59; Gladys Davidson Weinberg, "Hellenistic Glass from Tel Anafa in Upper Galilee," *Journal of Glass Studies* 12 (1970): 17–27; Gladys Davidson Weinberg, "Notes on Glass from Upper Galilee," *Journal of Glass Studies* 15 (1973): 35–51.

[47] Saul S. Weinberg, "Tel Anafa: A Problem-Oriented Excavation," *Muse* 3 (1969): 16–23.

[48] Herbert, ed., *Tel Anafa II, i*, 21; Kathleen Warner Slane, "The Fine Wares," in ibid., 247–418; and the following studies in Herbert, ed., *Tel Anafa, I, i,*: Donald T. Ariel and

Not everything was imported from far away, however; the site's spatter-ware pottery originated in the Ḥuleh Valley itself.[49] While some jars came from the Ḥuleh, others were brought in from the Phoenician coast and the eastern Mediterranean.[50] But very little was imported from Galilee and Judea. Herbert observes that "Tel Anafa's Late Hellenistic assemblages share nothing with the southern ceramic repertoire – no types in common, no overlap of forms or fabrics that would imply contact, connection, or exchange . . . The Hasmonean state presented a closed border, economically and probably socially as well."[51]

If such stark differences in the material culture of Tel Anafa and that of Jewish Palestine suggest that Tel Anafa's inhabitants were not Jews, who were they? Andrea M. Berlin's thorough analysis of the ceramic finds suggests a Greek cultural orientation, an impression seconded by the frequency of Greek graffiti on the site's red ware.[52] In particular, Berlin notes the presence of open-mouthed, wide-bellied casserole dishes, arguing that this particular form of casserole dish is found only at sites with a Greek presence or at least a Greek cultural orientation, rarely occurring, for example, at Hasmonean sites (with the notable exception of Jerusalem itself, reflecting the complexity of its cultural atmosphere).[53] A few locally made Italian-style pans add even more variety to the site's ceramic repertoire,[54] and a significant number of pig bones indicates that many of Tel Anafa's inhabitants were dining on decidedly non-Jewish dishes.[55] The discovery of figurines, including one of Pan, and a statue, perhaps of Demeter, also suggest the pagan character of the settlement.[56]

Gerald Rinkielszejn, "Stamped Amphora Handles," 183–240; Yaakov Meshorer, "Coins," 241–260; and Alla Stein, "A Tyrian Sealing," 261–263.

[49] Herbert, ed., *Tel Anafa II, i*, 9.

[50] Andrea Berlin, "The Plain Wares," in Herbert, ed., *Tel Anafa II, i*, 149–153.

[51] Herbert, ed., *Tel Anafa II, i*, 23.

[52] Berlin, "Plain Wares"; cf. her earlier work, "The Hellenistic and Early Roman Common-Ware Pottery from Tel Anafa" (Ph.D. Diss., University of Michigan, 1988). On the graffiti, see Slane, "Fine Wares," 342–346.

[53] Berlin, "Plain Wares," 95; note 214 lists sites where these casserole dishes are found. See also Herbert, ed., *Tel Anafa II, i*, 20–22.

[54] Berlin, "Plain Wares," 104–106. See also her discussion of the relationship between cook-ware forms and the dishes prepared in them in "Hellenistic and Early Roman Common-Ware Pottery," 67–94.

[55] Richard W. Redding, "The Vertebrate Fauna," in Herbert, ed., *Tel Anafa I, i*, 279–322, esp. 288.

[56] On the Pan figurine, see Sharon C. Herbert, "Tel Anafa, 1980," *Muse* 14 (1980): 24–30; on the Demeter statue, see Saul S. Weinberg, "Tel Anafa: The Second Season," *Muse* 4 (1970): 15–24 and "Tel Anafa: The Hellenistic Town," 105. On other figurines, see Weinberg, "Tel Anafa: The Hellenistic Town," 106, "Tel Anafa," *IEJ* 23 (1973), and Saul S. Weinberg, "Tel Anafa: The Third Season," *Muse* 5 (1971): 8–16.

Given the location of Tel Anafa, the obvious economic orientation to the coast, and the use of Phoenician construction techniques, the most likely candidates for its settlement in this period are Hellenized Phoenicians, probably from Tyre or even Sidon. Perhaps it was originally an outpost on the trade route connecting Damascus and Tyre.[57] It began to decline in the early first century BCE, as Seleucid influence weakened and the region grew more and more unstable. The number of occupants dwindled and the buildings were left to decay. By *c.* 75 BCE, Tel Anafa's abandonment was complete.[58] The timing of this decline strongly suggests that as Hasmonean influence in the region grew, culminating with Alexander Jannaeus's incorporation of the area into his kingdom, the inhabitants of Tel Anafa simply left.

New settlers arrived around the turn of the era, initiating a period of occupation which lasted until the middle of the first century CE. The new community had little in common with the previous settlement. Its eleven buildings were much simpler in design than the Late Hellenistic structures.[59] Its pottery was plainer and coarser. A small number of the plain ware vessels were Italian in origin, a few, Judean. The fine wares included imports from Italy, Asia Minor, and Cyprus, but in significantly smaller numbers than the fine wares of the Late Hellenistic community. Amphorae were brought in primarily from the Huleh and Ptolemais, rather than from the Aegean. In contrast to the Hellenistic settlement, the first-century CE community seems to have been economically oriented towards Caesarea Philippi and also towards Galilee.[60] It was dependent on Kefar Hananyah for much of its common ware, and 95 percent of the community's jars were Galilean. Such jars originally contained oil and wine; whereas the previous settlement had turned to the coast for such goods, the new one looked to the south.[61] In all probability, it was part of Philip's kingdom, perhaps started at the dawn of his reign and enjoying good relations with Antipas's kingdom. In the middle of the first century CE, however, it, too, was abandoned, for unknown reasons.[62]

Like the previous inhabitants, first-century CE Tel Anafa's occupants were probably not Jews. Pig bones from this period show that the diet

---

[57] Herbert, ed., *Tel Anafa, I, i*, 5–6; Herbert, ed., *Tel Anafa II, i*, 23–29; Herbert, "Anafa, Tel," *OEANE*, vol. I, 117. Note also the bilingual Greek-Phoenician inscription on a seal (Stein, "Tyrian Sealing," 261–263).

[58] Herbert, "Anafa, Tel," *NEAEHL*, vol. I, 60. The date for abandonment is suggested by the dates on coins and amphora handles.

[59] Ibid., 60–61.

[60] The frequent coins of Philip show that Tel Anafa participated in a trade network that included Caesarea Philippi (Meshorer, "Coins," in Herbert, ed., *Tel Anafa, I*).

[61] Berlin, "Plain Wares," 150–151; Slane, "Fine Wares," 246.

[62] Herbert suggests that it was abandoned when the Romans imposed direct rule of the region after Agrippa I's death in 44 CE (*Tel Anafa II, i*, 30–32).

was not kosher,[63] and, as with the Hellenistic settlement's pottery, many of the ceramic forms are unusual. The quantity of locally made Italian-style pans – 11 percent of the total number of cooking vessels, an extremely unusual proportion for Near Eastern sites – demonstrates, as did the Hellenistic casseroles for the earlier settlement, that the inhabitants had a non-Jewish diet. On the basis of these pans, found at other sites with a known Roman presence, Berlin proposes that some residents were Romans or Italians.[64] Why Romans or Italians would have settled in the area is unclear; Herbert suggests that they were mercenaries in the service of Philip.[65] If Tel Anafa's first-century CE occupants were Romans, they were among a very, very few in the region, and it is notable that similar Italic-style pans have not been discovered elsewhere in the vicinity.

Gamla

Of the first-century CE sites in the Golan, Gamla, located only a few kilometers east of the Sea of Galilee, is the most self-evidently Jewish.[66] Its synagogue is one of only a handful yet discovered from the first century CE,[67] and fragments of stone vessels prove that some of the inhabitants practiced Jewish ritual purity customs.[68] Mikvaot reflect the same concerns: one, a 4 m by 4.5 m basin, stood to the west of the synagogue; a second has been discovered near an olive press; and a third dates as early as the first century BCE.

Josephus provides considerable information about Gamla. Hellenistic remains and coins corroborate his account of the town's pre-Roman existence, and the conquest by Alexander Jannaeus probably marks the beginning of its Jewish character.[69] While Gabinius is said to have rebuilt and repopulated the town, the exact nature of his refoundation is unclear, given the site's subsequent Jewish occupation.[70] Gamla's single most famous inhabitant is probably Judas, also known as Judas the Galilean,

---

[63] Redding, "Vertebrate Fauna," 288.

[64] Berlin, "Plain Wares," 104–106; Herbert, ed., *Tel Anafa II, i*, 30–31.

[65] Herbert, ed., *Tel Anafa II, i*, 32.

[66] Steven Fine, "Gamla," *OEANE*, vol. II, 382; Shemaryahu Gutman, "Gamala," *NEAEHL*, vol. II, 459–463; Danny Syon, "The Coins from Gamala: Interim Report," *INJ* 12 (1992–1993): 34–55.

[67] In addition to Fine, "Gamla," and Gutman, "Gamala," see Shemaryahu Gutman, "The Synagogue at Gamla," in Levine, ed., *Ancient Synagogues Revealed*, 30–34 and Zvi Ma'oz, "The Synagogue of Gamla and the Typology of Second-Temple Synagogues," 35–41 in the same volume.

[68] Deines, *Jüdische Steinfegäße*, 153; Ma'oz, "Golan," *NEAEHL*, vol. II, 536.

[69] *War* 1.103–105; *Ant.* 13.393–397.

[70] *War* 1.165–166; note the omission of Gamla in the parallel passage, *Ant.* 14.75–76.

who, along with Saddok the Pharisee, led an unsuccessful revolt after the announcement of Quirinius's census in 6 CE.[71]

Gamla was part of Agrippa II's kingdom and initially remained loyal to him in the Jewish Revolt.[72] Josephus even refers enigmatically to Gamla's assault on the "Babylonians," apparently Babylonian Jews from Batanaea who were perhaps fleeing to Galilee for safety; the reason for the attack is unclear. In the same passage he refers to Gamla's action against the kinsmen of Philip, one of Agrippa's loyalists.[73]

Ultimately, Gamla chose to participate fully in the Revolt, casting its lot with the Jews of Galilee and Judea.[74] Josephus considered it within his area of responsibility and claims to have fortified it.[75] Coins unique to Gamla attest to its loyalty to Jerusalem, bearing the Hebrew inscription "For the redemption of H[oly] Jerusalem."[76] Agrippa II tried and failed to retake the town, and its conquest was left to Roman legions in 67 CE. Josephus describes the battle in epic terms. The town was clearly in a good defensive position, surrounded by steep ravines and its defenders supplemented by fugitives from other villages. The Romans eventually broke through its defenses, with the breach in the wall by the synagogue still visible today. To escape capture by the Romans, Josephus writes, "multitudes plunged headlong with their wives and children into the ravine which had been excavated to a vast depth beneath the citadel."[77] Fortress walls and the remains of four towers are still present, and ballista stones, arrowheads, sling stones, pieces of armor, and traces of fire attest to the ferocity of the siege.[78] Occupation of the site ceased with the city's destruction.

The Decapolis

The Hellenistic cities to the east of Galilee were known collectively as the Decapolis. Though "Decapolis" means, literally, "ten cities,"[79] lists

---

[71] *Ant.* 18.4; cf. *War* 2.118.   [72] *War* 3.56; *Life* 46–61.   [73] *Life* 177–184.
[74] *Life* 185–186.   [75] *War* 2.568, 574; *Life* 186.
[76] Meshorer, *Ancient Jewish Coinage*, vol. II, 129–131, 263; Syon, "Coins"; Fine, "Gamala," *OEANE*, vol. II, 382.
[77] *Life* 114, *War* 4.1–83; quote from *War* 4.80; cf. Suetonius, *Titus* 4.
[78] Gutman, "Gamala," *NEAEHL*, vol. II, 459–463.
[79] Jean-Paul Rey Coquais, "Decapolis," trans. Stephen Rosoff, *ABD*, vol. II, 116–121; S. Thomas Parker, "Decapolis," *OEANE*, vol. II, 127–130; S. Thomas Parker, "The Decapolis Reviewed," *JBL* 94 (1975): 437–441; Millar, *Roman Near East*, 408–414; Hans Bietenhard, "Die syrische Dekapolis von Pompeius bis Trajan," in Hildegard Temporini and Wolfgang Haase, eds., *Aufstieg und Niedergang der römischen Welt* 2.8 (Berlin: Walter de Gruyter, 1977), 220–261.

enumerating the cities vary and are not limited to ten.[80] The exact relationship between the cities is uncertain. Earlier scholarship often referred to them as a league or confederation, but no ancient source describes them in either fashion.[81] They were somewhat autonomous, with many issuing their own coinage, but they were also part of the Roman province of Syria. No "Decapolis" inscription, betraying a strong sense of group identity, occurs on any of their coins. During the Revolt, their only joint action was the formation of a delegation of leading citizens to petition Vespasian for action against Justus of Tiberias after his attacks in the region.[82] A late first-century CE inscription found at Madytos in Asia Minor refers to a soldier stationed in the Decapolis, which is identified as a distinct administrative unit within Syria. By that time, at least, the Decapolis was an official sub-district.[83] In 106 CE, only a few years after the inscription, the Decapolis cities were divided among the provinces of Syria, Arabia and Palestine.[84]

The cities shared common histories, extending back into the Hellenistic period, with most having earlier phases of occupation as well. Some had – or at least claimed – Greek foundations. Their political relationship with the Jewish territory to their west was sometimes uneasy. Scythopolis fell to Aristobulus and Antigonus,[85] and Alexander Jannaeus marched on Pella, Gerasa, Scythopolis, Gadara, and perhaps Dium, dying while campaigning in the territory of Gerasa.[86] In 63 BCE, Pompey removed Hippos, Scythopolis, Dium, and Pella from Jewish rule, rebuilt Gadara for his freedman Demetrius, and attached the cities to the province of Syria.[87] The Decapolis cities welcomed the Roman general and remembered his

[80] Pliny lists Damascus, Philadelphia, Raphana, Scythopolis, Gadara, Hippos, Dion, Pella, Galasa (presumably Gerasa), and Canatha (*Natural History* 5.16.74). The second-century CE writer Ptolemy repeats Pliny's list, with the exception of Raphana, and adds nine more: Heliopolis, Abila, Saana, Hina, Abila, Lysanius, Capitolias, Edrei, Gadara, and Samulis (*Geography* 5.14.22). Eusebius (*Onomasticon* 1.16) and Stephanius of Byzantium (*Ethnika*) provide other lists. The word "Decapolis" first appears in the Gospels (Mark 5:20, Mark 7:31 and Matt. 4:25) and in Josephus's works (*War* 3.446; *Life* 341, 410).

[81] See Parker, "Decapolis Reviewed."   [82] *Life* 341, 410.

[83] Benjamin Isaac, "The Decapolis in Syria: A Neglected Inscription," *Zeitschrift für Papyrologie und Epigraphik* 44 (1981): 67–74; Parker, "Decapolis," *OEANE*, vol. II, 127–128.

[84] Parker, "Decapolis," *OEANE*, vol. II, 129.

[85] *War* 1.64–66; *Ant.* 13.277–280; it was later part of Alexander Jannaeus's territory (*Ant.* 13.396).

[86] *War* 1.103–105; *Ant.* 13.393–398. Whether the Dium mentioned is that of the Decapolis is unclear.

[87] *War* 1.155–158, quote from 157; see also *Ant.* 14.75–76; cf. previous note on the identity of Dium.

liberation of them; the coins of several reflect a dating system commemorating his arrival.[88] Gabinius continued the reconstruction efforts begun by Pompey,[89] and issues of Scythopolis honor him.[90] Augustus detached Hippos and Gadara and returned them briefly to Jewish hands during the reign of Herod the Great; afterwards they returned to the province of Syria.[91] After the Caesarea Maritima massacre in 66 CE, Jews raided Syrian villages and the cities Philadelphia, Gerasa, Pella, Scythopolis, Hippos, and Gadara, and Jewish–gentile conflict broke out throughout the region. Scythopolis, Hippos, Damascus and Gadara killed many of their own Jewish inhabitants, though Gerasa refrained from such action.[92] Jews from Hippos and Gadara joined refugees from Trachonitis and Gaulanitis at Taricheae, across the Sea of Galilee.[93]

If legends of Greek foundations have any basis at all in truth, some cities' populations may have had a Greek component. Most of their inhabitants, however, were drawn from the surrounding regions. Nabateans had settled in some cities, most notably Gerasa,[94] and probably all of the cities (in addition to those specified by Josephus) had Jewish minorities. Archaeological evidence from the Hellenistic period is generally limited, given the disruption caused by the vast amount of later construction,[95] but the ample Roman-era remains – architecture, physical lay-outs, inscriptions, and cultic finds – all reflect strong Greek and Roman influence.[96] While an investigation of the ethos and population of every Decapolis city is not necessary for our purposes, those in closest proximity to Galilee deserve discussion.[97]

[88] Abila, Canatha, Dium, Gadara, Gerasa, Hippos, Pella, Philadelphia and Scythopolis date their coins from Pompey's liberation (Coquais, "Decapolis," 116; Meshorer, *City-Coins*, pages cited below).

[89] *War* 1.165–166; *Ant.* 14.75–76.

[90] Rachel Barkay, "Coins of Roman Governors Issued by Nysa-Scythopolis in the Late Republican Period," *INJ* 13 (1994–1999): 54–62.

[91] *War* 1.396, 2.97.   [92] *War* 2.457–480.   [93] *War* 3.542.

[94] David F. Graf, "Nabateans," *OEANE*, vol. IV, 82–85; David F. Graf, "The Nabataeans and the Decapolis," in P. W. M. Freeman and D. L. Kennedy, eds., *The Defence of the Roman and Byzantine East* (Oxford: BAR, 1986), 785–796; Hammond, *Nabataeans*, esp. 33–39; and Robert Wenning, "Die Dekapolis und die Nabataër," *ZDPV* 110 (1994): 2–35; cf. the reference to the Nabatean king Aretas in Damascus in 2 Cor. 11:32–33.

[95] Robert Houston Smith, "The Southern Levant in the Hellenistic Period," *Levant* 22 (1990): 123–130.

[96] Thomas Weber, "A Survey of Roman Sculpture in the Decapolis: Preliminary Report," *ADAJ* 34 (1990): 351–355; Henri Seyrig, "Temples, cultes, et souvenirs historiques de la Décapole," *Syria* 36 (1959): 60–78; Julian M. C. Bowsher, "Architecture and Religion in the Decapolis: A Numismatic Survey," *PEQ* 119 (1987): 62–69.

[97] As for the other cities, little data exists for Raphana and Canatha, and the site for Dium is disputed. Capitolias apparently was not founded until 97/98 CE and didn't peak until the end of the next century (C. J. Lenzen and F. A. Knauf, "Beit Ras/ Capitolias:

Hippos

Hippos stood perched on a promontory only two kilometers from the Sea of Galilee, directly opposite Tiberias. The city is unexcavated, though the town plan of rectangular insulae and perpendicular streets, dating to the second and third centuries CE, is still visible, along with remnants of a nymphaeum and a bathhouse.[98] Coins minted in 37 BCE and 67/68 CE bear the image of Tyche, and later issues depict Tyche, Zeus-Arotesios ("Zeus of the Heights"), and Hera, as well as tetrastyle temples.[99] A Greek inscription from the second or third century CE seemingly refers to the Nabatean deity Dushara, suggesting that some of the inhabitants may have been Nabateans.[100] Josephus refers to the slaughter of Hippos's Jews during the Revolt.[101] Many of the surviving Jews fled to Taricheae, where they participated in its defense.[102]

Abila

Little is known of Early Roman Abila, located eighteen to twenty kilometers east of Gadara. It may have been taken by Alexander Jannaeus and liberated by Pompey, though it is not mentioned in Josephus's discussions of those events.[103] The archaeological data published thus far have contained frustratingly little information about the exact dates of finds.

A Preliminary Evaluation of the Archaeological and Textual Evidence," *Syria* 64 [1987]: 21–46; C. J. Lenzen, "Beit Ras," *OEANE*, vol. I, 297–298) and Philadelphia was far to the south (J. P. Rey-Coquais, "Philadelphia [Amman]," in Richard Stillwell et al., eds., *The Princeton Encyclopedia of Classical Sites* [Princeton: Princeton University Press, 1976], 703–704; Adnan Hadidi, "The Roman Town Plan of Amman," in Roger Moorey and Peter Parr, eds., *Archaeology in the Levant* [Warminster: Aris and Phillips, 1978], 210–222). Damascus stood considerably distant to the northeast of the rest of the Decapolis cities, and very little has been excavated there, though the remains of an early-first-century CE temple to the Damascene Jupiter have been found (Pitard, "Damascus," *OEANE*, vol. I, 103–106; John McRay, "Damascus: The Greco-Roman Period," *ABD*, vol. II, 7–8; Klaus S. Freyberger, "Untersuchungen zur Baugeschichte des Jupiter-Heiligtums in Damaskus," *Damaszener Mitteilungen* 4 [1989]: 61–86 and Jean Sauvaget, "Le Plan antique de Damas," *Syria* 26 [1949]: 314–358).

[98] Clare Epstein, "Hippos," *NEAEHL*, vol. II, 634–636; Vassilios Tzaferis, "Susita Awaits the Spade," *BAR* 16:5 (1990): 50–58; Zeev Meshel, Tsvika Tsuk, Henning Fahlbusch, and Yehudah Peleq, *The Water-Supply System of Susita* (Tel Aviv: Institute of Archaeology; Lübeck: Fachhochschule, 1996).

[99] Meshorer, *City-Coins*, 72–75; Spijkerman, *Coins*, 168–179; Rosenberger, *City-Coins*, vol. III, 1–4.

[100] Asher Ovadiah, "Was the Cult of the God Dushara-Dusares Practised in Hippos-Susita?" *PEQ* 113 (1981): 101–104.

[101] *War* 2.459, 477.   [102] *War* 3.542.

[103] *Ant.* 13.393–397, 14.74–76; *War* 1.155–157. Nero gave an Abila to Agrippa II, but that was Abila of Perea, not the Decapolis Abila.

A large civic center, aqueducts, a nymphaeum complex, and a theater have been excavated, but when they were constructed is unclear.[104] A seal, discovered near a temple, depicts Artemis, and terracotta figurines, including one of Dionysos and another possibly of Pallas-Athene, have been found in tombs.[105] Artemis is also represented by a statue, most likely from the Hellenistic period though possibly a Roman copy of an earlier style.[106] Abila apparently did not mint coins until 161 CE; when it did so, they, like other coins of the region, bore images of deities and temples.[107]

Gerasa

Gerasa is best known among New Testament scholars as the city in whose territory Jesus encountered the "Gerasene Demoniac," sending his demons (collectively identifying themselves as "Legion") into pigs, sending the pigs into the Sea of Galilee, and sending the local inhabitants away frightened. Basic historiographical questions about the nature of exorcisms aside, the story is problematic, given that Gerasa is considerably distant from the Sea.[108] Its ruins, still visible today, are among the most impressive of the Roman Near East. As one of the most prosperous cities of the Decapolis, Gerasa's influence on the larger region was probably, at times, considerable.[109]

[104] W. Harold Mare, "Abila," *OEANE*, vol. I, 5–7; W. Harold Mare, "Abila," *NEAEHL*, vol. I, 1–3; W. Harold Mare, "The 1996 Season of Excavation at Abila of the Decapolis," *ADAJ* 41 (1997): 303–310.

[105] Michael Jeffrey Fuller, "Abila of the Decapolis: A Roman-Byzantine City in Transjordan" (Ph.D. Diss., Washington University, 1987), 358–367.

[106] W. Harold Mare, "The Artemis Statue Excavated at Abila of the Decapolis in 1994," *ADAJ* 41 (1997): 277–281.

[107] Meshorer, *City-Coins*, 78; Spijkerman, *Coins*, 48–57.

[108] Mark 5:1–20 and Luke 8:26–39 locate it in the region (χώρα) of Gerasa, while Matt. 8:28–34 situates it in the region of Gadara. Neither city is adjacent to the Sea of Galilee. This discrepancy has led to a confused textual record, and tradition has settled upon a lakeside site, Gergesa, as a more suitable candidate for the miracle. All three sites appear in the textual traditions of the Gospels. On Gergesa, see Vassilios Tzaferis, "Kursi," *OEANE*, vol. III, 314–315 and Vassilios Tzaferis, "Kursi," *NEAEHL*, vol. III, 893–896.

[109] Carl H. Kraeling, ed., *Gerasa: City of the Decapolis* (New Haven, Conn.: American Schools of Oriental Research, 1938); Carl H. Kraeling, "The History of Gerasa," in ibid., 27–72; C. B. Welles, "The Inscriptions," in ibid., 355–496; John McRay, "Gerasenes," *ABD*, vol. II, 991–992; Melissa M. Aubin, "Jerash," *OEANE*, vol. III, 215–219; Shimon Applebaum and Arthur Segal, "Gerasa," *NEAEHL*, vol. II, 470–479; and the popular guides by Rami Khouri, *Jerash: A Frontier City of the Roman East* (London and New York: Longman, 1986), and Ian Browning, *Jerash and the Decapolis* (London: Chatto & Windus, 1982).

Like other Decapolis cities, Gerasa emphasized its Greek roots. "Macedonians" donated a column to the city's arcade, according to a late second-century CE inscription; how far back the Macedonian component of the population dated is unknown.[110] A third-century CE pedestal inscription identified the displayed statue (now lost) as that of Perdiccas, perhaps a reference to Alexander the Great's officer, Perdiccas.[111] Late second- and third-century CE coins bear busts of Alexander the Great and name him founder, though earlier coins identify the city as the "city of the Antiochenes," suggesting a Seleucid foundation.[112]

Architectural remains abound, and because of the plentitude of inscriptions – over three hundred and fifty (mostly Greek, some Latin, and one Nabatean) – precise dating is possible for the construction of many of the buildings. One of the earliest datable structures is a temple to Zeus Olympios. One Zabdion, a priest of Tiberius Caesar, gave a gift for its construction *c.* 22/23 CE, invoking both Agathe Tyche and the Olympian Zeus and asking for the safety of the *Sebastoi* (Augustus and Tiberius) and the harmony of the *demos*. Two individuals identifying themselves as *gymnasiarchs* made donations for the construction of the temple *c.* 42–43 CE, as recorded by similarly worded inscriptions.[113]

Other features can also be dated to the first two centuries. One inscription from 73/74 CE records the construction of a temple to Hera.[114] By approximately the same time, a city gate had been completed, perhaps reflecting the completion of the city's walls, and a typical Hippodamian city plan, with a cardo and decumanii, was in use.[115] Near the end of the century, a 3000-person theater and a forum were built.[116] In the second

[110] Welles, "Inscriptions," #78.

[111] Ibid., #137; Kraeling, "History," 28–29; Jones, *Cities*, 129, 447.

[112] Meshorer, *City-Coins*, 94; Spijkerman, *Coins*, 156–167; for other traditions, see Kraeling, "History," 27–29.

[113] Welles, "Inscriptions," #2–4; see also Jacques Seigne, "Le sanctuaire de Zeus à Jérash: Eléments de chronologie," *Syria* 62 (1985): 287–295, and Millar, *Roman Near East*, 411–413. *Gymnasiarchs* are not the only officials mentioned in first-century inscriptions; another lists the *archontes*, including the president, a *dekaprotos*, and a scribe (*grammateus*) (Kraeling, "History," 44).

[114] Welles, "Inscriptions," #17.

[115] Kraeling, "History," 41; Asem N. Barghouti, "Urbanization of Palestine and Jordan in Hellenistic and Roman Times," in Adnan Hadidi, ed., *Studies in the History and Archaeology of Jordan* (Amman: Department of Antiquities, 1982), vol. I, 209–230. G. W. Bowersock credits Traianus, legate to Syria and father of the future emperor, for these developments ("Syria Under Vespasian," *Journal of Roman Studies* 63 [1973]: 133–140).

[116] Applebaum and Segal, "Gerasa," *NEAEHL*, vol. II, 473; Welles, "Inscriptions," #51–55; C. S. Fisher, "The 'Forum,'" 153–158 in Kraeling, ed., *Gerasa*.

century, a triumphal arch celebrating Hadrian's tour of the region was erected,[117] and two new temples were built, one between 110 and 150 CE, and the other, to Artemis, *c.* 150 CE.[118] A hippodrome, seating 15,000, was constructed *c.* 150 CE;[119] another theater, *c.* 162–166 CE; a bath complex, *c.* 150–200 CE; and a nymphaeum, *c.* 191 CE.[120] A third theater was built outside the city walls in the early third century,[121] and a second bath complex dates to the third century at the latest.[122] In short, Gerasa was the epitome of the Roman city in the east, especially in the second and third centuries.[123]

As such, its inhabitants worshipped numerous gods. Gerasa's first coins, minted in 67/68 CE, bore images of Zeus and Tyche; Artemis and Tyche often appear on second- and third-century issues.[124] Inscriptions, many from altars, indicate that shrines and temples were dedicated to numerous deities: Hera (first century CE), Apollo, Zeus Poseidon, Zeus Epicarpius, Nemesis (all from second century CE), and Zeus Helios Serapis (second to third century CE).[125] Non-Olympian deities were also worshipped, with invocations to Tyche Agathe especially frequent in the epigraphic corpus. The Nabatean god Pakidas is coupled with Hera in one first-century CE inscription and mentioned alone on a first-century CE altar.[126] Three second-century inscriptions honor an "Arabian God,"[127] and three second- to third-century inscriptions honor the "Heavenly Goddess."[128] Another inscription attests to veneration of Leucothea.[129] Priests of the imperial cult are also recorded in first- and second-century CE inscriptions.[130]

[117] Welles, "Inscriptions," #58.

[118] On the first temple, see C. S. Fisher and C. H. Kraeling, "Temple C," in Kraeling, ed., *Gerasa*, 139–148. Fisher and Kraeling tentatively identified the temple as a *heroon*, but L. H. Vincent suggested that it was a Nabatean temenos ("Le Dieu Saint Paqeidas a Gérasa," *RB* 49 [1940]: 98–129). On the second temple, see C. S. Fisher, "The Temple of Artemis," in Kraeling, ed., *Gerasa*, 125–138.

[119] Antoni A. Ostrasz, "The Hippodrome of Gerasa: A Report on Excavations and Research," *Syria* 66 (1989): 51–77.

[120] Aubin, "Jerash," *OEANE*, vol. III, 218; Welles, "Inscriptions," #65–71.

[121] Chester C. McCown, "The Festival Theater at the Birketein," in Kraeling, ed., *Gerasa*, 159–170.

[122] Kraeling, "History," 57.

[123] Jacques Seigne, "Jérash romaine et byzantine: développement urbain d'une ville provinciale orientale," 331–341 in Adnan Hadidi, ed., *Studies in the History and Archaeology of Jordan IV* (Amman: Department of Antiquities; Lyon: Maison de l'Orient Méditerranéen, Université Lumière, 1992).

[124] Meshorer, *City-Coins*, 94; Spijkerman, *Coins*, 156–167.

[125] Kraeling, "History," 56; on Helios, see also Welles, "Inscriptions," #195.

[126] Welles, "Inscriptions," #17–18.   [127] Ibid., #19–21.   [128] Ibid., #24–26.

[129] P.-L. Gatier, "Inscriptions religieuses de Gerasa," *ADAJ* 26 (1982): 269–275.

[130] Welles, "Inscriptions," #2, 10, 15, 121–123; Kraeling, "History," 44.

Who lived in the Roman-era city? The majority of the city's population probably consisted of Semitic inhabitants from the surrounding area. Quite possibly, some citizens had actual Greek lineage. Nabateans also lived there, as indicated by the veneration of Nabatean deities and a Nabatean inscription honoring a Nabatean king.[131] Inscriptions to Phoenician deities suggest that Phoenicians were also a component of the population.

Three first-century CE funerary inscriptions show that during or after the Revolt, Roman soldiers were either stationed or settled at Gerasa, for unclear purposes. The inscriptions, one Latin and two bilingual (Greek-Latin), commemorate members (all with Thracian names) of the *Ala I Thracum*, a unit known to have participated in the Revolt.[132] The Roman presence was not limited to the first century CE; three other inscriptions show that members of the Legio III Cyrenaicae were in Gerasa in the second or third century CE.[133]

Jews were a distinct minority, a fact obvious from their near invisibility in both the literary and archaeological records. Josephus mentions their presence and notes that Gerasa distinguished itself in its treatment of its Jewish inhabitants during the Revolt. According to him, "the people of Gerasa not only abstained from maltreating the Jews who remained with them, but escorted to the frontiers any who chose to emigrate."[134] The sparse material evidence for Jews in Early Roman Gerasa consists of architectural fragments found in early second-century CE fill which may have come from a synagogue.[135]

Gadara

Less is known of Gadara, ten kilometers southeast of the Sea of Galilee, than of Gerasa. Its prominence in the mid-first century BCE is demonstrated by Gabinius's selection of it as one of the capitals of his unions,[136] as well as by the city's coins, which, appearing in the first century BCE,

---

131 Welles, "Inscriptions," #1; Kraeling, "History," 3–39.

132 Welles, "Inscriptions," #199–201; Kraeling, "History," 45.

133 Welles, "Inscriptions," #211–213; cf. other Latin funerary inscriptions in #199–218.

134 *War* 2.480. The city's activity in the rest of the Revolt is unknown. Vespasian attacked a Gerasa (*War* 4.487), but Applebaum and Segal argue that this was probably not the Decapolis city, since it was never in Jewish hands ("Gerasa," *NEAEHL*, vol. II, 471), while Kraeling suggests that Vespasian attacked Jewish villages in the territory of Gerasa ("History," 45–46).

135 Aubin, "Jerash," *OEANE*, vol. III, 216; Applebaum and Segal, "Gerasa," *NEAEHL*, vol. II, 471. See the discussion of a later synagogue in F. M. Biebel, "The Synagogue Church," in Kraeling, ed., *Gerasa*, 318–324.

136 *War* 1.155, 170; *Ant.* 14.75, 91.

pre-date most Decapolis coinage. Gadara's pagan character is evident from Josephus's comment that its inhabitants complained about Herod the Great's harsh rule and his "violence, pillage, and overthrowing of temples."[137] Of the Gospels, only Matthew mentions it, locating Jesus's casting of demons into swine there, rather than at Gerasa.[138]

The site is under-excavated and under-published. Greco-Roman influence is reflected in a first-century BCE or CE Greek inscription on a pedestal mentioning a "guild of builders," and Latin funerary inscriptions refer to Roman soldiers from or at Gadara.[139] Other Roman-era remains include a cardo, a bath complex, a hippodrome, a theater, a street monument (formerly identified as a nymphaeum), and marble statues, but the exact dates of all of these features are uncertain.[140] City coins bear images of Tyche, Athena, Herakles, a river god, and the three graces.[141] In the second century CE, its inhabitants probably participated in the construction of nearby Hammath Gader (approximately three kilometers away), which had its own theater, colonnaded streets, and an elaborate bathing complex.[142]

Pella

Pella is located approximately nineteen kilometers south of the Sea of Galilee.[143] Though late traditions that Alexander or Seleucus I was its

---

[137] *War* 1.396; *Ant.* 15.217, 354–359 (quote from 356). At Herod's death, Gadara was passed to Syria rather than to Archelaus (*War* 2.97; *Ant.* 17.320).

[138] Matt. 8:28.

[139] Taha Batyneh, Wajih Karasneh, and Thomas Weber, "Two New Inscriptions from Umm-Qeis," *ADAJ* 38 (1994): 379–384.

[140] Svend Holm-Nielsen, Ute Wagner-Lux, and K. J. H. Vriezen, "Gadarenes," *ABD*, vol. II, 866–868; Adnan Hadidi, "Umm Qeis," *OEANE*, vol. V, 281–282; Svend Holm-Nielsen et al, "Umm Qeis (Gadara)," in Denyse Homès-Fredericq and J. Basil Hennessy, eds., *Archaeology of Jordan* (Leuven: Peeters, 1986), 597–611; Thomas Weber, "Gadara of the Decapolis: Preliminary Report on the 1990 Season at Umm Qeis," *ADAJ* 35 (1991): 223–231; Ute Wagner-Lux et al., "Preliminary Report on the Excavations and Architectural Survey in Gadara (Umm Qeis) in Jordan, Area I (1992)," *ADAJ* 37 (1993): 385–395; Thomas Weber with Rami Khouri, *Umm Qeis: Gadara of the Decapolis* (Amman: Al Qutba, 1989).

[141] Meshorer, *City-Coins*, 80–83; Spijkerman, *Coins*, 126–155.

[142] Yizhar Hirschfeld, "Hammath-Gader," *OEANE*, vol. II, 468–470; Michael Avi-Yonah, "Hammat Gader," *NEAEHL*, vol. II, 565–569; Yizhar Hirschfeld, "Hammat Gader," *NEAEHL*, vol. II, 569–573; Yizhar Hirschfeld and Giora Solar, "Sumptuous Roman Baths Uncovered Near Sea of Galilee," *BAR* 10:6 (1984): 22–40; Yizhar Hirschfeld and Giora Solar, "The Roman Thermae at Hammat Gader," *IEJ* 31 (1981): 197–219; Yizhar Hirschfeld, "The History and Town-Plan of Ancient Hammat Gader," *ZDPV* 103 (1987): 101–116. The synagogue uncovered by E. L. Sukenik dates to the fifth century CE (*The Ancient Synagogue of El-Hammeh* [Jerusalem: Rubin Mass, 1935]); the date of its earliest phase of use is unclear (see dictionary articles by Hirschfeld).

[143] Robert Houston Smith: "Excavations at Pella of the Decapolis, 1979–1985," *National Geographic Research* 1 (1985): 470–489; Robert Houston Smith, "Pella," *ABD*,

founder are unlikely,[144] its occupation extended back into the Hellenistic period and beyond. The charred remains of two houses[145] as well as burned soil and other remains[146] date to the approximate time of Alexander Jannaeus, perhaps collaborating Josephus's report that Jannaeus razed the town because it would not submit to Jewish customs.[147]

Most of the remains at Pella are from the Byzantine period, but some earlier constructions have been recovered. A small odeon and a nearby parvis and shops date to the late first or perhaps the early second century CE.[148] A bath complex, linked to a nearby spring by pipes, was constructed at some point,[149] and a nymphaeum, depicted and referred to on coins but not yet discovered, may have stood near the same spring.[150] Roman-era graves and grave goods have been discovered in two cemeteries.[151]

Religious life is attested vividly in two inscriptions. One, found on a column and dating to the second or third century, reads, "Dedicated to the Arabian Heavenly God and the gods who are worshipped at the same altar with him." Another, also found on a column and dating to the third

vol. v, 219–221 and "Pella," *NEAEHL*, vol. IV, 1174–1180; Robert Houston Smith, "Pella of the Decapolis," *Archaeology* 34:5 (1981): 46–53; Robert Houston Smith, *Pella of the Decapolis*, vol. I (Wooster, Ohio: The College of Wooster, 1973); Anthony McNicoll, Robert H. Smith, and Basil Hennessy, *Pella in Jordan 1: An Interim Report on the Joint University of Sydney and The College of Wooster Excavations at Pella 1979–1981* (Canberra: Australian National Gallery, 1982); Anthony W. McNicoll et al., *Pella in Jordan 2: The Second Interim Report of the Joint University of Sydney and The College of Wooster Excavations at Pella 1982–1985* (Sydney: Meditarch, 1992); Robert H. Smith and Leslie Preston Day, *Pella of the Decapolis 2: Final Report on the College of Wooster Excavations in Area IX, The Civic Complex, 1979–1985* (Wooster, Ohio: The College of Wooster, 1989); J. Basil Hennessy and Robert Houston Smith, "Pella," *OEANE*, vol. IV, 256–259.

[144] Smith, *Pella*, vol. I, 34–35.

[145] *War* 1.103–105; *Ant.* 13.392–397. (In *Antiquities*, Josephus interestingly refers to a city as Dion which in *War* he had called Pella.) On the burned houses, see Robert H. Smith and Anthony W. McNicoll, "The 1982 and 1983 Seasons at Pella of the Decapolis," *BASOR Supplement* 24 (1985): 21–50, esp. 29. Smith suggests that other evidence of this destruction may have been altered by later Roman construction ("Preliminary Report on a Second Season of Excavation at Pella, Jordan: Spring 1980," *ADAJ* 25 [1981]: 317).

[146] Robert H. Smith, Anthony W. McNicoll, J. B. Hennessy, "The 1980 Season at Pella of the Decapolis," *BASOR* 243 (1980): 1–30.

[147] *Ant.* 13.397. In *War* 1.156, however, Josephus specifies that Pella had not been destroyed by the Hasmoneans.

[148] Smith and Day, *Pella of the Decapolis 2*, 20–26; Smith, "Excavations," 478; McNicoll et al., *Pella in Jordan 2*, 120.

[149] Smith and Day, *Pella of the Decapolis 2*, 18; Smith, *Pella*, vol. I, 57–58.

[150] Abbreviations on a second-century and three third-century CE city coins refer to the nymphaeum, and images on third-century CE coins of an elaborate two-story facade with columns and a deity may depict it. See Smith, *Pella*, vol. I, 54–56 and Smith, "Excavations," 478–479; cf. Spijkerman, *Coins*, 215–216 and Meshorer, *City-Coins*, 92.

[151] Smith, *Pella*, vol. I, 182–195; McNicoll et al., *Pella in Jordan 2*, 124–144.

or fourth century CE, refers to the "Elders of Zeus-Ares."[152] A fragment of a statue (probably of a deity or the emperor) was found in the ruins of the civic complex, and an altar was found in the trash in the odeon.[153] The city's coins, minted for two centuries beginning with Domitian, depict Herakles, Apollo, Athena, Tyche, and Nike.[154]

Most of the city's inhabitants were probably from neighboring areas, though worship of the Arabian god suggests that Nabateans may also have been present. As for Pella's Jewish population in the pre-Revolt period, its size is unknown. Neither Josephus nor inscriptions attest to a Jewish presence there. Eusebius and Epiphanius report that Jewish-Christians fled from Jerusalem to Pella to escape the Revolt, and Epiphanius reports the activity of several Jewish-Christian groups in the vicinity of Pella.[155] A sarcophagus, designed and decorated in a fashion similar to Jewish sarcophagi found at several late first-century CE and early second-century CE Palestinian sites, may suggest a link to Palestinian Jews.[156]

Scythopolis

Scythopolis, located at the juncture of the Jordan and Jezreel valleys, was the largest city of the Decapolis and the only one located west of the Jordan.[157] It was built at the foot of an enormous tell, the result of centuries of occupation.[158] Persian figurines attest to a settlement's presence in that period, and ceramics and architecture, including portions of a third-century BCE amphitheater, remain from the Hellenistic city.[159]

[152] Smith and Day, *Pella of the Decapolis 2*, 132–136. Smith and Day provide an alternate suggestion for the second inscription, suggesting it refers to Dushara/Dusares (Δουσάρης), rather than to Zeus-Ares.

[153] Ibid., 119.

[154] Meshorer, *City-Coins*, 92; Spijkerman, *Coins*, 210–217.

[155] Eusebius, *Ecclesiastical History* 3.5.3–4; Epiphanius, *Treatises on Weights and Measures* 14B–15B and *Adv. Haereses* 29.7.7–8, 30.2.7–8; Smith, *Pella*, vol. I, 42–47. See differing views of these traditions in Gerd Lüdemann, "The Successors of Pre-70 Jerusalem Christianity: A Critical Evaluation of the Pella-Tradition," in E. P. Sanders, ed., *Jewish and Christian Self-Definition* (Philadelphia: Fortress, 1980), vol. I, 161–173 and Craig Koester, "The Origin and Significance of the Flight to Pella Tradition," *CBQ* 51 (1989): 90–106.

[156] Smith, *Pella*, vol. I, 143–149. Notably, the sarcophagus was discovered under the apse of a Byzantine church. If it originated in a Palestinian context, does it denote an early connection between the Pella church and Palestinian Jews, as per Eusebius and Epiphanius?

[157] *War* 3.446.

[158] Patrick E. McGovern, "Beth-Shan," *ABD*, vol. I, 693–696; Amihai Mazar, "Beth-Shean," *OEANE*, vol. I, 305–309; Amihai Mazar, "Beth-Shean: Tel Beth Shean and the Northern Cemetery," *NEAEHL*, vol. I, 214–223; Gideon Foerster, "Beth-Shean at the Foot of the Mound," *NEAEHL*, vol. I, 223–235.

[159] Gaby Mazar, Gideon Foerster, Yoram Tsafrir, and Fanny Vitto, "The Bet Shean Project," *ESI* 6 (1987–1988): 7–45, esp. 35–38; Shimon Applebaum, "When Did Scythopolis Become a Greek City?" in *Judaea in Hellenistic and Roman Times: Historical and Archaeological Essays* (Leiden: E. J. Brill, 1989), 1–8.

Most of Scythopolis's archaeological evidence is from the Roman and Byzantine eras, with very little of the pre-second-century CE city preserved. Tombs in the northern cemetery date to the Late Hellenistic and Early Roman periods,[160] and a little evidence of the Early Roman city remains, undestroyed by subsequent construction.[161] A monumental temple on the mound itself was in use in the first century CE; Greek epigraphic evidence found elsewhere at the site suggests it was dedicated to Zeus Akraios.[162]

The city's heyday, at least in terms of construction, was in the second century CE,[163] when an orthogonal city plan emerged and an amphitheater, a bathhouse, a palaestra,[164] and probably a nymphaeum with an adjacent columnar monument were all built. A second temple has been discovered in the lower civic center, and a theater seating 5,000 dates to the Severan period.[165] With its architectural features, Greek inscriptions, pagan cults, images, and statuary, Scythopolis, like Gerasa, stands distinct from both Sepphoris and Tiberias in the sheer obviousness of its Greco-Roman cultural milieu.[166]

Evidence of Olympian cults is prominent. One inscription (first or second century CE) is dedicated to Zeus Bacchus[167] and another to the "queen of all the earth."[168] Tyche is also mentioned in inscriptions, and fragments of a statue of Tyche have been found in the theater.[169] Hermes is represented by a marble bust and a head of a statue.[170] First-century CE coins depict Tyche and Nike, and later coins show temples and a variety of Greek deities.[171]

---

[160] A. Mazar, "Beth-Shean," *OEANE*, vol. I, 309.

[161] Gaby Mazar, "Bet Shean Project – 1988," *ESI* 7–8 (1988–1989): 15–32.

[162] Yoram Tsafrir, "Further Evidence of the Cult of Zeus Akraios at Beth Shean (Scythopolis)," *IEJ* 39 (1989): 76–78; Lifshitz, "Der Kult des Zeus Akraios"; and Henri Seyrig, "Note sur les cultes de Scythopolis à l'époque romaine," *Syria* 39 (1962): 207–211.

[163] *NEAEHL*, vol. I, Foerster, "Beth-Shean," 223–228.

[164] Gaby Mazar and Rachel Bar-Hathan, "The Beth She'an Excavation Project, 1992–1994," *ESI* 17 (1998): 7–38, esp. 12.

[165] G. Mazar et al., "Bet Shean Project," 19–22; Shimon Applebaum, "The Roman Theatre of Scythopolis," *Scripta Classica Israelica* 4 (1978): 77–105.

[166] Note also the statue of a man found in the theater (Foerster, "Beth-Shean," *NEAEHL*, vol. I, 226); the fragment of a statue with armor decorated with griffins, Medusa, and an eagle (ibid., 229–230); and the pedestal with a Greek inscription identifying the statue it once held as Marcus Aurelius (ibid., 227; Gideon Foerster and Yoram Tsafrir, "Nysa-Scythopolis – A New Inscription and the Titles of the City on its Coins," *INJ* 9 [1986–1987]: 53–58). See also the report of two (probably second-century CE) statues, one of Athena and one of an unidentified female deity, to the northwest of Scythopolis (Fanny Vitto, "Naharon, Tel," *NEAEHL*, vol. III, 1094–1095).

[167] Lifshitz, "Der Kult des Zeus Akraios," 186–190.

[168] G. Mazar et al., "Bet Shean Project," 29.   [169] Ibid., 21.   [170] Ibid., 18–19.

[171] Spijkerman, *Coins*, 186–209; Meshorer, *City-Coins*, 40–41; Rosenberger, *City-Coins*, vol. III, 27–38.

Dionysos-worship was particularly prevalent, a fact demonstrated by the city's alternative name, Nysa, which commemorates the burial place of Dionysos's nurse. Pliny the Elder refers to the city by this name, and the city's coins show that its people identified themselves as "Nysaean Scythopolitans."[172] Archaeological evidence includes an altar to Kurios Dionysos, decorated with masks of Dionysos and Pan, from 142 CE; a marble pedestal at the monument next to the nymphaeum, decorated with a bust of Dionysos (as well as images of Nereids and cupids); a statue of young Dionysos; and the frequent depiction of Dionysos on city coins.[173]

Scythopolis had a sizable Jewish population, though we catch glimpses of it only during political transitions and times of crisis.[174] During the Maccabean revolt, the Jews of Scythopolis pleaded to Judas to spare the city, bearing "witness to the goodwill that the people of Scythopolis had shown them and their kind treatment of them in times of misfortune."[175] The city's treatment of its Jewish population during the Revolt, however, displayed no such goodwill, if we trust Josephus's accounts. When Jewish raiders from surrounding areas attacked Scythopolis, the city's Jews participated in its defense. The other Scythopolitans, however, still leery of their Jewish residents, lured them into a nearby grove and massacred them.[176] Later in the Revolt, Scythopolis accepted Roman protection. A unit of cavalry was stationed there, and Vespasian used the city as a base for both the XV and the X legion.[177] The size and fate of the city's small surviving Jewish population in the aftermath of the Revolt is unknown, though, intriguingly, a dedicatory inscription to Zeus Akraios identifies the dedicant's father as Tobias – a Jewish name.[178]

---

[172] Pliny, *Natural History* 5.18.4, 5.18.74; David Flusser, "Paganism in Palestine," in S. Safrai et al., eds., *Compendia rerum Iudaicarum ad Novum Testamentum* (Assen and Amsterdam: Van Gorcum, 1976), vol. II, 1065–1069.

[173] Foerster, "Beth-Shean," *NEAEHL*, vol. I, 228–230; L. Di Segni, G. Foerster, and Y. Tsafrir, "The Basilica and an Altar to Dionysos at Nysa-Scythopolis," 59–75 in J. H. Humphrey, ed., *The Roman and Byzantine Near East*, vol. II; Lea Di Segni, "A Dated Inscription from Beth Shean and the Cult of Dionysos Ktistes in Roman Scythopolis," *Scripta Classica Israelica* 16 (1997): 139–161. See also Jesús M. Nieto Ibañez, "The Sacred Grove of Scythopolis (Flavius Josephus, *Jewish War* II 466–471)," *IEJ* 49 (1999): 466–471.

[174] See Gideon Fuks, "The Jews of Hellenistic and Roman Scythopolis," *JJS* 33 (1982): 407–416. Three first-century Greek-Hebrew inscriptions show that some Scythopolitan Jews were buried at Jerusalem.

[175] 2 Macc. 12:29–31.

[176] *War* 2.458, 466–477; *Life* 26. Foerster suggests that a mass burial of 142 skeletons is associated with this incident ("Beth-Shean," *NEAEHL*, vol. I, 234–235).

[177] *Life* 121; *War* 3.412 (cf. 446), 4.87.

[178] Tsafrir, "Further Evidence." The inscription illustrates the complexity of Jewish–gentile interaction. Was Tobias Jewish, with a daughter who participated in pagan cults?

The population mix for the city was probably similar to that of other Decapolis cities. Large numbers of locals, and perhaps a few Greeks, lived there. After the stationing of troops there during the Revolt and the arrival of the VI legion in the second century, Romans may have settled there. Byzantine legends explained the name "Scythopolis" by positing that Scythians had originally settled the town. No earlier literary evidence or physical remains corroborate this claim, but it is possible that Scythian soldiers or mercenaries were among its early settlers.[179]

The coastal area

The coast was primarily Phoenician territory, and by the first century CE, its cities had long been influenced by Hellenism. Ptolemais and Caesarea Maritima were the chief ports in the vicinity of Galilee, though Tyre and Sidon may have overshadowed them in importance for the larger region. Dor was less prominent in the Roman period than it had been in earlier years, but it was still functioning. Most cities probably had Greek minorities in addition to their native Phoenician inhabitants. Romans were especially visible at Ptolemais and Caesarea Maritima, particularly after the establishment of colonies in those cities (in the mid-first century CE for Ptolemais and after the Revolt for Caesarea Maritima). Merchants from other areas were probably also established at the ports to operate trade and travel services for their kinspeople. Each city had its own shrines, and Mount Carmel, in close proximity to Ptolemais, was regarded as sacred territory with an associated god.[180]

As in the other predominantly gentile cities surrounding Jewish territory, Jewish–gentile relations were at times tense. Ptolemais, Dor, and Strato's Tower (the precursor to Caesarea Maritima) had been attacked by Alexander Jannaeus. He had failed to conquer Ptolemais but had taken the other two, and they remained in Hasmonean hands until Pompey.[181] At Caesarea Maritima, Jewish–gentile incidents occurred that

Or were both Tobias and his daughter syncretistic Jews who blended pagan practices with Judaism? Or, was Tobias a pagan with a Jewish name?

[179] Flusser, "Paganism," 1065–1068.

[180] Iamblichus, *Vita Pythagorae* 3.15 (late third/early fourth century CE); Tacitus, *Histories* 2.78; Suetonius, *Vespasian* 5. A second- or third-century CE Greek inscription, found on a votive foot, records a dedication by a colonist of Caesarea, Gaius Iulius Eutychas, to the Heliopolitan Zeus Carmel (Michael Avi-Yonah, "Mount Carmel and the God of Baalbek," *IEJ* 2 [1952]: 118–124; Henry O. Thompson, "Carmel, Mount," *ABD*, vol. I, 874–875; note also J. H. Iliffe, "A Nude Terra-Cotta Statuette of Aphrodite," *IEJ* 3 [1934]: 106–111).

[181] *Ant.* 13.393–397; cf. *War* 1.103–105; on Pompey: *Ant.* 14.75–76, *War* 1.155–158.

were instrumental in sparking the Jewish Revolt.[182] Caesarea, Ptolemais, and the Tyrian village Kedesh were among the targets of Jewish raids at the outset of the Revolt. Ptolemais and Tyre attacked their own Jewish inhabitants, though Sidon spared its Jews.[183]

Caesarea Maritima

Recognizing the gains a new port would bring in economic terms and in personal stature, Herod the Great built Caesarea Maritima.[184] He chose the settlement Strato's Tower, itself a port with a long history, as the site of his new city.[185] Initial construction lasted from *c.* 22 to 10 BCE, and the result was a stunning accomplishment. Its streets were laid out from the start on a grid system, and Josephus describes the typical features of a Hellenistic city: a pagan temple, a theater, an efficient sewer system, an amphitheater, palaces, and other public buildings.[186] Herod's construction of palaces and his use throughout the city of white stone displayed "here, as nowhere else, the innate grandeur of his character."[187] Its harbor, in particular, was a technical masterpiece, comparable to that at Piraeus, with three colossal statues on either side of its entrance. Archaeologists have confirmed the accuracy of Josephus's description: the temple platform

---

[182] *War* 2.266–294; *Ant.* 20.173–178.   [183] *War* 2.458–460, 477–480.

[184] Robert L. Hohlfelder, "Caesarea," *ABD*, vol. I, 798–803; Kenneth G. Holum, "Caesarea," *OEANE*, vol. I, 399–404; Kenneth G. Holum and Avner Raban, "Caesarea," *NEAEHL*, vol. I, 270–272; Avraham Negev, Antonio Frovo, and Michael Avi-Yonah, "Caesarea: Excavations in the 1950's and 1960's," *NEAEHL*, vol. I, 272–280; Lee I. Levine and Ehud Netzer, "Caesarea: Excavations in the 1970's," *NEAEHL*, vol. I, 280–282; Kenneth G. Holum and Avner Raban, "Caesarea: The Joint Expedition's Excavations, Excavations in the 1980's and 1990's, and Summary," *NEAEHL*, vol. I, 282–286; Avner Raban, "Caesarea: Maritime Caesarea," *NEAEHL*, vol. I, 286–291; Giordano Dell'amore et al., eds., *Scavi di Caesarea Maritima* (Rome: Lerma di Bretschneider, 1966); Charles T. Fritsch, ed., *The Joint Expedition to Caesarea Maritima*, vol. I, *Studies in the History of Caesarea Maritima* (Missoula, Mont.: Scholars Press for ASOR, 1975); Lee I. Levine, *Caesarea under Roman Rule* (Leiden: E. J. Brill, 1975); Avner Raban and Kenneth G. Holum, eds., *Caesarea Maritima: A Retrospective after Two Millenia* (Leiden: E. J. Brill, 1996); John Peter Oleson et al., *The Harbours of Caesarea Maritima*, 2 vol. (Oxford: BAR, 1989, 1994); Jeffrey A. Blakely, *The Joint Expedition to Caesarea Maritima Excavation Reports*, vol. IV, *Caesarea Maritima: The Pottery and Dating of Vault 1: Horreum, Mithraeum, and Later Uses* (New York: Edwin Mellon Press, 1987); Yosef Porath, Avner Raban, and Joseph Patrick, "The Caesarea Excavation Project–March 1992–June 1994," *ESI* 17 (1998): 39–82; Kenneth G. Holum, A. Raban, and J. Patrick., eds., *Caesarea Papers 2* (Portsmouth, R.I.: Journal of Roman Archaeology, 1999).

[185] Gideon Foerster, "The Early History of Caesarea," in Fritsch, ed., *Joint Expedition*, 9–22.

[186] *War* 1.408–414; *Ant.* 15.331–341, 16.136–141.

[187] *War* 1.409–412; *Ant.* 15.331–339.

has been discovered, the theater has been excavated and restored, at least one palace uncovered, the imprint of the amphitheater is preserved, and the harbor itself is the object of ongoing underwater excavations.[188]

Thus, Caesarea Maritima was a center for Greco-Roman culture from its inception. Its very name honored the emperor, and Herod built a temple, "visible a great way off to those sailing into the harbor," with statues of Augustus and Roma.[189] At the completion of the city, Herod instituted quinquennial games named after Caesar, the first festival consisting of music and athletic contests, gladiatorial combat, horse and wild beast shows, and other entertainment.[190]

By the time of the Revolt, Caesarea Maritima had grown to "one of the largest cities in Judea with a population consisting chiefly of Greeks," with a wealthy Jewish minority, according to Josephus.[191] The population may have contained some of actual Greek lineage, with roots going back to Ptolemaic and Seleucid reigns, but more likely Josephus's term refers to Hellenized Syrians and Phoenicians.[192] Herod's original settlers probably had included soldiers or veterans drawn from the gentiles in his service.

Romans were a visible element of the city's population. Herod probably employed at least a few Roman architects and artisans in his construction projects. After the annexation of Judea, Caesarea served as the center of Roman administration,[193] with only the brief interlude of Agrippa I's

---

[188] Holum and Raban, "Caesarea: The Joint Expedition's Excavations," 283. On the temple platform, see Holum, "Caesarea," *OEANE*, vol. I, 399; Lisa C. Kahn, "King Herod's Temple of Roma and Augustus at Caesarea Maritima," in Raban and Holum, eds., *Caesarea Maritima*, 130–145; Kenneth G. Holum, "The Temple Platform: Progress Reports on the Excavations," in Holum, Raban, and Patrick, eds., *Caesarea Papers 2*, 13–34; and Farley H. Stanley, Jr., "The South Flank of the Temple Platform," 35–40 in the same volume; on the theater, see Dell'amore et al., eds., *Scavi*, 57–246; on the palace, three articles in Raban and Holum, eds., *Caesarea Maritima*: Ehud Netzer, "The Promontory Palace," 193–207; Kathryn Louise Gleason, "Rule and Spectacle: The Promontory Palace," 208–227; and Barbara Burrell, "Palace to Praetorium: The Romanization of Caesarea," 228–250. At some point a shrine was constructed in the eastern seats of the amphitheater; three small rooms with niches for statues as well as votive feet have been discovered there (Rivka Gersht, "Representations of Deities and the Cults of Caesarea," in Raban and Holum, eds., *Caesarea Maritima*, 306–307, 310–311). On the harbor, see Raban, "Caesarea: Maritime Caesarea," *NEAEHL*, vol. I, 286–291; Oleson et al, *Harbours*.

[189] *Ant.* 15.339; *War* 1.414.   [190] *War* 1.415; *Ant.* 16.136–149.

[191] *War* 2.268, 3.409; *Ant.* 20.175, 178; on the population of Caesarea Maritima, see the excellent collection in Terence L. Donaldson, ed., *Religious Rivalries and the Struggle for Success in Caesarea Maritima* (Waterloo, Ont.: Wilfrid Laurier University Press, 2000).

[192] Josephus prefers the terms "Syrians" and "Greeks" in describing the city's pagan inhabitants; see *War* 2.266–270, 284; 7.361–363; *Ant.* 20.173–178, 182–184.

[193] In addition to the Josephus passages cited in the following discussion, see Acts 23:23–33; 25:1–13.

rule in 41–44 CE. From that time on, Roman soldiers and veterans were a constant presence. These troops were not, for the most part, from Italy, having been levied mainly from Syria.[194] Caesarea itself provided large numbers of recruits to the Romans as auxiliaries.[195]

Roman cultural dominance is visible throughout the city's archaeological record. Most of its epigraphic corpus is Latin, and one early inscription records Pilate's dedication of a temple to Titus.[196] Caesarea was an early advocate for Vespasian, honoring him with an inscription on its war-time coins,[197] and he rewarded its loyalty by elevating it to the rank of a Roman colony.[198] A circus was built in the first half of the second century,[199] and an inscription reflects the presence of a Hadrianeum.[200]

Evidence of pagan cults, in addition to that of the emperor, is abundant.[201] Late in the first century CE, a mithraeum was built in a warehouse vault, and it continued to function until the third century.[202] Statues of pagan deities were common, with numerous gods depicted.[203] The city's coins, which begin with the issue in 68 honoring Vespasian, bear images of temples and deities, including Tyche, a harbor-god, Ares, Apollo, Dea Roma, Dionysos, Minerva, Nike, Poseidon, Serapis,

[194] *War* 2.268.

[195] Many of the Roman troops stationed in Judea came from Caesarea and Sebaste. See Aryeh Kasher, *Jews and Hellenistic Cities in Eretz-Israel: Relations of the Jews in Eretz-Israel with the Hellenistic Cities during the Second Temple Period (332 BCE-70 CE)* (Tübingen: J. C. B. Mohr [Paul Siebeck], 1990), 225–312. Like Ptolemais, because of the Roman presence, Caesarea Maritima received Jewish delegations on occasion; see *Ant.* 18.57–59, 20.113–114.

[196] Holum, "Caesarea," *OEANE*, vol. I, 399; Bradley H. McLean, "Epigraphical Evidence in Caesarea Maritima," in Donaldson, ed., *Religious Rivalries*, 57–64.

[197] Meshorer, *City-Coins*, 20–21.

[198] Pliny, 5.14.69; Levine, *Caesarea*, 34–45; Millar, "Roman *Coloniae*," 26–28.

[199] Holum and Raban, "Caesarea: The Joint Expedition's Excavations," 284.

[200] Gersht, "Representations," 305.

[201] R. Jackson Painter, "Greco-Roman Religion in Caesarea Maritima," in Donaldson, ed., *Religious Rivalries*, 105–125.

[202] The identification of the structure as a mithraeum is secure: benches lined its north and south walls, fragments of an altar remain, frescoes adorn its walls, holes allowed light in, and a medallion with images of Mithra was found. See Robert J. Bull, "The Mithraeum at Caesarea Maritima," *Textes et mémoires*, vol. IV (Leiden: E. J. Brill, 1978), 75–89; on the first-century use, see Blakely, *Joint Expedition*, 150; Holum and Raban, "Caesarea: The Joint Expedition's Excavations," 284; and R. Jackson Painter, "The Origins and Social Context of Mithraism at Caesarea Maritima," in Donaldson, ed., *Religious Rivalries*, 205–225.

[203] Images of Apollo, Aphrodite, Athena, Asklepios, Hygeia, Dionysos, Ephesian Artemis, Isis, Serapis, Mithra, Tyche, and either Cybele or Nemesis have been found. See Gersht, "Representations," 305; Negev, Frovo, and Avi-Yonah, "Caesarea," *NEAEHL*, vol. I, 273–274; Rivka Gersht, "The Tyche of Caesarea Maritima," *PEQ* 116 (1984): 110–114; cf. Joseph Patrick et al., "The Warehouse Complex and Governor's Palace," in Holum, Raban, and Patrick, eds., *Caesarea Papers 2*, 71–107.

and Zeus.[204] A Roman-era inscription reflects the worship of Jupiter Dolichenus.[205]

Relations between the city's Jewish and gentile inhabitants were often uneasy.[206] Pagans rejoiced at the death of Agrippa I, who had briefly reunited Jewish Palestine.[207] They desecrated images of his daughters by placing them on the roofs of brothels, and public celebrations filled the city, with feasts, toasts, and libations to Charon, the ferryman over the River Styx.[208] Tensions escalated under the Roman procurators who arrived after Agrippa's death. Felix's governorship was marked by the beginning of a lengthy dispute c. 59/60 CE between Caesarea's "Syrians" and Jews for equal political rights (*isopoliteia*).[209] Arguments and inconclusive legal actions escalated into open conflict, which continued until Felix dispersed the Jews with his troops, killing and wounding many. The dispute was not settled until c. 66 CE, during the procuratorship of Florus, when Nero himself annulled the equal rights of the city's Jewish community. Josephus emphasizes the disastrous consequences of this decision: "For the Jewish inhabitants of Caesarea, when they learned of Nero's rescript, carried their quarrel with the Syrians further and further until at last they kindled the flames of war."[210]

The specific event that precipitated the Jewish Revolt occurred soon after Nero's decision reached the city. A synagogue abutted property owned by a "Greek," and relations between the neighbors were not good. A dispute with this owner intensified Jewish–gentile tensions, and these tensions exploded after Jews arrived one Sabbath to discover a prankster sacrificing birds outside the synagogue entrance. After exchanging blows with the man's gentile supporters, the Jews fled to nearby Narbata, taking their Torah scroll. Rather than punishing the Caesareans responsible for the sacrifice, Florus arrested the Jewish leadership for removing the scroll, and then offended the whole region's Jews by pillaging the Jerusalem temple for money.[211]

The desecration of the temple quickly led to outright conflict in Jerusalem between the Jews and Romans. On the same day as the Jewish

---

[204] Meshorer, *City-Coins*, 20–21; Leo Kadman, *The Coins of Caesarea Maritima* (Jerusalem and Tel Aviv: Schocken Publishing House, 1957), 49–62, 98–194; Hamburger, "Coin Issues"; Rosenberger, *City-Coins*, vol. II, 1–28, vol. III, 79–80.

[205] Levine, *Caesarea*, 3–38.

[206] Foerster, "Early History," 9–22; Irving M. Levey, "Caesarea and the Jews," in Fritsch, ed., *Joint Expedition*, 43–78; Levine, *Caesarea*, 1–33; Kasher, *Jews and Hellenistic Cities*, 256–265.

[207] Acts 12:19–23.   [208] *Ant.* 19.356–359.

[209] *War* 2.266–270; *Ant.* 20.173–178.   [210] *Ant.* 20.182–184.

[211] *War* 2.284–296.

slaughter of the Roman garrison there, Caesarea's pagan majority attacked its Jewish community. Josephus claims that "within one hour more than twenty thousand [surely an exaggeration] were slaughtered, and Caesarea was completely emptied of Jews," with survivors apparently enslaved. This massacre at Caesarea prompted Jewish raids on gentile cities throughout Palestine, including Caesarea itself.[212]

Dor

Despite Caesarea's growing prominence, the Phoenician port of Dor continued to function in the Roman period. Like the other coastal cities, Dor had a long history; in Greek mythology, it was associated with Doros, the son of Poseidon. Its coins depict Zeus, Tyche-Astarte, Doros, and Nike. At least two temples existed there, begun in the Hellenistic period but still functioning in the Roman era. A bathhouse and a small theater were also constructed in the Roman period, though apparently after the first century CE.[213]

The size of Dor's Jewish community is unknown. Fragments of stone vessels and stone tables reflect a Jewish concern for ritual purity,[214] and Josephus reports an incident involving the city's synagogue: when several men placed a statue of the emperor there, Agrippa II protested immediately to Petronius, governor of Syria, who intervened promptly on behalf of the Jews. Despite this Jewish minority, Cestius Gallus considered Dor safe enough to hold his Jewish hostages from Sepphoris there during the Revolt.[215]

Ptolemais

Ptolemais, so-named because of its Ptolemaic foundation, was the chief port for Galilee, especially prior to the construction of Caesarea Maritima and probably afterwards, as well.[216] Strategically located, it stood at the entrance to the "Great Plain," where the coastal road met the route crossing Lower Galilee just north of Sepphoris. The city served as a center for

[212] *War* 2.457–460.
[213] E. Stern, "Dor," *NEAEHL*, vol. I, 357–368; Ephraim Stern, "Dor," *OEANE*, vol. I, 168–170; Ephraim Stern, *Dor: Ruler of the Seas* (Jerusalem: Israel Exploration Society, 1994), esp. 261–318; Kurt Raveh and Sean A. Kingsley, "Dor: Underwater Surveys," *NEAEHL*, vol. I, 371–372; Ya'akov Meshorer, "The Coins of Dora," *INJ* 9 (1986–1987): 59–72; Meshorer, *City-Coins*, 16; Rosenberger, *City-Coins*, vol. II, 31–37.
[214] E. Stern, "Dor," *NEAEHL*, vol. I, 364.   [215] *Ant.* 19.300–312; *Life* 30–31.
[216] *War* 2.188–191.

gentile resistance to the Maccabean conflicts[217] but was a Herodian favorite, receiving building projects, including a gymnasium, at Herod the Great's expense.[218]

In the mid-first century CE, a Roman colony was established there.[219] Pliny (*Natural History* 5.17.75) attributes its establishment to Claudius, but a coin minted under Nero depicts him plowing with an ox, presumably establishing the boundaries of the colony in a ceremony. Standards of four Roman legions form the backdrop for this image, attesting to the strong Roman presence there. Because of the security provided by this colony, Ptolemais frequently served as a way-station for Roman troops arriving by sea or marching down from Syria en route to Judea, Galilee, or further south.[220] Roman administrators at the city were frequently visited by delegations from neighboring peoples, including Jews assembled to protest Caligula's attempt to erect a statue in the temple, Sepphoreans seeking Roman protection during the Revolt, and citizens of the Decapolis seeking relief from the attacks of Justus.[221] Ptolemais served as a major Roman base during the Revolt, with Vespasian, Titus, and Roman officers billeting troops there.[222]

Archaeology has shed less light on ancient Ptolemais than the literary sources (in no small part due to the modern city, Acco).[223] The Persian period is well represented, and Hellenistic remains include portions of a temple and a Greek inscription dedicated to Zeus Soter dated to 130/129 BCE. The Roman strata are poorly preserved, though remains from a few buildings, including a bathhouse (exact date uncertain) have been found. The city's coinage, which begins in Alexander the Great's time and continues into the third century CE, frequently depicts deities, including Tyche, Serapis, and Zeus-Heliopolites.[224] A mid-second-century BCE inscription to Hadad and Atargatis found nine kilometers away shows

[217] 1 Macc. 5:21–22, 12:47–48. [218] *War* 1.422.

[219] Meshorer, *City-Coins*, 12; Shimon Applebaum, "The Roman Colony of Ptolemais-'Ake and its Territory," in *Judaea in Hellenistic and Roman Times: Historical and Archaeological Essays*, 70–96; and Millar, "Roman *Coloniae*," 23–26.

[220] *War* 1.290, 394; 2.67–68, 187–203, 501–507; 3.29, 64; *Ant.* 14.394, 452; 15.199; 17.287–288; 18.120, 262–263; *Life* 213–215, 343, 410.

[221] *War* 2.192–203, 3.29; *Ant.* 18.262–263; *Life* 343.

[222] *War* 2.458–460, 477–480.

[223] William G. Dever, "Akko," *OEANE*, vol. I, 54–55; Moshe Dothan and Zeev Goldmann, "Acco," *NEAEHL*, vol. I, 16–23; Moshe Dothan and Zeev Goldman, "Acco: Excavations in the Modern City," *NEAEHL*, vol. I, 23–27; Avner Raban, "Acco: Maritime Acco," *NEAEHL*, vol. I, 29–31; Moshe Dothan, "Akko," *ABD*, vol. I, 50–53.

[224] Meshorer, *City-Coins*, 12–15; Leo Kadman, *The Coins of Akko Ptolemais* (Jerusalem and Tel-Aviv: Schocken Publishing House, 1961); Rosenberger, *City-Coins*, vol. I, 17–32, vol. III, 69–72.

that local gods had not been entirely subsumed into the Greco-Roman pantheon.[225]

Tyre

To the northeast of Galilee stood the ancient Phoenician port, Tyre,[226] about which more is known than its neighbor Sidon.[227] Tyre was famous for its cult of Hercules, who apparently was identified with the Tyrian deity Melkart. Herodotus commented on the city's temple honoring Hercules, and the Maccabean Jason sent representatives to sacrifice to him during the quadrennial games.[228] A first-century CE inscription naming two *agoranomoi* illustrates the city's blending of Phoenician and Greco-Roman culture. One *agoranomos* bore a Latin name, and the other, a Greek name, though the second one's father bore a Phoenician name.[229] Herod was known to visit the city, bestowing upon it several sizable gifts (including an agora, halls, temples, and porticoes) and employing Tyrian soldiers.[230] Jews did not fare well during the Revolt; at its start, the city killed or imprisoned its Jewish inhabitants.[231] In the second century CE, Tyre boasted one of the largest hippodromes (seating 60,000) in the empire and an impressive (170 meter long) colonnaded street, as well as an arched entry way, an aqueduct, and a necropolis.

Kedesh/Kedasa

Tyre's territory extended considerably eastward into geographical Galilee. Josephus speaks of Kedesh as a "strong inland village of the

[225] Michael Avi-Yonah, "Syrian Gods at Ptolemais-Acho," *IEJ* 9 (1959): 1–12.

[226] Douglas R. Edwards and H. J. Katzenstein, "Tyre (Place)," *ABD*, vol. VI, 686–692; William A. Ward, "Tyre," *OEANE*, vol. V, 247–250; Maurice Chéab, "Tyr a L'époque romaine: Aspects de la cité a la lumière des textes et des fouilles," *Mélanges de l'université Saint Joseph* 38 (1962): 13–40; Jean-Paul Rey-Coquais, *Inscriptions de la nécrapole* (Paris: Libraire d'Amérique et d'Orient, 1977) in *Bulletin du Musée de Beyrouth* 29 (1977); Maurice H. Chéhab, *Fouilles de Tyr: La Nécrapole* in *Bulletin du Musée de Beyrouth* 34 (1984), 35 (1985) and 36 (1986); Martha Sharp Joukowsky, ed., *The Heritage of Tyre* (Dubuque, Iowa: Kendall/Hunt Publishing Company, 1992); and Nina Jidejian, *Tyre Through the Ages* (Beirut: Dar El-Mashreq Publishers, 1969).

[227] Issam Ali Khalifeh, "Sidon," *OEANE*, vol. V, 38–41; Philip C. Schmitz, "Sidon (Place)," *ABD*, vol. VI, 17–18.

[228] Herodotos, *Histories* 2.44; 2 Macc. 4:18–20.

[229] The names are, respectively, Gaius Julius Jucundus, Nicholas, and Baledo (Edwards and Katzenstein, "Tyre," *ABD*, vol. VI, 691).

[230] *Ant.* 14.297–299; *War* 1.231–238, 275, 422, 543.   [231] *War* 2.478.

Tyrians" which was "always at feud and strife with the Galileans."[232] He provides no details of this long-standing tension, other than repeating 1 Maccabees's description of conflicts in its vicinity between Jonathan and Demetrius, including Kedesh in his list of towns attacked by Jewish marauders at the onset of the Revolt, and noting Titus's encampment at the city.[233] Few archaeological finds from the first century CE have been recovered, but second- and third-century remains include an impressive temple, the only excavated Roman-era temple in geographical Galilee. The building was sizable: the temenos was 55 by 80 meters, the inner building approximately 17.6 by 20 meters, the height 12 meters. Four Greek inscriptions show that the temple was in use as early as 117/118 CE and that it was dedicated to the "Holy God of Heaven," a deity perhaps associated with Baal-Shamin.[234]

Qeren Naftali

The inland settlement on the peak of Qeren Naftali, like Kedesh, is located on the Galilee-Tyre border. Surveys and partial excavations have revealed the presence of a fortress and, on the slope below, a village. Ceramic evidence suggests the fortress, complete with towers, casemate walls, and large, round stones (probably intended to be sent rolling down upon attackers), was built c. 200 BCE, perhaps by the Seleucids. Walls and enclosures surrounding it probably came from besieging forces. The history of the fortification is unclear, but it seems to have gone out of use

---

[232] *War* 4.104. See also *Ant.* 13.154, where he says it lies "between the land of Tyre and that of Galilee."

[233] *Ant.* 13.154, 162; *War* 2.459, 4.104.

[234] Asher Ovadiah, Moshe Fischer, and Israel Roll, "Kedesh (In Upper Galilee): The Roman Temple," *NEAEHL*, vol. III, 857–859; Moshe Fischer, Asher Ovadiah, and Israel Roll, "The Epigraphic Finds from the Roman Temple at Kedesh in the Upper Galilee," *Tel Aviv* 13 (1986): 60–66; Moshe Fischer, Asher Ovadiah, and Israel Roll, "The Roman Temple at Kedesh, Upper Galilee: A Preliminary Study," *Tel Aviv* 11 (1984): 146–172; Mordechai Aviam, "The Roman Temple at Kedesh in the Light of Certain Northern Syrian City Coins," *Tel Aviv* 12 (1985): 212–214. Jodi Magness suggests that the temple was associated with Apollo ("Some Observations on the Roman Temple at Kedesh," *IEJ* 40 [1990]: 173–181), but Ovadiah, Roll, and Fischer reject this suggestion in "The Roman Temple at Kedesh in Upper Galilee: A Response," *IEJ* 43 (1993): 60–63. Earlier studies include C. Clermont-Ganneau, "Archaeological and Epigraphic Notes on Palestine," *PEQ* 35 (1903): 128–140; Moshe Fischer, Asher Ovadiah, and Israel Roll, "An Inscribed Altar from the Roman Temple at Kadesh (Upper Galilee)," *Zeitschrift für Papyrologie und Epigraphik* 49 (1982): 155–158; and Chester C. McCown, "Epigraphic Gleanings," *AASOR* 2–3 (1923): 109–11. New excavations at Kedesh under the direction of Sharon Herbert will shed additional light on the settlement.

in the late first century BCE. The village below, most likely built after its abandonment, has yielded two Greek dedicatory inscriptions, one to Athena, carved on a lintel and dating to the mid-first to mid-second century CE, and the other, from the third century CE, to Zeus Heliopolitanus.[235]

Jezreel Valley

The Jezreel Valley (known in antiquity as the "Plain of Esdraelon" or the "Great Plain") separates Galilee from Samaria, and its inhabitants were probably drawn from both regions. Josephus describes Ginae, "on the border between Samaria and the Great Plain," as a Samaritan village, for example, while rabbinic traditions describe Kefar 'Otnay (the village at which the Romans established their second-century CE base Legio) as a village of both Jews and Samaritans.[236] To the east stood Scythopolis, and overlooking the western end of the valley stood Gaba, a predominantly pagan city established by Herod.

Gaba

Herod the Great established Gaba on the edge of Galilee, settling veteran cavalrymen there, probably to guard the entrance of the Jezreel.[237] Two inscriptions reading "Gaba," one Greek and one Aramaic, found at Tel Shosh make it the most likely site for the city.[238] Archaeological finds are thus far limited, consisting of a few inscriptions, a third-century CE jug spout in the shape of a dramatic mask, a head of Aphrodite, and parts of an aqueduct system.[239] Given Herod's employment of gentiles in his

[235] Mordechai Aviam, "A Second-First Century B.C.E. Fortress and Siege Complex in Eastern Upper Galilee," in Edwards and McCollough, eds., *Archaeology and the Galilee*, 97–105; for the inscriptions, see E. W. G. Masterman, "Two Greek Inscriptions from Khurbet Harrawi," *PEQ* 20 (1908): 155–157. Aviam proposes that the fortress shifted hands from the Seleucids to the Hasmoneans to Hasmonean loyalists opposing Herod the Great before going out of use. The pagan village below the fortress, in his opinion, reflects the shrinking borders of Galilee after Antipas's exile. The dedicatory inscriptions may have originated in a large building, no longer visible, described by an earlier surveyor.

[236] On Ginae, see *Ant.* 20.118; on Kefar 'Otnay, see *m. Git.* 1.5; cf. *t. Git.* 1.4, 7.9, *t. Demai* 5.3; *t. Bekh* 7.3.

[237] *War* 3.36, *Ant.* 15.294.

[238] Some have identified Sha'ar Ha'amaqim as Gaba (see chapter 3), but the inscriptions are compelling evidence for accepting Tel Shosh as the location. See Ayriel Siegelmann, "The Identification of Gaba Hippeon," *PEQ* 116 (1984–1985): 89–93; Götz Schmitt, "Gaba, Getta und Gintikirmil," *ZDPV* 103 (1987): 22–48.

[239] The inscriptions include the two Gaba inscriptions (one on a lead weight), a Roman-era Greek inscription granting the title "first of the city" to a certain "Abdagos Alexander," and a Greek inscription mentioning "the high priest." See Ze'ev Safrai and M. Lin, "Mishmar

army and the attacks Gaba suffered from Jews at the start of the Revolt, its inhabitants were probably pagans. Some of these inhabitants served as auxiliaries to Agrippa II during the Revolt.[240] The city's second-century CE coins depict the deities Men and Tyche. Men's veneration was rare in the Near East but common in Asia Minor; combined with the coins' images of soldiers with Phrygian caps, the honoring of this deity may indicate a Phrygian background for some of the original settlers.[241]

The region of Samaria

Much of Samaria was quite fertile, and so, like Galilee, the region was fairly well settled, with numerous villages.[242] Both Jews and Samaritans lived there in the first century CE alongside a substantial pagan population. Some of these pagans were descendants of the colonists brought in by the Assyrians, and others may have been descendants of Hellenistic settlers. Pagans were especially numerous in Samaria's principal city, Sebaste, and at Neapolis, a Roman city established near Shechem after the Revolt.

The literary sources depict great animosity between Jews and Samaritans.[243] The destruction of the Samaritan temple at Gerizim by John Hyrcanus heightened tensions between the groups,[244] and John's report of the Samaritan woman's comment that her ancestors worshiped on "this mountain," rather than in Jerusalem, accurately depicts the lingering rivalry between the two holy sites.[245] In the first century CE, Jewish

Ha' Emeq," *ESI* 6 (1987–1988): 11; Raphael Giveon, "Geva, A New Fortress City: From Tuthmosis to Herod," *BAIAS* 3 (1983–1984): 45–46.

[240] *War* 2.458–460; *Life* 115–118.

[241] Siegelmann, "Identification," 91; Meshorer, *City-Coins*, 38 (though Meshorer believes the coins belong not to Herod's Gaba but to another Gaba); and Rosenberger, *City-Coins*, vol. II, 43–47.

[242] Shimon Dar, "Samaria (Archaeology of the Region)," *ABD*, vol. V, 926–931; Robert T. Anderson, "Samaritans," *ABD*, vol. V, 940–947; Ron Tappy, "Samaria," *OEANE*, vol. IV, 463–467; Shimon Dar, *Landscape and Pattern: An Archaeological Survey of Samaria 800 B.C.E.–636 C.E.*, 2 vols. (Oxford: BAR, 1986); Shimon Applebaum, "The Settlement Pattern of Western Samaria from Hellenistic to Byzantine Times: A Historical Commentary," in Dar, ed., *Landscape*, 257–269; Alan D. Crown, ed., *The Samaritans* (Tübingen: J. C. B. Mohr [Paul Siebeck], 1989); Jürgen Zangenburg, *SAMAREIA: Antike Quellen zur Geschichte und Kultur der Samaritaner in deutscher Übersetzung* (Tübingen and Basel: Francke Verlag, 1994).

[243] R. J. Coggins, *Samaritans and Jews: The Origins of Samaritanism Reconsidered* (Atlanta: John Knox Press, 1975), 138–148; and three essays in Crown, ed., *The Samaritans*: Menachem Mor, "The Persian, Hellenistic and Hasmonaean Period," 1–18; Menachem Mor, "The Samaritans and the Bar-Kochbah Revolt," 19–31; and Bruce Hall, "From John Hyrcanus to Baba Rabba," 32–54.

[244] *Ant.* 13.255–256.   [245] John 4:20; cf. *Ant.* 18.85.

pilgrimage festivals were particularly tense times. During the pro-curatorship of Coponius (6–9 CE), a group of Samaritans had disrupted Passover by scattering human bones in the temple precincts, effectively shutting the temple down, at least temporarily.[246] The murder of one or more Galilean pilgrims passing through Samaria en route to Jerusalem during the administration of Cumanus (48–62 CE) resulted in armed conflict between Samaritans and Jews from both Galilee and Judea, as well as Roman intervention.[247] Against such a backdrop, Luke's report that a Samaritan village denied Jesus passage as he traveled to Passover plausibly depicts Samaritan attitudes toward Galilean pilgrims.[248]

Sebaste

Herod constructed Sebaste on the site of the ancient city Samaria.[249] The mixed population of the area went back for centuries. According to late traditions, Alexander the Great had introduced Macedonian colonists at Samaria.[250] While the reliability of this report is uncertain, it is clear that construction occurred in the Early Hellenistic period: round towers may have been built shortly after the arrival of Alexander. Epigraphic evidence suggests that by Hasmonean times, the city included a temple to Serapis-Isis. Pompey freed the city from Hasmonean rule,[251] and Gabinius rebuilt it.[252]

Herod named his new foundation in honor of the emperor and settled veterans there.[253] Most likely, Jews and Samaritans from the surrounding regions dwelt side by side with pagans. Like Herod's other foundation, Caesarea Maritima, Sebaste boasted a temple to the emperor, remnants of which have been recovered, including a platform, an altar, monumental staircases, and a fragment of a statue (probably of Augustus). Another temple was dedicated to Kore, and statues of that goddess, as well as of Dionysos, Apollo, and Hercules have been recovered. Both temples were attacked in the Jewish Revolt. True to its name, Sebaste remained staunchly pro-Roman, providing manpower for Roman auxiliary units.[254] Despite damage suffered during the Revolt, it prospered in the second and third centuries, with many of the typical features of a Hellenistic city – a

---

[246] *Ant.* 18.29–30.   [247] *War* 2.232–246, *Ant.* 20.118–136; Tacitus, *Annals* 12.54.
[248] Luke 9:52–53.   [249] James D. Purvis, "Samaria (City)," *ABD*, vol. v, 915–921.
[250] Eusebius, *Chron.* 123; Curtius Rufus 4.8.9–11.   [251] *Ant.* 14.75, *War* 1.156.
[252] *Ant.* 14.87–88, *War* 1.166.
[253] Meshorer suggests that Herod minted coins at Samaria between 40 and 37 BCE (*Ancient Jewish Coinage*, vol. II, 11, 235).
[254] See discussion in Kasher, *Jews and Hellenistic Cities*, 225–312.

stadium, a gate, a theater, a basilica, and an aqueduct. The city's coins, unsurprisingly, depict deities.[255]

Neapolis

Vespasian established Neapolis at the foot of Mount Gerizim after the Revolt, naming it "Flavia Neapolis in Samaria," according to its earliest coins (issued in 81 CE). Not unexpectedly, most archaeological evidence dates to the second century and later. By early in that century, Neapolis had a hippodrome, theater, and public buildings, and an inscription from 123–124 CE suggests that it had a Greek constitution. On the northern slope of the mountain at Tel er-Ras, Hadrian built a temple to Zeus Hypsistos, which was accessed by a flight of hundreds of stairs. An image of the temple appears on mid-second-century coins, and excavations have also recovered remains from it. The city was granted the status of a Roman colony in 244 CE.[256]

Galilee and the neighboring areas

How much contact would Galileans have had with the peoples of these surrounding areas? The question is a significant one. Even though the evidence suggests that Galilee's own population was primarily Jewish, perhaps the region's "multicultural" reputation in scholarship would be justified if most of its inhabitants frequently encountered nearby gentiles, either on their own travels or as gentiles crossed Galilean territory. If the suggestion that major roads ran near or through Galilee is correct, then it is possible that Galileans met travellers from not only nearby regions but also more distant lands.

The chief difficulty in characterizing Early Roman Galilee's interactions (whether in terms of quality of relations or frequency of contact) with its neighbors or with people from further away is that, for the most part, literary sources are silent about the nature of "everyday contact." Josephus, our chief source, typically reports crisis, conflict, turmoil or political change, leaving the mundane undescribed.

---

[255] Meshorer, *City-Coins*, 44–45; Rosenberger, *City-Coins*, vol. III, 54–60.
[256] Applebaum, "Settlement Pattern," 262; Itzhak Magen, "Gerizim, Mount," *NEAEHL*, vol. II, 484–493; Itzhak Magen, "Shechem: Neapolis," *NEAEHL*, vol. IV, 1354–1359; Robert J. Bull, "Ras, Tell er- ," *OEANE*, vol. IV, 407–409; Robert J. Bull, "A Preliminary Excavation of the Hadrianic Temple at Tell-er Ras on Mt. Gerizim," *AJA* 71 (1967): 387–393; Robert J. Bull, "The Excavation of Tell er-Ras on Mt. Gerizim," *BA* 31 (1968): 58–72; Meshorer, *City-Coins*, 48–49; Rosenberger, *City-Coins*, vol. III, 5–26.

A summary of what we know of Galilee's relationship with Tyre illustrates the limits of our knowledge. Galilee's Jews were probably in touch with the Jewish community of Tyre. On a political level, however, Galilee and Tyre experienced occasional difficulties. In the last days of the Hasmonean kingdom, while Antigonus battled Herod, Marion of Tyre invaded Galilee and placed garrisons in three fortresses there. Herod routed the Tyrians and attempted to establish a more cordial relationship with the city.[257] Acts mentions a dispute between Agrippa I and the cities of Tyre and Sidon, though it provides no details about its nature.[258] The border between Tyre and Galilee shifted from time to time; Josephus describes Mount Carmel as Tyrian territory, for example, though he notes that it formerly belonged to Galilee.[259] Josephus includes the Tyrian settlement Kedesh among the villages sacked by Jews at the start of the Revolt, and he is quick to note that Galilee had a history of conflict with it.[260] Such events suggest that everyday relationships between Galilean villages and Tyre and its *komai* were occasionally strained. Despite this strain, however, Galilee and Tyre undoubtedly traded with each other.[261]

Our information about Galilee's dealings with other nearby cities is similarly limited. We can imagine the joy of the Decapolis cities when they were freed from Hasmonean rule and rebuilt by Pompey and Gabinius, joy evidenced by the dating systems on their coins, but we cannot gauge any lingering, consistent, enduring anti-Jewish hostility that affected their dealings with Galilee. Josephus writes of Jewish–gentile tensions within Dor and Caesarea Maritima in the years preceding the Revolt, but not of Galilean Jews' regular relations with the cities.[262] Though he reports one conflict between Galileans and Samaritans, he does not explicitly note the safety or danger typically involved with travel outside of Galilee. When the Revolt begins, Josephus portrays Jews from communities all over Palestine – Galilee, Judea, and Perea – lashing out in every direction against nearby predominantly gentile cities, with many of these cities retaliating by slaughtering their own Jewish inhabitants or attacking Jewish villages.

Josephus thus details the low points in relations between Galileans and their neighbors, not any type of norm. In fact, the conclusions we

---

[257] *Ant.* 14.297–299. Herod released captured Tyrian soldiers, giving them gifts (cf. *War* 1.238), sponsored numerous building projects (*War* 1.422), visited the city, and employed Tyrians in his army (*War* 1.231–238, 275, 543).

[258] Acts 12:20–22. Kasher suggests that it was a border dispute, and this is plausible, given Tyre's expansion eastward (*Jews and Hellenistic Cities*, 242).

[259] *War* 3.35.   [260] *War* 2.459.   [261] See discussion below.

[262] Kasher, *Jews and Hellenistic Cities*, 245–268.

can draw about "the norm" of Galilean contact with non-Galileans are limited and general. A review of road networks and economic contacts, as well as a consideration of the feasibility of travel and probability of regular encounters, shed some light on these interactions.

Galilee's road network

A well-developed road network rendered travel within Galilee and between it and the surrounding areas feasible (see Map 3).[263] Unfortunately, very little remains of the regional roads that connected village to village, but their presence is not in doubt. Ze'ev Safrai has mapped out the road systems connecting villages in the vicinity of Ḥorvat Ammudim, Arab, Chabulon, and Gush Ḥalav; similar systems must have connected other neighboring villages.[264] The wide distribution of pottery from Kefar Ḥananyah and Shiḥin to surrounding communities reflects the ability to travel within the region.[265]

The routes of the more significant roads can be traced. One branch of the ancient *Via Maris* ran along the Mediterranean, connecting Alexandria with Antioch in Syria. Two spurs of this highway cut across the Jezreel Valley, one running between Mount Tabor and the Hill of Moreh before heading to the northern tip of the Sea of Galilee and then on to Damascus, the other passing through Scythopolis, crossing the Jordan, and connecting with the King's Highway. The King's Highway ran along the fringe of the desert, linking Damascus to the north with Petra and the Red Sea to the south. These routes had served merchants, travellers, and armies for centuries.[266] The Romans gradually upgraded and paved portions of them for military purposes, choosing the segment between Antioch and Ptolemais as the first to be paved *c*. 52–54 CE.

---

[263] Isaac and Roll, *Roman Roads*, 1–10; Safrai, *Economy*, 274–289 (esp. 282–287); Strange, "First-Century Galilee," 81–90; E. Meyers, "Archaeological Response," 17–26; Zvi Ilan, "Eastern Galilee, Survey of Roman Roads," *ESI* 9 (1989–1990): 14–16; Israel Roll, "Survey of Roman Roads in Lower Galilee," *ESI* 14 (1994): 38–40; Strickert, *Bethsaida*, 36–41; McCollough and Edwards, "Transformations of Space," 135–142; the dated but still useful discussion in Avi-Yonah, *The Holy Land*, 181–187; and Israel Roll, "Roman Roads to Caesarea Maritima," in Raban and Holum, eds., *Caesarea Maritima*, 549–558.

[264] Safrai, *Economy*, 282–287. Safrai does not provide specific information on the dates of the archaeological remains of these roads, but they are probably representative of first-century networks. Samaria's road system is better preserved and is most likely similar to that of Galilee (Dar, *Landscape*, vol. I, 126–146).

[265] Strange, "First-Century Galilee," 82–84.

[266] Isaac and Roll, *Roman Roads*, 2–4; Yohanan Aharoni, *The Land of the Bible: A Historical Geography* (Philadelphia: The Westminster Press, 1967), 41–52.

East–west routes in the area generally followed the valleys.[267] Inscriptions from numerous milestones indicate that they were paved after the arrival of Roman troops in the region (especially during Hadrian's reign), but their existence prior to that can be assumed. One originated at Gerasa and ran through Pella to Scythopolis, crossing the Jezreel Valley and branching off to Ptolemais and Caesarea Maritima. It thus served to connect the *Via Maris* and the King's Highway.[268] Another linked Tiberias with Ptolemais, passing just to the north of Sepphoris; a spur off this road ran southward to Sepphoris and then on to the Jezreel Valley route.[269] Portions of an additional east–west road have been found north of Chorazin, suggesting that a road ran from Acco to the northern tip of the Sea of Galilee and perhaps beyond. Josephus mentions roads connecting Galilee with the Golan cities of Seleucia and Gamla, which were, perhaps, related to the road above Chorazin.[270] Further still to the north, a road linked Caesarea Philippi with both Damascus and Tyre, passing by the Upper Galilean villages of Gush Ḥalav and Nabratein.[271]

The major cities in the region all appear to have been connected. Roads circled the lake, with one stretching further north to Caesarea Philippi, joining the Damascus–Tyre route, and another heading south down the Jordan rift valley. Hippos, Gadara, Pella and Gerasa (and, in the second century CE, Capitolias) all had roads extending to Scythopolis, which served as a hub for roads in all directions. Other routes connected the Decapolis cities to the King's Highway. Gerasa, situated directly on the King's Highway, prospered from its role in the caravan trade.

Galilee and the trade routes

The inhabitants of Lower Galilee, thus, were not far removed from important regional thoroughfares. At least one (the Tiberias–Ptolemais route)

---

[267] Isaac and Roll, *Roman Roads*, 118, 120.

[268] The strategic importance of the Jezreel routes can be seen in Herod's establishment of a veterans' colony at Gaba, which guarded passage between Ptolemais and Jezreel, and the Roman establishment of their base, Legio, at Kefar 'Otnay, on the road to Caesarea Maritima. The Romans paved the Caesarea–Scythopolis road during the Revolt, making it the first paved Roman road in the province Judea; the other segment of the *Via Maris* in the Jezreel was never paved. The significance of the Jezreel as an east–west passage can be seen in earlier troop movements, such as Vitellius's march through the Great Plain in 37 CE (*Ant.* 18.120–122). As for the Pella and Gerasa connection, milestones from 112 CE indicate its renovation, proving its earlier use (Isaac and Roll, *Roman Roads*, 7–9; note also their discussion of ancient sites along the Legio–Scythopolis segment in 87–91).

[269] A milestone indicates that the Sepphoris–Jezreel connection was paved *c*. 120 CE (Isaac and Roll, "Judaea," 54–66), while the Tiberias–Ptolemais route was paved *c*. 135 CE (McCollough and Edwards, "Transformations of Space," 137–138).

[270] *Life* 398–400; Strickert, *Bethsaida*, 36–41.

[271] E. Meyers, "Galilean Regionalism: A Reappraisal," 123.

and perhaps another (passing above Chorazin and running to Ptolemais) crossed through the region itself. The King's Highway was not too far to the east, and the *Via Maris* lay just over the ridges separating Galilee from the coast, with two spurs running through the Jezreel, one of which went through Galilee itself. Because of these routes, some scholars have suggested that Galilee itself was bustling with merchants going between the coast and the East and between Alexandria and the cities to the north. In such arguments, Galilee itself is sometimes implied to be the crucial thoroughfare for caravans from Arabia and perhaps India and China, journeying to the ports of the Mediterranean. If this image is accurate, Galileans (particularly Lower Galileans), would have regularly met foreign traders, some, perhaps, from exotic locales to the east, others from the Hellenistic cities surrounding Galilee.[272]

This, in fact, does not seem to have been the case – at least not on any large scale. Despite the proximity of these major highways, it is highly unlikely that huge quantities of imported goods and numerous caravans moved through Galilee en route to elsewhere. The greater probability is that most "international" trade in the Roman period bypassed Galilee altogether. The spices, silk, gems, and other luxury items of China and India seem to have been transported primarily either through Mesopotamia to Syrian Antioch, or by ship to the Red Sea. Those sent by ship were deposited either in Alexandria, for the next leg of their journey, or at the Nabatean port, Aila. Goods arriving at Aila were carried either north through Petra along the King's Highway or northwest to the southern Palestinian port of Gaza. As for Arabian imports, caravans moved most of them through the desert to Damascus, relying on the King's Highway for north–south travel. Since most eastern trade occurred along these routes, the branch of the *Via Maris* running through the Jezreel, up to the Sea of Galilee, and on to Damascus does not seem to have been the route of choice for caravan traffic.[273]

Some eastern imports presumably made their way into Galilee, but these would have been for consumption by the wealthy, not for transit to

---

[272] Cf. Overman, "Who Were the First Urban Christians?" 161; Goodman, *State and Society*, 17; Freyne, *Galilee, Jesus and the Gospels*, 156; Dalman, *Sacred Sites*, 10–11, 62–63.

[273] Lionel Casson, "Rome's Trade with the East: The Sea Voyage to Africa and India," in *Ancient Trade and Society* (Detroit: Wayne State University Press, 1984), 182–198; Lionel Casson, "China and the West," in ibid., 247–272; Ajoy Kumar Singh, *Indo-Roman Trade* (New Delhi: Commonwealth Publishers, 1988), 20; E. H. Warmington, *The Commerce Between the Roman Empire and India* (Delhi: Vikas Publishing House Pvt. Ltd, 1974), 6–34; J. Innes Miller, *The Spice Trade of the Roman Empire: 29 B.C. to A.D. 641* (Oxford: Clarendon Press, 1969), 119–152; M. P. Charlesworth, *Trade Routes and Commerce of the Roman Empire*, 2nd. rev. edn. (Chicago: Ares Publishers, 1926), 35–74, 97–112; Safrai, *Economy*, 269–274.

the coastal cities. Ptolemais was a "seaside city of Galilee,"[274] not the chief port of the Roman Near East, and Caesarea Maritima, while important, served primarily as a port for Palestine, not as a major junction for eastern trade. These two cities facilitated trade with the Mediterranean, not with Arabia, India, and China. Other ports – Aila, Gaza, Alexandria, and, because of its link with Damascus, Tyre – received the bulk of the goods from the East.

Thus, the thoroughfares through Galilee and the Jezreel probably did not see much "international" trade coming from and going to Arabia and Asia. There is no indication in either the contemporary literary sources or the archaeological record that Galilee's roads were the preferred routes for ancient caravan traffic from afar. Instead, the most significant function of these roads was to facilitate trade and travel between the larger region (both Galilee and other nearby areas) and the coast, between Galilee and its immediate neighbors, and within Galilee itself.[275] Galilee's own trade went through Ptolemais, Tyre, Sidon, and Caesarea Maritima; more frequent rabbinic references to the first three cities may suggest they were the more significant trading partners for Galilee.[276] Some of the Decapolis's trade may have moved along the presumed route from the northern tip of the Sea of Galilee to Ptolemais or across the Sea of Galilee, to Tiberias and on through Lower Galilee to Ptolemais. Given the convergence of roads at Scythopolis, however, most of the Transjordan's trade probably went through it and then through the Jezreel to Caesarea Maritima.[277] Caesarea Maritima seems to have overshadowed Ptolemais as the chief port for the rest of northern and central Palestine, if not for Galilee itself; in the second century CE, Roman roads probably connected it with Gaba, Legio, Ginae, Samaria, Neapolis, and Antipatris.[278]

Galilee's own trade

That Galilee participated in both inter-regional and regional trade is beyond doubt.[279] In the Late Hellenistic and Early Roman eras, some

[274] *War* 2.188.

[275] These routes were paved to facilitate the movement of Roman troops, not goods or travelers. On trade in Roman Israel, see Safrai, *Economy*, 222–231. On the "internal trade" of Galilee, see Goodman, *State and Society*, 54–63.

[276] Goodman, *State and Society*, 19.   [277] Isaac and Roll, *Roman Roads*, 6.

[278] The presence of these roads is inferred from discovered milestones; the complete routes have not yet been discovered (Roll, "Roman Roads to Caesarea").

[279] Sean Freyne, in several studies: "Herodian Economics"; "Geography, Politics and Economics"; *Galilee, Jesus, and the Gospels*, 155–175; *Galilee from Alexander*, 170–176;

imported products, such as eastern terra sigillata tableware, perhaps from Cyprus, made their way inland from the coast. Other imported wares, from Asia Minor, Cyprus, and North Africa, become more common in the Late Roman and Byzantine periods.[280] Rabbinic texts mention numerous imports of foodstuffs and other items, though the references are late and their usefulness in determining earlier trade networks is uncertain.[281]

Galilee had its own products to offer. With its fertile land, it could provide significant amounts of food, including wine and grain, to the surrounding cities, especially those on the coast.[282] Tyre was probably dependent in part on the hinterland of Upper Galilee for its agricultural produce; the claim in Acts that Tyre and Sidon depended on Agrippa I's territory for food is most likely accurate.[283] Strabo notes that the Plain of Gennesareth was a major producer of balsam, which was probably exported widely.[284] Josephus records an incident during the Revolt in which Syrian Jews sought acceptable oil from Galilee, "a special home of the olive," and this export of oil was probably not a one-time event.[285] Villages and cities on the Sea of Galilee supplied fish for the region, and the very name of Taricheae reflects its role as a supplier of salted fish. Such trade could have involved a considerable number of Galileans. The transportation of a large amount of olive oil, for example – bulky freight, whether in skins, barrels, or amphorae – would have required a sizable escort.

Exports were not limited to agricultural products and fish. Kefar Ḥananyah supplied common tableware not only to the villages and cities of Galilee, but to the surrounding areas, as well. About 10–20 percent of

cf. Horsley in *Archaeology*, 66–87 and *Galilee*, 202–222; and Edwards, "Socio-Economic and Cultural Ethos."

[280] Adan-Bayewitz, *Common Pottery*, 246. See, e.g., Dennis E. Groh, "The Fine Wares from the Patrician and Lintel Houses," in E. Meyers, Strange, and C. Meyers, eds., *Excavations at Ancient Meiron, Upper Galilee, Israel 1971–1972, 1974–1975, 1977* (Cambridge, Mass.: The American Schools of Oriental Research, 1981), 129–138 and Dennis E. Groh, "The Late Roman Fine Wares of the Gush Ḥalav Synagogue," in E. Meyers, C. Meyers, and Strange, eds., *Excavations at the Ancient Synagogue*, 139–148. It is important to recognize that the presence of such imported objects reflects Galilee's contact with the coastal cities, not necessarily contact with the imports' places of origin.

[281] Edwards, "Socio-Economic and Cultural Ethos," 60–61.

[282] Goodman discusses Galilee's resources as depicted in the rabbinic texts (*State and Society*, 22–24); see also Bösen, *Galiläa*, 44–52, 173.

[283] Acts 12:20–22.

[284] Strabo, *Geography* 16.2.16; Freyne, *Galilee from Alexander*, 172–173.

[285] Contra Horsley, *Archaeology*, 68–69. See *War* 2.591–594; cf. version in *Life* 73–74, where Josephus specifies that the Jews are in Caesarea Philippi. Thomas R. Longstaff discusses this incident in "Gush Ḥalav in the Ancient Literary Sources," in E. Meyers, C. Meyers, and Strange, *Excavations at the Ancient Synagogue*, 16–22.

the tableware of the Golan originated there, and the Golan's own forms imitated those of Kefar Ḥananyah.[286] Small amounts of Kefar Ḥananyah ware have been discovered in Early Roman contexts at Ptolemais and as far north as Tel Anafa. The village also exported pottery to the Mount Carmel region, settlements in the Beth Shean valley, Pella, Tabgha and Susita, though whether trade with these communities dates as early as the Late Hellenistic or Early Roman period is unclear. (Notably, no Kefar Ḥananyah ware has been found in Samaria, perhaps reflecting Galilee's alienation from its southern neighbor.[287])

Galilee's trade with neighboring cities is also visible in its numismatic record, which includes coins from the coastal cities, the Decapolis, and elsewhere. These coins have at times been over-interpreted; we have no way of measuring how many times they changed hands before being deposited at the sites where archaeologists discovered them. Tyrian currency provides an example of the difficulty of interpretation. Excavations in Upper Galilee in the 1970s recovered a surprising amount of Tyrian coinage, extending from the Hellenistic era through the Roman period. These coins were interpreted as an indication that the settlements at which they were found had extensive trade relations with Tyre, and that Upper Galilee, consequently, was economically oriented toward Tyre.[288] Subsequent research has shown, however, that Tyrian coinage appears not only in Upper Galilee but also in Lower Galilee, and an alternative interpretation of its presence has emerged: it is common in the region because of the sheer amount minted. To a certain extent, Tyrian currency flooded the market, far outnumbering the coins produced by other city mints. The discovery of Tyrian civic coins at a Galilean site is not, therefore, *necessarily* due to that particular settlement's direct trade with Tyre; it may simply reflect Tyre's and that settlement's participation in the same trade network.[289] Despite the complexity of interpreting numismatic finds at individual sites, the amount of Tyrian currency in Galilee as a whole probably does reflect a considerable exchange of goods between the region and that port.

[286] Adan-Bayewitz, *Common Pottery*, 165, 211–213. Because most of the finds in the Golan are post-first-century CE, presumably the 10–20% figure includes finds from later strata. Adan-Bayewitz notes that the copying of Kefar Ḥananyah forms begins as early as the latter half of the first century BCE (165–189).

[287] Ibid., 213–220.

[288] The major statement of this position is Hanson, *Tyrian Influence*; cf. also Raynor, Meshorer, with Hanson, *Coins of Ancient Meiron*.

[289] See especially Dan Barag, "Tyrian Currency in Galilee," *INJ* 6/7 (1982–1983): 7–13; cf. Horsley, *Archaeology*, 67–70 and Adan-Bayewitz, *Common Pottery*, 244–246. Note the use of Tyrian currency in John of Gischala's sale of olive oil in *War* 2.591–594; cf. *Life*, 73–74.

Coins originating from other outside cities should be interpreted like-wise. They may reflect direct exchanges with their issuing city, or they may reflect a common economic network encompassing the whole region, a network in which various city coins were used freely as currency. In either circumstance, they unmistakably demonstrate Galilee's links with its neighbors.

Clay oil lamp finds also illustrate Galilee's contacts with other areas. Archaeological discoveries of lamp molds are rare in Palestine, suggesting that a few workshops provided the bulk of the lamps. Thus, commonality of specific lamp types at sites in Palestine and the Transjordan most likely reflects interaction between these regions. For example, the "Judean coastal lamp with circular nodules," which was probably manufactured beginning in the early first century BCE in the northern coastal region of Palestine, is found at Meiron and Sepphoris, as well as Ashdod, Jerusalem, Masada, and Maresha. The "Palestinian round lamp with decorated discus" probably was manufactured in the northern Jordan Valley, perhaps near Scythopolis, and is found at numerous sites in the coastal plain, Galilee, Judea, the Negev, Samaria, and the Decapolis. Neutron activation analysis demonstrates that a sherd of a "Herodian" lamp discovered at Meiron originated at Jerusalem, according to its chemical composition.[290] The distribution of lamps illustrates the economic connections of Palestinian communities, at least in regard to this industry.

Everyday contact

What of casual encounters between Galileans and their neighbors? The same roads that facilitated trade facilitated travel. Perhaps some Galileans journeyed outside the region on occasion; Jesus's reported trips to the associated villages, if not the cities themselves, of the Decapolis, Tyre, and Caesarea Philippi are, at the least, plausible. Some Galileans made pilgrimages to Jerusalem for Jewish festivals, but we have no way to gauge with any accuracy how often; most Galileans could not have gone regularly, given the distance. Aside from these journeys, we know little of Galileans' travel habits, particularly in regard to trips of considerable distance. It is impossible to determine the commonality of "leisure travel" through Galilee.[291] We can generalize that extended trips, for any purpose, would have required both financial resources and large amounts of time,

[290] Lapp, "Archaeology of Light," 14–79. On the "Judean coastal lamp with circular nodules," see 28–30; on the "Palestinian round lamp with decorated discus," see 39–44; on the Herodian lamp fragment, see 22–23.
[291] See Sanders, "Jesus in Historical Context," 445–446.

so there was a class dimension to travel. Those with means could travel further and more often than could those without. The communication between Jews in Judea and Galilee and those in gentile territory provides a tantalizing glimpse of the inter-connectedness of the region's Jews, but, again, we are unable to determine much more than that the communities were in touch with each other.[292]

In the border areas of Galilee, in contrast to the interior, daily contact with inhabitants from the villages and cities surrounding the region can be assumed. The argument of proximity is persuasive: Galilean settlements were simply too close for neighboring villages to have been totally isolated from them. Consider the area around the Sea of Galilee. A thirty-minute walk from Capernaum brought one into what was during the time of Jesus Philip's tetrarchy. The population did not instantly and dramatically change the moment one crossed the border – witness the lack of clear evidence for paganism at Bethsaida – but nonetheless, when one crossed the Jordan, one was, in effect, entering into predominantly gentile territory. This was all the more the case the further one walked south along the eastern coast of the lake, eventually arriving at the Decapolis city of Hippos. Travel by boat was also a possibility, of course, as the trips of both Jesus and Josephus illustrate. On the sea, fishermen, merchants, and travellers from both sides of the water would have sailed past each other, and often. Contact was virtually assured by the relatively small size of the lake.

Likewise, encounters between Galileans and their neighbors in the Golan would have been fairly frequent on the fringes of Upper Galilee. Similarities in the material cultures of Galilee and the Golan suggest that the two areas were very much in contact with each other, though most evidence post-dates the Early Roman period. Residents of the border regions of Upper Galilee also would have had some interaction with villages associated with Tyre, such as Kedesh.[293] During the Revolt, John of Gischala was in touch with Tyre enough to recruit mercenaries from it.[294]

Contact with the surrounding peoples can also be assumed near the coast and to the immediate south. Ptolemais was only a few miles from

---

[292] As examples of such communication, consider Agrippa II's intervention on behalf of Dor's Jews (*Ant.* 19.300–312; *Life* 30–31); the request from Caesarea Philippi for ritually pure oil (*Life* 73–74); and Josephus's discussion of the deputation sent from Jerusalem to investigate him (*Life* 196–198).

[293] *War* 2.458–460.

[294] *War* 2.588. One wonders, however, if Josephus ascribed Tyrian soldiers to John of Gischala to show that John's support came not from the majority of Galileans themselves but from outsiders.

Galilee; its easternmost villages must have been quite close to Galilean settlements. Phoenician cultural influence was visible in western Galilee; when the Roman Cestius marched on the village of Chabulon, he found houses built in the style of Tyre, Sidon, and Berytus.[295] Gaba was a brief walk from Beth She'arim, and villages in the Jezreel were in sight of some Lower Galilean communities. The territory of Scythopolis also stretched westward into the Jezreel, though its extent in the first century CE is unknown. Most likely, Galilean dealings with Samaritan villages below the Jezreel were less common, though probably not unheard of.

Conclusion

Josephus's general statement that Galilee was "encircled by foreign nations" is borne out both by specific details in his writings as well as by numerous archaeological finds. Literary sources and archaeological data corroborate each other in the images they suggest of the surrounding regions. These areas were predominantly gentile, though all had Jewish minorities. The unanimity and clarity of the remains of paganism in these territories starkly contrast with the minimal evidence for paganism within the interior of Galilee itself. Given the impressive abundance of evidence for paganism in these areas, the glaring lack of similar finds within Galilee suggests that evidence is sparse there because pagans were very few in number.

Who were these gentiles living near Galilee? Josephus frequently refers to "Syrians," presumably the indigenous gentiles. Phoenicians lived in the coastal areas, Itureans lived in the Golan, and at least some Nabateans lived in the Decapolis. The cities contained some "Greeks," but whether these "Greeks" were of actual Greek lineage or were fully Hellenized locals is unclear. Romans were present in some cities, most notably on the coast, but also in the Decapolis. As with Greeks, whether "Romans" were of actual Roman lineage or were locals with a Roman cultural orientation is debatable.

How much contact did Galileans have with their neighbors? These regions were close together and Galilean border settlements were typically only a very few miles from the cities and villages of the adjacent territories. Though frequent contact can be assumed on the borders, there is no reason to believe that such contacts were the norm for communities in the interior. The road system made longer trips from Galilee to more distant cities possible, at least for Galileans with sufficient financial resources,

[295] *War* 2.504.

but we have little reason to think that the majority of Galileans frequently undertook such journeys.

The contact that is most visible in the archaeological record is commercial in nature. While this economic relatedness required a certain degree of interaction between merchants and traders, meaningful generalization about the frequency of such interaction between most Galileans, who were affected by, but not necessarily engaged in, trade, and the neighboring regions is nigh impossible. As for the claim that Galilee was a chief route for caravan traffic from near and far, the evidence suggests that by the first century CE, the chief routes bypassed Galilee, though some were not too far away. In short, some contact with gentiles did occur in ancient Galilee, and in communities on the Galilee's fringes, interaction with neighboring gentiles was probably common. But nothing in the literary or archaeological record suggests that such contact was especially frequent.

CONCLUSION

The belief that pagans made up a large part, perhaps even the majority, of Galilee's population in the first century CE – a view that has influenced generations of New Testament scholars – exists despite the evidence, not because of it. The image of Galilee that results from an integration of information provided by Josephus and the Gospels with the discoveries of modern excavations is entirely different. The vast majority of first-century CE Galileans were Jews. Pagans were a small minority. The various arguments scholars have proposed for a diverse population simply do not hold up to critical examination. In fact, when checked against the evidence, they fall apart.

Scholars have often claimed that Galilee's history of successive invasions by foreign powers resulted in an eclectic mixture of inhabitants. Galilee *was* ruled again and again by non-Jewish peoples, first by the Assyrians and later by the Persians, Alexander the Great, the Ptolemies, the Seleucids, and eventually the Romans. It did *not* undergo successive repopulation efforts, however. After the Assyrian conquest, it seems to have lain largely uninhabited until the Persian period. When resettlement began, it was slow, apparently consisting mostly of Phoenicians from the coast. Galilee's population under Greek rule probably also included Phoenicians, as well as a few Itureans (particularly in the northern regions), and some Jews. The repopulation of the region was gradual, occurring over centuries, and seemingly not the result of any intentional efforts by the various ruling powers, none of whom introduced a substantial number of colonists.

The conquest that did drastically affect the composition of Galilee's population was not one of the pagan annexations, but the Hasmonean takeover in the late second century BCE. Aristobulus I gave the gentile inhabitants of Galilee an option: live as Jews or leave.[1] While some gentiles may have converted to Judaism and others may have taken their

---

[1] *Ant.* 13.318–319.

chances by ignoring the Hasmonean directive, many fled the region. They were replaced by new inhabitants, apparently Jews from the south. Most of the first-century CE inhabitants were probably descended from these Hasmonean settlers. Thus, the region's political and demographic history suggests just the opposite of what many scholars have claimed. Far from creating an eclectic population, that history resulted in a largely Jewish population.

A site-by-site sifting of the evidence from the Late Hellenistic and Early Roman periods corroborates the picture of a Jewish Galilee. The Gospels mention only one gentile in Galilee, at Capernaum.[2] Josephus, whose intimate familiarity with Galilee is evident in both *War* and *Life*, also refers to non-Jewish Galileans in this period only once, in his discussion of the massacre of Tiberias's Greeks by Jews.[3] Galilee's material culture likewise reflects its Jewish character. Claims that recent discoveries in Galilee have illuminated its multicultural population in the first century CE are ill-founded. Gentiles are invisible in the archaeological record of most communities, particularly in the interior. Pagan inscriptions occur only on the fringes of the region, figurines are rare, and cultic sites (occurring only in the border areas) are either post-first-century (Kedesh) or purported but not proven (Bethsaida). For the vast majority of sites, if the Late Hellenistic or Early Roman evidence points to a cultural orientation for its inhabitants, that orientation is Jewish.

No other Galilean site has received as much attention within recent New Testament scholarship as Sepphoris, which has been hailed as the chief example of the region's multicultural character and mixed population. Yet, evidence for paganism there in the first century is virtually non-existent, and even the evidence found in second-century contexts and later is limited in quantity and often ambiguous. Jewish remains, however, are abundant from all centuries of the Roman period. The claim that first-century CE Galilee's cities had numerous gentile inhabitants is common in scholarship, but Sepphoris, excavated far more extensively than Tiberias, provides little support for this claim.

The scarcity of clear proof of pagan inhabitants in Galilee is all the more notable given the abundance of pagan remains in the areas around it, in such places as Caesarea Maritima and Scythopolis. If gentiles were a large proportion of Galilee's population, we would expect to find similar evidence in Galilee. We do not. Literary sources are explicit in their descriptions of the surrounding territories as predominantly gentile, in contrast to depictions of a Jewish Galilee found in Josephus and the

---

[2] See discussion below.   [3] *Life* 65–67.

Gospels. The appropriate conclusion for these contrasts is obvious: we find so little evidence for pagans in Galilee because so few lived there. This conclusion is more than an argument from silence. Given the remarkable differences between the information we have for Galilee and that for the surrounding areas, it is the most straightforward reading of the evidence.

Galileans would have occasionally encountered gentiles from adjacent territories. The region was small, and many Galilean communities were not far from neighboring territories. Such encounters were probably common in border areas, particularly around the Sea of Galilee. They probably occurred less frequently in the region's interior. As for the travel of Galileans, the road network made trips to adjacent territories possible, but nothing indicates that Galilean jaunts to the encircling cities occurred with great regularity. Presumably, such travel would have been more common on the fringes of Galilee, where the distances to nearby cities were shorter. The type of interaction between Galilee and its neighbors most clearly attested is economic contact. Numismatic finds reflect regional trade, much of Galilee's produce was exported (particularly to Tyre), and Kefar Ḥananyah's pottery was distributed beyond Galilee's borders.

Galilee's role as a crossing ground for foreign merchants and caravans has been greatly exaggerated. Obviously, traders used the roads passing through and near Galilee, most notably the route through the Jezreel connecting Scythopolis with Caesarea Maritima, but most trade from Arabia and further east bypassed Galilee. Galilee's road network does not demonstrate its centrality in Near Eastern trade. Instead, it illustrates that Galilee, along with Judea and Samaria, was connected by highways to the larger Levant region. Such connections were typical; Galilee was hardly the exception.

Roman troops arrived in Galilee *c.* 120 CE. They had entered the region before only in times of trouble, such as the Revolt. Their assignment this time, however, was long-term, and they remained there for centuries, bringing with them support personnel and families. Shortly after their arrival, Sepphoris and Tiberias minted coins depicting pagan temples and Sepphoris took the name Diocaesarea, actions reflecting the growing influence of gentiles in the wake of the Romans' appearance. Because of this new pagan presence, it should be no surprise that artifacts indicating cultic practices are discovered from time to time, though not frequently, in second- through fourth-century CE contexts.

In sum, pagans were a small proportion of Galilee's population in the first century CE. The presence of a few gentiles is incontestable, but their numbers and influence have been greatly exaggerated in much biblical scholarship. When discussing the particularity of Galilee's culture, there is no reason to emphasize a large gentile presence, whether as residents or visitors. An exceptionally high degree of Jewish–gentile interaction does not seem to have been a distinctive characteristic of Galilee.

Was Galilee known as "Galilee of the Gentiles?"

If most Galileans were Jews, why was the region commonly known as "Galilee of the Gentiles," as generations of scholars have noted? The most straightforward response, surprisingly, is that it was not. The phrase "Galilee of the Gentiles" very rarely occurs in ancient literature. The one-word name "Galilee" is far more common, occurring in the vast majority of ancient references, as a survey of the pertinent passages clearly demonstrates.

The origin of Galilee's name is uncertain. The word גליל is used only six times in the Hebrew Bible in reference to territory in northern Palestine (Joshua 20:7, 21:32; 1 Kings 9:11; 2 Kings 15:29; 1 Chronicles 6:76; Isaiah 8:23 [9:1]). It seems to have originally signified "cylinder," but it came to mean both "circle" and "district." Any (or all) of these ideas could lie behind its application to the region.[4] Perhaps the name derives from the geography of the region, a circular area surrounded by the plain of Esdraelon to the south, the Jordan rift to the east, the coastal plain (or the coastal mountain range) to the west, and the mountains in the north.[5] Of the six biblical references, only one, Isaiah 8:23 (9:1), adds הגוים to גליל. If the two-word name גליל הגוים pre-dates the use of גליל alone – which is not clear – it might indicate that at an early time in Israel's history, Galilee was known as a "district" of nations. Alternatively, it might reflect the Israelite experience of being encircled by gentile cities.[6]

In the Septuagint, the word "Galilee" occurs twenty-seven times, but only three of these references add a genitive phrase. The phrase Γαλιλαία τῶν ἐθνῶν in the Septuagint Isaiah 8:23 closely echoes the Hebrew גליל הגוים. First Maccabees 5:15 and Joel 4:4 have Γαλιλαία ἀλλοφύλων, but the geographical referent in both passages is the coastal region, not all of Galilee.[7]

References to Galilee outside the Bible are surprisingly few in number, especially before the third century CE. The earliest, pre-dating even the

---

[4] See especially Alt, "Galiläsche Probleme," 363–374 and Bösen, *Galiläa*, 15–17.
[5] Cf. Freyne's discussion of the region's geography in *Galilee from Alexander*, 4–9.
[6] Ibid., 3.
[7] See discussion of 1 Macc. 5:15 and Joel 4:4 in chapter 2.

biblical texts, may be the "K-R-R" mentioned in a town list of Thutmoses III (fifteenth century BCE).[8] As for Greek and Latin pagan literature, the few texts that mention it at all use simply "Galilee."[9] The earliest of these is one of the Zenon papyri, dating to *c.* 259 BCE.[10] The handful of other pagan references occur primarily in geographical discussions, mostly from the second century BCE through the second century CE.[11]

The phrase "Galilee of the Gentiles" is also uncommon in Jewish documents from the Second Temple period and immediately afterwards. In the non-canonical texts among the Dead Sea Scrolls, Galilee – not "Galilee of the Gentiles" – is mentioned once.[12] Philo's writings likewise contain only a single reference to the region, as "Galilee."[13] Josephus refers to it 161 times, but never as "Galilee of the Gentiles." It is never mentioned in either the Jewish or the Christian documents of the Latin and Greek Pseudepigrapha.[14]

[8] Jan Jozef Simons, *Handbook for the Study of Egyptian Topographical Lists Relating to Western Asia* (Leiden: E. J. Brill, 1937), list 1, #80; cf. Frankel, "Galilee," *ABD*, vol. II, 879.

[9] Claims about ancient Greek and Latin texts are based on word searches using the Thesaurus Linguae Graecae database (Property of the Regents of U. Cal., 1999), PHI 5.3 (Packard Humanities Institute, 1991), PHI 7.0 (Packard Humanities Institute, 1991–1996), and CETEDOC Library of Christian Latin Texts (Universitas Catholica Lovaniensis, 1996).

[10] See Victor A. Tcherikover and Alexander Fuks, eds., *Corpus Papyrorum Judaicarum*, 3 vols. (Jerusalem: Magnes, Hebrew University Press; Cambridge, Mass.: Harvard University Press, 1957) vol. I, 124, no. 2e.

[11] Alexander Polyhistor, *Fragmenta* 18 and 24 (in Carl Müller, *Fragmenta historicorum Graecorum*, 5 vols. [Paris: Ambrosio Firmin Didot, 1853–1870], vol. III, 226, 229); Posidonius, *Fragmenta* 87. 70 (in F. Jacoby, ed., *Die Fragmente der griechischen Historiker*, 4 vols. [Leiden: Brill, 1926; repr. 1954–1960], vol. IIa, 264); Strabo, *Geogr.* 16.2.34.12, 16.2.40.20; Pliny, *Nat. Hist.* 5.70.2; Aelius Herodianus, *De prosodia catholica* (6 times) (in A. Lentz, ed., *Grammatici Graeci*, 4 vols. [Leipzig: Teubner, 1867; repr. Hildesheim: Olms, 1965], vol. III.1, 93, 130, 252, 253, 312, 315), περὶ παρωνύμων (2 times) (in ibid., vol. III. 2, 887), *Partitiones* (in J. F. Boissonade, ed., *Herodiani partitiones* [London, 1819; repr. Amsterdam: Hakkert, 1963], 217); Claudius Ptolemaeus, *Geographia* 5.16.4. (in C. F. A. Nobbe, ed., *Claudii Ptolemaei geographia* [Leipzig: Teubner, 1843; repr. Hildesheim: Olms, 1966]); cf. the reference to Galilean–Samaritan strife in Tacitus (*Annals* 12.54).

[12] See 4Q522 (4Q Prophecy of Joshua), Fragments 9 + 10, Column 1, line 10, according to the enumeration in The Dead Sea Scrolls Electronic Reference Library, vol. II (Foundation of Ancient Research and Mormon Studies and its Center for the Preservation of Ancient Religious Texts at Brigham Young University, 1999); cf. the different enumeration as 4Q522 Frag. 8, col. 1, line 10 in Florentine García Martinez, *The Dead Sea Scrolls Translated: The Qumran Texts in English* (trans. Wilfred G. E. Watson; Leiden: E. J. Brill, 1994), 227.

[13] *Embassy to Gaius* 326.

[14] Cf. Albert-Marie Denis, ed., *Concordance Grecque des Pseudépigraphes d'Ancien Testament* (Louvain-la-Neuve: Université Catholique de Louvain, Institut Orientaliste, 1987) and Albert-Marie Denis, ed., *Concordance Latine des Pseudépigraphes d'Ancien Testament* (Brepols-Turnhout: Universitas Catholica Louvaniensis, 1993); Denis includes

The phrase is no more common in rabbinic texts. Of the hundreds of references to Galilee in the Mishnah, the two Talmuds, the Tosefta, and the pre-medieval midrashim, only three, all in the Babylonian Talmud, add הגוים.[15] These three references are found in two passages, both of which include discussions of Isaiah 8:23. In the first of these passages, the gemara of *b. Sanhedrin* 94B quotes Isaiah 8:23 (including גליל הגוים), relating it to Sennacherib's attack on Jerusalem. It then applies a midrashic interpretation to גליל הגוים: God pledges that he will make him (i.e., Sennacherib) "*galil* among the nations" (אני אעשה לו גליל בגוים). The Hebrew wording is ambiguous but seems to have a derogatory connotation, as suggested by Rashi, who interpreted גליל as a reference to "rolling" – that is, rolling in shame before the nations.[16] The other passage, *b. Sanhedrin* 104B, quotes Isaiah 8:23 in the context of a discussion about interpretations of Lamentations. Neither passage relates גליל הגוים to contemporary Galilee or its inhabitants in any way.

Thus, the phrase "Galilee of the Gentiles" occurs only a handful of times out of hundreds of ancient pagan and Jewish references to the region. The obvious conclusion to draw from this pattern is that the single word "Galilee" was the region's common name. Why, then, have the ideas persisted that Galilee was widely known in the first century as "Galilee of the Gentiles" and that this name reflects its inhabitants?

The answer to this question appears to be the influence of Matthew 4:15–16. Of the sixty-one references to Galilee in the Gospels and Acts, this one alone mentions "Galilee of the Gentiles," reading "Land of Zebulun, land of Naphtali, on the road by the sea, across the Jordan, Galilee of the Gentiles – the people who sat in darkness have seen a great light, and for those who sat in the region and shadow of death, light has dawned." Notably, this passage does not reflect Matthew's independent usage of the phrase; Matthew is explicitly quoting Isaiah 8:23 to show that Jesus, in settling in Capernaum, fulfilled an ancient prophecy.[17] For

---

quotations of Polyhistor (see note 11 above) in the writings of Eupolemus, a mid second-century BCE Palestinian Jew.

[15] I rely here on the Bar Ilan University Responsa Project 7.0 (1999) computer database.

[16] See Adin Steinsaltz, ed., *The Talmud: The Steinsaltz Edition*, 21 vols. (New York: Random House, 1989–2000), vol. XX, 139–140; cf. the interpretation as "the butt of the nations' scorn" and the accompanying discussion in I. Epstein, ed., *The Babylonian Talmud*, 6 vols. (London: Soncino Press, 1935–1959), vol. 4:6, 636.

[17] Matthew's quotation differs from both the Masoretic Text and the Septuagint. See Robert H. Gundry, *The Use of the Old Testament in St. Matthew's Gospel with Special Reference to the Messianic Hope* (Leiden: E. J. Brill, 1967), 105–108 and Krister Stendahl, *The School of St. Matthew and its Use of the Septuagint and Masoretic Text of the Old Testament* (Philadelphia: Fortress Press, 1968), 104–106.

Matthew, Jesus's presence in Capernaum is one more example of the correlation of Jesus's activity to passages from scripture.[18]

Matthew's quotation of Isaiah may serve an additional purpose, as well. Throughout the Gospel, Matthew hints that gentiles will eventually be included in the kingdom. Thus, he mentions gentile women in Jesus's genealogy (1:3–6) and tells of the recognition of Jesus's kingship by pagan wise men (2:1–12). Jesus proclaims that his message of the kingdom is for the "lost sheep of Israel" (10:6, 15:24) but acknowledges the faith of the gentile centurion at Capernaum (8:5–13) and that of the Canaanite woman from the coast (15:24–28). After the resurrection, the disciples are directed to make disciples of "all nations" (28:16–20). In this context, Matthew's quotation of Isaiah and its phrase "Galilee of the Gentiles" probably reflects his theme of the slowly unfolding mission to the gentiles. The words "Galilee of the Gentiles" alert the reader that even those "who have sat in great darkness" – the gentiles – will, in time, see "a great light" (4:16).[19]

The name "Galilee of the Gentiles" may have reflected social realities in Isaiah's time, but Matthew does not employ it to tell the reader about Galilee in his own time. It does not seem to have much correlation to any of Jesus's depicted activity in Galilee, which Matthew explicitly characterizes as directed to Jews.[20] Matthew's use of the phrase reflects his themes of prophecy fulfillment and the coming post-resurrection mission to the gentiles. Matthew 4:15 does not indicate that gentiles were a large part of first-century CE Galilee's population, and it does not suggest that "Galilee of the Gentiles" was a commonly used name. In short, Matthew's reference to "Galilee of the Gentiles" tells us about Matthew, not about Galilee. This verse has received more attention than it deserves in scholarly discussions of Galilee's name and population.

Matthew's usage re-introduces this ancient name for Galilee, at least for Christian circles. Because of Matthew 4:15, the name "Galilee of the Gentiles" occasionally appears in ancient Christian literature, but

---

[18] Cf. Matt. 2:1–6, 13–15, 16–18, 23 and 3:1–3. On Matthew's use of Isaiah 8:23, see the representative discussions in Ulrich Luz, *Matthew 1–7: A Commentary* (Edinburgh: T&T Clark, 1989), 194–197; David Hill, *The Gospel of Matthew* (Grand Rapids, Mich.: Eerdmans; London: Marshall, Morgan and Scott, 1972), 104; Davies and Allison, *Matthew*, vol. I, 379; Saldarini, *Matthew's Christian-Jewish Community*, 75–76.

[19] Gundry, *Matthew*, 59–60; Davies and Allison, *Matthew*, 384–385. On Matthew and the mission to the gentiles, see also Jack Dean Kingsbury, *Matthew* (Philadelphia: Fortress Press, 1986), 78–81; Hill, *Matthew*, 41–44. For an alternate interpretation, see Warren Carter, "Evoking Isaiah: Matthean Soteriology and an Intertextual Reading of Isaiah 7–9 and Matthew 1:23 and 4:15–16," *JBL* 119:3 (2000): 503–520.

[20] Cf. Luz, *Matthew*, 193.

almost always in quotations of, allusions to, and commentary on scriptural references. When not discussing Matthew 4:15, Isaiah 8:23 or Joel 4:4, however, most early Christian writers, like Jewish and pagan writers, referred simply to "Galilee."[21]

Jesus's homeland was known as "Galilee." The belief that it was frequently called "Galilee of the Gentiles" in the first century is one more scholarly and popular misconception. The phrase "Galilee of the Gentiles," appearing only once in a first-century CE source, and that a quotation of an eighth-century BCE source, tells us nothing about the region's population in the Roman period.

The Historical Jesus's contact with gentiles

What can be said of Jesus's interaction with gentiles? The Gospels preserve stories of only two specific encounters in northern Palestine (one in Galilee and one near the coast), though some travel narratives imply that others occurred.[22] Determining the accuracy of the Gospels' reports is impossible; in each case, the story may have originated not with Jesus but in the early church, to lend credence to the gentile mission.[23] It is worth noting that they are historically plausible, however, given what we know of social conditions in Galilee.[24]

Contacts within Galilee

The four canonical Gospels are unanimous in the depiction of Jesus as a traveling preacher and wonder-worker who visited numerous Galilean communities.[25] Jesus is said to have passed through Upper Galilee[26] but the Gospels suggest he spent most of his time in Lower Galilee. They

[21] For example, use of the databases mentioned above revealed hundreds of references to Galilee in Christian texts from the second–fourth centuries CE, but only 68 to "Galilee of the Gentiles." Of these 68, all but nine were in references to Matt. 4:15/ Isa. 8:23 or, in a few cases, LXX Joel 4:4. Clearly, Galilee remained the name of choice in Christian texts, as in non-Christian texts.

[22] Other encounters with gentiles are depicted in the Passion narratives.

[23] Cf. Sanders, *Jesus and Judaism*, 218–221 and John Dominic Crossan, *The Historical Jesus: The Life of a Mediterranean Jewish Peasant* (San Francisco: HarperSanFrancisco 1991), 328.

[24] Cf. E. Meyers, "Jesus and His Galilean Context"; Freyne, "Jesus and the Urban Culture"; Freyne, "Geography, Politics and Economics"; Freyne, "Archaeology and the Historical Jesus," 117–144.

[25] Summary statements of Jesus's activity (e.g., Mark 1:39/ Matt. 4:23; Mark 6:6/ Matt. 9:35/ Luke 8:1), while typically occurring in redactional contexts, probably accurately reflect the itinerant nature of his ministry.

[26] Mark 7:24–30; cf. Matt. 15:21–28; Mark 8:27–33; Matt. 16:13–23.

identify only a few specific locales by name. Jesus is frequently associated with Nazareth,[27] and Luke explicitly situates his synagogue sermon there.[28] John identifies Cana as the site of two of Jesus's signs, and Luke describes Jesus's resurrection of a widow's son in Nain, a short distance to the south of Galilee in the Jezreel.[29] Most of the Galilean communities mentioned by name are near the Sea of Galilee: Capernaum, first and foremost;[30] Bethsaida;[31] Chorazin;[32] Gennesaret;[33] and Magdala.[34] These traditions, combined with the frequent stories of Jesus's travel by or across the lake,[35] suggest that the Sea of Galilee region was the primary area of his activity.

Some interaction with gentiles from neighboring regions would have been inevitable near the lake. The Gospels, however, describe only one encounter. All of the canonical Gospels support, to differing degrees, the gentile mission; presumably, the authors would have reported more such incidents, if they had constituted an important part of Jesus's ministry.[36] The fact that only one story is preserved suggests that Jesus's activity was directed to Jews, as depicted in the Gospels, and not to Galilee's gentile minority.

The reported encounter is, of course, that between Jesus and the centurion at Capernaum, who asks Jesus to heal his servant. Both synoptic versions of the story (Matthew 8:5–13/ Luke 7:1–10) specify that the centurion was a gentile, presenting him as a model of faith and, thus, a foil for Israel: "Truly I tell you," Jesus declares, "in no one in Israel have I found such faith" (Matthew 8:11/ cf. Luke 7:9).[37] Assuming the historicity of this event, there is little reason to suppose, as many scholars do, that the centurion was a Roman officer, since Romans were not yet stationed in Galilee.[38] More likely, he was a member of the forces of Herod Antipas,

[27] E.g., Mark 1:9, 24; 10:47, 14:67, 16:6; Matt. 21:11, 26:71; Luke 18:37, 24:19; John 1:45–46, 18:5–7, 19:19. See Bösen, *Galiläa*, 110–145.

[28] Luke 4:16–30; cf. Mark 6:1 and Matt. 13:54.

[29] John 2:1–11, 4:46–54; Luke 7:11–17.

[30] Mark 1:21, 2:1–12, 9:33; Matt. 4:13, 8:5–13, 17:24–27, cf. 9:1–8; Luke 4:23, 4:31, 7:1–10; John 2:12, 6:24, 6:59. On the Gospels' references to Capernaum, see Bösen, *Galiläa*, 83–97.

[31] Mark 8:22; Matt. 11:20–24; Luke 9:10, 10:13–15.

[32] Matt. 11:20–24, Luke 10:13–15.   [33] Mark 6:53, Matt. 14:34.

[34] Matt. 15:39.

[35] E.g. Mark 4:35–5:21/ Matt. 8:23–9:1/ Luke 8:22–39; Mark 4:1/ Matt. 13:1; Mark 6:32–53/ Matt. 14:13–36; Luke 5:1–11; Luke 6:1–25.

[36] Cf. Sanders, *Jesus and Judaism*, 218–221.

[37] Cf. the similar healing in John 4:46–53, where a royal official at Capernaum approaches Jesus.

[38] See discussion of Romans in Galilee in chapter 2 and of "Capernaum" in chapter 3. The word is ἑκατόνταρχος in Matthew and ἑκατοντάρχης in Luke, not κεντυρίων.

who probably employed foreigners in his service (a typical practice of the day).[39] Perhaps he was a Syrian, though the text does not provide us with enough information to determine this with certainty.

Contacts outside of Galilee

Reports of Jesus's encounters with gentiles from other regions are also few in number. Mark reports one with a woman from the coastal area northwest of Galilee. In Mark, this incident occurs in "the region of Tyre" (τὰ ὅρια Τύρου) (7:24–30). Matthew follows Mark and depicts Jesus going "to the districts of Tyre and Sidon" (εἰς τὰ μέρη Τύρου καὶ Σιδῶνος) (15:21–28).[40] In both Gospels, the woman approaches Jesus and begs him to cast out a demon from her daughter. Mark identifies her as both a Syro-Phoenician and a Greek, while Matthew changes Mark's terminology to characterize her as a Canaanite.[41] Jesus initially refuses her request as "taking the children's bread and throwing it to the dogs," thus comparing gentiles to dogs, but ultimately accedes to her request and performs a long-distance exorcism on her daughter. Matthew adds his own themes of the exclusive mission to the "lost sheep of the house of Israel" (15:24; cf. 10:6) and of the reward for a faithful response (cf. the story of the centurion, above).[42]

The historicity of this encounter is plausible, if unprovable. According to Mark, Jesus goes not into the city of Tyre, but rather into the city's "region." Because of the proximity of Tyre's territory to Galilee – the Tyrian village Kedesh was well inland – Jesus would not have had to venture far beyond Upper Galilee to enter into Tyre's territory. Roads made

[39] Cf. comments of Josephus on foreigners in Herod the Great's armies (*Ant.* 17.198–199).

[40] Note that a majority of manuscripts add καὶ Σιδῶνος to Mark, bringing it in line with Matthew's version. Perhaps Matthew adds "and Sidon" to the story to make explicit the contrast between this woman's faithful response and the lack of such a response by Bethsaida and Chorazin (11:21–22; cf. Luke 10:13–14). Others suggest that he adds Sidon to echo biblical references to the two cities, such as Jer. 25:22, 27:3, 47:4; Joel 3:4; Zech. 9:1–4, Judith 2:28 (Davies and Allison, *Matthew*, vol. II, 267–268, 545–546; Schweizer, *Good News*, 329–330). G. D. Kilpatrick suggests that Matthew adds "Sidon" because he writes for a church in the coastal area near Tyre and Sidon (*The Origins of the Gospel according to St. Matthew* [Oxford: Clarendon Press, 1946], 130–134). On the possibility that Matthew situates this story in northern Galilee, see Saldarini, *Matthew's Jewish-Christian Community*, 72–73 and n. 17 on 249; Davies and Allison, *Matthew*, vol. II, 546–548.

[41] On Matthew's reference to the woman as a Canaanite, see Davies and Allison, *Matthew*, vol. II, 547; Beare, *Gospel*, 341; Saldarini, *Matthew's Jewish-Christian Community*, 73.

[42] Cf. Saldarini, *Matthew's Jewish-Christian Community*, 73–74; Davies and Allison, *Matthew*, vol. II, 542–559; David E. Garland, *Reading Matthew* (New York: Crossroad, 1993), 162–166; Meier, *Matthew*, 170–173; Stock, *Method*, 256–268.

such travel possible, and Jewish–gentile contacts would not have been unusual on the Galilee–Tyre border. The historical Jesus need not have been seeking contact with gentiles, if he made such a journey. He could have been drawn to Tyre's large population of Jews, of which we have ample evidence. In any event, the report of his presence in the territory of Tyre and his encounter with a gentile woman need not be automatically discounted as later tradition.[43]

The other reports of Jesus's journeys outside of Galilee may also have a basis in actual trips.[44] If Jesus ventured into these regions, contact with pagans would have been unavoidable. Like Tyre, however, all of these regions contained Jews, so such trips do not necessarily indicate any intentional outreach to gentiles.

The visits to Bethsaida[45] and to the villages of Caesarea Philippi[46] are not problematic. Bethsaida, technically a part of Philip's territory, was so close to Galilee that it was sometimes considered part of it, and the villages of Caesarea Philippi could not have been far from Upper Galilee. A lengthy trip beyond the borders of Antipas's territory would not have been required to reach either location.

Trips to the Decapolis area were equally possible. Even the seemingly awkward itinerary in Mark 7:31 – from the region of Tyre, to Sidon, south-east to the Sea of Galilee, passing through the Decapolis – may reflect an actual route.[47] Sidon had a common border with Damascus, a Decapolis city, in the first century. If Jesus passed from Sidon through the territory of Damascus en route to the Sea of Galilee, he would have followed the route Mark depicts.[48] The possibility remains that the journey is a Marcan invention, but the unreliability of the passage cannot be assumed without argument.[49]

In their references to Jesus's travels to the Decapolis, the Gospels record only one event involving local people, an exorcism.[50] While the

---

[43] Cf. Gerd Theissen, *The Gospels in Context: Social and Political History in the Synoptic Tradition*, trans. Linda M. Maloney (Minneapolis: Fortress Press, 1991), 61–80.

[44] Note that Jesus's travels to the Decapolis, Tyre, Sidon, and Caesarea Philippi are absent from Luke, possibly because they detract from his Galilee to Jerusalem schema.

[45] Mark 8:22–26; Luke 9:10. John (1:43–44, 12:21) and Ptolemy (*Geography* 5.16.4) place it within Galilee.

[46] Mark 8:27–33; "region" of Caesarea Philippi in Matthew 16:13–23. Luke 9:18–22 deletes the reference to Caesarea Philippi.

[47] See the skeptical discussion in Elisabeth Struthers Malbon, "The Jesus of Mark and the Sea of Galilee," *JBL* 103 (1984): 242–255.

[48] Theissen, *Gospels in Context*, 242–243. On Damascus and the Decapolis, see Pliny, *Natural History* 5.16.74 and Ptolemy, *Geography* 5.14.22.

[49] Cf. the differing views of Theissen, *Gospels in Context*, 244–245 and Freyne, "Jesus and the Urban Culture," 600–602.

[50] Mark 5:1–20/ Luke 8:26–39/ Matt. 8:28–34.

demoniac – or demoniacs, in Matthew's version – is not explicitly identified as gentile(s), his non-Jewish identity is suggested by the presence of
the herd of swine into which the demons flee. The garbled transmission
of the story makes it impossible to determine what city the exorcism was
originally associated with, Gerasa or Gadara. Neither city was located
beside the Sea of Galilee, making both names problematic, given that the
possessed pigs plunge into the lake and drown. The details of this story
aside, it is worth noting that Jesus could theoretically have traveled to
the region of either Gerasa or Gadara, though, of the two, Gadara was
much closer to Galilee.

Jesus's popularity with crowds from neighboring regions

Gauging the historicity of the Gospels' claims that non-Galileans flocked
to see Jesus is even more difficult than gauging the historicity of Jesus's
own journeys. The most pertinent passage is Mark 3:7–8, which depicts a
great crowd from Galilee, Judea, Jerusalem, Idumea, beyond the Jordan,
Tyre, and Sidon, all gathered to see Jesus. Mark's use of the story to
develop his themes is obvious. The diversity and size of the group reflects
Jesus's growing popularity, Jesus performs his characteristic healings and
exorcisms, and he issues his typical command to the demons "not to make
him known."[51] Whether Mark has taken historically accurate traditions
and adapted them to his own use or has created the story to illustrate
his own themes is debatable. In either case, he does not specify that the
crowds are non-Jewish; he only notes their places of origin.[52]

Luke and Matthew each contain a sweeping summary statement of
great crowds from diverse places, but both passages seem to be based on
Mark 3:8. Luke 6:17–19 depicts a similar group as the audience for the
"Sermon on the Plain." His description of the crowd maintains Mark's
references to Judea, Jerusalem, Tyre, and Sidon, while deleting those
to Idumea and "beyond the Jordan." Matthew omits Mark 3:7–12, but
he includes a similarly worded description in Matthew 4:24–25 which
appears to have been influenced by Mark 3:7–8. In Matthew, Jesus travels
throughout Galilee, preaching, healing, and exorcising, with the result that
his "fame spread throughout all Syria" and people brought to Jesus their
sick and demon-possessed. Matthew concludes the summary of Jesus's
activity by noting that "great crowds followed him from Galilee and the

---

[51] Cf. Mark 1:21–28, 40–45.
[52] Cf. Mary Ann Tolbert, *Sowing the Gospel* (Minneapolis: Fortress Press, 1989), 142
and Morna D. Hooker, *The Gospel According to Saint Mark* (Peabody, Mass.: Hendrickson
Publishers, 1991), 109–110.

Decapolis and Jerusalem and Judea and from beyond the Jordan."[53] Like their source, Mark, neither Luke nor Matthew explicitly states that these crowds are non-Jewish.

Jesus's encounters with gentiles

Jesus would have met gentiles during his ministry, especially in the area around the Sea of Galilee. If he traveled to the regions surrounding Galilee, as suggested by Mark and Matthew, then contact with gentiles would have been even more likely. Measuring how often such interaction occurred is impossible, but the scarcity of traditions reporting such encounters is striking. In light of this study's findings, however, this scarcity is somewhat more understandable. If, as depicted in the synoptics, the geographical focus of Jesus's ministry was Galilee, then the people he would have had the most interaction with would have been Jews. His Galilean environment should not prompt scholarly speculation that frequent contact with gentiles was formative in the development of his ministry.

The cultural atmosphere of ancient Galilee

A detailed discussion of the variegated issues of how "Hellenistic" and "cosmopolitan" Galilee was in the first century CE is beyond the scope of this study, but the foregoing review of evidence does allow for a few observations.[54] The strongest implication of my findings for that discussion is that we cannot cite Galilee's remarkably diverse population as one example of how deeply Greco-Roman culture had penetrated the region. In particular, we cannot look to the presence of Greeks, Romans, or other Hellenized pagans there as either a partial explanation for increasing Greco-Roman cultural influence or, conversely, a result of increasing Greco-Roman cultural influence. When we discuss the interaction of Greco-Roman and local Galilean culture in the first century CE, we must keep in mind that the local culture is predominantly that of Jews.

What were the original sources of Hellenistic culture in Galilee? The region had been exposed to it centuries before, first with Alexander and then with the Ptolemaic and Seleucid kingdoms. Population shifts after the Hasmonean conquest disrupted continuity with the earlier population, but

---

[53] Saldarini suggests that Matthew regards these crowds as Jewish, given Jesus's focus on Israel (*Matthew's Jewish-Christian Community*, 76).

[54] On Hellenism in Galilee, see Sanders's important article, "Jesus' Galilee."

it is worth noting that Hasmonean settlers themselves would have brought Hellenism to Galilee, given the influence of Greek culture in Jerusalem.

In the first half of the first century CE, the Herodians were the primary advocates of Greco-Roman culture in Galilee. Antipas's rebuilding of Sepphoris, with its basilical building and at least some streets on a grid, provides an early glimpse of the tide of Romanization that would eventually wash over Galilee. His naming it "Autocratoris" probably reflects his desire to flatter the emperor, as his naming his next city "Tiberias" clearly does. Antipas built these cities to increase his own political stature, following a route to higher status his father had taken before him. Herodian family members, supporters, administrators, and civic elites were probably his main allies in this process of urbanization.

Their success at disseminating Roman culture appears to have been overstated in some recent studies, however. With no Latin inscriptions, no evidence of veneration of Roman gods, no literary reports of a Roman presence, and only a few Roman architectural forms, pre-Revolt Sepphoris and Tiberias were hardly typical Roman cities. In the first century CE, we see a foreshadowing of the developments that were to occur after the arrival of Roman troops *c*. 120 CE, not full-blown Romanization.

In terms of their architectural features and epigraphic corpus, the cities around Galilee are quite different. Caesarea Maritima, Paneas, and Scythopolis, much more than first-century Sepphoris and Tiberias, stand as regional exemplars of the Greco-Roman city. Galileans living in the border regions near them would have had some awareness of their cultural atmospheres, though generalizing about the extent and impact of that awareness is difficult.

What about the use of Greek in Galilee? Galilee's first-century CE epigraphic corpus is quite small. Aside from coins, we have only a handful of other Greek inscriptions, such as the tomb-robbing warning near Nazareth and the market weights from Tiberias. Greek numismatic inscriptions tell us that royalist and civic elites wanted their coins to look like – and thus compare favorably with – the coins issued by other authorities in the eastern Mediterranean region; they tell us little about the everyday language of the common people. It is obvious that Greek loan-words and names (as well as occasional Latin names) were used in Galilee, and there may have been some competence in Greek for those living in border regions, those involved in trade with the coastal cities, and educated civic elites. The first-century CE epigraphic evidence by no means makes clear, however, that Greek was widely used among the Galilean masses.

What of other aspects of Greco-Roman culture in Galilee proper? Greek terms were used in some communities to refer to civic officials.

Tiberias, for example, had a *boule* and *agoranomoi*, as made clear by both Josephus[55] and two recovered market weights. As for Greek philosophy, nothing explicitly points to its presence. The remarkable level of cultural diversity presupposed by some who depict Jesus as Cynic-like is largely unattested in the material and literary records.[56]

Evidence for Greco-Roman culture multiplies exponentially in the second and following centuries. One reason for this has already been proposed: the arrival of a Roman legion and support personnel *c*. 120 CE. Another factor is also important: the arrival of Jewish refugees from the south in the wake of the two revolts. As with the earlier Hasmonean settlers, these new arrivals would have brought with them the Hellenistic culture so prevalent in the environs of Jerusalem.

In stressing the changes that happened in Galilee in the second century, I am not suggesting that the first-century region was totally isolated from the larger cultural trends of the Roman Empire, an assertion impossible in light of recent scholarship. I am arguing, however, that the interplay of local and Greco-Roman culture manifested itself differently at different times. Mid-second-century CE Galilee was not the same as early first-century CE Galilee. In light of the changes that occurred in the second century, use of evidence from that period and afterwards to understand first-century Galilee is methodologically problematic and should be accompanied by careful justification of why that later data are relevant.

Conclusion

Conclusions drawn from archaeological data are always somewhat tentative, because one cannot take into consideration what has been lost forever or not yet recovered. New material from Galilee is being unearthed every summer, and, for that reason, syntheses of information such as this one are always provisional. This study is intended as a guide to what we presently know of first-century Galileans. Its findings will have to be revised and updated again and again in light of future excavations and publications.

---

[55] *War* 2.641, *Ant.* 18.149.

[56] Crossan, *Historical Jesus* and John Dominic Crossan, *Jesus: A Revolutionary Biography* (San Francisco: HarperSanFrancisco, 1994); Mack, *Myth of Innocence*; Robert W. Funk, Roy W. Hoover, and The Jesus Seminar, *The Five Gospels: The Search for the Authentic Words of Jesus* (New York: Macmillan, 1993); and F. Gerald Downing in several studies: *Christ and the Cynics*, JSOT Manuals 4 (Sheffield: JSOT, 1988); *Cynics and Christian Origins* (Edinburgh: T&T Clark, 1992); "Cynics and Christians," *NTS* 30 (1984): 584–593; and "Deeper Reflections on the Jewish Cynic Jesus," *JBL* 117 (1998): 97–104. See the important critique by Christopher M. Tuckett in "A Cynic Q," *Biblica* 70 (1989): 349–376.

One hopes that future developments will also facilitate the application of other methodological approaches and bring clarity to issues that, due to the nature of our evidence, are currently difficult to explore, such as the gender and class dimensions of Jewish–gentile contact.

The remarkable consistency of the archaeological materials published so far, however, along with that of the information provided by Josephus and the Gospels, suggests that future discoveries are more likely to corroborate than to refute this work's findings. Another figurine, dedicatory inscription to an Olympian deity, small incense altar, or other indisputably pagan artifact will inevitably turn up at some Galilean site in the Early Roman strata – of this we can be certain. Unless such artifacts become common finds at multiple sites, however, they do little to undermine the contention that Galilee was predominantly Jewish. The question, after all, is not whether or not there were any gentiles in Galilee; the question is one of relative proportion and influence.

Galilee in the first century CE appears to have been anything but a "Galilee of the Gentiles." It was not known by that name, and understandably so. Gentiles were a small portion of the population, not a sizable group and certainly not the majority. No evidence points to the presence of unusually high numbers of gentile merchants, traders, and other travelers in Galilee. Scholarly reconstructions that de-emphasize the Jewish character of Jesus's ministry or the Jewish roots of early Christianity by de-Judaizing Galilee distort Jesus, the Jesus movement, and their Galilean context. The evidence, both literary and archaeological, corroborates the Gospels' depictions of Jesus as a Jew preaching to and working primarily among other Jews. Oft-repeated claims to the contrary appear to be nothing more than a myth.

BIBLIOGRAPHY

The publisher has used its best endeavours to ensure that the URLs for external websites referred to in this book are correct and active at the time of going to press. However, the publisher has no responsibility for the websites and can make no guarantee that a site will remain live or that the content is or will remain appropriate.

Adam, A. K. M. "According to Whose Law? Aristobulus, Galilee and the ΝΟΜΟΙ ΤѠΝ ΙΟΥΔΑΙѠΝ." *JSP* 14 (1996): 15–21.

Adan-Bayewitz, David. *Common Pottery in Roman Galilee: A Study of Local Trade*. Ramat-Gan: Bar-Ilan University Press, 1993.

"Kefar Hananyah, 1986." *IEJ* 37 (1987): 178–179.

"Kefar Hananya, 1987." *IEJ* 39 (1989): 98–99.

"Kefar Hananya, 1989." *IEJ* 41 (1991): 186–188.

"Kefar Hananyah." *OEANE*, vol. III, 276–278.

Adan-Bayewitz, David and Mordechai Aviam. "Iotapata, Josephus, and the Siege of 67: Preliminary Report on the 1992–1994 Seasons." *Journal of Roman Archaeology* 10 (1997): 131–165.

Adan-Bayewitz, David, Mordechai Aviam, and Douglas R. Edwards. "Yodefat – 1992." *ESI* 16 (1997): 42–44.

Adan-Bayewitz, David and Isadore Perlman. "Local Pottery Provenience Studies: A Role for Clay Analysis." *Archaeometry* 27 (1985): 203–217.

"The Local Trade of Sepphoris in the Roman Period." *IEJ* 40 (1990): 153–172.

Aharoni, Yohanan. *The Land of the Bible: A Historical Geography*. Philadelphia: The Westminster Press, 1967.

Albright, William Foxwell. *Archaeology and the Religion of Israel*, 5th edn. Baltimore: Johns Hopkins Press, 1968.

"Contributions to the Historical Geography of Palestine." *AASOR* 2–3 (1921–1922): 24–47.

Review of Leroy Waterman, *Preliminary Report of the University of Michigan Excavations at Sepphoris, Palestine, in 1931. Classical Weekly* 31 (1938): 148.

Alt, Albrecht. "Galiläsche Probleme." In *Kleine Schriften zur Geschichte des Volkes Israel*, vol. II, 363–435. Munich: C. H. Beck'sche Verlagsbuchhandlung, 1953.

Die Landnahme der Israeliten in Palästina. Leipzig: Druckerei der Werkgemeinschaft, 1925.

"Das System der assyrischen Provinzen auf dem Boden des Reiches Israel." *ZDPV* 52 (1929): 220–242. Reprinted in *Kleine Schriften zur Geschichte des Volkes Israel*, vol. II, 188–205. Munich: C. H. Beck'sche Verlagsbuchhandlung, 1953.

Where Jesus Worked: Towns and Villages of Galilee Studied with the Help of Local History. Trans. Kenneth Grayson. London: Epworth Press, n. d.

Anderson, Hugh, ed. *Jesus.* Englewood Cliffs, N.J.: Prentice-Hall, 1967.

Anderson, Robert T. "Samaritans." *ABD*, vol. V, 940–947.

Applebaum, Shimon. "The Roman Colony of Ptolemais-'Ake and its Territory." In *Judaea in Hellenistic and Roman Times: Historical and Archaeological Essays*, 170–96. Leiden: E. J. Brill, 1989.

"The Roman Theatre of Scythopolis." *Scripta Classica Israelica* 4 (1978): 77–105.

"The Settlement Pattern of Western Samaria from Hellenistic to Byzantine Times: A Historical Commentary." In Shimon Dar, ed., *Landscape and Pattern: An Archaeological Survey of Samaria 800 B.C.E.–636 C.E.*, 257–269. Oxford: BAR, 1986.

"When Did Scythopolis Become a Greek City?" In *Judaea in Hellenistic and Roman Times: Historical and Archaeological Essays*, 1–8. Leiden: E. J. Brill, 1989.

Applebaum, Shimon and Arthur Segal. "Gerasa." *NEAEHL*, vol. II, 470–479.

Arav, Rami. "Bethsaida." *OEANE*, vol. I, 302–305.

"Bethsaida, 1989." *IEJ* 41 (1991): 184–185.

"Bethsaida – 1990/1991." *ESI* 12 (1993): 8–9.

"Bethsaida – 1992." *ESI* 14 (1994): 25–26.

"Bethsaida, 1996–1998." *IEJ* 49 (1999): 128–136.

"Bethsaida Excavations: Preliminary Report, 1987–1993." In Rami Arav and Richard Freund, eds., *Bethsaida: A City by the North Shore of the Sea of Galilee*, vol. I, 3–64. Kirksville, Mo.: The Thomas Jefferson University Press, 1995.

"Bethsaida Excavations: Preliminary Report, 1994–1996." In Rami Arav and Richard Freund, eds., *Bethsaida: A City by the North Shore of the Sea of Galilee*, vol. II, 3–114. Kirksville, Mo.: Truman State University Press, 1999.

"Et-Tell and El-Araj." *IEJ* 38 (1988): 187–188.

"Et-Tell (Bethsaida) – 1989." *ESI* 9 (1989–1990): 98–99.

"Golan." *ABD*, vol. II, 1057–1058.

"Hermon, Mount." *ABD*, vol. III, 158–160.

Arav, Rami and Richard A. Freund. "An Incense Shovel from Bethsaida." *BAR* 23:1 (1997): 32.

Arav, Rami and Richard A. Freund, eds. *Bethsaida: A City by the North Shore of the Sea of Galilee.* Vol. I, Bethsaida Excavations Project. Kirksville, Mo.: Thomas Jefferson University Press, 1995.

Bethsaida: A City by the North Shore of the Sea of Galilee. Vol. II, Bethsaida Excavations Project. Kirksville, Mo.: Truman State University Press, 1999.

Arav, Rami, Richard A. Freund, and John F. Shroder, Jr. "Bethsaida Rediscovered." *BAR* 26:1 (2000): 44–56.

Arav, Rami and J. Rousseau. "Bethsaïde, ville Perdue et Retrouvée." *RB* 100 (1993): 415–428.

Arenhoevel, Diego. *Die Theokratie nach dem 1 und 2 Makkabäerbuch*. Mainz: Matthias-Grünewald-Verlag, 1967.

Ariel, Donald T. "Two Rhodian Amphoras." *IEJ* 38 (1988): 31–35.

Ariel, Donald T. and Gerald Rinkielszejn. "Stamped Amphora Handles." In Sharon C. Herbert, ed., *Tel Anafa, I: Final Report on Ten Years of Excavation at a Hellenistic and Roman Settlement in Northern Israel*, 183–240. Ann Arbor, Mich.: Kelsey Museum, 1994.

Atkinson, Kenneth. "On Further Defining the First-Century C.E. Synagogue: Fact or Fiction?" *NTS* 43 (1997): 491–502.

Aubin, Melissa M. "Jerash." *OEANE*, vol. III, 215–219.

Avi-Yonah, Michael. "The Foundation of Tiberias." *IEJ* 1 (1950–1951): 160–169.

"Hammat Gader." *NEAEHL*, vol. II, 565–569.

The Holy Land. Grand Rapids, Mich.: Baker Book House, 1966.

"Mount Carmel and the God of Baalbek." *IEJ* 2 (1952): 118–124.

"Sepphoris." *EAEHL*, vol. IV, 1051–1055.

"Some Comments on the Capernaum Excavations." In Lee I. Levine, ed., *Ancient Synagogues Revealed*, 60–62. Jerusalem: Israel Exploration Society, 1982.

"Synagogues." *EAEHL*, vol. IV, 1129–1138.

"Syrian Gods at Ptolemais-Acho." *IEJ* 9 (1959): 1–12.

Aviam, Mordechai. "Galilee: The Hellenistic to Byzantine Periods." *NEAEHL*, vol. II, 453–458.

"Gush Ḥalav." *ESI* 3 (1984): 35.

"Gush Halav." *ESI* 5 (1986): 44–45.

"Magdala." *OEANE*, vol. III, 399–400.

"The Roman Temple at Kedesh in the Light of Certain Northern Syrian City Coins." *Tel Aviv* 12 (1985): 212–214.

"A Second-First Century B.C.E. Fortress and Siege Complex in Eastern Upper Galilee." In Douglas R. Edwards and C. Thomas McCollough, eds., *Archaeology and the Galilee: Texts and Contexts in the Greco-Roman and Byzantine Periods*, 97–105. Atlanta: Scholars Press, 1997.

"Tel Yodefat, Oil Press." *ESI* 9 (1989/1990): 106.

Avigad, Nahman. *Beth She'arim*. Vol. III, *Catacombs 12–23*. New Brunswick, N.J.; Rutgers University Press, 1976.

"Chorazin: The Synagogue." *EAEHL*, vol. I, 301–303.

"Kefar Neburaya." *EAEHL*, vol. III, 710–711.

"A Votive Altar from Upper Galilee." *BASOR* 167 (1962): 18–22.

Avigad, Nahman and Benjamin Mazar. "Beth She'arim." *EAEHL*, vol. I, 229–247.

"Beth She'arim." *NEAEHL*, vol. I, 236–248.

Bagatti, Bellarmino. "Le Antichità di Kh. Qana e di Kefr Kenna in Galilea." *LA* 15 (1964–1965): 251–292.

The Church from the Circumcision. Jerusalem: Franciscan Printing Press, 1971.

Excavations in Nazareth. Trans. E. Hoade. Jerusalem: Franciscan Printing Press, 1969.

"Nazareth." *EAEHL*, vol. III, 919–922.

"Ritrovamenti Nella Nazaret Evangelica." *LA* 5 (1955): 5–44.

Gli Scavi di Nazaret. Vol. I. Jerusalem: Tipografia Dei PP Francescani, 1967.

"Una singolare tomba a Nazaret." *Rivista di Archeologia Cristiana* 43 (1967): 7–14.

Bagnall, Roger S. "Palestine, Administration of (Ptolemaic)." *ABD*, vol. V, 90–92.

Bahat, D. "A Roof Tile of the Legio VI Ferrata and Pottery Vessels from Horvat Hazon." *IEJ* 24 (1974): 160–169.

Bar-Adon, P. "Beth Yerah." *IEJ* 5 (1955): 273.

Bar-Kochva, Bezalel. *Judas Maccabeus: The Jewish Struggle against the Seleucids*. Cambridge: Cambridge University Press, 1989.

"Manpower, Economics, and Internal Strife in the Hasmonean State." In H. Van Effenterre, ed., *Armées et Fiscalité dans le Monde Antique*, 168–196. Paris: Editions du Centre National de la Recherche Scientifique, 1977.

Barag, Dan. "Tyrian Currency in Galilee." *INJ* 6/7 (1982–1983): 7–13.

Barghouti, Asem N. "Urbanization of Palestine and Jordan in Hellenistic and Roman Times." In Adnan Hadidi, ed., *Studies in the History and Archaeology of Jordan*, vol. I, 209–230. Amman: Department of Antiquities, 1982.

Barkay, Rachel. "Coins of Roman Governors Issued by Nysa-Scythopolis in the Late Republican Period." *INJ* 13 (1994–1999): 54–62.

Batey, Richard A. "Is not this the Carpenter?" *NTS* 30 (1984): 249–258.

Jesus and the Forgotten City: New Light on Sepphoris and the Urban World of Jesus. Grand Rapids, Mich.: Baker Book House, 1991.

"Jesus and the Theatre." *NTS* 30 (1984): 563–574.

"Sepphoris: An Urban Portrait of Jesus." *BAR* 18:3 (1992): 50–63.

Batyneh, Taha, Wajih Karasneh, and Thomas Weber. "Two New Inscriptions from Umm-Qeis." *ADAJ* 38 (1994): 379–384.

Bauer, Walter. "Jesus der Galiläer." In *Aufsätze und kleine Schriften*, ed. G. Strecker, 91–108. Tübingen: JCB Mohr (Paul Siebeck), 1967. Originally in *Festgabe für Adolf Jülicher zum 70 Geburtstag*, 16–34, Tübingen: J. C. B. Mohr (Paul Siebeck), 1927.

Beare, Francis Wright. *The Gospel According to Matthew*. San Francisco: Harper and Row, 1981.

Ben-Tor, Amnon. "Hazor: Fifth Season of Excavations (1968–1969)." *NEAEHL*, vol. II, 604–605.

Berlin, Andrea M. "The Archaeology of Ritual: The Sanctuary of Pan at Banias/ Caesarea Philippi." *BASOR* 315 (1999): 27–46.

"From Monarchy to Markets: The Phoenicians in Hellenistic Palestine." *BASOR* 306 (1997): 75–88.

"The Hellenistic and Early Roman Common-Ware Pottery from Tel Anafa." Ph.D. Diss., University of Michigan, 1988.

"The Plain Wares." In Sharon C. Herbert, ed., *Tel Anafa II, i: The Hellenistic and Roman Pottery*, ix–246. Ann Arbor, Mich.: Kelsey Museum; Columbia, Mo.: Museum of Art and Archaeology of the University of Missouri, 1997.

Berman, A. "Kafr Kanna." *ESI* 7–8 (1988–1989): 107–108.

Bertram, W. "Der Hellenismus in der Urheimat des Evangeliums." *Archiv für Religionswissenschaft* 32 (1935): 265–281.

Biebel, F. M. "The Synagogue Church." In *Gerasa: City of the Decapolis*, ed. Carl H. Kraeling, 318–324. New Haven, Conn.: American Schools of Oriental Research, 1938.

Bietenhard, Hans. "Die syrische Dekapolis von Pompeius bis Trajan." In Hildegard Temporini and Wolfgang Haase, eds., *Aufstieg und Niedergang der römischen Welt*, 2.8, 220–261. Berlin and New York: Walter de Gruyter, 1977.

Biran, Avraham. "Dan (Place)." *ABD*, vol. II, 12–17.

"Dan, Tel." *NEAEHL*, vol. I, 323–332.

"To the God who is in Dan." In Avraham Biran, ed., *Temples and High Places in Biblical Times*, 142–151. Jerusalem: Nelson Glueck School of Biblical Archaeology of Hebrew Union College – Jewish Institute of Religion, 1981.

Blakely, Jeffrey A. *The Joint Expedition to Caesarea Maritima Excavation Reports*. Vol. IV, *Caesarea Maritima: The Pottery and Dating of Vault 1: Horreum, Mithraeum, and Later Uses*. New York: Edwin Mellon Press, 1987.

Boatwright, Mary T. "Theaters in the Roman Empire." *BA* 53 (1990): 184–192.

Bösen, Willibald. *Galiläa als Lebensraum und Wirkungsfeld Jesu*. Basle and Vienna: Herder Freiburg, 1985.

Boissonade, J. F., ed. *Herodiani partitiones*. London, 1819; repr. Amsterdam: Hakkert, 1963.

Boling, Robert G. *Judges*. Garden City, N.Y.: Doubleday, 1977.

Boobyer, G. "Galilee and Galileans in St. Mark's Gospel." *Bulletin of the John Rylands Library* 35 (1953): 334–348.

Borg, Marcus J. *Meeting Jesus Again for the First Time*. San Francisco: Harper-SanFrancisco, 1994.

"The Palestinian Background for a Life of Jesus." In *Searching for Jesus*, 37–58. Washington, D.C.: Biblical Archaeology Society, 1994.

Bornkamm, Günther. *Jesus of Nazareth*. Trans. Irene and Fraser McLuskey with James M. Robinson. San Francisco: Harper & Row, 1960.

Bowersock, Glen W. *Hellenism in Late Antiquity*. Ann Arbor: University of Michigan Press, 1990.

"Syria Under Vespasian." *Journal of Roman Studies* 63 (1973): 133–140.

Bowsher, Julian M. C. "Architecture and Religion in the Decapolis: A Numismatic Survey." *PEQ* 119 (1987): 62–69.

Braund, David. *Rome and the Friendly King: The Character of the Client Kingship*. London and Canberra: Croom Helm; New York: St. Martin's Press, 1984.

Bright, John. *A History of Israel*, 3rd edn. Philadelphia: Westminster Press, 1981.

Brooke, Alan England and Norman McLean, eds. *The Old Testament in Greek*. Vol. I, part 4, *Joshua, Judges, and Ruth*. Cambridge: Cambridge University Press, 1917.

Broshi, Magen and Israel Finkelstein. "The Population of Palestine in Iron Age II." *BASOR* 287 (1992): 47–60.

Browning, Ian. *Jerash and the Decapolis*. London: Chatto & Windus, 1982.

Browning, W. R. F. "Galilee." In W. R. F. Browning, ed., *A Dictionary of the Bible*, 145. Oxford and New York: Oxford University Press, 1996.

Bull, Robert J. "The Excavation of Tell er-Ras on Mt. Gerizim." *BA* 31 (1968): 58–72.

"The Mithraeum at Caesarea Maritima." *Textes et mémoires*, vol. IV, 75–89. Leiden: E. J. Brill, 1978.

"A Preliminary Excavation of the Hadrianic Temple at Tell-er Ras on Mt. Gerizim." *AJA* 71 (1967): 387–393.

"Ras, Tell er- ." *OEANE*, vol. IV, 407–409.

Burrell, Barbara. "Palace to Praetorium: The Romanization of Caesarea." In Avner Raban and Kenneth G. Holum, eds., *Caesarea Maritima: A Retrospective after Two Millenia*, 228–250. Leiden: E. J. Brill, 1996.

Cahill, Jane M. "Chalk Vessel Assemblages of the Persian/Hellenistic and Early Roman Periods." *Qedem* 33 (1992): 190–274.

Carpenter, Humphrey. *Jesus*. Oxford: Oxford University Press, 1980.

Carter, Warren. "Evoking Isaiah: Matthean Soteriology and an Intertextual Reading of Isaiah 7–9 and Matthew 1:23 and 4:15–16." *JBL* 119:3 (2000): 503–520.

Case, Shirley Jackson. *Jesus: A New Biography*. Chicago: University of Chicago Press, 1927.

"Jesus and Sepphoris." *JBL* 45 (1926): 14–22.

Casson, Lionel. "China and the West. " In *Ancient Trade and Society*, 247–272. Detroit: Wayne State University Press, 1984.

"Rome's Trade with the East: The Sea Voyage to Africa and India." In *Ancient Trade and Society*, 182–198. Detroit: Wayne State University Press, 1984.

Chamberlain, Houston Stewart. *Foundations of the Nineteenth Century*. Trans. John Lees. 2 vols. London: John Lane The Bodley Head, 1910.

Chance, J. Bradley. *Jerusalem, The Temple, and the New Age in Luke-Acts*. Macon, Ga.: Mercer University Press, 1988.

Chancey, Mark. "The Cultural Milieu of Ancient Sepphoris." *NTS* 47 (2001): 127–145.

Chancey, Mark and Eric M. Meyers. "How Jewish was Sepphoris in Jesus' Time?" *BAR* 26:4 (2000): 18–33, 61.

Charlesworth, M. P. *Trade Routes and Commerce of the Roman Empire*, 2nd. rev. edn. Chicago: Ares Publishers, 1926.

Fouilles de Tyr: La Nécropole. In *Bulletin du Musée de Beyrouth* 34 (1984), 35 (1985) and 36 (1986).

Chéab, Maurice H. "Tyr a l'époque romaine: Aspects de la cité à la lumière des textes et des fouilles." *Mélanges de l'université Saint Joseph* 38 (1962): 13–40.

Clark, K. W. "Galilee." In George Arthur Buttrick et al., eds., *Interpreter's Dictionary of the Bible*, 5 vols., vol. II, 344–347. New York and Nashville: Abingdon, 1962.

Clermont-Ganneau, C. "Archaeological and Epigraphic Notes on Palestine." *PEQ* 35 (1903): 128–140.

Coggins, R. J. *Samaritans and Jews: The Origins of Samaritanism Reconsidered*. Atlanta: John Knox Press, 1975.

Cohen, Getzel. *The Seleucid Colonies*. Wiesbaden: Franz Steiner Verlag GMBH, 1978.

Cohen, Shaye D. *Josephus in Galilee and Rome: His Vita and Development as a Historian*. Leiden: E. J. Brill, 1979.

"Religion, Ethnicity and Hellenism in the Emergence of Jewish Identity." In Per Bilde et al., eds., *Religion and Religious Practice in the Seleucid Kingdom*, 204–223. Aarhus: Aarhus University Press, 1990.

Collins, John J. *Daniel, First Maccabees, Second Maccabees with an Excursus on the Apocalyptic Genre*. Wilmington, Del.: Michael Glazier, Inc., 1981.

Conzelmann, Hans. *The Theology of St. Luke*. Trans. Geoffrey Buswell. London: Faber & Faber, 1960.

Corbo, Virgilio C. *Cafarnao*. Vol. I, *Gli Edifici della Città*. Jerusalem: Franciscan Printing Press, 1975.

"Capernaum." *ABD*, vol. I, 866–869.

"Capernaum." *OEANE*, vol. I, 416–419.

"La Casa di S. Pietro a Cafarnao." *LA* 18 (1968): 5–54.

"La Città Romana di Magdala: Rapporto preliminare dopo la quarta campagna di scavo, 1975." In Emmanuele Testa, ed., *Studia Hierosolymitana in onore del P. Bellarmino Bagatti*. Vol. I, *Studi Archeologici*, 355–378. Jerusalem: Franciscan Printing Press, 1976.

"Edifici antichi soto la sinagoga di Cafarnao." In Emmanuele Testa, ed., *Studia Hierosolymitana in onore del P. Bellarmino Bagatti*. Vol. I, *Studi Archeologici*, 159–176. Jerusalem: Franciscan Printing Press, 1976.

The House of St. Peter at Capharnaum. Trans. Sylbester Saller. Jerusalem: Franciscan Printing Press, 1969.

"Il Mausoleo di Cafarnao." *LA* 27 (1977): 145–155.

"La mini-synagogue de Magdala." *Le Monde De La Bible* 57 (1989): 15.

"Resti della Sinagoga del Primo Secolo a Cafarnao." In Emmanuele Testa, ed., *Studia Hierosolymitana III in onore del P. Bellarmino Bagatti*. Vol. III, *Nell' Ottavo centenario Francescano* (1182–1982), 313–357. Jerusalem: Franciscan Printing Press, 1982.

"Scavi archeologici a Magdala, 1971–1973." *LA* 24 (1974): 19–37.

Corbo, Virgilio C., Stanislao Loffreda, and Augustus Spijkerman. *La Sinagoga di Cafarnao dopo gli Scavi del 1969*. Jerusalem: Tipografia dei PP. Francescani, 1970.

Crossan, John Dominic. *The Birth of Christianity*. San Francisco: HarperSan-Francisco, 1998.

The Historical Jesus: The Life of a Mediterranean Jewish Peasant. San Francisco: HarperSanFrancisco, 1991.

Jesus: A Revolutionary Biography. San Francisco: HarperSanFrancisco, 1994.

Crown, Alan D., ed. *The Samaritans*. Tübingen: J. C. B. Mohr (Paul Siebeck), 1989.

Dalman, Gustaf. *Sacred Sites and Ways: Studies in the Topography of the Gospels*. Trans. Paul P. Levertoff. New York: Macmillan, 1935.

Damati, Emanuel. "A Greek Inscription from a Mausoleum in Tiberias." *Atiqot* 38 (1999): 227–228.

"Meiron." *ESI 10* (1991): 72–73.

Dancey, J. C. *A Commentary on 1 Maccabees*. Oxford: Basil Blackwell, 1954.

Dar, Shimon. "The Greek Inscriptions from Senaim on Mount Hermon." *PEQ* 120 (1988): 26–44.

"Hermon, Mount." *NEAEHL*, vol. II, 616–617.

Landscape and Pattern: An Archaeological Survey of Samaria 800 B.C.E.– 636 C.E. 2 vols., Oxford: BAR, 1986.

"Samaria (Archaeology of the Region)." *ABD*, vol. V, 926–931.

Settlements and Cult Sites on Mount Hermon, Israel: Ituraean Culture in the Hellenistic and Roman Periods. Oxford: BAR, 1993.

Dar, Shimon and Yohanon Mintzker. "Sena'im, Mount." *NEAEHL*, vol. IV, 1322–1324.

Davies, W. D. *The Gospel and the Land: Early Christianity and Jewish Territorial Doctrine*. Sheffield: JSOT Press, 1994.

Davies, W. D. and Dale C. Allison. *A Critical and Exegetical Commentary on the Gospel According to Saint Matthew*. 3 vols. Edinburgh: T&T Clark, 1988–1997.

Deines, Roland. *Jüdische Steingefäße und pharisäische Frömmigkeit.* Tübingen: J. C. B. Mohr (Paul Siebeck), 1993.

Dell'amore, Giordano et al., eds. *Scavi di Caesarea Maritima.* Rome: Lerma di Bretschneider, 1966.

Delorme, Jean. *Gymnasion: Etude sur les Monuments consacré a l'éducation en Grèce.* Paris: Editions E. de Boccard, 1960.

Delougaz, Richard and Richard C. Haines. *A Byzantine Church at Khirbat al-Karak.* Chicago: University of Chicago Press, 1960.

Dessel, J. P. "'Ein Zippori, Tel." *OEANE,* vol. II, 227–228.

Dever, William G. "Akko." *OEANE,* vol. I, 54–55.

⸻. "Israel, History of (Archaeology and the 'Conquest')." *ABD,* vol. III, 545–558.

⸻. "'Will the Real Israel Please Stand Up?' Archaeology and Israelite Historiography: Part I." *BASOR* 297 (1995): 61–80.

⸻. "'Will the Real Israel Please Stand Up?' Part II: Archaeology and the Religions of Ancient Israel." *BASOR* 298 (1995): 37–58.

Di Segni, Lea. "A Dated Inscription from Beth Shean and the Cult of Dionysos Ktistes in Roman Scythopolis." *Scripta classica Israelica* 16 (1997): 139–161.

Di Segni, L., G. Foerster, and Y. Tsafrir. "The Basilica and an Altar to Dionysos at Nysa-Scythopolis." In J. H. Humphrey, ed., *The Roman and Byzantine Near East,* vol. II, 59–75. Portsmouth, R.I.: Journal of Roman Archaeology, 1999.

Dibelius, Martin. *Jesus.* Trans. Charles B. Hedric and Frederick C. Grant. Philadelphia: Westminster Press, 1949.

Donaldson, Terence L., ed. *Religious Rivalries and the Struggle for Success in Caesarea Maritima.* Waterloo, Ont.: Wilfrid Laurier University Press, 2000.

Donner, Herbert. "The Separate States of Israel and Judah." In John H. Hayes and J. Maxwell Miller, eds., *Israelite and Judaean History,* 381–434. Philadelphia: Westminster Press, 1977.

Doran, Robert. "The First Book of Maccabees." In Leander Keck et al., eds., *The New Interpreter's Bible,* vol. IV. Nashville: Abingdon Press, 1996.

Dothan, Moshe. "Akko." *ABD,* vol. I, 50–53.

⸻. *Hammath Tiberias: Early Synagogues and the Hellenistic and Roman Remains.* Jerusalem: Israel Exploration Society; Haifa: University of Haifa Department of Antiquities and Museums, 1983.

⸻. "Hammath-Tiberias." *NEAEHL,* vol. II, 573–577.

⸻. "The Synagogue at Hammath-Tiberias." In Lee I. Levine, ed., *Ancient Synagogues Revealed,* 63–69. Jerusalem: Israel Exploration Society; Detroit: Wayne State University Press, 1982.

⸻. "Tiberias, Hammath." *EAEHL,* vol. IV, 1178–1184.

Dothan, Moshe and Zeev Goldmann. "Acco." *NEAEHL,* vol. I, 16–23.

⸻. "Acco: Excavations in the Modern City." *NEAEHL,* vol. I, 23–27.

Downing, F. Gerald. *Christ and the Cynics.* JSOT Manuals 4. Sheffield: JSOT, 1988.

⸻. *Cynics and Christian Origins.* Edinburgh: T&T Clark, 1992.

⸻. "Cynics and Christians." *NTS* 30 (1984): 584–593.

⸻. "Deeper Reflections on the Jewish Cynic Jesus." *JBL* 117 (1998): 97–104.

Edwards, Douglas R. "First-Century Urban/Rural Relations in Lower Galilee: Exploring the Archaeological and Literary Evidence." In D. J. Lull, ed.,

Society of Biblical Literature 1988 Seminar Papers, 169–182. Atlanta: Scholars Press, 1988.

"Jotapata." *OEANE*, vol. III, 251–252.

"The Socio-Economic and Cultural Ethos of the Lower Galilee in the First Century: Implications for the Nascent Jesus Movement." In Lee I. Levine, ed., *The Galilee in Late Antiquity*, 39–52. New York and Jerusalem: The Jewish Theological Seminary of America, 1992.

Edwards, Douglas R., Mordechai Aviam, and David Adan-Bayewitz. "Yodefat, 1992." *IEJ* 45 (1995): 191–197.

Edwards, Douglas R. and C. Thomas McCollough, eds. *Archaeology and the Galilee: Texts and Contexts in the Greco-Roman and Byzantine Periods*. Atlanta: Scholars Press, 1997.

Edwards, Douglas R. and H. J. Katzenstein. "Tyre (Place)." *ABD*, vol. VI, 686–692.

Elliot-Binns, L. E. *Galilean Christianity*. London: SCM Press, 1956.

Eph'al, Israel. "Assyrian Dominance in Palestine." In Abraham Malamat, ed., *The Age of the Monarchies*, 276–289, 364–368. The World History of the Jewish People 1.4.2. Israel: Jewish History Publications; New Brunswick: Rutgers University Press, 1979.

Epstein, Clare. "Hippos." *NEAEHL*, vol. II, 634–636.

Epstein, I. ed. *The Babylonian Talmud*. 6 vols. London: Soncino Press, 1935–1959.

Eshel, Hanan. "A Note on 'Miqvaot' at Sepphoris." In Douglas R. Edwards and C. Thomas McCollough, eds., *Archaeology and the Galilee: Texts and Contexts in the Graeco-Roman and Byzantine Periods*, 131–134. Atlanta: Scholars Press, 1997.

"They're Not Ritual Baths." *BAR* 26:4 (2000): 42–45.

"We Need More Data." *BAR* 26:4 (2000): 49.

Fairweather, W. and J. Sutherland Black. *The First Book of Maccabees*. Cambridge: Cambridge University Press, 1936.

Faust, Avraham. "Ethnic Complexity in Northern Israel during Iron Age II." *PEQ* 132 (2000): 2–27.

Feig, Nurit. "Meron." *ESI* 7–8 (1988/1989): 127–128.

"Nazareth 'Illit.'" *IEJ* 33 (1986): 116–117.

Feldman, Louis H. "How Much Hellenism in Jewish Palestine?" *Hebrew Union College Annual* 57 (1986): 83–111.

Jew and Gentile in the Ancient World: Attitudes and Interactions from Alexander to Justinian. Princeton: Princeton University Press, 1993.

Fine, Steven. "Chorazin." *ABD*, vol. I, 490–491.

"Gamla." *OEANE*, vol. II, 382.

Fine, Steven, ed. *Sacred Realm: The Emergence of the Synagogue in the Ancient World*. New York and Oxford: Oxford University Press and Yeshiva University Museum, 1996.

Fine, Steven and Meyers, Eric M. "Synagogues." *OEANE*, vol. V, 118–123.

Finkelstein, Israel and Nadav Na'aman, eds. *From Nomadism to Monarchy: Archaeological and Historical Aspects of Early Israel*. Jerusalem: Yad Izhak Ben Zvi and Israel Exploration Society; Washington: Biblical Archaeology Society, 1994.

Fiorenza, Elisabeth Schüssler. *Jesus: Miriam's Child, Sophia's Prophet: Critical Issues in Feminist Christology.* New York: Continuum, 1994.

Fischel, H. A. *The First Book of Maccabees.* New York: Schocken Books, 1948.

Fischer, Moshe, Asher Ovadiah, and Israel Roll. "The Epigraphic Finds from the Roman Temple at Kedesh in the Upper Galilee." *Tel Aviv* 13 (1986): 60–66.

"An Inscribed Altar from the Roman Temple at Kadesh (Upper Galilee)." *Zeitschrift für Papyrologie und Epigraphik* 49 (1982): 155–158.

"The Roman Temple at Kedesh, Upper Galilee: A Preliminary Study." *Tel Aviv* 11 (1984): 146–172.

Fischer, Thomas. "Palestine, Administration of (Seleucid)." Trans. Frederick H. Cryer. *ABD*, vol. V, 92–96.

Fisher, C. S. "The 'Forum.'" In Carl H. Kraeling, ed., *Gerasa: City of the Decapolis*, 153–158. New Haven, Conn.: American Schools of Oriental Research, 1938.

"The Temple of Artemis." In Carl H. Kraeling, ed., *Gerasa: City of the Decapolis*, 125–138. New Haven, Conn.: American Schools of Oriental Research, 1938.

Fisher, C. S. and C. H. Kraeling. "Temple C." In Carl H. Kraeling, ed., *Gerasa: City of the Decapolis*, 139–148. New Haven, Conn.: American Schools of Oriental Research, 1938.

Fitzmeyer, Joseph A. "Did Jesus Speak Greek?" *BAR* 18:5 (1992): 58–63, 76–77.

The Gospel According to Luke (I–IX). Garden City, N.Y.: Doubleday and Co., Inc., 1981.

Flusser, David. "Paganism in Palestine." In S. Safrai et al., eds., *Compendia rerum Iudaicarum ad Novum Testamentum* 1.2, 1065–1100. Assen and Amsterdam: Van Gorcum, 1976.

Foerster, Gideon. "The Ancient Synagogues of the Galilee." In Lee I. Levine, ed., *The Galilee in Late Antiquity*, 289–320. New York and Jerusalem: The Jewish Theological Seminary, 1992.

"Beth-Shean at the Foot of the Mound." *NEAEHL*, vol. I, 223–235.

"The Early History of Caesarea." In Charles T. Fritsch et al., eds., *The Joint Expedition to Caesarea Maritima*. Vol. I, *Studies in the History of Caesarea Maritima*, 9–22. Missoula, Mont.: Scholars Press for ASOR, 1975.

"Excavations at Ancient Meron (Review Article)." *IEJ* 37 (1987): 262–269.

"Jericho: Exploration since 1973." *NEAEHL*, vol. II, 683–691.

"Notes on Recent Excavations at Capernaum." *IEJ* 21 (1971): 207–211.

"Notes on Recent Excavations at Capernaum." In Lee I. Levine, ed., *Ancient Synagogues Revealed*, 57–59. Jerusalem: Israel Exploration Society, 1982.

"Tiberias." *EAEHL*, vol. IV, 1173–1176.

"Tiberias: Excavations in the South of the City." *NEAEHL*, vol. IV, 1470–1473.

Foerster, Gideon and Yoram Tsafrir. "Nysa-Scythopolis – A New Inscription and the Titles of the City on its Coins." *INJ* 9 (1986–1987): 53–58.

Forrer, E. *Die Provinzeinteilung des assyrischen Reiches.* Leipzig, 1920.

Fortner, Sandra. "The Fishing Implements and Maritime Activities of Bethsaida-Julias (et-Tell)." In Rami Arav and Richard A. Freund, eds., *Bethsaida: A City by the North Shore of the Sea of Galilee*. Vol. II, Bethsaida Excavations Project, 269–282. Kirksville, Mo.: Truman State University Press, 1999.

Frankel, Rafael. "Galilee (Pre-Hellenistic)." *ABD*, vol. II, 879–895.

"Har Mişpe Yamim – 1988/1989." *ESI* 9 (1989–1990): 100–102.

"Upper Galilee in the Late Bronze-Iron I Transition." In Israel Finkelstein and Nadav Na'aman, eds., *From Nomadism to Monarchy: Archaeological and Historical Aspects of Early Israel*, 18–34. Jerusalem: Yad Izhak Ben Zvi and Israel Exploration Society; Washington: Biblical Archaeology Society, 1994.

Frankel, Rafael and Raphael Ventura. "The Miṣpe Yamim Bronzes." *BASOR* 311 (1998): 39–55.

Frankfort, H. *The Art and Architecture of the Ancient Orient*. Baltimore: Penguin, 1954.

Freund, Richard. "The Incense Shovel of Bethsaida and Synagogue Iconography in Late Antiquity." In Rami Arav and Richard A. Freund, eds., *Bethsaida: A City by the North Shore of the Sea of Galilee*, vol. II, Bethsaida Excavations Project, 413–457. Kirksville, Mo.: Truman State University Press, 1999.

Frey, Jean-Baptiste. *Corpus Inscriptionum Iudaicarum*, vol. II. Rome: Pontificio Instituto di Archeologia Cristiana, 1952.

Freyberger, Klaus S. "Untersuchungen zur Baugeschichte des Jupiter-Heiligtums in Damaskus." *Damaszener Mitteilungen* 4 (1989): 61–86.

Freyne, Sean. "Archaeology and the Historical Jesus." In John R. Bartlett, ed., *Archaeology and Biblical Interpretation*, 117–144. London and New York: Routledge, 1997.

"Behind the Names: Galileans, Samaritans, *Ioudaioi*." In *Galilee through the Centuries: Confluence of Cultures*, ed. Eric M. Meyers, 39–56. Winona Lake, Ind.: Eisenbrauns, 1999.

Galilee from Alexander the Great to Hadrian: 323 BCE to 135 CE: A Study of Second Temple Judaism. Wilmington, Del.: Michael Glazier; Notre Dame, Ind.: University of Notre Dame Press, 1980. Reprint, Edinburgh: T&T Clark, 1998.

"Galilee: Galilee in the Hellenistic through Byzantine Periods." *OEANE*, vol. II, 370–376.

"Galilee (Hellenistic/Roman)." *ABD*, vol. II, 895–899.

"Galilee–Jerusalem Relations in the Light of Josephus' *Life*." *NTS* 33 (1987): 600–609.

Galilee, Jesus, and the Gospels. Philadelphia: Fortress Press, 1988.

"The Geography, Politics and Economics of Galilee and the Quest of the Historical Jesus." In Bruce Chilton and Craig A. Evans, eds., *Studying the Historical Jesus: Evaluations of the State of Current Research*, 75–121. Leiden: E. J. Brill, 1994.

"Herodian Economics in Galilee: Searching for a Suitable Model." In Philip F. Esler, ed., *Modelling Early Christianity: Social Scientific Studies of the New Testament in its Context*, 23–46. London and New York: Routledge, 1995.

"Jesus and the Urban Culture of Galilee." In Tord Fornberg and David Hellholm, eds., *Texts and Contexts: Biblical Texts in their Textual and Situational Contexts: Essays in Honor of Lars Hartman*, 597–622. Oslo: Scandinavia University Press, 1995.

"Urban–Rural Relations in First Century Galilee: Some Suggestions from the Literary Sources." In Lee I. Levine, ed., *The Galilee in Late Antiquity*, 75–94. New York and Jerusalem: The Jewish Theological Seminary of America, 1992.

Friedland, E. "Graeco-Roman Sculpture in the Levant: The Marbles from the Sanctuary of Pan at Caesarea Philippi (Banias)." In J. H. Humphrey, ed., *The*

Roman and Byzantine Near East, vol. II, 7–22. Portsmouth, R.I.: Journal of Roman Archaeology.

Fritsch, Charles T., ed. *The Joint Expedition to Caesarea Maritima*. Vol. I, *Studies in the History of Caesarea Maritima*. Missoula, Mont.: Scholars Press for ASOR, 1975.

Fuks, Gideon. "The Jews of Hellenistic and Roman Scythopolis." *JJS* 33 (1982): 407–417.

"Tel Anafa: A Proposed Identification." *Scripta Classica Israelica* 5 (1979): 178–184.

Fuller, Michael Jeffrey. "Abila of the Decapolis: A Roman-Byzantine City in Transjordan." Ph.D. Diss., Washington University, 1987.

Funk, Robert W. *Honest to Jesus: Jesus for a New Millennium*. San Francisco: HarperSanFrancisco, 1996.

Funk, Robert W., Roy W. Hoover, and The Jesus Seminar. *The Five Gospels: The Search for the Authentic Words of Jesus*. New York: Macmillan, 1993.

Gal, Zvi. "Galilee: Chalcolithic to Persian Periods." *NEAEHL*, vol. II, 449–453.

"Galilee: Galilee in the Bronze and Iron Ages." *OEANE*, vol. II, 369–370.

"Iron I in Lower Galilee and the Margins of the Jezreel Valley." In Israel Finkelstein and Nadav Na'aman, eds., *From Nomadism to Monarchy: Archaeological and Historical Aspects of Early Israel*, 35–46. Jerusalem: Yad Izhak Ben Zvi and Israel Exploration Society; Washington: Biblical Archaeology Society, 1994.

"Israel in Exile." *BAR* 24:3 (1998): 48–53.

"The Late Bronze Age in Galilee: A Reassessment." *BASOR* 272 (1988): 79–84.

Lower Galilee during the Iron Age. Winona Lake, Ind.: Eisenbrauns, 1992.

"The Lower Galilee in the Iron Age II: Analysis of Survey Material and its Historical Interpretation." *Tel Aviv* 15–16 (1988–1989): 56–64.

"A Stone-Vessel Manufacturing Site in the Lower Galilee." *'Atiqot* 20 (1991): 179–180.

"Galilee." In John L. McKenzie, ed., *Dictionary of the Bible*, 293–294. Milwaukee: Bruce Publishing Company, 1965.

"Galilee." In John E. Steinmueller and Kathryn Sullivan, eds., *Catholic Biblical Encyclopedia: New Testament*, 248–249. New York: Joseph F. Wagner, Inc.: 1950.

Galili, Ehud, Uzi Dahari and Jacob Sharvit. "Underwater Survey along the Coast of Israel." *ESI* 10 (1991): 160–165.

Garland, David E. *Reading Matthew*. New York: Crossroad, 1993.

Gatier, P.-L. "Inscriptions religieuses de Gerasa." *ADAJ* 26 (1982): 269–275.

Gersht, Rivka. "Representations of Deities and the Cults of Caesarea." In Avner Raban and Kenneth G. Holum, eds., *Caesarea Maritima: A Retrospective after Two Millenia*, 305–324. Leiden: E. J. Brill, 1996.

"The Tyche of Caesarea Maritima." *PEQ* 116 (1984): 110–114.

Gitin, Seymour. "Philistines: Late Philistines." *OEANE*, vol. IV, 311–313.

Giveon, Raphael. "Geva, A New Fortress City: From Tuthmosis to Herod." *BAIAS* 3 (1983–1984): 45–46.

Glass, Stephen J. "The Greek Gymnasium: Some Problems." In Wendy J. Raschke, ed., *The Archaeology of the Olympics*, 155–173. Madison: University of Wisconsin Press, 1988.

Gleason, Kathryn Louise. "Rule and Spectacle: The Promontory Palace." In Avner Raban and Kenneth G. Holum, eds., *Caesarea Maritima: A Retrospective after Two Millenia*, 208–227. Leiden: E. J. Brill, 1996.

Goguel, Maurice. *Jesus and the Origins of Christianity*. 3 vols. New York: Harper Brothers, 1960.

Goldstein, Jonathan A. *1 Maccabees*. Garden City, N.Y.: Doubleday and Co., Inc. 1976.

Goodman, Martin. "Galilean Judaism and Judaean Judaism." In William Horbury, W. D. Davies, and John Sturdy, eds., *The Cambridge History of Judaism*, vol. III, 596–617. Cambridge: Cambridge University Press, 1999.

State and Society in Roman Galilee, AD 132–212. Totowa, N.J: Rowman and Allanheld, 1983.

Gordon, Douglas L. "Hammath Tiberias." *OEANE*, vol. II, 470–471.

Graf, David F. "Nabateans." *OEANE*, vol. IV, 82–85.

"The Nabataeans and the Decapolis." In P. W. M. Freeman and D. L. Kennedy, eds., *The Defence of the Roman and Byzantine East*, 785–796. Oxford: BAR, 1986.

Grant, F. C. "Jesus Christ." In George Arthur Buttrick et al., eds., *Interpreter's Dictionary of the Bible*, vol. II, 869–896. New York and Asheville: Abingdon, 1962.

Grantham, Billy J. "Sepphoris: Ethnic Complexity at an Ancient Galilean City." Ph.D. Diss., Northwestern University, 1996.

Green, Joel B. *The Gospel of Luke*. Grand Rapids, Mich.: William B. Eerdmans, 1997.

Green, John T. "Bethsaida-Julias in Roman and Jewish Military Strategies, 66–73 C.E." In Rami Arav and Richard A. Freund, eds., *Bethsaida: A City by the North Shore of the Sea of Galilee*. Vol. I, Bethsaida Excavations Project, 203–227. Kirksville, Mo.: Thomas Jefferson University Press, 1995.

"The Honorific Naming of Bethsaida-Julias." In Rami Arav and Richard A. Freund, eds., *Bethsaida: A City by the North Shore of the Sea of Galilee*. Vol. II, Bethsaida Excavations Project, 307–331. Kirksville, Mo.: Truman State University Press, 1999.

Gregg, Robert C. and Dan Urman. *Jews, Pagans, and Christians in the Golan Heights*. Atlanta: Scholars Press, 1996.

Groh, Dennis E. "The Fine Wares from the Patrician and Lintel Houses." In Eric M. Meyers, James F. Strange, and Carol L. Meyers, eds., *Excavations at Ancient Meiron, Upper Galilee, Israel 1971–1972, 1974–1975, 1977*, 129–138. Cambridge, Mass.: The American Schools of Oriental Research, 1981.

"The Late Roman Fine Wares of the Gush Ḥalav Synagogue." In Eric M. Meyers, Carol L. Meyers, with James F. Strange, eds., *Excavations at the Ancient Synagogue of Gush Ḥalav*, 139–148. Winona Lake, Ind.: Eisenbrauns, 1990.

Grootkerk, Salomon E. *Ancient Sites in Galilee: A Toponymic Gazetteer*. Leiden: Brill, 2000.

Grundman, Walter. *Jesus der Galiläer und das Judentum*. Leipzig: Verlag Georg Wigand, 1941.

Guignebert, Ch. *The Jewish World in the Time of Jesus*. Trans. S. H. Hooke. New York: E. P. Dutton and Co., 1939.

Gundry, Robert H. *Matthew: A Commentary on His Handbook for a Mixed Church under Persecution*, 2nd. edn. Grand Rapids, Mich.: William B. Eerdmans, 1994.

The Use of the Old Testament in St. Matthew's Gospel with Special Reference to the Messianic Hope. Leiden: E. J. Brill, 1967.

Guthe, Hermann. "Beiträge zur Ortskunde Palästinas: Kana in Galilee." *Mitteilungen und Nachrichten des deutschen Palästina-Vereins* 18 (1912): 81–86.

Gutman, Shemaryahu. "Gamala." *NEAEHL*, vol. II, 459–463.

"The Synagogue at Gamla." In Lee I. Levine, ed., *Ancient Synagogues Revealed*, 30–34. Jerusalem: Israel Exploration Society; Detroit: Wayne State University Press, 1982.

Hachlili, Rachel. "Burials: Ancient Jewish." *ABD*, vol. I, 789–794.

Hadidi, Adnan. "The Roman Town Plan of Amman." In Roger Moorey and Peter Parr, eds., *Archaeology in the Levant*, 210–222. Warminster: Aris and Phillips, 1978.

"Umm Qeis." *OEANE*, vol. V, 281–282.

Hagner, Donald A. *Matthew 1–13*. Dallas: Word Books, 1993.

Hall, Bruce. "From John Hyrcanus to Baba Rabba." In Alan D. Crown, ed., *The Samaritans*, 32–54. Tübingen: J. C. B. Mohr (Paul Siebeck), 1989.

Halpern, Baruch. "Settlement of Canaan." *ABD*, vol. V, 1120–1143.

Hamburger, H. "The Coin Issues of the Roman Administration from the Mint of Caesarea Maritima." *IEJ* 20 (1970): 81–91.

Hammond, P. C. *The Nabataeans: Their History, Culture and Archaeology*. Gothenburg, Sweden: Paul Aströms Verlag, 1973.

Hanson, Richard S. *Tyrian Influence in the Upper Galilee*. Cambridge, Mass.: American Schools of Oriental Research, 1980.

Harnack, Adolf von. *What is Christianity?* Trans. Thomas Bailey Saunders. Philadelphia: Fortress Press, 1957.

Harrington, Daniel J. *The Gospel of Matthew*. Collegeville, Minn.: A Michael Glazier Book published by The Liturgical Press, 1991.

Hartel, Mosheh. "Khirbet Zemel, 1985/1986." *IEJ* 37 (1987): 270–272.

Hengel, Martin. The *"Hellenization" of Judaea in the First Century after Christ*. London: SCM Press; Philadelphia: Trinity Press International, 1989.

Judaism and Hellenism: Studies in their Encounter in Palestine during the Early Hellenistic Period. 2 vols. Trans. John Bowden. London: SCM Press; Philadelphia: Trinity Press International, 1974.

Hennessy, Anne. *The Galilee of Jesus*. Rome: Editrice Pontificia Università Gregoriana, 1994.

Hennessy, J. Basil and Robert Houston Smith. "Pella." *OEANE*, vol. IV, 256–259.

Herbert, Sharon C. "Anafa, Tel." *NEAEHL*, vol. I, 58–61.

"Anafa, Tel." *OEANE*, vol. I, 117–118.

"Tel Anafa, 1980." *Muse* 14 (1980): 24–30.

Tel Anafa, I: Final Report on Ten Years of Excavation at a Hellenistic and Roman Settlement in Northern Israel. 2 vols. Ann Arbor, Mich.: Kelsey Museum, 1994.

Herbert, Sharon C., ed. *Tel Anafa II, i: The Hellenistic and Roman Pottery*. Ann Arbor, Mich.: Kelsey Museum; Columbia, Mich.: Museum of Art and Archaeology of the University of Missouri, 1997.

Herion, Gary A. "Hammath." *ABD*, vol. III, 37–38.

Hermann, Siegfried. *A History of Israel in Old Testament Times*. Philadelphia: Fortress Press, 1981.

Heschel, Susannah. "Nazifying Christian Theology: Walter Grundmann and the Institute for the Study and Eradication of Jewish Influence on German Church Life." *Church History* 63 (1994): 587–605.

"Post-Holocaust Jewish Reflections on German Theology." In Carol Rittner and John K. Roth, eds., *From the Unthinkable to the Unavoidable*, 57–69. Westport, Conn. and London: Greenwood Press, 1997.

"Transforming Jesus from Jew to Aryan: Theological Politics in Nazi Germany." *Dialog* 35 (1996): 181–187.

Hestrin, Ruth. "Beth Yeraḥ." *NEAEHL*, vol. I, 255–259.

Hill, David. *The Gospel of Matthew*. Grand Rapids, Mich.: Eerdmans; London: Marshall, Morgan and Scott, 1972.

Hirschfeld, Yizhar. "Excavations at Tiberias Reveal Remains of Church and Possibly Theater." *BA* 54 (1991): 170–171.

"Hammath-Gader." *OEANE*, vol. II, 468–470.

"Hammat Gader." *NEAEHL*, vol. II, 569–573.

"The History and Town-Plan of Ancient Ḥammat Gader." *ZDPV* 103 (1987): 101–116.

"Tiberias." *ESI* 9 (1989/1990): 107–109.

"Tiberias." *ESI* 16 (1997): 35–42.

"Tiberias." *NEAEHL*, vol. IV, 1464–1470.

"Tiberias." *OEANE*, vol. V, 203–206.

"Tiberias: Preview of Coming Attractions." *BAR* 17:2 (1991): 44–51.

Hirschfeld, Yizhar and Giora Solar. "The Roman Thermae at Ḥammat Gader." *IEJ* 31 (1981): 197–219.

"Sumptuous Roman Baths Uncovered Near Sea of Galilee." *BAR* 10:6 (1984): 22–40.

Hoglund, Kenneth G. and Eric M. Meyers. "The Residential Quarter on the Western Summit." In Rebecca Martin Nagy, Carol L. Meyers, Eric M. Meyers, and Zeev Weiss, eds., *Sepphoris in Galilee: Crosscurrents of Culture*, 39–43. Winona Lake, Ind.: Eisenbrauns, 1996.

Hohlfelder, Robert L. "Caesarea." *ABD*, vol. I, 798–803.

Holloman, Henry W. "Galilee, Galileans." In Walter A. Elwell et al., eds., *Baker Encyclopedia of the Bible*, 2 vols., vol. I, 834–836. Grand Rapids, Mich.: Baker Book House, 1986.

Holm-Nielsen, Svend et al. "Umm Qeis (Gadara)." In Denyse Homès-Fredericq and J. Basil Hennessy, eds., *Archaeology of Jordan*, 597–611. Leuven: Peeters, 1986.

Holm-Nielsen, Svend, Ute Wagner-Lux, and K. J. H. Vriezen. "Gadarenes." *ABD*, vol. II, 866–868.

Holum, Kenneth G. "Caesarea." *OEANE*, vol. I, 399–404.

"The Temple Platform: Progress Reports on the Excavations." In Kenneth G. Holum, A. Raban, and J. Patrick, eds., *Caesarea Papers 2*, 13–34. Portsmouth, R.I.: Journal of Roman Archaeology, 1999.

Holum, Kenneth G. and Avner Raban. "Caesarea." *NEAEHL*, vol. I, 270–272.

"Caesarea: The Joint Expedition's Excavations, Excavations in the 1980's and 1990's, and Summary." *NEAEHL*, vol. I, 282–286.

Holum, Kenneth G., A. Raban, and J. Patrick., eds. *Caesarea Papers 2.* Portsmouth, R.I.: Journal of Roman Archaeology, 1999.

Hooker, Morna D. *The Gospel According to Saint Mark.* Peabody, Mass.: Hendrickson Publishers, 1991.

Horsley, Richard A. "Archaeology and the Villages of Upper Galilee: A Dialogue with Archaeologists." *BASOR* 297 (1995): 5–16.

Archaeology, History and Society in Galilee: The Social Context of Jesus and the Rabbis. Valley Forge, Penn.: Trinity Press International, 1996.

Galilee: History, Politics, People. Valley Forge, Penn.: Trinity Press International, 1995.

"The Historical Jesus and Archaeology of the Galilee: Questions from Historical Jesus Research to Archaeologists." In Eugene H. Lovering, Jr., ed., *Society of Biblical Literature 1994 Seminar Papers*, 91–135. Atlanta: Scholars Press, 1994.

Ibañez, Jesús M. Nieto. "The Sacred Grove of Scythopolis (Flavius Josephus, *Jewish War* II 466–471)." *IEJ* 49 (1999): 466–471.

Ilan, David. "Dan, Tel." *OEANE*, vol. II, 107–112.

Ilan, Zvi. "Arbel, Survey of Caves." *ESI* 9 (1989–1990): 17–18.

"Eastern Galilee, Survey of Roman Roads." *ESI* 9 (1989–1990): 14–16.

"Galilee, Survey of Synagogues." *ESI* 5 (1986): 35–37.

"H. Kefar Hananya, Survey." *IEJ* 33 (1983): 255.

"Har Evyatar, Caves of Refuge." *ESI* 7–8 (1988–1989): 75.

"Horvat Arbel." *ESI* 6–7 (1988–1989): 8–9.

"Horvat Arbel." *IEJ* 39 (1989): 100–102.

"Meroth." *NEAEHL*, vol. III, 1028–1031.

Ilan, Zvi and Emmanuel Damati. "Kh. Marus (Merot), 1985–1986." *IEJ* 37 (1987): 54–57.

"Khirbet Marus – 1984," *ESI* 3 (1984): 73–76.

"Meroth (Kh. Marus) – 1986." *ESI* 5 (1986): 64–68.

"The Synagogue at Meroth." *BAR* 15:2 (1989): 20–36.

Ilan, Zvi and Avraham Isdarechet. "Arbel." *NEAEHL*, vol. I, 87–89.

Iliffe, J. H. "A Nude Terra-Cotta Statuette of Aphrodite." *IEJ* 3 (1934): 106–111.

Irvine, Stuart A. "The Southern Border of Syria Reconstructed." *CBQ* 56 (1994): 21–41.

Isaac, Benjamin. "The Decapolis in Syria: A Neglected Inscription." *Zeitschrift für Papyrologie und Epigraphik* 44 (1981): 67–74.

The Limits of Empire: The Roman Army in the East, rev. edn. Oxford: Clarendon Press, 1992.

Isaac, Benjamin and Israel Roll. "Judea in the Early Years of Hadrian's Reign." *Latomus* 38 (1979): 54–66.

"Legio II Traiana – A Reply." *Zeitschrift für Papyrologie und Epigraphik* 47 (1982): 131–132.

"Legio II Traiana in Judaea." *Zeitschrift für Papyrologie und Epigraphik* 33 (1979): 149–156.

Roman Roads in Judaea I: The Legio–Scythopolis Road. BAR International Series 141, Oxford: BAR, 1982.

Jacoby, F. ed. *Die Fragmente der griechischen Historiker.* 4 vols. Leiden: Brill, 1926; repr. 1954–1960.

Jidejian, Nina. *Tyre Through the Ages*. Beirut: Dar El-Mashreq Publishers, 1969.

Joffe, Alexander H. "Beth Yerah." *OEANE*, vol. I, 312–314.

Jones, A. H. M. *The Cities of the Eastern Roman Provinces*, 2nd edn. Oxford: Oxford University Press, 1971.

The Greek City from Alexander to Justinian. Oxford: Clarendon Press, 1940.

Joukowsky, Martha Sharp, ed. *The Heritage of Tyre*. Dubuque, Iowa: Kendall/ Hunt Publishing Company, 1992.

Kadman, Leo. *The Coins of Akko Ptolemais*. Jerusalem and Tel Aviv: Schocken Publishing House, 1961.

The Coins of Caesarea Maritima. Jerusalem and Tel Aviv: Schocken Publishing House, 1957.

Kahane, P. P. "Rock-Cut Tombs at Ḥuqoq: Notes on the Finds." *Atiqot* 3 (1961): 128–147.

Kahn, Lisa C. "King Herod's Temple of Roma and Augustus at Caesarea Maritima." In Avner Raban and Kenneth G. Holum, eds., *Caesarea Maritima: A Retrospective after Two Millenia*, 130–145. Leiden: E. J. Brill, 1996.

Kasher, Aryeh. *Jews and Hellenistic Cities in Eretz-Israel: Relations of the Jews in Eretz-Israel with the Hellenistic Cities during the Second Temple Period (332 BCE–70 CE)*. Tübingen: J. C. B. Mohr (Paul Siebeck), 1990.

Jews, Idumaeans and Ancient Arabs. Tübingen: J. C. B. Mohr, 1988.

Kee, Howard Clark. "The Changing Meaning of Synagogue: A Response to Richard Oster." *NTS* 40 (1994): 281–283.

"Defining the First-Century C.E. Synagogue: Problems and Progress." *NTS* 41 (1995): 481–500.

"Early Christianity in the Galilee: Reassessing the Evidence from the Gospels." In Lee I. Levine, ed., *The Galilee in Late Antiquity*, 3–22. New York and Jerusalem: The Jewish Theological Seminary of America, 1992.

"The Transformation of the Synagogue after 70 C.E.: Its Import for Early Christianity." *NTS* 36 (1990): 1–24.

Kelber, Werner H. *The Kingdom in Mark: A New Place and a New Time*. Philadelphia: Fortress Press, 1974.

Keller, Joan. "The Glass from Sepphoris (1983–1991): A Preliminary Report." http://www.colby.edu/rel/Glass.html.

Kennedy, David. "Legio VI Ferrata: The Annexation and Early Garrison of Arabia." *Harvard Studies in Classical Philology* 84 (1980): 283–309.

Keppie, Lawrence. "Legions in the East from Augustus to Trajan." In Philip Freeman and David Kennedy, eds., *The Defence of the Roman and Byzantine East*, vol. II, 411–429. Oxford: *BAR*, 1986.

Khalifeh, Issam Ali. "Khirbet Marus." *ESI* 1 (1982): 70.

"Sidon." *OEANE*, vol. V, 38–41.

Khouri, Rami. *Jerash: A Frontier City of the Roman East*. London and New York: Longman, 1986.

Kilpatrick, G. D. *The Origins of the Gospel according to St. Matthew*. Oxford: Clarendon Press, 1946.

Kindler, Arie. *The Coins of Tiberias*. Tiberias: Hamei Tiberia, 1961.

Kingsbury, Jack Dean. *Matthew*. Philadelphia: Fortress Press, 1986.

Klausner, Joseph. *Jesus of Nazareth: His Life, Times and Teachings*. New York: Macmillan, 1929.

Klein, Samuel. "Die ältesten jüdischen Siedlungen in Galiläa." In *Galiläa von der Makkabäerzeit bis 67*, 1–21. Vienna: Verlag "Menorah," 1928.

Kloppenborg, John S. "Ethnic and Political Factors in the Conflict at Caesarea Maritima." In Terence L. Donaldson, ed., *Religious Rivalries and the Struggle for Success in Caesarea Maritima*, 227–248. Waterloo, Ontario: Wilfrid Laurier University Press, 2000.

———. "The Sayings Gospel Q: Recent Opinion on the People Behind the Document." *Currents in Research: Biblical Studies* 1 (1993): 9–34.

Kloppenborg Verbin, John S. *Excavating Q: The History and Setting of the Sayings Gospel*. Minneapolis: Fortress Press, 2000.

Knauf, Ernest Axel. "Ituraea." *ABD*, vol. III, 583–584.

Koester, Craig. "The Origin and Significance of the Flight to Pella Tradition." *CBQ* 51 (1989): 90–106.

Kopp, Clemons. "Beiträge zur Geschichte Nazareths." *JPOS* 18 (1938): 187–233.

———. *The Holy Places of the Gospels*. New York: Herder and Herder, 1963.

———. "Korazin." *ESI* 1 (1982): 64–67.

Kraeling, Carl H. "The History of Gerasa." In Carl H. Kraeling, ed., *Gerasa: City of the Decapolis*, 27–72. New Haven, Conn.: American Schools of Oriental Research, 1938.

Kraeling, Carl H., ed. *Gerasa: City of the Decapolis*. New Haven, Conn.: American Schools of Oriental Research, 1938.

Kuhn, Heinz-Wolfgang. "Zum neuesten Stand der Grabungen auf et-Tell." *Welt und Umwelt der Bibel* 10:4 (1998): 78–80.

Kuhn, Heinz-Wolfgang and Rami Arav. "The Bethsaida Excavations: Historical and Archaeological Approaches." In Birger A. Pearson et al., eds., *The Future of Early Christianity*, 77–107. Minneapolis: Fortress Press, 1991.

Kutsko, John. "Caesarea Philippi." *ABD*, vol. I, 803.

Lapp, Eric Christian. "The Archaeology of Light: The Cultural Significance of the Oil Lamp from Roman Palestine." Ph.D. Diss., Duke University, 1997.

Laughlin, John C. H. "Capernaum: From Jesus' Time and After." *BAR* 19:5 (1993): 54–61.

Lawlor, John Irving. *The Nabataeans in Historical Perspective*. Grand Rapids, Mich.: Baker Book House, 1974.

Lee, Bernard J. *The Galilean Jewishness of Jesus*. New York and Mahwah: Paulist Press, 1988.

Lentz, A. ed. *Grammatici Graeci*. 4 vols. Leipzig: Teubner, 1867; repr. Hildesheim: Olms, 1965.

Lenzen, C. J. "Beit Ras." *OEANE*, vol. I, 297–298.

Lenzen, C. J. and F. A. Knauf. "Beit Ras/ Capitolias: A Preliminary Evaluation of the Archaeological and Textual Evidence." *Syria* 64 (1987): 21–46.

Levey, Irving M. "Caesarea and the Jews." In Charles T. Fritsch et al., eds., *The Joint Expedition to Caesarea Maritima*. Vol. I, *Studies in the History of Caesarea Maritima*, 43–78. Missoula, Mont.: Scholars Press for ASOR, 1975.

Levine, Lee I. "Beth She'arim." *OEANE*, vol. I, 309–311.

———. *Caesarea under Roman Rule*. Leiden: E. J. Brill, 1975.

———. "Jewish-Greek Conflict in First Century Caesarea." *Journal of Jewish Studies* 25 (1974): 381–397.

Judaism and Hellenism in Antiquity: Conflict or Confluence? Peabody, Mass.: Hendrickson Publishers, 1998.

Review of Moshe Dothan, *Hammath Tiberias: Early Synagogues and the Hellenistic and Roman Remains. IEJ* 34 (1984): 284–288.

Levine, Lee I., ed. *Ancient Synagogues Revealed.* Jerusalem: Israel Exploration Society; Detroit: Wayne State University Press, 1982.

The Galilee in Late Antiquity. New York and Jerusalem: The Jewish Theological Seminary of America, 1992.

Levine, Lee I. and Ehud Netzer. "Caesarea: Excavations in the 1970's." *NEAEHL,* vol. I, 280–282.

Lifschitz, Baruch. "Der Kult des Zeus Akraios und des Zeus Bakchos in Beisan (Skythopolis)." *ZDPV* 77 (1961): 186–190.

"Sur la date du transfert de la Legio VI Ferrata en Palestine." *Latomus* 19 (1960): 109–111.

Lightfoot, Robert Henry. *Locality and Doctrine in the Gospels.* New York and London: Harper and Brothers Publishers, n. d.

Loffreda, Stanislao. *Cafarnao.* Vol. II, *La Ceramica.* Jerusalem: Franciscan Printing Press, 1974.

"Capernaum." *NEAEHL,* vol. I, 291–295.

"Capernaum." *OEANE,* vol. I, 416–419.

"Ceramica ellenistica-romana nel sottosuolo della sinagoga di Cafarnao." In Emmanuele Testa, ed., *Studia Hierosolymitana III in onore del P. Bellarmino Bagatti: Studi Archeologici,* 273–312. Jerusalem: Franciscan Printing Press, 1982.

"The Late Chronology of the Synagogue of Capernaum." In Lee I. Levine, ed., *Ancient Synagogues Revealed,* 52–56. Jerusalem: Israel Exploration Society; Detroit: Wayne State University Press, 1982.

"Un lotto di ceramica da Karm er-Ras presso Kafr Kanna." *LA* 25 (1975): 193–198.

Recovering Capharnaum, 2nd edn. Jerusalem: Franciscan Printing Press, 1993.

Lohmeyer, Ernst. *Galiläa und Jerusalem.* Göttingen: Vandenhoeck and Ruprecht, 1936.

Long, Thomas G. *Matthew.* Louisville: Westminster John Knox Press, 1997.

Longstaff, Thomas R. W. "Gush Ḥalav in the Ancient Literary Sources." In Eric M. Meyers, Carol L. Meyers, and James F. Strange, eds., *Excavations at the Ancient Synagogue of Gush Ḥalav,* 16–22. Winona Lake, Ind.: Eisenbrauns, 1990.

"Nazareth and Sepphoris: Insights into Christian Origins." *Anglican Theological Review Supplementary Series* 11 (1990): 8–15.

Lüdemann, Gerd. "The Successors of Pre-70 Jerusalem Christianity: A Critical Evaluation of the Pella-Tradition." In E. P. Sanders, ed., *Jewish and Christian Self-Definition,* vol. I, 161–173. Philadelphia: Fortress, 1980.

Luz, Ulrich. *Matthew 1–7: A Commentary.* Edinburgh: T&T Clark, 1989.

MacAlister, R. W. Stewart and Emil G. Kraeling. "Galilee." In James Hastings, Frederick C. Grant, and H. H. Rowley, eds., *Dictionary of the Bible,* 313–314. New York: Charles Scribner's Sons, 1963.

Mack, Burton L. *The Lost Gospel: The Book of Q and Christian Origins.* San Francisco: HarperCollins, 1993.

A Myth of Innocence: Mark and Christian Origins. Philadelphia: Fortress Press, 1988.

Mackowski, Richard M. "Scholars' Qanah: A Re-examination of the Evidence in Favor of Khirbet Qanah." *Biblische Zeitschrift* 23 (1979): 278–284.

Magen, Itzhak. "Ancient Israel's Stone Age: Purity in Second Temple Times." *BAR* 24:5 (1998): 46–52.

"Gerizim, Mount." *NEAEHL*, vol. II, 484–493.

"Jerusalem as a Center of the Stone Vessel Industry during the Second Temple Period." In Hillel Geva, ed., *Ancient Jerusalem Revealed*, 244–256. Jerusalem: Israel Exploration Society; Washington, D.C.: Biblical Archaeology Society, 1994.

"Shechem: Neapolis." *NEAEHL*, vol. IV, 1354–1359.

"The Stone Vessel Industry during the Second Temple Period." In *"Purity Broke Out in Israel,"* 7–28. Catalogue no. 9, The Reuben and Edith Hecht Museum, University of Haifa, 1994.

Magness, Jodi. "Some Observations on the Roman Temple at Kedesh." *IEJ* 40 (1990): 173–181.

Maisler, B., M. Stekelis, and M. Avi-Yonah. "The Excavations at Beth Yerah (Khirbet el-Kerak) 1944–1946." *IEJ* 2 (1952): 165–173, 218–229.

Malbon, Elisabeth Struthers. "The Jesus of Mark and the Sea of Galilee." *JBL* 103 (1984): 242–255.

Malinowski, Frances Xavier. "Galilean Judaism in the Writings of Flavius Josephus." Ph.D. Diss., Duke University, 1973.

Ma'oz, Zvi Uri. "Banias." *NEAEHL*, vol. I, 136–143.

"Coin and Temple – The Case of Caesarea Philippi-Paneas." *INJ* 13 (1994–1999): 90–100.

"Golan." *OEANE*, vol. II, 417–424.

"Golan Heights." *ABD*, vol. II, 1055–1065.

"Golan: Hellenistic Period to the Middle Ages." *NEAEHL*, vol. II, 534–546.

"The Synagogue of Gamla and the Typology of Second-Temple Synagogues." In Lee I. Levine, ed., *Ancient Synagogues Revealed*, 35–41. Jerusalem: Israel Exploration Society; Detroit: Wayne State University Press, 1982.

Mare, W. Harold. "Abila." *NEAEHL*, vol. I, 1–3.

"Abila." *OEANE*, vol. I, 5–7.

"The 1996 Season of Excavation at Abila of the Decapolis." *ADAJ* 41 (1997): 303–310.

"The Artemis Statue Excavated at Abila of the Decapolis in 1994." *ADAJ* 41 (1997): 277–281.

Markoe, Glenn. "Phoenicians." *OEANE*, vol. IV, 325–331.

Marshall, I. Howard. *The Gospel of Luke*. Grand Rapids, Mich.: William B. Eerdmans Publishing Co., 1978.

Martinez, Florentine García. *The Dead Sea Scrolls Translated: The Qumran Texts in English*. Trans. Wilfred G. E. Watson. Leiden: E. J. Brill, 1994.

Marxsen, Willi. *Mark the Evangelist*. Trans. James Boyce et al. Nashville: Abingdon, 1969.

Masterman, E. W. G. "Cana of Galilee – at Khirbet Kana." *Palestine Exploration Fund Quarterly Statement* (1914): 179–183.

"Two Greek Inscriptions from Khurbet Ḥarrawi." *PEQ* 20 (1908): 155–157.

Mazar, Amihai. "Beth-Shean." *OEANE*, vol. I, 305–309.

"Beth-Shean: Tel Beth Shean and the Northern Cemetery." *NEAEHL*, vol. I, 214–223.

Mazar, Benjamin. *Beth She'arim*. Vol. I, *Catacombs 1–4*. New Brunswick, N.J.: Rutgers University Press, 1973.

Mazar, Gaby. "Bet Shean Project–1988." *ESI* 7–8 (1988–1989): 15–32.

Mazar, Gaby and Rachel Bar-Hathan. "The Beth She'an Excavation Project, 1992–1994." *ESI* 17 (1998): 7–38.

Mazar, Gaby, Gideon Foerster, Yoram Tsafrir, and Fanny Vitto. "The Bet Shean Project." *ESI* 6 (1987–1988): 7–45.

McCane, Byron. "Burial Techniques." *OEANE*, vol. I, 386–387.

"Jews, Christians, and Burial in Roman Palestine." Ph.D. Diss., Duke University, 1992.

"Ossuary." *OEANE*, vol. IV, 187–188.

McCollough, C. Thomas and Douglas R. Edwards. "Transformations of Space: The Roman Road at Sepphoris." In Douglas R. Edwards and C. Thomas McCollough, eds., *Archaeology and the Galilee: Texts and Contexts in the Greco-Roman and Byzantine Periods*, 135–142. Atlanta: Scholars Press, 1997.

McCown, Chester C. "Epigraphic Gleanings." *AASOR* 2–3 (1923): 109–11.

"The Festival Theater at the Birketein." In Carl H. Kraeling, ed., *Gerasa: City of the Decapolis*, 159–170. New Haven, Conn.: American Schools of Oriental Research, 1938.

"The Problem of the Site of Bethsaida." *JPOS* 10 (1930): 32–58.

McGovern, Patrick E. "Beth-Shan." *ABD*, vol. I, 693–696.

McLean, Bradley H. "Epigraphical Evidence in Caesarea Maritima." In Terence L. Donaldson, ed., *Religious Rivalries and the Struggle for Success in Caesarea Maritima*, 57–64. Waterloo, Ontario: Wilfrid Laurier University Press, 2000.

McNicoll, Anthony W., Robert H. Smith, and Basil Hennessy. *Pella in Jordan 1: An Interim Report on the Joint University of Sydney and The College of Wooster Excavations at Pella 1979–1981*. Canberra: Australian National Gallery, 1982.

McNicoll Anthony W. et al. *Pella in Jordan 2: The Second Interim Report of the Joint University of Sydney and The College of Wooster Excavations at Pella 1982–1985*. Sydney: Meditarch, 1992.

McRay, John. "Damascus: The Greco-Roman Period." *ABD*, vol. II, 7–8.

"Gerasenes." *ABD*, vol. II, 991–992.

Meier, John P. *A Marginal Jew*. 2 vols. New York: Doubleday, 1991, 1994.

Matthew. Collegeville, Minn.: A Michael Glazier Book published by The Liturgical Press, 1990.

Mendenhall, George E. "The Hebrew Conquest of Palestine." *BA* 25 (1962): 66–87.

Meshorer, Yaakov. *Ancient Jewish Coinage*. 2 vols. Dix Hills, N.Y.: Amphora Books, 1982.

"Ancient Jewish Coinage Addendum I." *INJ* 11 (1990–1991): 104–132.

City-Coins of Eretz-Israel and the Decapolis in the Roman Period. Jerusalem: The Israel Museum, 1985.

"Coins." In Sharon C. Herbert, ed., *Tel Anafa, I: Final Report on Ten Years of Excavation at a Hellenistic and Roman Settlement in Northern Israel*, 241–260. Ann Arbor, Mich.: Kelsey Museum, 1994.

"The Coins of Caesarea Paneas." *INJ* 8 (1984–1985): 37–58.

"The Coins of Dora." *INJ* 9 (1986–1987): 59–72.

Jewish Coins of the Second Temple Period. Trans. I. H. Levine. Tel Aviv: Am Hassefer Publishers Ltd. and Massada, 1967.

"The Lead Weight: Preliminary Report." *BA* 49 (1986): 16–17.

"Sepphoris and Rome." In O. Morkholm and N. M. Waggoner, eds., *Greek Numismatics and Archaeology: Essays in Honor of Margaret Thompson*, 159–171. Belgium: Cultura Press, 1979.

Meyers, Carol L. "Gush Ḥalav." *OEANE*, vol. II, 442–443.

"Of Seasons and Soldiers: A Topological Appraisal of the Premonarchic Tribes of Galilee." *BASOR* 252 (1983): 47–59.

"Sepphoris and Lower Galilee: Earliest Times through the Persian Period." In Rebecca Martin Nagy, Carol L. Meyers, Eric M. Meyers, and Zeev Weiss, eds., *Sepphoris in Galilee: Crosscurrents of Culture*, 15–20. Winona Lake, Ind.: Eisenbrauns, 1996.

Meyers, Carol L. and Eric M. Meyers. "Sepphoris." *OEANE*, vol. IV, 527–536.

Meyers, Carol L., Eric M. Meyers, Ehud Netzer, and Zeev Weiss. "The Dionysos Mosaic." In Rebecca Martin Nagy, Carol L. Meyers, Eric M. Meyers, and Zeev Weiss, eds., *Sepphoris in Galilee: Crosscurrents of Culture*, 111–115. Winona Lake, Ind.: Eisenbrauns, 1996.

"Sepphoris (Ṣippori), 1986 (I) – Joint Sepphoris Project." *IEJ* 37 (1987): 275–288.

Meyers, Eric M. "Ancient 'Gush Ḥalav' (Gischala), Palestinian Synagogues and the Eastern Diaspora." In Joseph Gutmann, ed., *Ancient Synagogues: The State of Research*, 61–78. Chico, Cal.: Scholars Press, 1981.

"Ancient Synagogues: An Archaeological Introduction." In Steven Fine, ed., *Sacred Realm: The Emergence of the Synagogue in the Ancient World*, 3–20. New York and Oxford: Oxford University Press and Yeshiva University Museum, 1996.

"Ancient Synagogues in Galilee: Their Religious and Cultural Setting." *BA* 43 (1980): 97–108.

"An Archaeological Response to a New Testament Scholar." *BASOR* 297 (1995): 17–26.

"Archaeology and Rabbinic Tradition at Khirbet Shema', 1970 and 1971 Campaigns." *BA* 35 (1972): 1–31.

"Archaeology in Palestine in Recent Decades: Achievements and Goals." In William Horbury, W. D. Davies, and John Sturdy, eds., *Cambridge History of Judaism*, vol. III, 59–74. New York and Cambridge: Cambridge University Press, 1999.

"The Challenge of Hellenism for Early Judaism and Christianity." *BA* 55 (1992): 84–91.

"The Cultural Setting of Galilee: The Case of Regionalism and Early Judaism." In Hildegard Temporini and Wolfgang Haase, eds., *Aufstieg und Niedergang der römischen Welt*, 2.19.1, 686–702. Berlin and New York: Walter de Gruyter, 1979.

"The Current State of Galilean Synagogue Studies." In Lee I. Levine, ed., *The Synagogue in Late Antiquity*, 127–138. Philadelphia: American Schools of Oriental Research, 1987.

"Early Judaism and Christianity in the Light of Archaeology." *BA* 51 (1988): 69–79.

"Excavations at Gush Halav in Upper Galilee." In Lee I. Levine, ed., *Ancient Synagogues Revealed*, 75–77. Jerusalem: Israel Exploration Society; Detroit: Wayne State University Press, 1982.

"Galilean Regionalism: A Reappraisal." In W. S. Green, ed., *Approaches to Ancient Judaism*, vol. V, 115–131. Missoula, Mont.: Scholars Press for Brown University, 1978.

"Galilean Regionalism as a Factor in Historical Reconstruction." *BASOR* 221 (1976): 93–101.

"Gush Halav." *NEAEHL*, vol. II, 546–549.

"Identifying Religious and Ethnic Groups through Archaeology." In Avraham Biran and Joseph Aviram, eds., *Biblical Archaeology Today, 1990: Proceedings of the Second International Congress in Biblical Archaeology*, 738–745. Jerusalem: Israel Exploration Society and Israel Academy of Sciences and Humanities, 1993.

"Jesus and His Galilean Context." In Douglas R. Edwards and C. Thomas McCollough, eds., *Archaeology and the Galilee: Texts and Contexts in the Graeco-Roman and Byzantine Periods*, 57–66. Atlanta: Scholars Press, 1997.

Jewish Ossuaries: Reburial and Rebirth. Rome: Biblical Institute Press, 1971.

"Meiron." *ABD*, vol. IV, 682–683.

"Meiron." *EAEHL*, vol. III, 856–862.

"Meiron." *NEAEHL*, vol. III, 1024–1027.

"Meiron." *OEANE*, vol. III, 469–470.

"Nabratein." *OEANE*, vol. IV, 85–87.

"Nabratein (Kefar Neburaya)." *NEAEHL*, vol. III, 1077–1079.

Review of Moshe Dothan, *Hammath Tiberias: Early Synagogues and the Hellenistic and Roman Remains*, *JAOS* 104 (1984): 577–578.

"Roman Sepphoris in Light of New Archeological Evidence and Recent Research." In Lee I. Levine, ed., *The Galilee in Late Antiquity*, 321–338. New York and Jerusalem: The Jewish Theological Seminary of America, 1992.

"Second Temple Studies in the Light of Recent Archaeology: Part I: The Persian and Hellenistic Periods." *Currents in Research: Biblical Studies* 2 (1994): 25–42.

"Secondary Burials in Palestine." *BA* 33:1 (1970): 2–29.

"Sepphoris on the Eve of the Great Revolt (67–68 C.E.): Archaeology and Josephus." In Eric M. Meyers, ed., *Galilee through the Centuries*, 127–140. Winona Lake, Ind.: Eisenbrauns, 1999.

"Synagogue." *ABD*, vol. VI, 251–260.

"Shema', Khirbet." *EAEHL*, vol. IV, 1095–1097.

"Shema', Khirbet." *NEAEHL*, vol. IV, 1359–1361.

"Shema', Khirbet." *OEANE*, vol. V, 26–27.

"Shema,' Khirbet." *ABD*, vol. V, 1197–1198.

"Synagogues of Galilee." *Archaeology* 35 (1982): 51–58.

"The Torah Shrine in the Ancient Synagogue: Another Look at the Evidence." *JSQ* 4 (1997): 303–338.

"Yes, They Are." *BAR* 26:4 (2000): 46–49, 60.

Meyers, Eric M., ed., *Galilee through the Centuries: Confluence of Cultures.* Winona Lake, Ind.: Eisenbrauns, 1999.

Meyers, Eric M. and A. Thomas Kraabel. "Archaeology, Iconography, and Non-literary Written Remains." In Robert A. Kraft and W. E. Nickelsburg, eds., *Early Judaism and its Modern Interpreters,* 175–210. Atlanta: Scholars Press, 1986.

Meyers, Eric M., A. Thomas Kraabel, and James F. Strange. *Ancient Synagogue Excavations at Khirbet Shema', Upper Galilee, Israel, 1970–1972.* Durham, N.C.: Duke University Press, 1976.

Meyers, Eric M. and Carol L. Meyers. "Finders of a Real Lost Ark." *BAR* 7:6 (1981): 24–39.

Meyers, Eric M., Carol L. Meyers, and Kenneth G. Hoglund. "Sepphoris (Sippori), 1993." *IEJ* 44 (1994): 247–259.

"Sepphoris, (Sippori) 1994." *IEJ* 45 (1995): 68–71.

"Zippori (Sepphoris) – 1994." *ESI* 16 (1997): 46–47.

Meyers, Eric M., Carol L. Meyers, and Ehud Netzer. "Sepphoris (Sippori) 1987, (I)." *IEJ* 37 (1987): 275–288.

"Sepphoris, (Sippori) 1985, (I)." *IEJ* 35 (1985): 295–297.

Meyers, Eric M., Carol L. Meyers, with James F. Strange. *Excavations at the Ancient Synagogue of Gush Ḥalav.* Winona Lake, Ind.: Eisenbrauns, 1990.

Meyers, Eric M., Ehud Netzer, and Carol L. Meyers. "Artistry in Stone: The Mosaics of Ancient Sepphoris." *BA* 50 (1987): 223–231.

Sepphoris. Winona Lake, Ind.: Eisenbrauns, 1992.

"Sepphoris: Ornament of All Galilee." *BA* 49 (1989): 4–19.

"Sepphoris (Sippori), 1987 and 1988." *IEJ* 40 (1990): 219–221.

Meyers, Eric M. and James F. Strange. *Archaeology, the Rabbis, and Early Christianity.* Nashville: Abingdon, 1981.

"The Cultural Setting of Galilee: The Case of Regionalism and Early Palestinian Judaism." In *Archaeology, the Rabbis, and Early Christianity,* 31–47. Nashville: Abingdon, 1981.

Meyers, Eric M., James F. Strange, and Dennis E. Groh. "The Meiron Excavation Project: Archeological Survey in Galilee and Golan, 1976." *BASOR* 230 (1978): 1–24.

Meyers, Eric M., James F. Strange, and Carol L. Meyers. "The Ark of Nabratein – A First Glance." *BA* 44 (1981): 237–243.

Excavations at Ancient Meiron, Upper Galilee, Israel 1971–1972, 1974–1975, 1977. Cambridge, Mass.: The American Schools of Oriental Research, 1981.

"Nabratein, 1980." *IEJ* 31 (1981): 108–110.

"Preliminary Report on the 1980 Excavations at en-Nabratein, Israel." *BASOR* 244 (1981): 1–25.

"Second Preliminary Report on the 1981 Excavations at en-Nabratein, Israel." *BASOR* 246 (1982): 35–54.

Meyers, Eric M., James F. Strange, Carol L. Meyers, and Richard S. Hanson. "Preliminary Report on the 1977 and 1978 Seasons at Gush Halav (El Jish)." *BASOR* 233 (1979): 33–58.

Millar, Fergus. "The Roman *Coloniae* of the Near East: A Study of Cultural Relations." In Heikki Solin and Mika Kajava, eds., *Roman Eastern Policy and Other Studies in Roman History,* 7–58. Helsinki: Societas Scientiarum Fennica, 1990.

The Roman Near East: 31 B.C.–A.D. 337. Cambridge, Mass. and London: Harvard University Press, 1993.

Miller, J. Innes. *The Spice Trade of the Roman Empire: 29 B.C. to A.D. 641.* Oxford: Clarendon Press, 1969.

Miller, Stuart S. "Hellenistic and Roman Sepphoris: The Historical Evidence." In Rebecca M. Nagy, Carol L. Meyers, Eric M. Meyers, and Zeev Weiss, eds., *Sepphoris in Galilee: Crosscurrents of Culture*, 15–29. Winona Lake, Ind.: Eisenbrauns, 1996.

"Intercity Relations in Roman Palestine: The Case of Sepphoris and Tiberias." *Association for Jewish Studies Review* 12 (1987): 1–24.

"Jewish Sepphoris: A Great City of Scholars and Scribes." In Rebecca M. Nagy, Carol L. Meyers, Eric M. Meyers, and Zeev Weiss, eds., *Sepphoris in Galilee: Crosscurrents of Culture*, 59–65. Winona Lake, Ind.: Eisenbrauns, 1996.

"New Perspectives on the History of Sepphoris." In Eric M. Meyers, ed., *Galilee through the Centuries: Confluence of Cultures*, 145–160. Winona Lake, Ind.: Eisenbrauns, 1999.

"Sepphoris, the Well-Remembered City." *BA* 55 (1992): 74–83.

Studies in the History and Traditions of Sepphoris. Leiden: E. J. Brill, 1984.

Mor, Menahem. "The Persian, Hellenistic and Hasmonaean Period." In Alan D. Crown, ed., *The Samaritans*, 1–18. Tübingen: J. C. B. Mohr (Paul Siebeck), 1989.

"The Roman Army in Eretz-Israel in the Years AD 70–132." In Philip Freeman and David Kennedy, eds., *The Defence of the Roman and Byzantine East*, vol. II, 757–601. Oxford: BAR, 1986.

"The Samaritans and the Bar-Kochbah Revolt." In Alan D. Crown, ed., *The Samaritans*, 19–31. Tübingen: J. C. B. Mohr (Paul Siebeck), 1989.

"The Mosaic Pavements of Roman and Byzantine Zippori," www.hum.huji.ac.il/archaeology/zippori/mosaic.htm.

Motyer, J. A. *The Prophecy of Isaiah.* Leicester: Inter-Varsity Press, 1993.

Müller, Carl. *Fragmenta historicorum Graecorum.* 5 vols. Paris: Ambrosio Firmin Didot, 1853–1870.

Murray, Michele. "Jews and Judaism in Caesarea Maritima." In Terence L. Donaldson, ed., *Religious Rivalries and the Struggle for Success in Caesarea Maritima*, 127–152. Waterloo, Ontario: Wilfrid Laurier University Press, 2000.

Nagakubo, Senzo. "Investigations into Jewish Concepts of Afterlife in the Beth She'arim Greek Inscriptions." Ph.D. Diss., Duke University, 1974.

Nagy, Rebecca Martin, Carol L. Meyers, Eric M. Meyers, and Zeev Weiss, eds. *Sepphoris in Galilee: Crosscurrents of Culture.* Winona Lake, Ind.: Eisenbrauns, 1996.

Najjar, Arfan and Nissim Najjar. "Nazareth." *ESI* 16 (1997): 49.

Najjar, Nissim. "Dabburiyya." *ESI* 16 (1997): 50–51.

"Kafr Kanna (A)." *ESI* 16 (1997): 47–48.

"Nazareth 'Illit." *ESI* 1 (1982): 78–79.

Negev, Avraham. "Petra." *NEAEHL*, vol. IV, 1181–1193.

Negev, Avraham, Antonio Frovo, and Michael Avi-Yonah. "Caesarea: Excavations in the 1950's and 1960's." *NEAEHL*, vol. I, 272–280.

Netzer, Ehud. "The Promontory Palace." In Avner Raban and Kenneth G. Holum, eds., *Caesarea Maritima: A Retrospective after Two Millenia*, 193–207. Leiden: E. J. Brill, 1996.

"A Synagogue from the Hasmonean Period Recently Exposed in the Western Palace of Jericho." *IEJ* 49 (1999): 203–221.

Netzer, Ehud and Zeev Weiss. *Zippori*. Jerusalem: n.p., distributed by Israel Exploration Society, 1994.

Nobbe, C. F. A., ed. *Claudii Ptolemaei geographia*. Leipzig: Teubner, 1843; repr. Hildesheim: Olms, 1966.

"Notes and News." *IEJ* 3 (1953): 265–266.

Oakman, Douglas E. "The Archaeology of First-Century Galilee and the Social Interpretation of the Historical Jesus." In Eugene H. Lovering, Jr., ed., *Society of Biblical Literature 1994 Seminar Papers*, 220–251. Atlanta: Scholars Press, 1994.

Oded, Bustenay. *Mass Deportations in the Neo-Assyrian Empire*. Wiesbaden: Reichert, 1979.

Oehler, W. "Die Ortschaften und Grenzen Galiläas nach Josephus." *ZPDV* 28 (1905): 1–26, 49–74.

Oleson, John Peter et al. *The Harbours of Caesarea Maritima*. 2 vols. Oxford: BAR, 1989, 1994.

Olson, Dennis T. "The Book of Judges." In Leander Keck et al, eds., *The Interpreter's Bible*, vol. II. Nashville: Abingdon Press, 1998.

Oppenheimer, Aharon. "Roman Rule and the Cities of the Galilee in Talmudic Literature." In Lee I. Levine, ed., *The Galilee in Late Antiquity*, 115–125. New York and Jerusalem: The Jewish Theological Seminary of America, 1992.

Orfali, Gaudence. *Capharnaüm et ses Ruines*. Paris, 1922.

Ostrasz, Antoni A. "The Hippodrome of Gerasa: A Report on Excavations and Research." *Syria* 66 (1989): 51–77.

Oswalt, John N. *The Book of Isaiah: Chapters 1–39*. Grand Rapids, Mich.: William B. Eerdmans Publishing Co., 1986.

Ovadiah, Asher. "Was the Cult of the God Dushara-Dusares Practised in Hippos-Susita?" *PEQ* 113 (1981): 101–104.

Ovadiah, Asher, Moshe Fischer, and Israel Roll. "Kedesh (In Upper Galilee): The Roman Temple." *NEAEHL*, vol. III, 857–859.

Ovadiah, Asher, Israel Roll, and Moshe Fischer. "The Roman Temple at Kedesh in Upper Galilee: A Response." *IEJ* 43 (1993): 60–63.

Overman, J. Andrew. "Recent Advances in the Archaeology of the Galilee in the Roman Period." *Currents in Research: Biblical Studies* 1 (1993): 35–57.

"Who Were the First Urban Christians? Urbanization in Galilee in the First Century." In David J. Lull, ed., *Society of Biblical Literature 1988 Seminar Papers*, 160–168. Atlanta: Scholars Press, 1988.

Painter, R. Jackson. "Greco-Roman Religion in Caesarea Maritima." In Terence L. Donaldson, ed., *Religious Rivalries and the Struggle for Success in Caesarea Maritima*, 105–125. Waterloo, Ontario: Wilfrid Laurier University Press, 2000.

"The Origins and Social Context of Mithraism at Caesarea Maritima." In Terence L. Donaldson, ed., *Religious Rivalries and the Struggle for Success in*

Caesarea Maritima, 205–225. Waterloo, Ontario: Wilfrid Laurier University Press, 2000.

Parker, S. Thomas. "Decapolis." *OEANE*, vol. II, 127–130.

"The Decapolis Reviewed." *JBL* 94 (1975): 437–441.

Patrick, Joseph et al. "The Warehouse Complex and Governor's Palace." In K. G. Holum, A. Raban, and J. Patrick, eds., *Caesarea Papers 2*, 71–107. Portsmouth, R.I.: Journal of Roman Archaeology, 1999.

Pitard, Wayne T. "Damascus." *OEANE*, vol. I, 103–106.

Pixner, Bargil. "Searching for the New Testament Site of Bethsaida." *BA* 48 (1985): 207–216.

Porath, Yosef, Avner Raban, and Joseph Patrick. "The Caesarea Excavation Project – March 1992–June 1994." *ESI* 17 (1998): 39–82.

Porter, Stanley E. "Jesus and the Use of Greek in Galilee." In Bruce Chilton and Craig A. Evans, eds., *Studying the Historical Jesus: Evaluations of the State of Current Research*, 123–154. Leiden: E. J. Brill, 1994.

Purvis, James D. "Samaria (City)." *ABD*, vol. V, 915–921.

Qedar, Shraga. "Two Lead Weights of Herod Antipas and Agrippa II and the Early History of Tiberias." *INJ* 9 (1986–1987): 29–35.

R., E. T. [no further identification of author provided]. "A Rock-Cut Tomb at Nazareth." *QDAP* 1 (1932): 53.

Raban, Avner. "Acco: Maritime Acco." *NEAEHL*, vol. I, 29–31.

"Caesarea: Maritime Caesarea." *NEAEHL*, vol. I, 286–291.

Raban, Avner and Kenneth G. Holum, eds. *Caesarea Maritima: A Retrospective after Two Millenia*. Leiden: E. J. Brill, 1996.

Rainey, Anson F. "Toponymic Problems." *Tel Aviv* 8 (1981): 146–151.

Rajak, Tessa. "Justus of Tiberias." *Classical Quarterly* 23 (1973): 345–368.

Rappaport, Uriel. "How Anti-Roman was the Galilee?" In Lee I. Levine, ed., *The Galilee in Late Antiquity*, 95–102. New York and Jerusalem: The Jewish Theological Seminary of America, 1992.

Rast, Walter E. *Through the Ages in Palestinian Archaeology*. Philadelphia: Trinity Press International, 1992.

Ravani, B. "Rock-Cut Tombs at Ḥuqoq: The Excavations." *Atiqot* 3 (1961): 121–127.

Raveh, Kurt and Sean A. Kingsley. "Dor: Underwater Surveys." *NEAEHL*, vol. I, 371–372.

Raynor, Joyce and Yaakov Meshorer, with Richard S. Hanson. *The Coins of Ancient Meiron*. Winona Lake, Ind.: ASOR, Eisenbrauns, 1988.

Redding, Richard W. "The Vertebrate Fauna." In Sharon C. Herbert, ed., *Tel Anafa, I: Final Report on Ten Years of Excavation at a Hellenistic and Roman Settlement in Northern Israel*, 279–322. Ann Arbor, Mich.: Kelsey Museum, 1994.

Redditt, Paul L. "Arbela." *ABD*, vol. I, 354.

Reed, Jonathan L. *Archaeology and the Galilean Jesus: A Re-examination of the Evidence*. Harrisburg, Penn.: Trinity Press International, 2000.

"'Israelite Village Communities,' and the Sayings Gospel Q." In Eric M. Meyers, ed., *Galilee through the Centuries*, 87–108. Winona Lake, Ind.: Eisenbrauns, 1999.

"Places in Early Christianity: Galilee, Archaeology, Urbanization, and Q." Ph.D. Diss., Claremont Graduate School, 1994.

"Population Numbers, Urbanization, and Economics: Galilean Archaeology and the Historical Jesus." In Eugene H. Lovering, Jr., ed., *Society of Biblical Literature 1994 Seminar Papers*, 203–219. Atlanta: Scholars Press, 1994.

"The Population of Capernaum." *Occasional Papers of the Institute for Antiquity and Christianity* 24 (1992): 1–19.

"The Social Map of Q." In John S. Kloppenborg, ed., *Conflict and Invention*, 17–36. Valley Forge, Penn.: Trinity Press International, 1995.

Reich, Ronny. "The Hot Bath-House (*balneum*), the *Miqweh*, and the Jewish Community in the Second Temple Period." *JJS* 39 (1988): 102–107.

"The Persian Building at Ayyelet ha-Shaḥar: The Assyrian Palace of Hazor?" *IEJ* 25 (1975): 233–237.

"Ritual Baths." *OEANE*, vol. IV, 430–431.

Reicke, Bo. *The New Testament Era*. Trans. David E. Green. Philadelphia: Fortress Press, 1968.

Renan, Ernest. *The Life of Jesus*, 13th edn. London: Mathieson and Co., n. d.

Rey-Coquais, Jean-Paul. "Decapolis." Trans. Stephen Rosoff. *ABD*, vol. II, 116–121.

Inscriptions de la nécrapole. Paris: Libraire d'Amérique et d'Orient, 1977. In *Bulletin du Musée de Beyrouth* 29 (1977).

"Philadelphia (Amman)." In Richard Stillwell et al., eds., *The Princeton Encyclopedia of Classical Sites*, 703–704. Princeton: Princeton University Press, 1976.

Richardson, Peter. "Archaeological Evidence for Religion and Urbanism in Caesarea Maritima." In Terence L. Donaldson, ed., *Religious Rivalries and the Struggle for Success in Caesarea Maritima*, 11–34. Waterloo, Ontario: Wilfrid Laurier University Press, 2000.

Herod: King of the Jews and Friend of the Romans. Columbia: University of South Carolina Press, 1996.

Roll, Israel. "Roman Roads to Caesarea Maritima." In Avner Raban and Kenneth G. Holum, eds., *Caesarea Maritima: A Retrospective after Two Millenia*, 549–558. Leiden: E. J. Brill, 1996.

"Survey of Roman Roads in Lower Galilee." *ESI* 14 (1994): 38–40.

Romanoff, Paul. *Jewish Symbols on Ancient Jewish Coins*. New York: American Israel Numismatic Association, Inc., 1971.

Rosenberger, M. *City-Coins of Palestine*. 3 vols. Jerusalem, 1972–1977.

Ross, Arthur M. "Galilee." In J. D. Douglas, Merrill C. Tenney et al., eds., *The New International Dictionary: Pictorial Edition*, 368–369. Grand Rapids, Mich.: Zondervan Publishing House; Basingstoke: Marshall Pickering, 1987.

Russell, D. S. *The Jews from Alexander to Herod*. Oxford: Oxford University Press, 1967.

Rutgers, Leonard V. "Archaeological Evidence for the Interaction of Jews and Non-Jews in Late Antiquity." *AJA* 96 (1992): 101–118.

"Incense Shovels at Sepphoris?" In Eric M. Meyers, ed., *Galilee through the Centuries: Confluence of Cultures*, 177–198. Winona Lake, Ind.: Eisenbrauns, 1999.

Safrai, Ze'ev. *The Economy of Roman Palestine*. London and New York: Routledge, 1994.

"The Roman Army in the Galilee." In Lee I. Levine, ed., *The Galilee in Late Antiquity*, 103–114. New York and Jerusalem: The Jewish Theological Seminary of America, 1992.

Safrai, Ze'ev and M. Lin. "Mishmar Ha' Emeq." *ESI* 6 (1987–1988): 11.

Saldarini, Anthony J. "The Gospel of Matthew and Jewish–Christian Conflict in the Galilee." In Lee I. Levine, ed., *The Galilee in Late Antiquity*, 23–38. New York and Jerusalem: The Jewish Theological Seminary of America, 1992.

— *Matthew's Christian-Jewish Community*. Chicago and London: University of Chicago Press, 1994.

Sanders, E. P. *The Historical Figure of Jesus*. London: Allen Lane, The Penguin Press, 1993.

— *Jesus and Judaism*. Philadelphia: Fortress Press, 1985.

— "Jesus in Historical Context." *Theology Today* 50 (1993): 429–448.

— "Jesus' Galilee." In Ismo Dunderberg, Kari Syreeni, and Christopher Tuckett, eds., *Pluralism and Conflicts: Festschrift Heikki Räisänen*, Leiden: Brill, forthcoming.

— "Jesus' Relation to Sepphoris." In Rebecca Martin Nagy, Carol L. Meyers, Eric M. Meyers, and Zeev Weiss, eds., *Sepphoris in Galilee: Crosscurrents of Culture*, 75–79. Winona Lake, Ind.: Eisenbrauns, 1996.

— *Jewish Law from Jesus to the Mishnah*. London: SCM Press; Philadelphia: Trinity Press International, 1990.

— *Judaism: Practice and Belief: 63 BCE–66 CE*. London: SCM Press; Philadelphia: Trinity Press International, 1992.

Sauvaget, Jean. "Le Plan antique de Damas." *Syria* 26 (1949): 314–358.

Sawicki, Marianne. *Crossing Galilee: Architectures of Contact in the Occupied Land of Jesus*. Harrisburg, Penn.: Trinity Press International, 2000.

Schmitt, Götz. "Gaba, Getta und Gintikirmil." *ZDPV* 103 (1987): 22–48.

Schmitz, Philip C. "Sidon (Place)." *ABD*, vol. VI, 17–18.

Schottroff, Willy. "Die Ituräer." *ZDPV* 98 (1982): 125–152.

Schürer, Emil. *The History of the Jewish People in the Age of Jesus Christ*. Rev. and ed. Geza Vermes and Fergus Millar. 3 vols. Edinburgh: T&T Clark, 1973–1987.

Schwabe, Moshe. "Ein griechisches Grabepigramm aus Tiberias." *JPOS* 16 (1936): 158–165.

Schwabe, Moshe and Baruch Lifshitz. *Beth She'arim*. Vol. II, *The Greek Inscriptions*. New Brunswick, N.J.: Rutgers University Press, 1974.

Schwartz, Seth. "Israel and the Nations Roundabout: 1 Maccabees and the Hasmonean Expansion." *JJS* 41 (1991): 16–38.

— "The 'Judaism' of Samaria and Galilee in Josephus's Version of the Letter of Demetrius I to Jonathan (*Antiquities* 13.48–57)." *HTR* 82 (1989): 377–391.

Schweizer, Eduard. *The Good News According to Matthew*. Atlanta: John Knox Press, 1975.

Segal, Arthur and Yehuda Naor. "Sha'ar Ha'amaqim." *NEAEHL*, vol. IV, 1339–1340.

— "Sha'ar Ha'amaqim, 1991." *ESI* 12 (1993): 22–23.

Seigne, Jacques. "Jérash romaine et byzantine: développement urbain d'une ville provinciale orientale." In Adnan Hadidi, ed., *Studies in the History and Archaeology of Jordan IV*, 331–341. Amman: Department of Antiquities; Lyon: Maison de l'Orient Méditerranéen, Université Lumière, 1992.

— "Le sanctuaire de Zeus à Jérash:Eléments de chronologie." *Syria* 62 (1985): 287–295.

Seyrig, Henri. "Irenopolis-Neronias-Sepphoris." *Numismatic Chronicle* 10 (1950): 284–289.

"Irenopolis-Neronias-Sepphoris: An Additional Note." *Numismatic Chronicle* 15 (1955): 157–159.

"Note sur les cultes de Scythopolis à l'époque romaine." *Syria* 39 (1962): 207–211.

"Temples, cultes, et souvenirs historiques de la Décapole." *Syria* 36 (1959): 60–78.

Shatzman, Israel. *The Armies of the Hasmoneans and Herod.* Tübingen: J. C. B. Mohr (Paul Siebeck): 1991.

Shroder, Jr., John F. and Moshe Inbar. "Geologic and Geographic Background to the Bethsaida Excavations." In *Bethsaida: A City by the North Shore of the Sea of Galilee.* Vol. I, Bethsaida Excavations Project, ed. Rami Arav and Richard A. Freund, 65–98. Kirksville, Mo.: Thomas Jefferson University Press, 1995.

Siegelmann, Ayriel. "The Identification of Gaba Hippeon." *PEQ* 116 (1984–1985): 89–93.

Simons, Jan Jozef. *Handbook for the Study of Egyptian Topographical Lists Relating to Western Asia.* Leiden: E. J. Brill, 1937.

Singh, Ajoy Kumar. *Indo-Roman Trade.* New Delhi: Commonwealth Publishers, 1988.

Slane, Kathleen Warner. "The Fine Wares." In Sharon C. Herbert, ed., *Tel Anafa II, i: The Hellenistic and Roman Pottery,* 247–418. Ann Arbor, Mich.: Kelsey Museum; Columbia, Mich.: Museum of Art and Archaeology of the University of Missouri, 1997.

Smallwood, E. Mary. *The Jews under Roman Rule.* Leiden: E. J. Brill, 1976.

Smith, Mark D. "A Tale of Two Julias: Julia, Julias, and Josephus." In *Bethsaida: A City by the North Shore of the Sea of Galilee.* Vol. 2, Bethsaida Excavations Project, ed. Rami Arav and Richard A. Freund, 333–346. Kirksville, Mo.: Truman State University Press, 1999.

Smith, Morton. "The Gentiles in Judaism 125 B.C.E.–66 C.E." In Shaye J. D. Cohen, ed., *Studies in the Cult of Yahweh,* vol. I, 263–319. Leiden: E. J. Brill, 1996.

Smith, Robert Houston. "Excavations at Pella of the Decapolis, 1979–1985." *National Geographic Research* 1 (1985): 470–489.

"Pella." *ABD,* vol. V, 219–221.

"Pella." *NEAEHL,* vol. IV, 1174–1180.

"Pella of the Decapolis." *Archaeology* 34:5 (1981): 46–53.

Pella of the Decapolis, vol. I. Wooster, Ohio: The College of Wooster, 1973.

"Preliminary Report on a Second Season of Excavation at Pella, Jordan: Spring 1980." *ADAJ* 25 (1981): 311–326.

"The Southern Levant in the Hellenistic Period." *Levant* 22 (1990): 123–130.

Smith, Robert H. and Leslie Preston Day. *Pella of the Decapolis 2: Final Report on the College of Wooster Excavations in Area IX, The Civic Complex, 1979–1985.* Wooster, Ohio: The College of Wooster, 1989.

Smith, Robert H. and Anthony W. McNicoll. "The 1982 and 1983 Seasons at Pella of the Decapolis." *BASOR Supplement* 24 (1985): 21–50.

Smith, Robert H., Anthony W. McNicoll, and J. B. Hennessy. "The 1980 Season at Pella of the Decapolis." *BASOR* 243 (1980): 1–30.

Smith, Robert W. "Chorazin." *ABD*, vol. I, 911–912.

Soggin, J. Alberto. *Judges*. Philadelphia: Westminster Press, 1981.

Spijkerman, Augustus. *Cafarnao*. Vol. III, *Catalogo della Monete Città*. Jerusalem: Franciscan Printing Press, 1975.

The Coins of the Decapolis and Provincia Arabia. Jerusalem: Franciscan Printing Press, 1978.

Stanley, Farley H., Jr. "The South Flank of the Temple Platform." In K. G. Holum, A. Raban, and J. Patrick, eds., *Caesarea Papers 2*, 35–40. Portsmouth, R.I.: Journal of Roman Archaeology, 1999.

Stein, Alla. "A Tyrian Sealing." In Sharon C. Herbert, ed., *Tel Anafa, I: Final Report on Ten Years of Excavation at a Hellenistic and Roman Settlement in Northern Israel*, 261–263. Ann Arbor, Mich.: Kelsey Museum, 1994.

Steinsaltz, Adin, ed. *The Talmud: The Steinsaltz Edition*. 21 vols. New York: Random House, 1989–2000.

Stemberger, Günter. "Galilee – Land of Salvation?" In W. D. Davies, ed., *The Gospel and the Land: Early Christianity and Jewish Territorial Doctrine*, 409–438. Sheffield: JSOT Press, 1994.

Stendahl, Krister. *The School of St. Matthew and its Use of the Septuagint and Masoretic Text of the Old Testament*. Philadelphia: Fortress Press, 1968.

Stepansky, Yosef. "Two Mausolea on the Northern Fringes of the Roman-Period Cemetery of Tiberias." *Atiqot* 38 (1999): 226–227.

Stern, Ephraim. "Dor." *NEAEHL*, vol. I, 357–368.

"Dor." *OEANE*, vol. I, 168–170.

Dor: Ruler of the Seas. Jerusalem: Israel Exploration Society, 1994.

Material Culture of the Land of the Bible in the Persian Period 538–332 B.C. Warminster: Aris and Phillips, 1982.

Stern, Menahem. *Greek and Latin Authors on Jews and Judaism*. 3 vols. Jerusalem: The Israel Academy of Sciences and Humanities, 1974.

"The Reign of Herod and the Herodian Dynasty." In S. Safrai et al., eds., *Compendia Rerum Iudaicarum ad Novum Testamentum* 1.1, 1065–1100. Assen/ Amsterdam: Van Gorcum, 1974.

Stock, Augustine. *The Method and Message of Matthew*. Collegeville, Minn.: A Michael Glazier Book published by The Liturgical Press, 1989.

Strange, James F. "Archaeology and the Religion of Judaism in Palestine." In Hildegard Temporini and Wolfgang Haase, eds., *Aufstieg und Niedergang der römischen Welt*, 2.19.1, 646–685. Berlin and New York: Walter de Gruyter, 1979.

"Beth-saida." *ABD*, vol. I, 692–693.

"Cana of Galilee." *ABD*, vol. I, 827.

"The Capernaum and Herodium Publications." *BASOR* 226 (1977): 65–73.

"The Capernaum and Herodium Publications, Part 2." *BASOR* 233 (1979): 63–69.

"First-Century Galilee from Archaeology and from the Texts." In Eugene H. Lovering, Jr., ed., *Society of Biblical Literature 1994 Seminar Papers*, 81–90. Atlanta: Scholars Press, 1994.

"Magdala." *ABD*, vol. IV, 463–464.

"Nazareth." *ABD*, vol. IV, 1050–1051.

"Nazareth." *OEANE*, vol. IV, 113–114.

"Sepphoris." *ABD*, vol. V, 1090–1093.

"Six Campaigns at Sepphoris: The University of South Florida Excavations, 1983–1989." In Lee I. Levine, ed., *The Galilee in Late Antiquity*, 339–356. New York and Jerusalem: The Jewish Theological Seminary of America, 1992.

"Some Implications of Archaeology for New Testament Studies." In James H. Charlesworth and Walter P. Weaver, eds., *What has Archaeology to do with Faith?*, ed. 23–59. Philadelphia; Trinity Press International, 1992.

"Survey of Lower Galilee, 1982." *IEJ* 32 (1982): 254–255.

"Tiberias," *ABD*, vol. vi, 547–549.

"The University of South Florida Excavations at Sepphoris, Israel: Report of the Excavations: 3 May–18 July, 1993." http://www.colby.edu/rel/Sep93.html.

"The University of South Florida Excavations at Sepphoris, Israel: Report of the Excavations: 12 June–14 July 1995." http://www.colby.edu/rel/Sep95.html.

"The University of South Florida Excavations at Sepphoris, Israel: Report of the Excavations: 14 June–15 July, 1994." http://www.colby.edu/rel/Sep94.html.

Strange, James F., Dennis E. Groh, and Thomas R. W. Longstaff. "Excavations at Sepphoris: Location and Identification of Shikhin." *IEJ* 44 (1994): 216–227.

"The Location and Identification of Ancient Shikhin (Asochis)." www.colby.edu/rel/shikhin.html.

"Sepphoris (Ṣippori) 1987." *IEJ* 38 (1988): 188–190.

"Sepphoris." *RB* 96 (1989): 240–242.

"Sepphoris, 1996." *IEJ* 49 (1999): 122–123.

Strange, James F., Dennis E. Groh, Thomas R. W. Longstaff, with David Adan-Bayewitz, Frank Asaro, Isadore Perlman, and Helen V. Michel, "Excavations at Sepphoris: Location and Identification of Shikhin." *IEJ* 45 (1994): 171–187.

Strange, James F., Dennis E. Groh, Thomas R. W. Longstaff and C. Thomas McCollough. "Sepphoris, 1998," *IEJ* 49 (1999): 126–128.

"The University of South Florida Excavations at Sepphoris, Israel: Report of the Excavations: May 11–July 14, 1998." http://www.colby.edu/rel/Sep98.html.

Strange, James F., Dennis E. Groh, and C. Thomas McCollough. "Sepphoris, 1997." *IEJ* 49 (1999): 124–126.

"The University of South Florida Excavations at Sepphoris, Israel: Report of the Excavations: May 8–23, 1997." http://www.colby.edu/rel/Sep97.html.

Strange, James F. and Thomas R. W. Longstaff. "Sepphoris (Ṣippori)–1986 (II)." *IEJ* 37 (1987): 287–280.

Strange, James F., Thomas R. W. Longstaff, and Dennis E. Groh. "The University of South Florida Excavations at Sepphoris, Israel: Report of the Excavations: 10 June–12 July, 1996." http://www.colby.edu/rel/Sep96.html.

"Zippori–1991." *ESI* 13 (1993): 29–30.

Strange, James F., Ehud Netzer and Zeev Weiss. "Sepphoris (Ṣippori) 1991–1992." *IEJ* 43 (1993): 190–196.

Strange, James F. and Hershel Shanks. "Has the House where Jesus Stayed in Capernaum been Found?" *BAR* 8:6 (1982): 26–37.

"Synagogue Where Jesus Preached Found at Capernaum." *BAR* 9:6 (1983): 25–28.

Strickert, Fred. "2 Esdras 1.11 and the Destruction of Bethsaida." *Journal for the Study of the Pseudepigrapha* 16 (1997): 111–122.

Bethsaida: Home of the Apostles. Collegeville, Minn.: Michael Glazier, Liturgical Press, 1998.

"The Coins of Philip." In *Bethsaida: A City by the North Shore of the Sea of Galilee.* Vol. I, Bethsaida Excavations Project, ed. Rami Arav and Richard A. Freund, 165–189. Kirksville, Mo.: Thomas Jefferson University Press, 1995.

"The Destruction of Bethsaida: The Evidence of 2 Esdras 1:11." In *Bethsaida: A City by the North Shore of the Sea of Galilee.* Vol. II, Bethsaida Excavations Project, ed. Rami Arav and Richard A. Freund, 347–392. Kirksville, Mo.: Truman State University Press, 1999.

"The Founding of Bethsaida-Julias: Evidence from the Coins of Philip." *Shofar* 13/4 (1995): 40–51.

Sukenik, E. L. *The Ancient Synagogue of El-Ḥammeh.* Jerusalem: Rubin Mass, 1935.

Sukenik, L. "The Ancient City of Philoteria (Beth Yeraḥ)." *JPOS* 2 (1922): 101–107.

Syon, Danny. "The Coins from Gamala: Interim Report." *INJ* 12 (1992–1993): 34–55.

Tadmor, H. *The Inscriptions of Tiglath-Pileser III King of Assyria.* Jerusalem: Israel Academy of Sciences and Humanities, 1994.

Tal, Oren. "Roman-Byzantine Cemeteries and Tombs around Apollonia." *Tel Aviv* 22 (1995): 107–120.

Tappy, Ron. "Samaria." *OEANE*, vol. IV, 463–467.

Taylor, Joan E. "Capernaum and its 'Jewish-Christians:' A Re-examination of the Franciscan Excavations." *BAIAS* 9 (1989–1990): 7–28.

Christians and the Holy Places: The Myth of Jewish-Christian Origins. Oxford: Clarendon Press, 1993.

Tcherikover, Victor. *Hellenistic Civilization and the Jews.* Trans. S. Applebaum. 3 vols. Philadelphia: Jewish Publication Society of America; Jerusalem: Magnes, Hebrew University Press, 1957–1964.

Tcherikover, Victor A. and Alexander Fuks, eds. *Corpus Papyrorum Judaicarum.* Jerusalem: Magnes, Hebrew University Press; Cambridge, Mass.: Harvard University Press, 1957.

Testa, Emmanuele. *Cafarnao.* Vol. IV, *Graffiti della Casa di S. Pietro.* Jerusalem: Franciscan Printing Press, 1972.

Nazareth Giudo-Cristiana. Jerusalem: Tipografia dei PP Francescan, 1969.

Il Simbolismo dei Giudo-Cristiani. Jerusalem: Tipografia dei PP Francescan, 1962.

Theissen, Gerd. *The Gospels in Context: Social and Political History in the Synoptic Tradition.* Trans. Linda M. Maloney. Minneapolis: Fortress Press, 1991.

Thompson, Henry O. "Carmel, Mount." *ABD*, vol. I, 874–875.

Tisera, Guido. *Universalism According to the Gospel of Saint Matthew.* Frankfurt am Main: Peter Lang, 1993.

Tolbert, Mary Ann. *Sowing the Gospel.* Minneapolis: Fortress Press, 1989.

Tsafrir, Yoram. "Further Evidence of the Cult of Zeus Akraios at Beth Shean (Scythopolis)." *IEJ* 39 (1989): 76–78.

Tsafrir, Yoram, Leah Di Segni and Judith Green. *Tabula Imperii Romani: Iudaea, Palaestina: Eretz Israel in the Hellenistic, Roman and Byzantine Periods.* Jerusalem: Israel Academy of Sciences and Humanities, 1994.

Tsuk, Tsvika. "The Aqueducts of Sepphoris." In Eric M. Meyers, ed., *Galilee through the Centuries: Confluence of Cultures*, 161–176. Winona Lake, Ind.: Eisenbrauns, 1999.

"The Aqueducts of Sepphoris." In Rebecca Martin Nagy, Carol L. Meyers, Eric M. Meyers, and Zeev Weiss, eds., *Sepphoris in Galilee: Crosscurrents of Culture*, 45–49. Winona Lake, Ind.: Eisenbrauns, 1996.

"Bringing Water to Sepphoris." *BAR* 26:4 (2000): 34–41.

"Şippori: The Aqueducts." *ESI* 1 (1982): 105–107.

"Şippori: The Aqueducts." *ESI* 9 (1989–1990): 20.

Tuckett, Christopher M. "A Cynic Q." *Biblica* 70 (1989): 349–376.

Q and the History of Early Christianity. Edinburgh: T&T Clark, 1996.

Tzaferis, Vassilios. "Banias." *OEANE*, vol. I, 270–271.

"Cults and Deities Worshipped at Caesarea Philippi-Banias." In Eugene Ulrich et al., eds., *Priests, Prophets, and Scribes*, 190–204. Sheffield: Sheffield Academic Press, 1992.

"Kursi." *NEAEHL*, vol. III, 893–896.

"Kursi." *OEANE*, vol. III, 314–315.

"New Archaeological Evidence on Ancient Capernaum." *BA* 46 (1983): 198–204.

"Susita Awaits the Spade." *BAR* 16:5 (1990): 50–58.

Tzaferis, Vassilios and Bellarmino Bagatti. "Nazareth." *NEAEHL*, vol. III, 1103–1106.

Tzaferis, Vassilios et al. *Excavations at Capernaum*, vol. I, *1978–1982*. Winona Lake, Ind.: Eisenbrauns, 1989.

Uqsa, Hana Abu. "Migdal." *ESI* 13 (1993): 28.

Uqsa, Hana Abu and Nissim Najjar. "Kafr Kanna (B)." *ESI* 16 (1997): 48–49.

Urman, Dan. *The Golan: A Profile of a Region during the Roman and Byzantine Periods*. Oxford: BAR, 1985.

"The Golan During the Roman and Byzantine Periods: Topography, Settlements, Economy." Ph.D. Diss., New York University, 1979.

Vale, Ruth. "Literary Sources in Archaeological Description: The Case of Galilee, Galilees, and Galileans." *Journal for the Study of Judaism* 18 (1987): 209–226.

Vermes, Geza. *Jesus and the World of Judaism*. London: SCM Press, 1983.

Jesus the Jew. Philadelphia Fortress Press, 1975.

Vincent, L. H. "Le Dieu Saint Paqeidas a Gérasa." *RB* 49 (1940): 98–129.

Vitto, Fanny. "Gush Halav." *RB* 82 (1975): 277–278.

"Gush Halav: The Mausoleum." *NEAEHL*, vol. II, 549–550.

"Kiriat Tiv'on." *RB* 79 (1972): 574–576.

"Naharon, Tel." *NEAEHL*, vol. III, 1094–1095.

"Qiryat Tiv'on." *IEJ* 24 (1974): 279.

"Tiberias: The Roman Tomb." *NEAEHL*, vol. IV, 1473.

Wagner-Lux, Ute et al. "Preliminary Report on the Excavations and Architectural Survey in Gadara (Umm Qeis) in Jordan, Area I (1992)." *ADAJ* 37 (1993): 385–395.

Waldbaum, James C. "Greeks *in* the East or Greeks *and* the East? Problems in the Definition and Recognition of Presence." *BASOR* 305 (1997): 1–17.

Ward, William A. "Phoenicia." *OEANE*, vol. IV, 313–317.

"Tyre." *OEANE*, vol. V, 247–250.

Warmington, E. H. *The Commerce Between the Roman Empire and India*. Delhi: Vikas Publishing House Pvt. Ltd, 1974.

Waterman, Leroy. *Preliminary Report of the University of Michigan Excavations at Sepphoris, Palestine, in 1931*. Ann Arbor: University of Michigan Press, 1937.

Weber, Thomas. "Gadara of the Decapolis: Preliminary Report on the 1990 Season at Umm Qeis." *ADAJ* 35 (1991): 223–231.

"A Survey of Roman Sculpture in the Decapolis: Preliminary Report." *ADAJ* 34 (1990): 351–355.

Weber, Thomas with Rami Khouri. *Umm Qeis: Gadara of the Decapolis*. Amman: Al Qutba, 1989.

Weinberg, Gladys Davidson. "Hellenistic Glass from Tel Anafa in Upper Galilee." *Journal of Glass Studies* 12 (1970): 17–27.

"Notes on Glass from Upper Galilee." *Journal of Glass Studies* 15 (1973): 35–51.

Weinberg, Saul S. "Anafa, Tel." *EAEHL*, vol. I, 65–69.

"Tel Anafa." *IEJ* 23 (1973): 113–117.

"Tel Anafa: A Problem-Oriented Excavation." *Muse* 3 (1969): 16–23.

"Tel Anafa (Shamir)." *IEJ* 18 (1968): 195–196.

"Tel Anafa: The Hellenistic Town." *IEJ* 21 (1971): 86–109.

"Tel Anafa: The Second Season." *Muse* 4 (1970): 15–24.

"Tel Anafa: The Third Season." *Muse* 5 (1971): 8–16.

Weiss, Zeev. "Sepphoris." *NEAEHL*, vol. IV, 1324–1328.

"The Sepphoris Synagogue Mosaic." *BAR* 26:5 (2000): 48–61, 70.

"Social Aspects of Burial in Beth She'arim: Archeological Finds and Talmudic Sources." In Lee I. Levine, ed., *The Galilee in Late Antiquity*, 357–372. New York and Jerusalem: The Jewish Theological Seminary of America, 1992.

Weiss, Zeev and Ehud Netzer. "Architectural Development of Sepphoris during the Roman and Byzantine Periods." In Douglas R. Edwards and C. Thomas McCollough, eds., *Archaeology and the Galilee: Texts and Contexts in the Graeco-Roman and Byzantine Periods*, 117–130. Atlanta: Scholars Press, 1997.

"Hellenistic and Roman Sepphoris: The Archaeological Evidence." In Rebecca Martin Nagy, Carol L. Meyers, Eric M. Meyers and Zeev Weiss, eds., *Sepphoris in Galilee: Crosscurrents of Culture*, 29–37. Winona Lake, Ind.: Eisenbrauns, 1996.

"The Mosaics of the Nile Festival Building." In Rebecca Martin Nagy, Carol L. Meyers, Eric M. Meyers, and Zeev Weiss, eds., *Sepphoris in Galilee: Crosscurrents of Culture*, 127–131. Winona Lake, Ind.: Eisenbrauns, 1996.

Promise and Redemption: A Synagogue Mosaic from Sepphoris. Jerusalem: Israel Museum, 1996.

"The Synagogue Mosaic." In Rebecca Martin Nagy, Carol L. Meyers, Eric M. Meyers, and Zeev Weiss, eds., *Sepphoris in Galilee: Crosscurrents of Culture*, 133–139. Winona Lake, Ind.: Eisenbrauns, 1996.

"Zippori–1992–1993." *ESI* 14 (1994): 40–46.

Weitzman, Steven. "Forced Circumcision and the Shifting Role of Gentiles in Hasmonean Ideology." *HTR* 92 (1999): 37–59.

Welles, C. B. "The Inscriptions." In Carl H. Kraeling, ed., *Gerasa: City of the Decapolis*, 355–496. New Haven, Conn.: American Schools of Oriental Research, 1938.

Wenning, Robert. "Die Dekapolis und die Nabataër." *ZDPV* 110 (1994): 2–35.

Wilson, John F. and Vassilios Tzaferis. "Banias Dig Reveals King's Palace." *BAR* 24:1 (1998): 54–61, 85.

Witherington, III, Ben. *The Jesus Quest: The Third Search for the Jew of Nazareth*. Downers Grove, Ill.: InterVarsity Press, 1995.

Yeivin., S. "Historical and Archaeological Notes." In Leroy Waterman, ed., *Preliminary Report of the University of Michigan Excavations at Sepphoris, Palestine, in 1931*, 17–34. Ann Arbor: University of Michigan, 1937.

Yeivin, Zeev. "Ancient Chorazin Comes Back to Life." *BAR* 13:5 (1987): 22–39.

"Chorazain." *EAEHL*, vol. I, 299–301.

"Chorazin." *NAEAHL*, vol. I, 301–304.

"Korazim–1983/1984." *ESI* 3 (1984): 66–71.

Yogev, O. and E. Eisenberg. "Beth Yerah." *ESI* 4 (1985): 14–16.

Younger, Jr., K. Lawson. "The Deportations of the Israelites." *JBL* 117 (1998): 201–227.

Zangenberg, Jürgen. "Jüngste Ausgrabungen im neutestamentlichen Sepphoris." *Weld und Umwelt der Bibel* 10:4 (1998): 76–77.

SAMAREIA: Antike Quellen zur Geschichte und Kultur der Samaritaner in deutscher Übersetzung. Tübingen and Basel: Francke Verlag, 1994.

INDEX OF PASSAGES

Antiquities

Life

Philo

Embassy to Gaius

Rabbinic passages

Other ancient texts

SELECTIVE INDEX OF PLACES

SELECTIVE INDEX OF PEOPLE AND TOPICS